Mutual Fund Investing For Canadians

FOR DUMMIES®

by Andrew Bell and
Matthew Elder

John Wiley & [

D1377189

Mutual Fund Investing For Canadians For Dummies®
Published by
John Wiley & Sons Canada, Ltd.
6045 Freemont Blvd.
Mississauga, ON L5R 4J3
www.wiley.com

For general information on John Wiley & Sons Canada, Ltd., including all books published by Wiley Publishing Inc., please call our warehouse, Tel. 1-800-567-4797. For reseller information, including discounts and premium sales, please call our sales department, Tel. 416-646-7992. For press review copies, author interviews, or other publicity information, please contact our publicity department, Tel. 416-646-4582, Fax 416-236-4448.

Library and Archives Canada Cataloguing in Publication Data

Bell, Andrew, 1960–
    Mutual fund investing for Canadians for
dummies / Andrew Bell, Matthew Elder.

ISBN 978-0-470-15764-0

    1. Mutual funds. I. Elder, Matthew II. Title.
HG5154.5.B438 2008   332.63'27   C2008-905703-1

1 2 3 4 5 RRD 13 12 11 10 09

WILEY

About the Authors

Andrew Bell was an investment reporter and editor with *The Globe and Mail* for 12 years. He joined Business News Network as a reporter in 2001.

Bell, an import from Dublin, Ireland, was for 10 years the main compiler of Stars & Dogs in Saturday's *Globe*. The roundup of hot and damp stocks and mutual funds was an invaluable therapeutic aid in relieving his own myriad jealousies, regrets, and resentments. He has also taken to the stage, where he practises a demanding "method" that involves getting the audience and other performers as off-balance and upset as possible.

He lives in Cabbagetown, Toronto, with his wife and daughter.

Matthew Elder is a writer and communications consultant based in Toronto. Previously he was vice-president, content and editorial, of Morningstar Canada. A Montreal native, he was a columnist and editor specializing in personal finance with *The Gazette* for 10 years before moving to the *Financial Post* in 1995, where he was mutual funds editor and columnist until joining Morningstar in 2000.

Matthew lives and works out of a Toronto condo tower, and frequently takes his trade (and recreation) to family retreats on Georgian Bay and the Laurentians. He is married to a financial planner and has two twentysomething sons.

Acknowledgements

Andrew thanks his colleagues for their support and indulgence, especially Eric Reguly, Lori Vanden Bergh, Steve Northfield, Mike Den Tandt, and Dave Pyette. His wife, Tara Ellis, cheerfully put up with months of whining, procrastination, and self-pity. And so did talented editors Joan Whitman and Melanie Rutledge. Thanks also to Ellen Roseman, who first got Andrew writing about funds.

Matthew is grateful for valuable input and assistance from a variety of experts. Foremost among them were Morningstar analysts David O'Leary, Brian O'Neil, and Mark Chow, who put together the lists of Dummies Approved funds that are scattered across various chapters. Matthew is grateful to Rudy Luukko, whose encyclopedic knowledge of the funds industry was tapped frequently. A special thank you to Scott Mackenzie, CEO of Morningstar, for supplying us with reams of data, gleaned mostly from the firm's invaluable PALTrak desktop software, with interpretive help from Anastasia Aulsebrook, Tom Teder, and John Campea. Thanks, too, to the Investment Funds Institute of Canada for permission to excerpt some of their extensive industry data. There was much appreciated input from *The Globe and Mail*'s Rob Carrick, the dean of Canadian personal finance writers. Input from Moshe Milevsky of York University, Malcolm Hamilton, senior actuary at Mercer, and veteran independent mutual fund analyst Dan Hallett was also greatly appreciated. Thanks to Robert Hickey and Lindsay Humphreys of Wiley, and to Kelli Howey for her copy editing. Perhaps most important, Matthew is grateful to his wife and financial adviser Jane Baker for putting up with months of silly questions and incessant complaining.

Publisher's Acknowledgements

We're proud of this book; please send us your comments through our Dummies online registration form located at www.dummies.com/register/.

Some of the people who helped bring this book to market include the following:

Acquisitions, Editorial, and Media Development

Editor: Robert Hickey

    (Previous Edition: Melanie Rutledge)

Project Manager: Elizabeth McCurdy

Project Editor: Lindsay Humphreys

Copy Editor: Kelli Howey

Cover photo: Credit: ©iStockphoto.com/ Nell Redmond

Cartoons: Rich Tennant

    (www.the5thwave.com)

Composition Services

Vice-President Publishing Services: Karen Bryan

Project Coordinator: Lynsey Stanford

Layout and graphics: Melissa Bronnenberg, Sarah E. Philippart, Christin Swinford

Proofreader: Laura L. Bowman

Indexer: Claudia Bourbeau

John Wiley & Sons Canada, Ltd.

    Bill Zerter, Chief Operating Officer

    Jennifer Smith, Vice-President and Publisher, Professional and Trade Division

Publishing and Editorial for Consumer Dummies

    Diane Graves Steele, Vice-President and Publisher, Consumer Dummies

    Joyce Pepple, Acquisitions Director, Consumer Dummies

    Kristin A. Cocks, Product Development Director, Consumer Dummies

    Michael Spring, Vice-President and Publisher, Travel

    Kelly Regan, Editorial Director, Travel

Publishing for Technology Dummies

    Andy Cummings, Vice-President and Publisher, Dummies Technology/General User

Composition Services

    Gerry Fahey, Vice-President of Production Services

    Debbie Stailey, Director of Composition Services

Contents at a Glance

Table of Contents

Part IV: The Nuts and Bolts of Keeping Your Portfolio Going 299

Chapter 21: The Internet: The Place to Go for Fund Information 301

Chapter 22: RRSPs: Fertilizer for Your Mutual Funds. 311

Chapter 23: Taxes: Timing Is Everything 321

Introduction

∙ ∙

Mutual funds have been a target of criticism over the years. The rap is that their fees are too high, they don't do any better than the market as a whole, and you get sold stuff you don't want — or, worse, stuff that's inappropriate to your financial needs. In some individual cases, those criticisms can be true.

Many funds *are* overpriced; in other words, their annual charges, often used to pay the very people who sell you funds, are too high to allow you to end up with a decent return. Many funds are little better than marketing ploys, and still more just drag their hapless customers through years of lousy returns.

But, despite it all, mutual funds work. And they work well. Conservative funds that invested in quality stocks and bonds — and cautious investors who made sure they didn't risk all their money in stocks — have achieved decent long-term returns. But here's the great part: Picking conservative funds with good returns and putting them together in a smart financial plan isn't that hard or time-consuming. Just follow the simple (and often obvious) guidelines in this book, and you'll do fine.

Life is short and we're all overloaded. So much mud-wrestling, so little time. We've written *Mutual Fund Investing For Canadians For Dummies* as though we're sitting with you in a coffee shop giving you the basic facts on mutual funds and investing — only the essential stuff you need to earn a decent return on your money. We hope you never feel, while reading this book, that we're droning on about something that doesn't affect your life. Most people relegate mutual funds to the grey parking lot of their lives that's reserved for stuff like plumbing or Kansas — something to think about if you have to, but otherwise no thanks. That's a pity; funds really can make a difference in your financial picture.

They aren't very complicated, either — a mutual fund is really just a handy invention that allows hordes of people to pool their cash into a professionally managed investment vehicle that handles the bookkeeping. It then buys things such as shares in companies and bonds issued by governments, things that a lot of ordinary people find confusing. Funds are so powerful and simple that they've helped to transform the economy of the capitalist world.

Until the mass-market mutual fund came along, investing in shares and buying bonds was mostly a privilege of the rich, just like tax evasion and dull conversations about the unreliability of nannies. These days, mutual funds have helped millions of ordinary people, especially in North America, to gather unprecedented wealth.

This book is meant to help you be part of that phenomenon. With a little education, you too can jump on the bandwagon and make yourself some cold, hard cash. Getting up to speed about mutual funds doesn't take long and it can be sinfully profitable. For more and more Canadians — especially the self-employed or those working for small companies — the returns they get from their funds will determine when they can stop working and what kind of retirement income to expect.

How This Book Is Different

Pick up nearly any book or article about investing and you'll probably see a picture of the author — a fresh-faced thing with cute tousled hair or a solemn corrupt senator-type trying to look prosperous. Oh, nothing's more glamorous than the hectic, glittering life of the investment author!

And then every book has its promises: The special formulas, the daring analyses, the hinted-at guarantee that at last you've found the route to riches. But what we all-knowing money gurus rarely get around to explaining is: How come, if we're such fantastic investors, we have to do something as wretched as write a book? Why aren't we striding the trading floor at RBC Dominion Securities, barking orders over a cell phone at quivering central bankers, and restructuring the automobile industry before lunch?

The evidence shows that hardly anybody, including the investment professional, is consistently good at picking shares and bonds that go up in price. Despite all the fancy talk and arcane theories, stock and bond prices move in unpredictable patterns — like the weather or the population of porcupines in New Brunswick.

So yeah, we admit it: This book contains no magic, just some plain logic and simple facts you could find out for yourself by fooling around with mutual funds for a few years. But lots of people don't have the time or inclination to do that — this book is for you, folks.

Besides, the investment market can be an awfully expensive place to learn investing lessons. So read on, and gain the benefit of our (often painful) experiences.

About the Information in This Book

Markets are in a state of constant movement, and the statistics that tell investors how well they're doing change continually. With mutual funds you don't need to keep an eye on their performance quite as closely as you would if you invested in individual stocks, because equity funds are diversified, longer-term investments. However, knowing what your rate of return has been over time, and how that compares to other funds and the relevant benchmark (such as the Standard & Poor's/Toronto Stock Exchange composite index) can be useful. For this reason we include numerous examples of fund performance in this book, using data provided by Morningstar, the world's leading source of investment fund data. This means we had to choose a point in time to capture this data — we selected June 30, 2008, and in most cases we refer to this date as "mid-2008."

In most cases, we use data for the median mutual fund in a particular category. As we explain in Chapter 2, a *median value* provides a more useful snapshot of a particular group of funds because it represents the midpoint between the highest and lowest values. A simple average, which is frequently used elsewhere to track asset-class performance, is often misleading because the smaller funds in the group have the same impact on the average value as larger funds.

Mutual fund medians exclude the impact of segregated funds, which are the same as mutual funds except they include a guarantee of part or all of your original investment. Segregated funds' higher annual fees (due to the guarantee, which brings with it the extra cost of insurance) can have an unfairly negative impact on a category's median return. (See Chapter 19 for more on seg funds, as they're known.) In some cases where it seems useful to do so, we provide overall median values that include both types of funds.

When describing the size of the Canadian fund industry, in most cases we use total assets data from the Investment Funds Institute of Canada References. However, IFIC's data reflect only the figures supplied by its members, which excludes not only insurance companies' seg funds but also some mutual fund companies, which for one reason or another have decided not to join IFIC. (An important example of the latter is CI Funds, which had more than $60 billion in mutual fund assets as of mid-2008.) Nonetheless, IFIC's numbers provide an excellent representation of the fund industry's size and activity.

How This Book Is Organized

The best first move is to look at the table of contents to get an idea of what's here. If you already know the basics, just jump to the topics you have trouble with. In the case of subjects with lots of further complications, like official rules and so on, we give you Web addresses so you can do further reading.

Think of the book as being like a set of Russian dolls, nesting inside each other. The smallest doll is Chapter 1, What Is a Mutual Fund? If you're not quite clear on the basics of investing in funds, you can read that chapter and get all the truly important information. It's designed to be a brief primer that gives you the essential core of mutual fund investing. The next level, providing more information on the drawbacks and advantages of funds, is Part I, which was written as a complete introduction to mutual funds. It provides more detail on each topic than we get into in Chapter 1. Then, to explore any aspect of funds in yet more depth, you can simply start jumping around the book. The whole thing is pretty flexible.

So don't worry about reading every chapter. You should be out partying anyway. Jump right to the section you're interested in, because each is understandable without reading others first. Throughout the book, we've avoided jargon wherever possible — where we're forced to use a technical term, we explain it right away.

The sections that follow describe the parts in this book and what they cover.

Part I: Meet the Mutual Fund

This first section is a summary of how funds work and the reasons to buy them, as well as what type to buy. Packed with definitions and plain-English explanations, this part is built for the novices who have been left scratching their heads about fund basics. You need to get your financial house in order before diving into the fund pool, so this part also features a crash course on financial planning and much, much more.

Part II: Buying Options: Looking for a Helping Hand

In Part II we walk through all the possible sources of help you might consider, from your friendly neighbourhood bank to a discount broker. Packed with inside information about who does what, this part will help you figure out exactly what you're looking for in terms of financial advice, and how much that advice should set you back.

Part III: The Fund Stuff: Building a Strong Portfolio

Herein lies the industry's entire menu of funds, give or take a handful. These days funds exist for every type of investor, from the daredevil who would just as soon go to the racetrack to the notorious mattress stuffer who can't part with a single dime. This part runs through the many fund types and helps you match your financial goals to what these beasts have to offer. All the biggies are here — equity funds, money market funds, and index funds, plus a look at fund packages. Each chapter includes suggestions for winning funds, prepared for this book by analysts at Morningstar, the country's leading mutual fund research firm.

Part IV: The Nuts and Bolts of Keeping Your Portfolio Going

Getting started in funds may seem like the hard part, but keeping your portfolio humming along and turning a profit is a challenge all its own. In this part we offer some valuable advice on tracking your progress and optimizing the mighty combination of your registered retirement savings plan and mutual funds. We also take a long hard look at taxes and your funds.

Part V: The Part of Tens

The Part of Tens is a collection of quick factoids about funds. We list ten common investing foul-ups in funds, which we hope you'll find entertaining as well as disturbing. We also list ten things to consider when hiring a salesperson — and a to-do list to consult if you're wondering whether to dump one.

Icons Used in This Book

Ever go over one of those speed bumps — the British call them "sleeping policemen" — at full throttle? Catches your attention. This finance stuff can get heavy after the 200th page. So, to keep you alert, throughout the book we sprinkle icons in the margin to wake you up and highlight important information that's too good to miss. It might be a grim admonition, a neat piece of advice, or a nugget of wisdom. Here's what to look out for.

This icon — judiciously used — denotes a product or particular fund that does a good job and offers you benefits. But watch out — funds have an annoying habit of dropping to the bottom of the performance table right after writers recommend them. In part that's because the type of investments the fund buys have already shot up in value.

Remember icons flag an important piece of information that's like the crucial clue in an Agatha Christie novel. The bit where the jealous sister-in-law couldn't possibly have heard the 1 a.m. time check on the radio when she said she did — *because the clocks went forward that night*. Our turning points won't be so complicated. They're simply realities about mutual funds that are worth always bearing in mind.

Relax: You can get away without reading this stuff. But for those who like a good conspiracy story, this icon denotes interesting, if not throwaway, information. It flags a place where we talk about the internal workings of a fund. But you can invest in funds perfectly well without reading it. In practice, Technical Stuff usually involves the money that fund managers and salespeople get from the funds they market. That's the thing that kind of drives the whole show forward.

The Tip icons point to methods or suggestions that save you money, improve your returns, or reduce your risk. They're also quick-and-dirty shortcuts. Or they mark practicalities that fund companies may not mention.

Warning icons flag a dangerous reef that you have to skirt — something that could cost you lots of money, either by hitting you with excessive management and sales fees, by leaving you vulnerable to nasty losses, or by dragging down your overall returns.

Part I
Meet the Mutual Fund

The 5th Wave   By Rich Tennant

"Choosing the right mutual fund is like choosing the right hat. You find one that fits you best and then you stick with it."

In this part . . .

Here's all you need to build a perfectly good mutual fund portfolio. We explain why you should own at least some funds. We also describe how funds work and set out the basic mechanics of buying funds and using them to make money. We also look at how funds fit beautifully into just about everyone's financial plan, and show you some of the alternative investments you can buy.

Chapter 1

What Is a Mutual Fund?

In This Chapter

▷ Understanding mutual funds

▷ Looking at how funds can make you money

▷ Identifying the four types of mutual funds

▷ Knowing where to buy funds

*U*nless you've been living in a cave high in the mountains for the past decade, railing against the evils of humankind, you've heard a lot about mutual funds. Chances are you or someone in your family already owns some. Mutual funds seem complicated — even though they are incredibly popular — so lots of people shy away. Many people aren't sure where to start, or they just buy the first fund their banker or financial planner suggests. All too often Canadians end up disappointed with their funds' performance, because they've been sold something that's either unsuitable or just too expensive. It's a shame, because building a portfolio of excellent funds is easy if you follow a few simple rules and use your own common sense. This stuff isn't complicated — a mutual fund is just a money-management service that operates under clear rules. Yes, it involves a lot of marketing mumbo-jumbo and arcane terminology, but the basic idea could be written on a postage stamp: In return for a fee, the people running the fund promise to invest your money wisely and give it back to you on demand.

The fund industry is competitive and sophisticated, which means plenty of good choices are out there. In this chapter, we show how funds make you money — especially if you leave your investment in place for several years. We also touch on the different types available, and quickly describe the main places you can go to buy funds. We discuss these topics in greater detail later in the book, but after you read this first chapter you'll know the basics.

Mutual Fund Basics

A mutual fund is a pool of money that a company gets from investors like you and me and divides up into equally priced units. Each unit is a tiny slice of the fund. When you put money into the fund or take it out again, you either buy or sell units. For example, say a fund has total assets — that is, money held in trust for investors — of $10 million and investors have been sold a total of 1 million units. Then each unit is worth $10. If you put money into the fund, you're simply sold units at that day's value. If you take money out, the fund buys units back from you at the same price. (Handling purchase and sale transactions in units makes it far simpler to do the paperwork.) And the system has another huge advantage: As long as you know how many units you own, you can simply check their current price to find out how much your total investment is worth. For example, if you hold 475 units of a fund whose current unit price is $15.20, then you know your holding has a value of 475 times $15.20, or $7,220.

Owning units of a mutual fund makes you — you guessed it — a unitholder. In fact, you and the other unitholders are the legal owners of the fund. But the fund is run by a company that's legally known as the fund manager — the firm that handles the investing and also deals with the fund's administration. The terminology gets confusing here because the person (usually an employee of the fund manager) who chooses which stocks, bonds, or other investments the fund should buy is also usually called the fund manager. To make things clear, we refer to the company that sells and administers the fund as the management company or fund sponsor. We use the term fund manager for the person who picks the stocks and bonds. His or her skill is one of the main benefits you get from a mutual fund. Obviously, the fund manager should be experienced and not too reckless — after all, you're trusting him or her with your money.

Under professional management, the fund invests in stocks and bonds, increasing the pool of money for the investors and boosting the value of the individual units. For example, if you bought units at $10 each and the fund manager managed to pick investments that doubled in value, your units would grow to $20. In return, the management company slices off fees and expenses. (In the world of mutual funds, just like almost everywhere else, you don't get something for nothing.) Fees and expenses usually come to between 0.3 percent and 3 percent of the fund's assets each year, depending on how a fund invests. Some specialized funds charge much more.

Confused? Don't be, it isn't rocket science. This example should help. Units in Canada's biggest mutual fund, Investors Dividend Fund — run by the country's largest fund company, Investors Group — were bought from and sold to people like you and me at $21.83 each at the end of March 2008. So if you invested $1,000 in the fund that day, you owned 45.8 units ($1,000 divided by $21.83). The price you pay for each unit is known as the fund's net asset value per unit. The net asset value is the fund's assets minus its liabilities, hence the "net" (which means after costs and debts are taken away), divided by the number of units outstanding.

So a fund company buys and sells the units to the public at their net asset value. This value increases or decreases proportionally as the value of the fund's investments rises or falls. Let's say in March you pay $10 each for 100 units in a fund that invests in oil and gas shares, always a smelly and risky game. Now, say, by July, the value of the shares the fund holds has dropped by one-fifth. Then your units are worth just $8 each. So your original $1,000 investment is now worth only $800. But that August, a bunch of companies in which the fund has invested strike oil in Alberta. That sends the value of their shares soaring and lifts the fund's units to $15 each. The value of your investment has now grown to $1,500.

Where can you go from here? You've made a tidy profit after a bit of a letdown, but what happens next? Well, that depends on you. You can hang in there and see if more oil's in them there hills, or you can cash out. With most funds, you can simply buy or sell units at that day's net asset value. That flexibility is one of the great beauties of mutual funds. Funds that let you come and go as you please in this way are known as open-end funds, as though they had a giant door that's never locked. Think of a raucous Viking banquet where guests are free to come and go at will because the wall at one end of the dining hall has been removed.

That means most mutual funds are marvelously flexible and convenient. The managers allow you to put money into the fund on any business day by buying units, and you take money out again at will by selling your units back to the fund. In other words, an investment in a mutual fund is a liquid asset. A liquid asset is either cash or it's an investment that can be sold and turned into good old cash at a moment's notice. The idea is that cash and close-to-cash investments, just like water, are adaptable and useful in all sorts of situations. The ability to get your cash back at any time is called liquidity in investment jargon, and professionals prize it above all else — more than they prize red Porsches with very loud sound systems or crystal goblets in lovely velvet-lined boxes with their initials engraved in gold.

The other type of fund is a *closed-end fund.* Investors in these funds often are sold their units when the fund is launched, but to get their money back they must find another investor to buy the units on the stock market like a share, often at a loss. The fund usually won't buy the units back, or may buy only a portion. You can make money in closed-end funds, but it's very tricky. As craven brokerage analysts sometimes say when they hate a stock but can't pluck up the courage to tell investors to sell it: "Avoid."

The Nitty Gritty: How a Fund Makes You Money

We'll stick with the example of Investors Dividend, a huge and well-run fund generally available only through Investors Group agents across the country. Investors Dividend's $12.3 billion in assets as of mid-2008 made it Canada's biggest mutual fund. That's $1 million 12,400 times over, or about $373 for each of the approximately 30 million people living in Canada. The fund, which dates to 1961, invests in shares of large Canadian banks and blue-chip companies. This behemoth lumbers along in the middle of the performance pack of similar funds. Like other mutual fund companies, Investors Group, based in Winnipeg, sells units of Investors Dividend to the public every business day and buys them back from other investors at the same price.

The somewhat sleazy dawn of the mutual fund

The modern mutual fund evolved in the 1920s in the United States. In 1924, one Edward Leffler started the world's first open-end fund, the Massachusetts Investors Trust. It's still going. Mr. Leffler's fund had to be purchased through a broker, who charged a sales commission, adding to an investor's cost. Four years later, Boston investment manager Scudder Stevens & Clark started First Investment Counsel Corp., the first no-load fund (a fund you buy with no sales commission). The fund was called no-load because instead of purchasing it through a commission-charging broker, investors bought it directly from the company.

Nothing was wrong with those early open-end funds. They were run well and they survived the Great Crash of 1929 and the subsequent Depression, in part because the obligation to buy and sell their shares every day at an accurate value tended to keep managers honest and competent. But closed-end funds were the main game in the 1920s. (Closed-end funds don't buy back your units on demand, meaning you're locked into the fund until you find another investor to buy your units from you on the open market.) And a crooked game it was. By 1929, investors were paying ridiculous prices for closed-end shares. Brokers charged piratical sales commissions of 10 percent, annual expenses topped 12.5 percent, and funds kept their holdings secret. Needless to say, most collapsed in the Crash and ensuing Depression.

Following that debacle, mutual funds in Canada and the United States were far more tightly regulated, with laws forcing them to disclose their holdings at least twice a year and report costs and fees to investors. Plenty of badly run funds are still out there, not to mention plenty of greedy managers who don't put their unitholders' interests first, but at least now clear rules that protect investors who keep their eyes open exist.

With most companies' funds you're free to come and go as you please, but companies often impose a small levy on investors who sell their units within 90 days of buying them. That's because constant trading raises expenses for the other unitholders and makes the fund manager's job harder. The charge (which should go to the fund, and usually does) is generally 2 percent of the units sold, but it can be more. Check this out before you invest, especially if you're thinking of moving your cash around shortly after you buy.

Returns — What's in it for you?

The main reason why people buy mutual funds is to earn a return. A return is simply the profit you get in exchange for either investing in a business (by buying its shares) or for lending money to a government or company (by buying its bonds). It's money you get as a reward for letting other people use your cash — and for putting your money at risk. Mutual fund buyers earn the same sorts of profits but they make them indirectly because they're using a fund manager to pick their investments for them. The fund itself earns the profits, which are either paid out to the unitholders or retained within the fund itself, increasing the value of each of its units.

When you invest money, you nearly always hope to get:

- **Trading profits** or capital gains (the two mean nearly the same thing) when the value of your holdings goes up. Capital is just the money you've tied up in an investment, and a capital gain is simply an increase in its value. For example, say you buy gold bars at $100 each and their price rises to $150. You've earned a capital gain of $50, on paper at least.

- **Income** in the form of interest on a bond or loan, or dividends from a company. Interest is the regular fee you get in return for lending your money, and dividends are a portion of a company's profits paid out to its shareowners. For example, say you deposit $1,000 at a bank at an annual interest rate of 5 percent; each year you'll get interest of $50 (or 5 percent of the money you deposited). Dividends are usually paid out by companies on a per-share basis. Say, for example, you own 10,000 shares and the company's directors decide to pay a dividend of 50 cents per share. You'll get a cheque for $5,000.

You also hope to get the money you originally invest back at the end of the day, which doesn't always happen. That's part of the risk you assume with almost any investment. Companies can lose money, sending the value of their shares tumbling. Or inflation can rise, which nearly always makes the value of both shares and bonds drop rapidly. That's because inflation eats away at the value of the money, which makes it less attractive to have the money tied up in such long-term investments where it's vulnerable to steady erosion.

Here's an example to illustrate the difference between earning capital gains and dividend income. Say you buy 100 shares of a company — a Costa Rican crocodile farm, for example — for $115 each and hold them for an entire year. Also, say you get $50 in dividend income during the year because the company has a policy of paying four quarterly dividends of 12.5 cents, or 50 cents per share, annually (that is, 50 cents times the 100 shares you own — $50 right into your pocket).

Now imagine the price of the stock rises in the open market by $12, from $115 to $127. The value of your 100 shares rises from $11,500 to $12,700, for a total capital gain of $1,200.

Your capital gain is only on paper unless you actually sell your holdings at that price.

Add up your gains and income, and that's your total return — $50 in dividends plus a capital gain of $1,200, for a total of $1,250.

Another example should make this crystal clear. Investors Dividend units were sold to the public at $24.77 on the first day of April 2007 and rose to $25.48 by the end of May. Things weren't so good the rest of the year: The unit price went up and down until October, when it began a prolonged fall, to $21.83 by the end of March 2008. That was a loss of 2.9 cents on every unit an investor held.

The fund also paid out a quarterly distribution, a special or scheduled payment to unitholders, of 14.5 cents per unit at the end of June and September 2007; 15.2 cents at the end of December 2007; and 16.0 cents at the end of March 2008, for a total distribution of 58.7 cents. Distributions are made when a fund has earned capital gains, interest, or dividends from its investments.

So what was the investor's return during the year? On a per-unit basis, she started with $24.77 at risk and during the following 12 months suffered a capital loss of $2.94. However, thanks to the 58.7 cents of distributions, this loss was trimmed to about $2.44 a unit. That represented about 9.8 percent of the starting figure of $24.77, so the *percentage* return, the amount she earned or lost by being invested, was a loss of 9.8 percent. Calculating the return is actually a little more complicated than that because most investors would have simply reinvested the quarterly distribution in more units immediately after being paid out. In fact, returns for mutual funds always assume that all distributions are reinvested in more units. Investors Dividend's official return for the year ended March 31, 2008, was a loss of 9.5 percent.

Returns as a percentage

Returns on mutual funds, and nearly all other investments, are usually expressed as a percentage of the capital the investor originally put up. That way you can easily compare returns and work out whether or not you did well.

After all, if you tied up $10 million in an investment to earn only $1,000, you wouldn't be using your cash very smartly. That's why the return on any investment is nearly always stated in percentages by expressing the return as a proportion of the original investment. In the example of the crocodile farm, the return was $50 in dividends plus $1,200 in capital appreciation, which is just a fancy term for an increase in the value of your capital, for a total of $1,250. At the beginning of the year you put $11,500 into the shares by buying 100 of them at $115 each. To get your percentage return (the amount your money grew expressed as a percentage of your initial investment), divide your total return by the amount you initially invested and then multiply the answer by 100. The return of $1,250 represented 10.9 percent of $11,500, so your percentage return during the year was 10.9 percent. It's the return produced by an investment over several years, however, that people are usually interested in. Yes, it's often useful to look at the return in each individual year — for example, a loss of 10 percent in Year 1, a gain of 15 percent in Year 2, and so on. But that's a long-winded way of expressing things. It's handy to be able to state the return in just one number that represents the average yearly return over a set period. It makes it much easier, for instance, to compare the performance of two different funds. The math can start getting complex here, but don't worry — we stick to the basic method used by the fund industry.

Fund returns are expressed, in percentages, as an average annual compound return. That sounds like a mouthful, but the concept is simple. Say you invested $1,000 in a fund for three years. In the first year, the value of your investment dropped by 10 percent, or one-tenth, leaving you with $900. In Year 2, the fund earned you a return of 20 percent, leaving you with $1,080. And in Year 3, the fund produced a return of 10 percent, leaving you with $1,188. So, over the three years, you earned a total of $188, or 18.8 percent of your initial $1,000 investment. When mutual fund companies convert that return to an "average annual" number, they invariably express the number as a "compound" figure. That simply means the return in Year 2 is added (or compounded) onto the return in Year 1, and the return in Year 3 is then compounded onto the new higher total, and so on. A return of 18.8 percent over three years works out to an average annual compound return of about 5.9 percent.

As the example demonstrates, the actual value of the investment fluctuated over the three years, but say it actually grew steadily at 5.9 percent. After one year, the $1,000 would be worth $1,059. After two years, it would be worth $1,121.48. And after three years, it would be worth $1,187.65. The total differs from $1,188 by a few cents because we rounded off the average annual return to one decimal place, instead of fiddling around with hundredths of a percentage point.

Remember these important points when looking at an average annual compound return:

- ✔ **Average:** That innocuous-looking average usually smoothes out some mighty rough periods. Mutual funds can easily lose money for years on end — it happened, for example, when the world economy was hurt by inflation and recession in the 1970s.

✔ **Annual:** Obviously, this means per year. And mutual funds should be thought of as long-term holdings to be owned for several years. The general rule in the industry is that you shouldn't buy an equity fund — one that invests in shares — unless you plan to own it for five years. That's because stocks can drop sharply, often for a year or more, and you'd be silly to risk money you might need in the short term (to buy a house, say) in an investment that might be down from its purchase value when you go to cash it in. With money you'll need in the near future, you're better off to stick to a super-stable, short-term bond or money market fund that will lose little or no money (more about those later).

Of course, mutual fund companies sometimes use the old "long-term investing" mantra as an excuse. If their funds are down, they claim it's a long-term game and that investors should give their miraculous strategy time to work. But if the funds are up, the managers run ads screaming about the short-term returns.

✔ **Compound:** This little word, which means "added" or "combined" in this context, is the plutonium trigger at the heart of investing. It's the device that makes the whole thing go. It simply means that to really build your nest egg, you have to leave your profits or interest in place and working for you so you can start earning income on income. After a while, of course, you start earning income on the income you've earned, until it becomes a very nicely furnished hall of mirrors.

Another example will help. Mr. Simple and Ms. Compound each have $1,000 to invest, and the bank's offering 10 percent a year. Now, let's say Mr. Simple puts his money into the bank, but each year he takes the interest earned and hides it under his mattress. Simple-minded, huh? After ten years, he'll have his original $1,000 plus the ten annual interest payments of $100 each under his futon, for a total of $2,000. But canny Ms. Compound leaves her money in the account, so each year the interest is added to the pile and the next year's interest is calculated on the higher amount. In other words, at the end of the first year, the bank adds her $100 in interest to her $1,000 initial deposit and then calculates the 10-percent interest for the following year on the higher base of $1,100, which earns her $110. Depending on how the interest is calculated and timed, she'll end the ten years with about $2,594, or $594 more than Mr. Simple. That extra $594 is interest earned on interest.

How funds can make you rich

The real beauty of mutual funds is the way they can grow your money over many years. "Letting your money ride" in a casino — by just leaving it on the odd numbers in roulette, for example — is a dumb strategy. The house will eventually win it from you because the odds are stacked in the casino operator's favour. But letting your money ride in a mutual fund over a decade or more can make you seriously rich.

An investment in Investors Dividend Fund from its launch in 1961 through the end of June 2008 produced an annual average compound return of about 8 percent. If your granny had been prescient enough to put $10,000 into the fund when it was launched, instead of blowing all her dough on sports cars and wild men, it would have been worth $5.4 million by mid-2008.

The main reason why Canadians had more than $697 billion in mutual funds at the end of 2007 is that funds let you make money in the stock and bond markets almost effortlessly. By the way, that $697 billion figure, which works out to an incredible $21,121 or so for everyone in the country, doesn't even include billions more sitting in segregated funds, which are mutual fund–like products sold by life insurance companies. They're called segregated because they're kept separate from the life insurer's regular assets. You can read more on seg funds in Chapter 19.

Of course, no law says you have to buy mutual funds in order to invest. You might make more money investing on your own behalf, and lots of people from all walks of life do. But it's tricky and dangerous. So millions of Canadians too busy or scared to learn the ropes themselves have found that funds are a wonderfully handy and reasonably cheap alternative. The Canadian fund industry association, the Investment Funds Institute of Canada, reports the public had more than 52 million accounts with its member firms at the end of 2007. Buying funds is like going out to a restaurant compared with buying food, cooking a meal, and cleaning up afterward. Yes, eating out is expensive, but it sure is nice not to have to face those cold pots in the sink covered in slowly congealing mustard sauce.

What mutual funds buy

Mutual funds and other investors put their money into just two long-term investments:

- ✔ **Stocks and shares:** Tiny slices of companies that trade in a big, sometimes chaotic but reasonably well-run electronic vortex called, yes, the stock market.
- ✔ **Bonds:** Loans made to governments or companies, which are packaged up so that investors can trade them to one another.

Folk memories run deep, and after ugly stock market meltdowns in the 1920s and 1970s, mutual funds and stocks in general had unhealthy reputations for many years. For generations, Canadians, like people all over the world, preferred to buy sure things, usually bonds or fixed-term deposits from banks, the beloved guaranteed investment certificate (GIC). But as inflation and interest rates started to come down in the 1990s, it became harder and harder to find a GIC that paid a decent rate of interest — research shows most people are truly happy when they get 8 percent.

As Table 1-1 shows, the Canadian mutual fund industry really started growing like a magic mushroom on a wet morning in Victoria in the mid-1990s, after rates on five-year GICs dropped well below that magic 8 percent. At that point, Canadians decided they were willing to take a risk on equity funds.

Table 1-1 shows the growth of the Canadian mutual fund industry from 1970 to the end of March 2008.

Table 1-1	Growth of the Mutual Fund Industry in Canada		
Year	Total Assets ($Billions)	Year	Total Assets ($Billions)
1970	2.5	1989	23.5
1971	2.5	1990	24.9
1972	2.7	1991	49.9
1973	2.2	1992	67.3
1974	1.6	1993	114.6
1975	1.8	1994	127.3
1976	1.8	1995	146.2
1977	1.8	1996	211.8
1978	1.9	1997	283.2
1979	2.7	1998	326.6
1980	3.6	1999	389.7
1981	3.5	2000	418.9
1982	4.1	2001	426.4
1983	5.8	2002	391.3
1984	6.7	2003	438.9
1985	10.2	2004	497.3
1986	17.5	2005	570.0
1987	20.4	2006	660.2
1988	20.8	2007	697.3
		2008	700.1

Industry statistics provided by the Investment Funds Institute of Canada.

Types of Funds

Mutual funds fall into four main categories. Later in the book we devote chapters to each type, but this is a quick breakdown of the bare facts. The four main types of mutual funds are:

- **Equity funds:** By far the most popular type of fund on the market, equity funds hold stocks and shares. Stocks are often called "equity" because every share is supposed to entitle its owner to an equal portion of the company. In mid-2008, Canadians had $178 billion in Canadian stock funds, $93 billion in global stock funds, and another $20 billion in U.S. equity funds. These funds represent an investment in raw capitalism — ownership of businesses. We look at the range of equity funds available to you in Chapters 10, 11, and 12.

- **Balanced funds:** The next biggest category is balanced funds. They generally hold a mixture of just about everything — from Canadian and foreign stocks to bonds from all around the world, as well as very short-term bonds that are almost as safe as cash. Chapter 13 gives you the scoop on balanced funds.

- **Bond funds:** These beauties, also referred to as "fixed-income" funds, essentially lend money to governments and big companies, collecting regular interest each year and (nearly always) getting the cash back in the end. We offer the thrilling details about these funds in Chapter 14.

- **Money market funds:** They hold the least volatile and most stable of all investments — very short-term bonds issued by governments and large companies that usually provide the lowest returns. These funds are basically savings vehicles for money you can't afford to take any risks with. They can also act as the safe little cushion of cash found in nearly all well-run portfolios. Chapter 17 fills you in about these funds.

Where-to-Buy Basics

Chapter 3 goes into detail about some of the legal and bureaucratic form-filling involved in buying a fund (don't worry, it's not complicated). In essence, you hand over your money and a few days later you get a transaction slip or confirmation slip stating the number of units you bought and what price you paid. You can buy a mutual fund from thousands of people and places across Canada, in one of four basic ways:

- **Buying from professional advisers:** The most common method of making a fund purchase in Canada is to go to a stockbroker, financial planner, or other type of adviser who offers watery coffee, wisdom, and suggestions on what you should buy. These people will also open an account for you in which to hold your mutual funds. They are essentially salespeople and they nearly always make their living by collecting sales commissions on the funds they sell you, usually from the fund company itself. Their advice may be excellent and they can justifiably claim to impose needed discipline on their clients by getting them into the healthy habit of saving. But always remember that they have to earn a living: The funds they offer will tend to be the ones that pay them the best commissions.

Examples of fund companies that sell exclusively through salespeople, planners, and stockbrokers are Mackenzie Financial Corp., Fidelity Investments Canada Ltd., AIM Trimark Funds, CI Fund Management Inc., AGF Management Ltd., and Templeton, all based in Toronto. Investors Group Inc. of Winnipeg, Canada's biggest fund company, also sells through salespeople, but the sales force is affiliated with the company.

✔ **Bank purchases:** The simplest way to buy funds is to walk into a bank branch. You also can call your bank's toll-free telephone number. But, increasingly, people are buying funds online, at banks' Web sites. Banks never charge sales commissions to investors who buy their funds. The disadvantage to this approach is limited selection, because most bank branches are set up to sell only their company's funds. And not all bank staff are equipped or trained to give you detailed advice about investing. But the beauty of this approach is that you can have all your money — including your savings and chequing accounts and even your mortgage or car loan — in one place, making it simple to transfer money from one account to another. Buying your mutual funds at your bank can also earn you special rates on loans.

✔ **Buying direct from fund companies:** For those who like to do more research on their own, excellent "no-load" companies sell their funds directly to investors. They're called no-load funds because they're sold with no sales commissions. No-load funds can avoid levying sales charges because they don't market their wares through salespeople. Because these funds don't have to make payments to the advisers who sell them, they often come with lower expenses. Examples of no-load companies include Beutel Goodman; GBC; Leith Wheeler; Mawer; McLean Budden; Phillips, Hager & North; Sceptre; and Saxon. Once again, limited selection of funds is a drawback.

✔ **Buying from discount brokers:** Finally, for the real do-it-yourselfers who like to make just about every decision independently, you can find discount brokers that operate on the Internet or over the phone. Mostly but not always owned by the big banks, they sell nearly every fund from nearly every company, usually free of commissions and sales pitches.

Discount brokers are a huge force in the United States and they've gained popularity in Canada. The advantages, and they're significant, are low costs and a wide selection of funds. But don't expect personal help from a discounter. We talk more about discount brokers in Chapter 6.

Chapter 2

Buying and Selling Basics

In This Chapter

▷ Exploring reasons to choose mutual funds

▷ Looking at potential drawbacks of funds

▷ Considering load versus no-load funds

Mutual funds were one of the 20th century's great wealth-creating innovations. Funds transformed stock and bond markets by giving people of modest means easy access to investments previously limited to the rich. The fund-investing concept is likely to remain popular for years, letting ordinary and not-so-ordinary people build their money in markets that would otherwise intimidate them. That's because the idea of packaging expert money management in a consumer product, which is then bought and sold in the form of units, is so brilliantly simple. Even journalists can understand it.

In this chapter, we take another look at funds, assessing their great potential as well as their nasty faults. We wrap up with a chat about the relative merits of no-load and load funds.

Reasons to Buy Funds

In Chapter 1, we discuss how and why mutual funds work and why they make sense in general. Here we give you some specific, significant reasons to make them a big part of your financial plan.

Offering safety in numbers: Public scrutiny and accountability

Perhaps the best thing about mutual funds is that their performance is public knowledge. When you own a fund, you're in the same boat as thousands of other unitholders, meaning the fund company is pressured to keep up the performance. If the fund lags its rivals for too long, unitholders will start redeeming, or cashing in, their units, which is the sort of thing that makes a manager stare at the ceiling at 4 a.m., sweat rolling down his or her grey face. Fund companies are obliged to let the sun shine into their operations — and sunlight is the best disinfectant — by sending unitholders clear annual financial statements of the fund's operations. These statements are tables of figures showing what the fund owns at the end of the year, what expenses and fees it paid to the management company, and how well it performed. Statements are audited (that is, checked) by big accounting firms. The management company must also at least offer to send you the semi-annual statements, showing how the fund was doing halfway through the year. (To get the semi-annual statement, you often have to mail back a fiddly little card requesting it. Make sure you do. It costs you nothing, and knowing that investors are interested in what's happening to their money helps to keep fund companies on their toes. If you want to reduce paper burden, make a note of looking for this information on the fund company's Web site.) For more on the financial statements for funds, see Chapter 3.

A lot of the information in the statements is hard to understand and not particularly useful, but always check one thing: Look at the fund's main holdings. If you bought what you thought was a conservative Canadian stock, for example, then you want to see lots of bank stocks and other companies you've at least heard of.

Don't confuse the financial statements — which describe how the fund is doing — with your own individual account statement. Your account statements are personal mailings that show how many units you own, how many you've bought and sold, and how much your holdings are worth. Companies usually must send you personal account statements at least twice a year. Some fund sellers, such as banks, send quarterly statements, and discount brokers often mail them monthly. Fund companies also have Internet-based and telephone-based services that let you verify the amount of money in your account every day. See Chapter 3 for more on account statements.

The next section helps you decipher price and performance figures. When you know what to look for, you can accurately track your funds' performance. We're not saying your fund manager won't give you the straight story, but getting a second opinion is never a bad plan, especially when it comes to your cash.

Finding and reading price tables

Time was you could check a mutual fund's unit price, or net asset value per share, in most daily newspapers. (A fund's NAVPS is its total assets under management divided by the numbers or shares of units held by its investors; less the management fees and other operating expenses charged to the fund by its portfolio managers or administrators.) But daily tables are now virtually extinct, and the few that remain are on the endangered species list. Although the two national dailies, *The Globe and Mail* and the *National Post,* still publish weekly price summary tables, these include only a handful of the larger, more popular funds. Only the *Post* continues to offer a (very short) daily table. It takes a lot of news-page space to print more than 7,000 fund prices, so the newspaper industry now uses the Internet to provide this information. If you're Internet-savvy, you also can look up fund prices on individual fund company Web sites. We talk more about how to look up fund prices and check performance in Chapter 21.

Most mutual funds calculate and publish a value for their units every day that stock and bond markets are open. Some small or very specialized funds do this only monthly or weekly, and some take a day or two getting the information out, but unit prices for most widely available funds are available the next day on fund information Web sites and, to a limited extent, in major newspapers. The listing also usually shows the change in unit price from the previous day. See Figure 2-1 for a Saturday listing for Investors Dividend Fund from the *Financial Post*.

Figure 2-1:
A Saturday
mutual
fund listing
from the
Financial
Post.

Fund	NAVPS	$ ch	Yr %ch	Fund	NAVPS	$ ch	Yr %ch	Fund	NAVPS	$ ch	Yr %ch
Mthly Div	19.51	+.01	−1.3	Cnd Equ(L)	652.63	−.86	—	Income Tr	12.14	+.13	—
Mthly Hilm	10.08	+.08	−.9	CndEqu (G)	19.45	−.19	—	**National Band Funds(n)**			
Mthly Hinll	13.83	+.12	−.8	Consery Pr	14.60	+.00	—	Bond	11.07	−0.1	+1.4
Great-West NL				Div (L)	24.73	+.27	—	C Cash	10.00	unch	−1.3
CdnRE1(G)7	17217.90	+.05	—	Divers (L)	236.63	+.61	—	Cdn Equity	10.05	+.05	—
Highstreet				Equity(MF)	13.42	+.23	—	Cdn Opp	11.52	+.02	—
Balanced	15.2	+.03	−3.2	Glo Eq (L)	7.77	+.10	—	Dividend	16.01	+.07	—
Cdn Bond	10.33	−.01	+1.8	Gr&In(AGF)	16.92	−.23	—	Glo Equ	7.40	+.02	—
Cdn Equity	29.24	+.12	−1.6	Gr&Inc(MF)	14.22	+.17	—	Global Bd	8.26	−.02	—
HSBC Funds Inv Ser CS(n)				Inc (L)	17.29	+.03	—	MMF	10.00	.00	−1.2
Balanced I	21.29	+.03	—	Income(MF)	16.86	+.06	—	Mortgage	10.79	unch	+2.2
Chinese-I	18.85	−.03	—	Int Equ	13.39	+.15	—	Mthly Inc	10.92	+.05	—
DivIncl	28.09	+.18	—	MMF (L)	24.49	+.00	—	Sml Cap	36.48	+.21	—

Checking and reading mutual fund performance

Newspapers' monthly fund performance reports have gone the way of the dodo bird. This is unfortunate if you liked to opened up those broad pages full of wide tables and highlight and circle things. Checking fund performance is now strictly an Internet operation. Assuming you are comfortable online, this is a very good thing. Apart from saving countless trees that used to be chopped up into newsprint pulp, you can get more immediate information and easily compare a fund against its peers and other investments. Go to Chapter 21 for more on how to make the most of the Internet for fund research.

Because mutual fund investing is primarily a longer-term undertaking, performance statistics should command more of your attention than daily prices do. How often should you check your fund's performance? Unfortunately, this question has no easy answer. But it's a good idea to look every three months or so to see how your manager is doing. Even if you bought your funds through a financial planner or other salesperson — who's supposed to be looking out for your interests — it never hurts to keep an eye on how well the recommendations are turning out.

Figure 2-2 is a sample from Morningstar.ca showing the returns for the Canadian Equity Balanced category, ranked by five-year compound annual return. Funds that buy the same sorts of investments are listed together, by category. Determining how a fund is categorized isn't easy nowadays, because data providers, who are members of the Canadian Investment Funds Standards Committee, use more than 40 asset categories. Your first step, then, is to enter the name of a fund in a Web site's general fund search tool, and then check its category on the page that appears.

Change Criteria	Results of Search	New Search | Definitions					
Daily Performance							
Fund Name (Click to select all)	1 D	▼1 W	1 Mth	3 Mth	YTD	NAVPS($)	
Trimark Select Balanced	0.7	1.9	-4.6	-5.7	-6.1	8.49	
Manulife GIF MLIP B Trimark Sel Balanced	0.7	1.9	-4.6	-5.7	-6.3	9.93	
Manulife GIF MLIA B Trimark Sel Balanced	0.7	1.9	-4.6	-5.7	-6.3	9.93	
Manulife GIFe 2 Trimark Sel Balanced	0.7	1.9	---	-5.8	-6.4	12.20	
Manulife GIFe 1 Trimark Sel Balanced	0.7	1.9	---	-5.9	-6.6	13.68	
Manulife GIF MLIP A Trimark Sel Balanced	0.7	1.9	---	-5.8	-6.5	10.03	
Manulife GIF MLIA A Trimark Sel Balanced	0.7	1.9	-4.7	-5.8	-6.5	10.03	
Manulife GIF CAP A Trimark Sel Balanced	0.7	1.9	-4.7	-5.8	-6.5	10.03	
Manulife GIF 2 Trimark Sel Balanced	0.7	1.9	---	-5.8	-6.4	12.20	
Manulife GIF 1 Trimark Sel Balanced	0.7	1.9	---	-5.9	-6.6	14.31	
Trimark Select Balanced Segregated	0.7	1.8	-4.8	-6.1	-6.8	6.30	
Great-West Life Balanced (AT) B	0.6	1.8	-4.4	-5.4	-5.9	332.32	
Great-West Life Balanced (AT) A	0.6	1.8	-4.4	-5.4	-6.0	322.91	
Investors Dividend B	0.6	1.8	-4.5	-4.8	-8.6	20.86	
Investors Dividend A	0.6	1.8	-4.5	-4.8	-8.5	20.99	
IG GWL Dividend Segregated	0.6	1.8	-4.5	-4.9	-8.7	17.40	
London Life Balanced (AIM Trimark)	0.6	1.8	-4.5	-5.5	-6.2	11.77	
Quadrus Trimark Balanced	0.6	1.8	-4.5	-5.5	-6.1	10.00	
Trimark Diversified Income Class A	0.4	1.7	-4.0	-4.9	-5.5	9.16	
Trimark Monthly Income Private Pool A	0.4	1.7	-3.9	-4.9	-5.7	9.22	
Investors Dividend C	0.6	1.7	-4.6	-4.8	-8.7	20.52	
Mac Maxxum Monthly Income Series T8	0.4	1.6	-3.8	-5.2	-7.0	10.33	
Mac Maxxum Monthly Income Series T6	0.4	1.6	-3.8	-5.2	-7.0	12.86	
Mac Maxxum Monthly Income Seg	0.4	1.6	-3.8	-5.3	-7.1	7.05	
Mac Maxxum Monthly Income	0.4	1.6	-3.8	-5.2	-7.0	10.08	

Results: 1-25 of 312 Next 25   Click column heading to rank

Data as of 18 Jul 08

Figure 2-2: An extract from Morningstar.ca showing returns for funds in the Canadian Equity Balanced category, ranked by five-year compound annual return.

The table provides the fund name at far left and, at the far right, its price, or net asset value per share, at the end of the most recent business day. In between are the percentage changes in price over one day, one week, one month, and three months, as well as the change from the beginning of the year. This is but one of many pages available on Morningstar.ca that provide data for this and all other fund categories. Similar information is available on Globefund.com. Go to Chapter 21 for the full story on researching funds on the Internet.

Making sense of the numbers

What can you do with this jumble of numbers? The unit price is useful information, because by multiplying the price by the number of units you own you can work out the value of your holdings. You can also make sure the unit price in the newspaper matches the price shown on the statement you get from your broker or fund company, in order to double-check their bookkeeping. Keep the newspaper's mutual fund reports for June 30 and December 31 in your little sequined satchel until you've done your checking, because you'll be getting reports from your fund company showing the value of your holdings as of those dates.

The unit price is also handy if you're hazy on which fund you actually own. Don't laugh — a lot of smart people aren't always sure. With more than 7,000 funds, versions of funds, and fund-like products available in Canada, it's easy to get confused. Often, several different versions of a particular fund are on sale, depending on how you buy it (such as a front-end or back-end load) and other factors such as investment guarantees. If your account statement shows you own a fund with a unit price of $10.95, for instance, and the newspaper reports the same price, chances are you're talking about the same fund. However, you might have to go so far as to check your statements for the precise name of the fund, including the series or class letter — or even check the fund sales code, which is used by fund salespeople when making transactions.

The meat of the subject is contained in the performance numbers. These returns are after the fund's fees and expenses have been deducted. Some exceptions to this practice exist in the monthly report — that is, funds that levy extra charges that reduce the performance shown — but the returns for all of the biggest companies are after charges. The companies that deduct fees and expenses after the returns shown in such tables are generally fund companies that sell funds as part of a comprehensive financial package. Clients get a customized statement that lists their fees separately, instead of lumping in the charges with the fund's overall return. Always check whether the returns you're being shown are before or after the deduction of all charges and costs.

Putting your eggs in many baskets

Another good reason to buy mutual funds is the fact that they instantly mitigate your risk by letting you own lots of stocks and bonds, ideally in many different markets. Diversification, spreading your dollars around, is the cornerstone of successful investing. Diversifying means you won't be slaughtered by a collapse in the price of one or two shares.

Some people learn about diversification the hard way. Investors think they've lucked into the next big thing, hand over their entire fortune, and then lose it all in a cruel market correction. Pinning your hopes on just one stock or handful of stocks is never a wise move, so don't let this happen to you.

Mutual funds let ordinary investors buy into faraway markets and assets. It would be difficult and expensive for most ordinary people to purchase shares in Asia or Europe, or bonds issued by Latin American governments (go easy on those, though), if they couldn't buy them through mutual funds. Although events of global impact such as terrorist activity, natural disasters, and the surging price of oil have an impact on markets worldwide, some respond positively to developments, and others respond negatively. It's tough to keep track of it all and predict which markets will be affected and by how much. So, we ask: Why even try? History demonstrates that a portfolio with lots of different and varied asset classes will tend to suffer fewer speed bumps.

Most equity mutual funds own shares in at least 50 companies — fund managers who try to go with more "concentrated" portfolios have been known to get their fingers burned. In fact, academic research suggests that only seven stocks may be enough to provide adequate diversification for an investor, but seeing dozens of names in a portfolio offers a lot more reassurance.

Getting good returns from professional management

One of the most entertaining and informative books ever written on the subject of investing is A Fool and His Money: The Odyssey of an Average Investor by John Rothchild. First published in 1988, the book describes Mr. Rothchild's own abject failure in the market and includes his observation that most amateur investors are less than frank about how they've actually done. Even if they've had their heads handed to them, they tend to claim they ended up "about even." The moral of the story: Even if your relatives and pals claim to have made a fortune in the market, treat their boasts with a goodly dose of skepticism.

Yes, bad funds abound. But chances are you'll do better in a mutual fund than you would investing on your own. At least the people running funds are professionals who readily dump a stock when it turns sour, instead of hanging on like grim death, as we amateurs tend to do. The habit of selling quickly and taking the loss while it's still small is said to be one of the main traits that distinguishes the pro from the amateur.

Making investing convenient

Funds are just so darned handy, no wonder hundreds of millions of people around the world buy them. Yes, you could make your own lip balm. You could gather the eucalyptus bark and the deer's eyelid secretions, and boil them up in a big copper pot for days while chanting your head off. But it's easier just to walk into the drugstore and buy a stick. Likewise, it's a snap to sign a cheque or let the fund company deduct cash from your bank account regularly — a lot easier than worrying about the market and finding out the difference between investing in a long-dated strip bond and an exciting, newly listed, Internet solutions startup with scalable technology.

Critics of funds claim, with some justification, that the industry has brain-washed members of the public into thinking they're too stupid to invest for themselves. And it does seem fund companies want us to believe it's neces-sary to have some 25-year-old pup in a suit do it for us, in return for a fat fee. But the reality is that most people are just too busy, confused, or plain lazy to figure out the investing game. This book will make you an educated fund investor, whether you choose to deal with that young pup or go it alone. In Chapter 4, we list a few sample portfolios that are about as easy to buy as a candy bar — and a lot better for you.

The difference between the average and the median

Sometimes figuring out whether a fund has done better than other funds in its group is harder than it looks. When you look at a newspaper fund report, you'll come across two terms used to describe the typical fund's performance: The average and the median. The average and the median are both numbers that attempt to show how funds in a particular category have done. That way, if you're interested in a fund you can compare its performance with that of its rivals. For example, if you're considering buying your bank's U.S. equity fund, it's a good idea to see how it has done compared with other funds in the U.S. equity category. However, sometimes the average can be distorted upward or downward by a few extreme cases, so the median acts as a middle point, giving a good idea of what the typi-cal return for funds was. Here's how it works:

✔ The **average** is calculated by simply adding up the return figures for all funds for a particular period and then dividing by the number of funds involved.

✔ The **median** is the halfway mark. Half of the funds were below that point and half were above.

Normally, the two numbers are very similar, but a sprinkling of very high or low returns in the sample can pull them apart. An "average" figure can be a misleading comparative, because it gives equal weight to each and every member of that group — regardless of the significance of each member. To be truly useful, an average must be "weighted" according to, in the case of a fund category, each individual fund's assets.

For an example, take a look at the Canadian small/mid-cap equity category, which includes more volatile funds that focus on stocks of smaller companies. In 2006, the average fund in this category gained 14.0 percent, while the median return was just 10.9 percent. Why such a great difference? Because the average was pumped up by enormous returns — as high as 60.5 percent — from a handful of funds that happened to ride some red-hot little shares. Although 2006 was a good year for this type of fund, about one-third of them made less than 10 percent — nowhere near the stratospheric numbers put in by the category leaders.

Investing without breaking the bank

The typical Canadian stock fund rakes off about 2.3 percent of your money each year in fees and costs. That's a hefty charge, but the fund company also relieves you of a lot of drudgery and tiresome paperwork in return. Funds offer a lot of convenience. The fund company keeps your money safe and handles the recordkeeping for your savings. It all leaves you free and clear to get on with your first love, naked samba dancing.

In fact, mutual funds are a positive bargain if you're just starting to invest. Quite a few companies will let you put as little as $500 into their funds, and you can often open up a regular investment plan — where the money is simply taken out of your bank account — for as little as $50 a month. That's a pretty good deal when you realize that fund companies actually lose money on small accounts. If an investor has, say, $1,000 in an equity fund with a management expense ratio (MER) of 2.3 percent, then the company is collecting only $23 in fees and expenses, barely enough to cover postage and administration costs let alone turn a profit. Even the cheapest "discount" stockbroker in Canada will let you do only one trade for about 25 bucks.

The costs of a mutual fund investment are buried in the MER and the relatively incomprehensible statement of operations, but at least you can work them out with a bit of digging. Try asking traditional full-service stockbrokers for a clear explanation of their commission rates. You'll get a lot of mumbling and long sentences containing the phrase "it depends," but no clear answers.

Why dollar-cost averaging may be a fairy tale

Pick up nearly any fund company's colourful and relentlessly upbeat brochure (they're written by chipmunks and tiny bluebirds that are cruelly force-fed a diet of snack cakes and fuchsia blossoms). Just before you pass out with boredom, you'll almost certainly see a phrase along these lines: "Investing small amounts regularly means you buy more units when prices are low and fewer units when they're high, reducing the average cost of the units you purchase." Well, maybe. But that's about as useful as saying it's a bad idea to go up to muscular guys in Sudbury, Ontario, and imitate them in a mocking, mincing, way. Sort of obvious. The industry even has a name for the strategy — dollar-cost averaging.

Don't get us wrong: Putting small amounts into a decently run mutual fund over many years is a great way to build wealth. But independent researchers are skeptical as to whether dollar-cost averaging actually means better returns. If the strategy worked, you'd expect it to produce the best results with volatile funds — those whose unit prices bounce around the most — because you'd be buying lots when they were in the dumps and very few when they were riding high. Chicago-based researcher Ibbotson Associates, famed for compiling widely used figures on investment returns, looked at ten pairs of funds with the same compound annual returns over a decade but very different volatility. Even using the fund industry's beloved

dollar-cost averaging strategy, the less volatile fund produced the better return seven out
of ten times. So invest small amounts regularly, because it's a great way to grow your
money. But don't assume you're getting units at
bargain basement prices. The evidence seems
to be that the best way to make money in the
stock and bond markets is simply to invest your
cash as early as possible — and let time and
compound returns work their magic.

Watching over your investment

Mutual fund companies are pretty closely watched, not only by overworked
provincial securities regulators, but also, believe it or not, by rival companies. Competing companies don't want a rotten peach spoiling the reputation of the whole barrel. The Investment Funds Institute of Canada (IFIC),
the industry lobby group, is a mouthpiece for the companies, naturally. But
it also generally keeps an eye on things. And Toronto, where most of the
industry is based, is a village where everyone knows everyone. You'd be
surprised how many industry executives tell reporters about skullduggery
off the record — always about competing fund sellers, of course. Yes, greed
abounds. Despite some improvements in recent years, fees are still too high,
unitholder reports are often difficult to decipher, salespeople are given
goodies, and funds are sometimes used as horns of plenty when managers
divert their trading, and the resulting flow of commissions, to their brokerage buddies. The good news is most companies are simply making too much
money honestly to risk it all by running scams.

The stocks, bonds, and other securities a fund buys with your money don't
even stay in the coffers of the fund company: Under provincial securities laws,
the actual assets of the fund must be held by a separate "custodian," usually
a big bank or similar institution. You're most likely to get swindled by your
salesperson, but in Chapter 8 we set out some of the best ways to protect
yourself. Just stick with regular mutual funds, those that come with a document called a "simplified prospectus" and are managed by widely known companies, and you should be okay.

Cashing out — Getting your money if you need it

If you decide to move your hard-earned cash out of a fund, your fund company will normally get your money to you within three days. Removing
money from a fund effortlessly whenever you like may not seem like a big
deal — but in the world of investing, being able to do so whenever you
want to, with no hassles or questions, is as good as a torrid fling with Ryan
Reynolds or Shania Twain, your choice.

Don't forget that lots of other investments, including guaranteed investment certificates, hit you with a penalty if you take your cash out early. Selling a stock invariably costs you a brokerage commission with no guarantee you'll get a decent price for your shares. Sell a bond and you're often at the mercy of your dealer, who can pluck a price out of the air.

Perils and Pitfalls of Funds

So now that you're convinced funds are the right place to be, we're going to throw you for a bit of a loop. An informed investor is a wealthy investor, after all, and it's important to realize that funds aren't perfect. None of these disadvantages mean you shouldn't buy mutual funds. But keeping them in mind will help you stay out of overpriced and unsuitable investments.

Excessive costs

When you start amassing serious money in mutual funds, your costs can get outrageous. For example, if you invest $100,000 in a set of typical equity funds with a management expense ratio of 2.3 percent, the fund company is siphoning off $2,300 of your money every year. The math gets truly chilling when you extrapolate the cost of management fees over long periods. Over 20 years, at an MER of 2.3 percent, the fund company will end up with an incredible 50 percent or so of the total accumulated capital. How so? Simply by slicing that little 2.3 percent off the top each year.

In theory, that's what it costs to pay a fund manager to actively invest on your behalf. But if you're content to accept whatever return — good or bad — the overall market can achieve, then you can save a bundle by owning index funds or, better still, exchange-traded funds (ETFs). Index funds are funds with low expenses that simply track the whole stock or bond market by producing a return in line with a market index, such as the Standard & Poor's/Toronto Stock Exchange composite index of approximately 300 well-known companies. An ETF is similar to an index fund except it trades on a stock exchange. They don't have a portfolio manager as they simply own all of the stocks in an index. A typical index fund, such as RBC Canadian Index, has expenses of 0.71 percent, and the main Canadian market ETF, iShares Canadian Composite Index, charges just 0.25 percent. See Chapter 15 for more on index funds and ETFs.

Style drift — When managers get lost in the jungle

In the past, some managers would drift or depart from the type of investments they told you they'd buy when you signed on, usually because they were chasing hot returns or because they were scared. You can keep tabs on the biggest portfolio holdings in your fund by checking the fund company's Web site — more on that in Chapter 21 — but your only legal entitlement to a full list of all of the portfolio contents is when the company sends you annual and semi-annual financial statements, but these typically do not arrive until three months following the period end.

The most prominent type of drift involves value and growth investing styles. The most glaring example of a value manager holding a growth stock was Nortel Networks in the late 1990s, which value managers held in their portfolios long after its price had multiplied many times. However, style drift has largely been a non-issue in recent years. One could argue that various Canadian equity funds run by AIM Trimark — a known value manager — are slipping into the growth stock arena by holding Research in Motion (RIM), the wireless device pioneer with a stock price many times greater than when Trimark Select Canadian Fund bought its shares in 2002. However, RIM was clearly a value play back then, so the issue becomes: How long should a value manager hold a stock that no longer provides value because its price is sky high?

Whether or not such examples represent style drift is highly debatable. It's an example of how you as an investor need to monitor your fund investments. Ultimately, it's your responsibility to make sure you're headed in the right direction.

When bad managers attack

They may be smart and they may be professionals, but fund managers sure can blow it, leaving behind nothing but a lot of little scraps of grey polyester and a bunch of ugly minus signs in front of their returns. Put down whatever you're eating — what you're about to see would make a 400-pound wild boar queasy — and have a look at Table 2-1. It shows some of the worst-performing Canadian equity funds during the past decade, with assets over $50 million. If you hung around with any of these lads for the whole of the decade, you missed out on a lot of fun.

Table 2-1	Slow Lane: Canadian Equity Underperformers in the Ten Years to June 2008 % Returns		
Fund Name	*1-Year Return*	*5-Year Annual*	*10-Year Annual*
IA Clarington Canadian Growth	−2.5	13.3	3.8
CIBC Canadian Equity Value	−4.8	8.2	3.8
Templeton Canadian Stock	−13.6	7.0	4.2
Desjardins Canadian Equity	−2.5	14.4	4.7
CIBC Canadian Equity	−1.9	13.0	5.3
MD Select	−5.9	12.1	5.6
National Bank Canadian Equity	−1.0	12.3	5.7
Altamira Capital Growth	14.7	18.0	6.3
Median Canadian equity mutual fund	**0.3**	**16.3**	**8.5**
S&P/TSX composite index	**6.7**	**18.2**	**9.0**

It's very rarely as terrifying as that, though. Companies usually replace managers of big funds after just a couple years of bad performance. Having a decent Canadian equity fund, in particular, is a marquee attraction for a company. It's the fund category carrying the most prestige, partly because it wins the most attention from the media. You can be sure that just about every manager running a large equity or balanced fund, Canadian or global, is working his or her silk socks off trying to top the performance league. Every so often, companies get in bidding wars for managers with a great reputation. So everyone running a fund is trying to get public notice for earning hot returns, because it increases his or her market value.

Can't see the forest for the funds

By mid-2008, Canada had an unbelievable 8,500 or so funds and fund-like products, counting segregated funds, U.S.–dollar editions, different versions with varying sales charges, and "guaranteed" funds with endlessly changing small print. There were funds that could be traded without racking up taxable capital gains, "market-neutral" funds that were supposed to shake off the effects of a bad stock market, funds that stuck to the safe and predictable world of income trusts, and funds that really didn't seem to have any very good reason for existing, to be honest. Table 2-2 tells the tale of this proliferation, showing the total number of investment funds in Morningstar's database at the end of each year since 1998.

Table 2-2	The Number of Investment Funds from 1998 to 2008
Year	*Number of Funds*
1998	2,441
1999	3,146
2000	3,979
2001	4,951
2002	5,859
2003	6,350
2004	6,639
2005	6,491
2006	7,338
2007	8,440
Mid-2008	8,479

Source: Morningstar

This ridiculous profusion of products exists for several reasons:

✔ Fund companies have learned the folly of relying too much on just one or two funds. The danger, for them, is that if performance goes in the tank then investors head for the door, pulling out tens of millions of dollars. Better to offer many varied funds so that if one turns cold, the others are still cooking.

✔ Like being a superhero, the fund business is, well, glamorous, and every-one wants in. But unlike pulling on the black tights, running a mutual fund is also profitable. When a fund company can get its assets above $100 million or so, it's difficult to lose money because those 2-percent management fees keep rolling in. And all sorts of newcomers have been coming into the fund industry, including insurance companies and even financial planning chains. But they love to offer their own house-brand funds because they get to keep all the fees instead of splitting the take with a separate name-brand fund company such as Mackenzie Financial Corp. or AGF Management Ltd. Clients are often happier with a name they've heard of, though, so insurance companies have taken to hiring well-known mutual fund companies as managers of their funds. However, the fund remains the insurance company's own product — and the insurer gets to keep the lion's share of the management fee.

✔ The investment game, with its hype and image obsession, is essentially a branch of showbiz. Every year you have something new to keep the salespeople awake and the investors hungry.

✔ Finally, in fairness to the industry, some of the new funds are meant to satisfy consumers' demands. Investors' thirst for income-producing investments in recent years brought a raft of funds that invest in income trusts and other income-generating securities. Although income trusts have lost their tax advantage over dividend-paying stocks, income-producing investments remain a popular tool for many boomer-age and older investors.

Vague explanations of poor performance

No matter how badly a fund did, the analysis given to investors is frequently a languid description of the stock or bond market and a few of the manager's choice reflections on the future of civilization. All written in a sort of Old Etonian detached and refined tone, as though the person running the fund was really just dabbling, old chap. Don't really have to work at all, don't you know, what with the estate in Scotland and the trust funds. Only really drop by the office for half an hour every two weeks or so, dash it all. Damn busy with the golf and usually comatose by 5 p.m.

What unitholders deserve, but too often are denied, is an honest discussion of whether their fund kept up with the market and its peers. Securities regulators are putting the squeeze on companies to improve their reports, but it'll take time. You shouldn't have to pull on a grubby deerstalker hat and smoke a smelly pipe to discover what went wrong with performance and what the manager plans to do about it.

In the meantime, if your fund lags the market and other funds in the same category, ask for a clear explanation from your broker or financial planner if you got advice when buying funds. If you bought a no-load fund, look for a written set of reasons in the company's regular mailings to unitholders. Because no-load companies deal directly with their investors — instead of going through a salesperson — their reports are often clearer than the information provided by companies that market their funds through advisers.

Another big problem in the reporting of performance is that all too often it's not at all clear who is actually running your fund and how long they've been doing it. Fund companies rarely, if ever, print the length of a manager's tenure, and they usually don't warn investors in a timely way if he or she quits or is fired. Yes, a few veteran managers have been running the same fund for years. And some companies such as Fidelity Investments Canada Ltd. make it reasonably plain who's actually calling the shots. But at many companies, managers come and go with such unpredictable frequency that it's difficult if not impossible to keep track of them. Rather than worry about finding a genius to pick your stocks, you're much better off looking at the fund itself. Make your decision about investing with an eye to how the fund has performed and what it currently holds, rather than trying to figure out who is in the top spot.

Prospectuses that don't say enough

It's often hard to tell from a company's Web site, promotional handouts, and even official reports to unitholders whether the returns from its funds have been any good. That's because most companies, incredibly, still don't show their performance against an appropriate market benchmark, such as the Standard & Poor's/Toronto Stock Exchange composite index (S&P/TSX) for Canadian equity funds or the MSCI World Index for global equity funds. However, things have gotten better since the fund industry began producing prospectuses that are fairly easy to understand. A prospectus is the document that must be given to the purchasers of a fund, describing its rules and risks. A prospectus must provide performance numbers that compare a fund to a benchmark, such as the S&P/TSX for Canadian equity funds. Prospectuses also give the fund's returns on a year-by-year calendar basis, which is invaluable for checking whether unitholders have enjoyed steady returns or suffered through insane swings.

However, prospectuses are still of only limited usefulness because they don't say why the fund has lagged or outperformed its benchmark. Fortunately, a fairly new, additional document, the *management report of fund performance,* has taken a big step toward providing useful comparative data and explanations of a fund's recent performance. More on these in Chapter 3.

Too many funds and too few long-term results

Fund managers love to talk about how investing is a long-term game — especially when they're losing money — but have you noticed how many ads you see touting performance over periods as short as one year? And companies seem unable to resist launching new funds that invest in the hottest new asset class — just in time to lose money for investors when the bubble bursts. It happened with science and technology funds in the early 2000s. At the beginning of the decade, the number of funds in this category had multiplied to more than 120, but the group then tanked with huge losses in 2001 and 2002. Today, fewer science and technology funds exist, but the group's median compound annual returns are mostly negative over most time spans. Did Canadians really need such a selection of science and technology funds? As the performance numbers attest, they arguably didn't need any of the wretched things. The median science and technology fund lost nearly 5 percent during the 10 years ended June 2008.

It's easy to get dizzy amid the flashing lights and loud music, and jump aboard the fund industry's carousel of new products. But steer clear of the fancy stuff and stick to plain old conservative equity and bond funds with your serious long-term money, and you'll end up ahead.

Load versus No-Load — The Great Divide

You can buy mutual funds in two main ways:

- ✔ **Through a professional seller:** You can get a salesperson such as a broker or financial planner to help. The broker has to earn a living, so you'll almost certainly end up buying load funds — a load is a sales charge or commission that's paid to the broker, either by you or by the fund company.

- ✔ **Going it alone:** You can pick your funds on your own, with perhaps some advice from a bank staffer or mutual fund employee. In that case, you'll often end up buying no-load funds, which don't levy a sales commission.

Grey areas abound. You can buy load funds on your own and pay no commissions (through a discount broker, which will provide little or no advice). Some brokers will sell you no-load funds or load funds on which they waive commissions. And banks can fall in between the two stools. But those are the two essential methods.

Load funds — The comfort zone

Most mutual funds in Canada are sold to investors by a salesperson who is in turn paid by way of a sales commission. Millions of people love the feeling of having an advocate and adviser who seems to know his or her way through the jungle of investing. And why not hire a professional? After all, you probably don't fix your plumbing yourself or remove your own appendix (too hard to get the stains out of the kitchen tiles).

Your adviser might work for a stockbroker, a financial planning firm, or an insurance brokerage — or he or she might be self-employed. But the important point is this: If you buy funds through a salesperson, your primary relationship is with them, not with the fund company.

Any fund company should be able to answer your questions about your account. Always make sure you get a regular account statement from the fund company itself (unless you're with one of the big stockbrokers; the big brokers usually handle all of the recordkeeping). But load companies, such as CI Funds, AIM Trimark, and Fidelity Investments Canada, won't even sell you funds directly. You have to open an account with a broker or planner, who will then put the order through for you. The companies' systems and much of their marketing are designed to deal with salespeople, not members of the public, so your buy and sell orders must come from your broker.

Seeing which companies sell load funds

Table 2-3 shows Canada's 20 biggest mutual fund companies (excluding CI Funds) at the end of June 2008 and the method they use to sell their funds. As you can see, 11 of the 20 giants are load companies. Eight of the no-load sellers are banking institutions, and one sells funds only to doctors and their families.

Table 2-3	Canada's 20 Biggest Fund Companies and How They Sell Their Funds	
Assets (as of June Company)	*2008 (in $Billions)*	*Selling Style*
Royal Bank of Canada	109.8	No-load
IGM Financial (Investors Group)	104.2	Load
Toronto-Dominion Bank	57.6	No-load
Canadian Imperial Bank of Commerce	51.0	No-load
Fidelity Investments Canada	44.2	Load
AIM Trimark	38.2	Load
Bank of Montreal	37.9	No-load

(continued)

Table 2-3 *(continued)*

Assets (as of June Company)	2008 (in $Billions)	Selling Style
AGF Management	27.1	Load
Franklin Templeton Investments	24.9	Load
Dynamic Funds	23.9	Load
Bank of Nova Scotia	19.6	No-load
MD Management	15.4	No-load
National Bank Group	11.9	No-load
Desjardins Group	11.3	No-load and load
Manulife Investments	10.1	Load
IA Clarington Investments	7.6	Load
HSBC Investments Canada	5.4	No-load
AIC Limited	5.1	Load
Brandes Investment Partners	5.1	Load
Northwest & Ethical Investments	4.5	Load

Source: Investment Funds Institute of Canada

Decoding sales commissions

Sales commissions on load funds come in a bewildering number of variations and forms. And discount brokers have dreamed up even more ways to make the whole thing even more complicated (see Chapter 6 for details). But when you buy a load fund from a broker or planner, you have three basic options.

You can negotiate and pay an upfront commission — known as a sales charge or front load — to the salesperson. Savvy investors usually pay 2 percent or less. That entitles you to sell the fund at any time with no further charges, and it sometimes gets you lower annual expenses.

Alternately, you can buy funds on a "low-load" basis. Some firms refer to this as "no-load," even though you must buy them through an adviser. There's no free lunch, of course, as a low-load fund generally will have higher annual expenses than the front-end version of the same fund.

Finally, you can buy funds with a back-end load or redemption charge. In that case, the fund company itself pays the commission to the broker — usually 5 percent in the case of an equity fund or a balanced fund and less for a bond fund. However, you, the investor, are on the hook for a "redemption charge" if you sell the fund within a set number of years. Table 2-4 shows the redemption charge formula for funds at Investors Group.

Table 2-4	Selling Periods and Redemption Charges at Investors Group
Sell During	**Applicable Redemption Charge**
First and second years	5.5%
Third year	5.0%
Fourth year	4.5%
Fifth year	4.0%
Sixth year	3.0%
Seventh year	1.5%
After that	0%

Note that Investors Group charges the same fee for redemptions made during the first two years following purchase; many other companies will charge less in the second year than the first. For example, Fidelity's redemption charge in the first year is 6 percent, and 5.5 percent in years 2 and 3, before dropping to 4.5 percent in year 4.

The redemption charge is based either on the original purchase cost of the units you're redeeming or their value at the time you sell. The policy varies by company. For example, Investors Group charges it on the value at the time of redemption, while Fidelity bases this fee on the value at the time of purchase. The first option is slightly better for you because, presumably, the value of your units will have increased by the time you redeem. For example, say you invest $10,000 in a fund on a back-end-load basis and the fund gains 20 percent, leaving you with $12,000. Say you decide to redeem half of your holding, incurring a 4.5-percent back-end load. If the redemption charge is based on your original investment, you pay $225 (which is 4.5 percent of $5,000), but if it's based on the current market value, you pay $270 (4.5 percent of $6,000).

But a difficulty exists for the fund industry with back-end loads. If the adviser doesn't have to wangle a commission out of the client every time he or she buys a fund, more of a temptation exists for brokers and planners to switch customers from fund to fund, collecting commissions from the fund companies along the way. So the fund industry borrowed a technique from the life insurers, who have been dealing with salespeople's naughty tricks for generations, and introduced the trailer fee. Trailers are essentially yet another commission — usually between 0.5 percent and 1 percent of the value of the client's holding annually — that's paid by the company to the salesperson each year as long as his or her customer stays in the fund. It's a payment for loyalty. The trailer comes out of the management fee, not out of your account, so you never see it.

Many load companies pay a higher trailer to salespeople when they sell the fund on a front-load basis, getting their sales commission directly from the investor. That's because the company itself hasn't had to pay the charge. So on front-load fund sales, where the investor negotiates and pays the commission, a company might pay a trailer of 1 percent of the client's holding of equity funds each year; but on deferred-load sales, where a company paid the original sales commission, the trailer might be only 0.5 percent. It all gets pretty confusing — and it gets more complicated as you go further in — but that's the basis of the commission structure in mutual funds. Chapter 8 provides tips on how to deal with salespeople.

No-load funds — The direct approach

The other great branch of the fund industry is the no-load sector — funds that sell directly to the public with no sales commissions. Here, life is much simpler. A no-load shop will open an account for you when you contact them; you do this without the involvement of a broker, planner, or any other kind of adviser. You're not charged to buy or sell a fund, although remember that to discourage in-and-out trading you often face a penalty of 2 percent or so if you dump a fund within three months of buying.

The banks dominate the no-load fund business through their vast customer bases, discount brokerage arms, and branch networks. Until recently they had difficulty building a strong record, and big market share, in equity funds. However, the Big Five banks have made gains in this area through improved performance and marketing through their branch networks, which has helped propel them to the top rungs of the fund-asset rankings.

Because no-load funds usually don't pay sales commissions to brokers — although they sometimes pay trailer fees to persuade advisers to sell their funds — their annual expenses and fees should be much lower than those of load funds. Should be, but aren't. Bankers aren't known for cutting fees where they can get away with keeping them high, and most no-load funds in Canada are only slightly cheaper than broker-sold funds. In other words, you can expect to part with more than 2 percent of your assets each year when you invest in most equity or balanced funds, no matter where you buy them. Some bank-run equity funds charge less than 2 percent — mostly income-oriented dividend funds, which generally are less complicated to manage than more aggressive stock funds.

The banks and a few other no-load-fund sellers also are the place to find index funds, which have ultra-low expenses — mostly less than 1 percent. **An index fund** costs very little to manage because its portfolio simply tracks the whole market by mimicking an index. These are known as passively managed funds, with no investment decisions necessary on the part of the managers. Because index funds generate such small management fees, load companies can't afford to sell them and also pay commissions to brokers. See Chapter 15 for more about index funds — and even less expensive passive investments known as exchange-traded funds, or ETFs.

No-load fund sellers' main bread and butter, like other fund companies, are actively managed funds — some of which also have relatively low expenses. An example is Phillips, Hager & North Ltd. of Vancouver, which has two excellent "actively managed" funds with expenses of less than 2 percent. Actively managed funds, unlike index funds, buy and sell particular stocks in an attempt to beat the market and other managers. However, no-load shops' bargain funds often have relatively high minimum investments in order to keep costs low (servicing tiny accounts isn't profitable, remember). PH&N requires a minimum account size of $25,000 with the company. See Chapter 9 for more on dealing directly with no-load companies.

How an Irish charmer revolutionized the mutual fund

Until the late 1980s, investors had to cough up the sales charge for load mutual funds themselves — it ran as high as 10 percent of the investor's money in some iniquitous cases. But in 1987 a brilliant fund marketer named Jim O'Donnell at Mackenzie Financial had a brainwave: Consumers loathed having to part with cash off the top just to pay a salesperson; they wanted to see all their money going to work for them right away. So why not have the company pay the commission to the broker and get the money back through the management fee?

There was at least one problem with the strategy: Investors who hadn't paid a sales charge upfront might be inclined to simply dump the fund whenever they wanted. They hadn't paid a sales load, after all, so they wouldn't feel like they were wasting the commission. So Mackenzie also introduced its redemption charges, which kicked in if you cashed out early. The back-end idea was a smash hit and the company's first back-end-load fund, the Industrial Horizon Fund, attracted hundreds of millions of dollars within months of its launch in 1987. The rest of the load fund industry soon copied it.

Chapter 3

Paperwork and Your Rights

. . . .

In This Chapter

▷ Making a fund purchase

▷ Figuring out a prospectus in a few seconds

▷ Getting to know the management report of fund performance

▷ Hearing what your account statement has to say

▷ Checking on how your investment is growing through annual reports

. . . .

*E*ver get work done on your house and notice how contractors talk? They use expressions such as "six of one and half a dozen of another" or "you could do that," and they'll pound 'em out in a barrage that leaves you more confused than before. People in the investment business like to drone on in the same way. They produce documents that explain every angle and aspect, but skip the stuff you really want to know: Is this fund any good and how has it done?

Investors hate getting piles of paper in the mail, but the glossy brochures keep coming. To some extent, the verbiage isn't the companies' fault. Securities law obliges those selling investments to disclose trivia their clients couldn't care less about. Still, it's pretty simple to filter out the noise in the mailings you get from a fund company — and cut straight to the information that really matters. And the documents from fund companies have improved, especially prospectuses, the all-important fact sheets that tell you about the promise and perils of a fund before you buy it. Industry regulators have gone further, requiring fund companies to provide performance update reports, written in plain English, to unitholders twice a year.

In general, the documents and forms you have to deal with are pretty straightforward. Mutual fund forms are set up to be easy to fill out. Some special questions apply for opening a registered retirement savings plan, or you may need to fill in sections of your tax return to report investment income and gains, but they tend to be simple.

In this chapter we go over the important paperwork, to demystify your account statement (the regular mailing that shows how you're doing) and walk you through a simplified prospectus (the brochure that describes the fund). As always, what to watch out for are the costs loaded on your account — and we show you where to sniff around.

Sign Me Up

The big thing to decide straightaway is whether you're investing inside a registered retirement savings plan — a special tax-sheltered account in which investment profits pile up tax-free — or in an ordinary, taxable account in which your money is subject to taxes (see Chapter 22 for more on how RRSPs work). You can expect to fill out two main types of forms when you buy mutual funds:

- ✔ An account application form — which may just be called a "retirement savings plan" form if it's for an RRSP.

- ✔ A form allowing the fund company to take fixed amounts out of your bank account for investment in funds, if you've decided to start a regular investing program. People usually have the money taken out monthly, but some fund companies allow you to use different periods, such as every week.

Starting a program of regular investments of small amounts into even a conservative mutual fund is one of the best ways of getting rich painlessly. For example, putting just $100 each month into the Royal Bank of Canada's biggest balanced fund (which holds a relatively stable mixture of stocks and bonds) from mid-1998 to mid-2008 left an investor with about $18,000.

Filling in your account (or RRSP) application form

When you decide to buy a mutual fund, the first thing you'll be asked to fill out is an "account application" form — which tells the company who you are, what you want to buy, and how much you want to spend. An account is like a little shelf on which all your investments are kept at the broker's or the mutual fund company's office.

The account application is the document that tells the fund company the following:

- ✔ Your name
- ✔ Address
- ✔ Level of investment knowledge
- ✔ The amount of money you want to put into each fund

For investors, it's actually one of the most useful and informative documents mutual fund sellers print. That's because it contains hard information the fund company needs itself, so the new account form is free of vagueness and verbosity. For example, in the space where the form asks how much you want to invest in each fund, it nearly always clearly states the minimum investment.

Before you agree to buy anything, have a good look at the application form. And if you have any questions at all, approach your seller for a clear explanation. The form will also sometimes disclose what extra fees — such as charges for administration — you're expected to cough up. That's not a sudden attack of candour on the company's part — it's simply that the bureaucrats need to know how you'll be paying, directly or by having it taken out of your account.

The form for opening a new account includes some odd-looking questions. The fund company or broker wants to know

- ✔ How experienced you are as an investor
- ✔ Your income
- ✔ Your net worth (the value of your personal assets after your debts are taken away)

They're not just being nosy here. One of the pillars of provincial securities law is a requirement that people selling investments should recommend only securities that are suitable for the customer — a principle referred to in the jargon as Know Your Client or KYC. In fact, the account application form is often just referred to as the KYC. The idea is this: An elderly investor on a limited income shouldn't have a big chunk of his or her portfolio rammed into a Low-Coupon Speculative High-Yield Unsecured Sub-Saharan Junk Bond Fund.

The KYC can be a useful protection for you if it turns out later that your adviser put you into funds that were too risky for your circumstances, but it also works to the salesperson's advantage. He or she has an automatic out if you lost money on a volatile fund but you claimed when you opened the account that you knew a fair bit about investing. This is no place to put on a brave face — if you're a complete novice, say so and be proud of it. Pretending to know more than you do could really get you into hot water here if a dispute erupts between you and your broker about an investment that went sour.

If you're investing with a bank or other no-load, direct fund seller, the application form will be issued by the company and it'll be clear that your deposit's going straight to them. But if you're buying funds through a financial planner or other independent fund salesperson, make sure you fill out an application form issued by the fund company itself. For your own security and convenience it's important that you're recorded as a customer on the books of the fund company, giving you an extra measure of protection if the dealer or financial planner makes an error or even runs into cash-flow or regulatory problems. For example, if you're investing in a Franklin Templeton Investments Corp. fund, see that the form you fill out is a Franklin Templeton form.

When money is held on the books of the mutual fund company itself, the account is said to be in client name. In other words, the account bears the name of the individual investor at the head office of the fund company. It's a good arrangement for you because that way, if you ever have a dispute with your broker or you want to move your account elsewhere, your units and your name are in the fund company's records, making it much easier to shift your money.

Nearly every big financial planning chain and mutual fund dealer is set up so that mutual fund units are held in client name on the books of the fund company. That means you can expect to get statements at least twice a year from both the dealer and the fund companies you've invested with; always check them against each other. However, with traditional stockbrokers such as RBC Dominion Securities Inc., or with discount brokers such as TD Waterhouse Inc., your money may be held only on the broker's books. In that case, the fund company may have no record of your account. Wherever you invest, it usually pays to keep an eye on the securities listed for your account and the transactions shown.

Discount brokers and traditional stockbrokers tend to have sophisticated back offices or administration systems because their clients usually own stocks and bonds as well as funds. That means mutual funds are held in the same big pot as other securities, so these brokers don't pass their clients names on to the mutual fund company. Unfortunately, that means the fund company may have no record of your investment, and therefore isn't able to send you an annual and semi-annual statement of your personal holdings. That could make it harder to resolve any disputes with your broker over what you bought and how much it's worth. And very early in your investing career, someone is certain to get an order wrong. As in any business, mistakes can happen when dealing with discount brokers, mutual fund companies, and fund dealers. However, the good news is that these are large organizations that have the resources to fix errors. But get everything in writing, retain copies of all of the forms you fill out, and keep brief notes of the orders you issue over the phone or online. Retain transaction confirmation numbers until you see evidence in your account that a purchase or sale has been conducted properly and according to your wishes.

Getting confirmed

Fund companies are required to send you a confirmation or transaction slip in the mail a few days after a transaction. This document confirms you've purchased units and for what amount, and whether you bought them with an upfront or "front-end" commission, on a "low-load" basis, or with a back-end load or redemption charge (assuming it's a fund that's sold with commissions). A back-end load or redemption charge applies when you sell fund units. Read the confirmation or transaction slip very carefully, and if you spot any errors, immediately contact the salesperson (or fund company, if you purchased directly) to get the mistake fixed.

Also, when writing your cheque to pay for your funds, make it payable to the fund company. Or, if it must be made out to your adviser's firm as opposed to the fund company, write "in trust" on the cheque. That gives you extra protection if the dealer hits financial problems, potentially tying your money up in bankruptcy proceedings.

The main thing, when you've decided what fund to buy, is keeping a brief note of what you asked for and what you were told. And hang on to copies, photocopies, or scanned images of everything. If a dispute arises, an investor who can calmly produce notes from his or her meetings with the adviser, along with copies of documents, will be taken far more seriously.

Prospectuses — Not Always Your Friend

A mutual fund *prospectus* is the document that must be given to you when you buy a mutual fund. It's the crucial method the fund industry uses to set out the purpose of the fund, describe the fees, costs, and charges, and warn buyers of the risks involved in investing in the fund. Always ask to see the prospectus before you buy a fund (the salesperson should offer it) and then make sure you read at least these two sections:

- ✔ The investment objectives of the fund — that is, the sort of things it invests in.

- ✔ The charges and fees — if they aren't clearly explained, then get your salesperson to help.

Prospectuses traditionally were written using vague language, laden with legalese or with so many technical terms that it was impossible to figure out whether a fund was worth buying. But during the past decade, securities regulators have forced fund companies to produce prospectuses and other documents that are clear and concise. Nowadays, prospectuses (and their new companions, management reports of fund performance) are summaries that allow investors to put their finger on important information quickly.

The prospectus itself actually comes in two parts. Part A is a very broad, catchall piece that serves to provide the bulk of the information required to inform you (and, perhaps more important, satisfy the lawyers that the regulatory requirements are being met). It covers absolutely every minute detail that could possibly be applied to all funds offered by a company. In some cases, such as when a fund company has various "families" or brands of funds, more than one Part A prospectus exists; be sure to obtain the one that applies to your fund.

A second document — somewhat predictably labelled Part B — provides information specific to your fund. Most fund companies have a list of Part B prospectuses, grouping related funds into individual documents. However, individual funds each have their own sections within this document. This is the part of the prospectus that contains the all-important historical performance and portfolio holdings information. The third piece of the disclosure puzzle is the management report of fund performance (MRFP), which mercifully is a self-contained piece. (We talk about the MRFP in the next section.)

You've been warned

Andrew once asked a famous lawyer, renowned for his courtroom wiles and enormous fees, what Andrew should do if he were ever arrested (assuming, of course, he was innocent). You can probably guess what the lawyer told him: Keep your mouth shut. Try it — any lawyer will tell you the same. The point we're trying to make here is that, innocent or guilty, the cops are not your friend when you're a suspect. They defend society; they do a tough and thankless job and we're glad they're there to take a bullet for us. But if you're arrested, the cops are not on your side. Your lawyer is your friend, as long as you pay your bill, so say nothing until he or she arrives. The mutual fund prospectus is not entirely your friend, or at least it's not a true do-anything-for-you, hoops-of-steel, give-you-her-last-smoke type of friend. The prospectus, the document describing a mutual fund that's given to purchasers, is designed to inform you, but it's also there to protect the fund salesperson and fund company. Because after it's been given to you, the law assumes you've been adequately warned about the dangers and disadvantages of the fund. No point whining about the losses on funny foreign currencies when you were told of the danger right there on page 137.

Mutual fund prospectuses — which usually cover all or at least several of the funds in a company's lineup under one cover — have always contained the following information:

- **The name of the fund and its investment objectives:** For example, providing a steady income while preserving capital for a money market fund, or capital gains for a stock fund. Usually it's a bland motherhood statement that tells you little — after all, it would be an odd equity fund that didn't seek capital gains. Perhaps someday they'll invent a fund that tries to lose as much money as possible, and also dream up a way to get investors to buy it. We hope we're still alive to see it: no doubt the wretched thing will find itself stuck with shares that go up like a rocket!

- **The risks of investing in the fund:** A good prospectus will warn of the dangers of losing money in bonds if inflation returns or interest rates turn up. And you can count on seeing a warning that an equity fund will be vulnerable if the stock market tanks. Special warnings about the dangers of foreign funds are almost always included, such as the chance of currency losses if the Canadian dollar climbs relative to overseas currencies — a danger that countless investors who were heavily diversified in foreign funds discovered to be very real in recent years. And small-company fund prospectuses invariably point to the unpleasant volatility and unique dangers of small stocks. But, once again, the risks section usually consists of stating the bleeding obvious, as our Australian friends would say.

✔ **The company's idea of an appropriate investor:** Look for clues as to the sort of investor who should buy the fund and the sort who should avoid it. For example, Franklin Templeton Investments — one of the more conservative fund companies — warns prospective investors in its emerging markets fund that they must be "willing to accept high investment risk." After reading that, you have no cause to whine if you get beaten up by volatile markets in Brazil, Russia, or Thailand. Sure enough, although Templeton Emerging Markets has made tons of money for its investors in recent years — including returns in excess of 20 percent in 2005 and 2006 — it also has produced some spectacular losses in other years. Most infamously, it crashed 27 percent in 2000 — but the crash came on the heels of a 43 percent gain the year before!

✔ **The costs and fees imposed on investors:** By law you'll find the management fees for a fund and the expenses that have recently been charged to investors. You'll also see any sales charges or commissions. Because most load funds can be bought with a front-end or a deferred load, you'll usually find both options explained (refer to Chapter 2 for more about front-end and deferred-load funds). Along with the charges to investors, the prospectus must also list the commissions, annual fees, and other incentives given to salespeople. In principle, that's a great idea because it tells fund buyers how their advisers may be biased or influenced. Unfortunately, though, disclosure of commissions is often hedged around with "up to" or "may," leaving most investors no wiser than before. The prospectus also includes a table showing the hypothetical total of expenses and fees an investor in the fund could expect to pay over periods ranging from one to ten years. It's a fairly useful indication as to how much mutual fund investing can cost.

Pulling out of the deal

A mutual fund prospectus (the term comes from a Latin word meaning "view") is one of the central pieces of mutual fund regulation. In fact, it's considered so important that in most provinces you have two business days after you get the prospectus to cancel your purchase of a fund for any reason. So even if you pull on a clown costume and dance around as you demand your money back, they have to pay up, no matter how silly your explanation.

Interestingly, in many provinces you also have the right to cancel your mutual fund purchase within 48 hours of getting your order confirmation.

But don't expect the fund company or broker to welcome your business in the future if you cancel your order without a reasonable justification. The law assumes that until you've had a chance to read the prospectus you haven't been properly told about the fund. But after you've read it, you're pretty well on your own. Unless you can show that the fund isn't sticking to the promises made in the prospectus, the people selling and running the fund can reasonably argue that all the risks and expenses have been explained to you — and you'll have a tough time cancelling your agreement to buy the fund.

Prospectuses for bank-sold funds will also talk vaguely about "incentives" given to their employees, and nearly all mutual fund companies will reserve the right to "participate" (as one fund seller delicately puts it) in advertising by brokers and in "conferences" for salespeople. In other words, the fund managers hand over money to help brokers pay for these things. However, the good — or bad — old days of flying to Maui for a "seminar" at a fund company's expense are over. The public, media, and regulators just got so tired of the piggery that the fund industry agreed to introduce a sales code, which bans the worst of the excesses.

Always remember that a fund company often has two sets of customers: its unitholders (the people who actually own the funds), and the brokers and financial planners who sell its wares. If a fund company doesn't keep its sales people happy, it's in trouble.

More charges to look for

Here are some of the other charges the prospectus must disclose:

- ✔ **Fees for administering registered retirement savings plans, registered retirement income funds, and registered educational savings plans:** These range from zero to about $75 annually. Ask if you can pay them separately by cheque — especially where it'll save your precious RRSP dollars — but some companies claim that their systems are set up only to take the money directly out of your account (which is handier for them).

- ✔ **Fees for closing your account and moving the money to another institution:** Expect to pay $40 or $50.

- ✔ **Fees for short-term trading:** If you sell a fund within a short period after buying it, usually one to three months, you'll often face a penalty of 2 percent of the amount you sold. That's because funds are supposed to be a long-term holding, and investors who hop on and off over and over again increase costs for everyone.

Introducing the Management Report of Fund Performance

In 2005, regulators forced the funds industry to produce annual and semi-annual summaries of fund performance and holdings. These reports, called *management reports of fund performance* (MRFP), also include basic information on the fund's investment mandate and its recent risk experience, and, perhaps most useful of all, a discussion of the fund's recent performance.

Although a fund company must provide you with a copy of a fund's prospectus and its periodic MRFPs, the most recent MRFP is the only document you really need to read to gain a clear picture of a fund's mandate and how the fund's been faring. If the fund seller doesn't give you a copy, ask for it or download it from the fund company's Web site or from SEDAR, the official online depositary of all securities documents filed in Canada. (We discuss SEDAR more in this chapter as well as in Chapter 21, which covers fund research sources.)

Looking at what goes into an MRFP

An MRFP must contain certain information for the specified period and be presented in a prescribed sequence. The format ensures that consistent and up-to-date information will be available for every mutual fund sold in Canada. Here's a summary of the information that must be included in an MRFP:

- **Investment objectives:** A summary of the fund's fundamental investment objective and strategies.

- **Risk experience:** How changes to the investment fund over the financial year affected the overall level of risk associated with an investment in the investment fund.

- **Results of operations:** This section covers the fund's performance during the period in question, as compared to its benchmark index. It summarizes noteworthy changes in portfolio holdings, the impact of these changes on the fund's stated objectives, and details of any borrowing in which the fund might have engaged. Portfolio holdings are expressed in terms of individual investments as well as industry sectors, geographic regions, bond investment quality, and currency, as applicable.

- **Recent developments:** This section includes a discussion of market events and how the fund's overall strategies might have been amended (or not) to respond to the situation. It also must disclose any changes in portfolio managers, or in accounting policies.

- **Related party transactions:** Any transactions involving parties related to the fund must be disclosed.

- **Financial highlights:** These are tables showing a breakdown of the calculation of the net asset value per share (NAVPS), various ratios including the management expense ratio and portfolio turnover ratio.

- **Management fees:** A breakdown of the services received by the fund that constitute its management fees.

- **Past performance:** Tables show the fund's rates of return for the past ten calendar years, plus one-, three-, five-, and ten-year compound annual returns.

When securities regulators first unveiled the MRFP concept, fund company executives, investment advisers, and investors all greeted it with groans because they feared it would be yet one more level of tedious and expensive documentation. But, in practice, MRFPs have turned out to be a source of pretty good information, all presented in a document typically less than a dozen pages long.

Checking out an MRFP

Have a look at the 2007 annual MRFP for a large equity income fund, CI Signature Dividend. Figures 3-1 and 3-2 show some key information about the fund's performance and portfolio holdings:

✔ **Year-by-year returns:** These are great for letting you know what kind of swings in value you can expect. These bar charts show returns for four classes of the CI Signature Dividend fund. The mainstream units, class A, had slightly lower returns than the other classes, which have lower annual expenses because they're sold only by advisers who charge a separate management fee directly to their clients. Regardless of the class, the bars clearly denote the fund's good years and bad.

Signature Dividend Fund

Management Report of Fund Performance for the year ended March 31, 2007

PAST PERFORMANCE

This section describes how the Fund has performed in the past. Remember, past returns do not indicate how the Fund will perform in the future. The information shown assumes that distributions made by the Fund in the periods shown were reinvested in additional units of the relevant classes of the Fund. In addition, the information does not take into account sales, redemption, distribution or other optional charges that would have reduced returns or performance.

Year-by-Year Returns

The following chart shows the Fund's annual performance for each of the years shown and illustrates how the performance has changed from year to year. In percentage terms, the chart shows how much an investment made on the first day of each financial year would have grown or decreased by the last day of each financial year, except where noted.

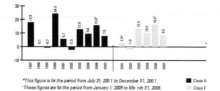

*This figure is for the period from July 31, 2001 to December 31, 2001.
¹These figures are for the period from January 1, 2005 to March 31, 2006.

■ Class A
▨ Class F

Annual Compound Returns

The following table shows the Fund's annual compound returns, compared to the benchmark consisting of 60% S&P/TSX Composite Index and 40% BMO Capital Markets 50 Preferred Shares Total Return Index

The S&P/TSX Composite Index tracks the performance of approximately 220 stocks and trusts listed on The Toronto Stock Exchange. It may be the best broad index available for Canadian equities. The indexes weighting is based on market capitalization. However, because of investment limits imposed on mutual funds and varying investment approaches among portfolio advisors, it may be more helpful to compare a fund's performance to that of other mutual funds with similar objectives and investment styles.

The BMO Capital Markets 50 Preferred Shares Total Return Index is a market capitalization weighted index that includes the 50 most liquid preferred issues with a P3 rating by Standard & Poor's.

A discussion of the performance of the Fund as compared to the benchmark can be found in the Results of Operations section of this report.

	One Year	Three Years	Five Years	Ten Years	Since Inception
Class A (%)	7.9	10.2	8.2	8.6	N/A
Blended Index (%)	8.6	12.1	10.1	8.4	N/A
S&P/TSX Composite Index (%)	11.4	17.7	13.1	10.3	N/A
BMO Capital Markets 50 Preferred Shares Total Return Index (%)	4.3	3.8	5.3	4.7	N/A

Figure 3-1: Management report of fund performance showing performance information for the CI Signature Dividend fund.

✔ **Annual compound returns:** This shows the rates of return, compounded annually, over one-, three-, five-, and ten-year periods ended March 31, 2007. It also shows the fund's compound annual return since its inception in October 1996, compared with the performance of two benchmark indices, the Standard & Poor's/Toronto Stock Exchange composite index and the BMO Capital Markets 50 Preferred Shares Total Return Index. The former tracks the broad Canadian stock market, and the latter is a barometer of the performance of preferred shares. *Preferreds,* as they're called, are the traditional form of dividend-paying stock, but nowadays fewer companies issue them, preferring (no pun intended) to pay dividends to shareholders via common stock. We'll spare you a lengthy discussion on the reasons why — although the serious lag in performance by preferreds, as shown in this table, might have something to do with it. Suffice it to say that the BMO preferred index is a worthwhile benchmark to use in this case. Blended returns of the two indices also are provided. The A units (which are fee-inclusive and are what most people buy) have outperformed the blended index over the long term (10 years) but lagged the broader S&P/TSX.

✔ **Portfolio breakdown:** This table shows in which TSX sectors the fund invests, as well as other types of investments such as cash and options contracts. In CI Signature Dividend's case, more than half the portfolio was in the Financials sector as of March 2007 — not surprising, given the fund's mandate to produce dividend income.

What is the S&P/TSX composite index?

The S&P/TSX composite is Canada's main stock market barometer, measuring the value of nearly 300 of our most important publicly traded companies, such as Royal Bank of Canada or Trans-Canada PipeLines Ltd. It's a fine way of checking how good the returns from stocks in general have been. For example, the index climbed above 15,000 for the first time in May 2008, doubling its value in less than five years. High prices for energy and other commodities have propelled the TSX's surge.

Every country has benchmarks for measuring returns from its local stock market. The United States has the old-fashioned Dow Jones industrial average, a relic of the 1800s that contains 30 giant companies. But the more representative Standard & Poor's index of 500 companies and the technology-heavy Nasdaq Stock Market Composite Index also exist. The wildest index name we've come across is Finland's: The Hex index.

The S&P/TSX composite used to contain a fixed 300 companies — when it was known as the TSE 300 — but the Canadian market turned out to be too small to produce 300 companies large enough for big pension funds and mutual funds to invest in. After persistent criticism that the index was full of little stocks that were hard to trade, the exchange brought in Standard & Poor's Corp. of New York to redesign the market benchmark. The revamped edition was launched in 2002. These days, the index has no fixed number of stocks — as of mid-2008, it contained approximately 260 companies.

Signature Dividend Fund

Summary of Investment Portfolio as at March 31, 2007

Portfolio Breakdown		Top 25 Holdings (excluding Cash & Equivalents)	
Category	Percentage of Net Asset Value (%)	Security Name	Percentage of Net Asset Value (%)
Financials	53.7	Toronto-Dominion Bank	3.6
Energy	10.6	Royal Bank of Canada	2.2
Telecommunication Services	8.5	BNP Paribas	2.1
Materials	7.3	Enbridge Inc.	2.0
Industrials	6.9	Suncor Energy Inc.	1.8
Utilities	5.2	Manulife Financial Corp.	1.7
Short Term Investments	4.0	BCE Inc.	1.5
Consumer Staples	2.5	TransCanada Corp.	1.4
Consumer Discretionary	0.7	Canadian Imperial Bank of Commerce	1.3
Other Assets	0.4	BCE Inc., 4.4% Preferred, Series AF 16	1.3
Cash & Equivalents	0.1	Bank of Nova Scotia	1.2
Option Contracts	0.1	BCE Inc., 5.45% Preferred, Series AA	1.2
		ING Groep NV	1.2
		Enel SpA	1.2
		St. Lawrence Cement Group Inc., Class A	1.2
		Bank of Montreal	1.2
		BCE Inc., 5.55% Preferred, Series 19	1.1
		Manulife Financial Corp., 4.65% Preferred, Series 2, Class A	1.1
		George Weston Ltd., 5.15% Preferred, Series 2	1.1
		Imperial Oil Ltd.	1.1
		Power Financial Corp.	1.1
		Toronto-Dominion Bank, 4.85% Preferred, Series O	1.1
		Cameco Corp.	1.1
		Brookfield Asset Management Inc., Preferred, Series 2	1.1
		Citigroup Inc.	1.1
		Total Net Asset Value (thousands of dollars)	**$2,182,194**

Figure 3-2: Management report of fund performance showing portfolio holdings information for the CI Signature Dividend fund.

✔ **Top-25 holdings:** The big holdings of an equity fund represent the manager's true loves. They're a reliable guide to the personality of the fund. Check 'em out — if they're natural resource producers or small companies you've never heard of, or bonds issued by technology outfits or developing nations, you're in for interesting times, as the old Chinese curse puts it. The top holdings of CI Signature Dividend are all big blue companies that normally pay dividends. Their shares aren't likely to shoot up ten times in value, but they're not likely to go bust either.

The financial section (see Figure 3-3) has some lines of tabular data well worth noting, specifically the following:

✔ **Net assets:** Asset growth (or shrinkage) is a key indicator of a fund's health. As you can see, this fund's assets have leaped in recent years, due to the strong showing by Canadian stocks as well as in response to investors' thirst for income-producing investments.

✔ **Management expense ratio (MER):** This is useful information when you're looking for low-cost funds (and you are). Seeing the figures for five years shows whether the fund company has been able to reduce its MER, particularly if its assets have risen significantly. In mutual funds, economies of scale don't seem to apply. But, in this case, bravo to CI: Signature Dividend's MER has come down a bit.

Signature Dividend Fund

Management Report of Fund Performance for the year ended March 31, 2007

FINANCIAL HIGHLIGHTS

The following tables show selected key financial information about the Fund and are intended to help you understand the Fund's financial performance for the periods indicated. This information is derived from the Fund's audited annual financial statements.

The Fund's Net Asset Value per Unit ($) [1] [2]

CLASS A (Commencement of operations October 29, 1996)	Year ended March 31, 2007	Period from January 1, 2005 to March 31, 2006	Year ended December 31, 2004	Year ended December 31, 2003	Year ended December 31, 2002
	$	$	$	$	$
Net asset value, beginning of period [2]	14.54	13.12	12.53	11.56	12.32
Increase (decrease) in operations:					
Total revenue	0.54	0.63	0.50	0.49	0.63
Total expenses	(0.26)	(0.31)	(0.24)	(0.23)	(0.23)
Realized gain (loss) for the period	1.07	0.94	0.56	0.39	(0.34)
Unrealized gain (loss) for the period	(0.23)	0.77	0.34	0.89	(0.40)
Total increase (decrease) from operations [2]	1.12	2.03	1.16	1.54	(0.34)
Distributions					
From income (excluding dividends)	-	-	-	-	-
From dividends	(0.24)	(0.25)	(0.24)	(0.36)	(0.28)
From capital gains	(0.80)	(0.33)	(0.34)	(0.12)	-
Return of capital	-	(0.02)	-	-	(0.20)
Total annual distributions [2] [3]	(1.04)	(0.60)	(0.58)	(0.48)	(0.48)
Net asset value, end of period shown [2]	14.61	14.54	13.12	12.53	11.56
Ratios & Supplemental Data					
Net Assets ($000's)	1,286,810	1,228,771	739,301	510,274	297,791
Number of units outstanding (000's)	88,053	84,524	56,368	40,713	25,764
Management expense ratio (%) [4]	1.81	1.84	1.92	1.96	1.94
Portfolio turnover rate (%) [5]	52.87	60.03	53.31	62.00	90.00
Trading expense ratio (%) [6]	0.06	0.12	N/A	N/A	N/A

*Footnotes for the tables are found at the end of the Financial Highlights section.

Figure 3-3: Management report of fund performance showing some of the financial information for CI Signature Dividend fund.

The mysterious annual information form

Pick up any mutual fund prospectus and you'll notice that it's referred to as the "simplified" version. As you get further into mutual funds, and hopefully more interested in them, you might get a hankering to look at the "complicated" version. Well, actually, no such thing exists. The prospectus given to investors is called "simplified" because it's only part of the full prospectus document: The rest of it, technically speaking, is the fund's annual and semi-annual statements and a little-known document called the "annual information form." The AIF is available if you ask for it (the prospectus should provide a contact address or phone number), or you can download it from the Internet at www.sedar.com, the central clearinghouse where just about all Canadian public companies and mutual funds must file their reports and other required disclosure documents. The AIF contains things like the names of the trustees for the funds (who are supposed to be looking out for the interest of the investors), more detail on the commissions paid to brokers and other salespeople, and a bit more information about the outside portfolio managers hired to help run the funds.

✔ **Portfolio turnover rate:** This measures the speed at which the manager changes the fund's holdings — a 100-percent turnover rate is high, indicating that trading equivalent to the value of the entire fund took place during the year. High turnover in a fund, of course, means higher transaction costs and greater expenses to the fund. This value has been a staple of U.S. fund reporting for years and was adopted as a Canadian requirement during the recent reporting upgrade. As for our example, CI Signature Dividend's turnover rate has been fairly low, no doubt a contributing factor to its lower MER.

Your Account Statement

Account statements, which show how much your holdings are worth and how much you've bought and sold since the last report from your fund company, are one area where the fund industry still needs to make progress. Investors often have trouble understanding what they actually own and even more difficulty figuring out their rates of return. Every company uses its own system and layout, and jargon such as "book value" isn't much help.

You may get an account statement only twice a year if you invest through a stockbroker or financial planner. The broker or planner and the fund company you've used will often both send you statements for the six months ending June 30 and for the year ending December 31. Usually the people who invest through a salesperson aren't interested in monitoring their investments frequently (that's why they hired someone to advise them), so twice-yearly statements are fine. Sometimes, a company will agree to send you statements more frequently — so try asking — but the fund seller's system may not be set up to do this. However, as more brokerages and planning firms make statement downloading available via their Web sites, monthly frequency is becoming more common.

If you hold your funds directly with a bank or no-load company, then you'll probably get a statement every quarter. That's because investors who go directly to their bank or to a fund company usually enjoy making their own decisions about investing — so they want to check their holdings more frequently. Finally, if you invest through a discount broker, your statement will often arrive monthly, especially if you've done some buying or selling in your account during the previous month. Discount brokerage customers tend to be very interested in investing, so they insist on regular updates. All companies still send out account statements, but just about every large fund seller also now lets you check your account and recent transactions over the phone or at their Internet site.

Besides your name, address, account number, and the nature of your account (that is, taxable or tax-deferred), your statement will almost certainly show the following:

✔ The total value of your investment in each fund you hold, plus a total value for your account.

✔ The number of fund units you held and their price or net asset value at the end of the reporting period. Remember to check these against the unit value shown for the fund in your newspaper's monthly report for the period — and it's not a bad idea to verify that the number of units matches the number shown in your previous statement, adjusting for any sales or purchases you may have made or for any distributions (in the form of new units) the fund declared.

✔ Any purchases or redemptions of units, and at what prices.

Beyond that, statements vary, but many big fund companies also provide the following information:

✔ The change in the value of your account, and ideally of your investment in each fund, since your last statement.

✔ The book value of your holdings. This technically means the amount you've ever put into the fund, which is useful for calculating whether you're using up your complete foreign content limit in a tax-sheltered plan. That's because the foreign content is calculated as a percentage of the book value, not of the current market value.

Some more service-oriented firms calculate compound rates of return for client portfolios. Although we think this should be a standard service in this era of high technology and regulation, it is an extreme exception to the rule. If your adviser provides this information to you, express how much you appreciate it. If on the other hand they don't provide portfolio compounded returns, bug them about doing so.

Annual and Semi-Annual Financial Statements (Or Annual Reports)

At least once a year, a glossy brochure turns up in the mail filled with rows of dull-looking figures and dry terms such as "statements of operations" or, Andrew's favourite, "net realized gain (loss) on sale of investment (excluding short-term notes)." These are the fund's financial statements, which, like the prospectus, usually group several funds into one document. Fund companies produce the statements twice a year. They have to send the report for the fund's financial year-end to all unitholders, but they're generally allowed to send the half-year report only to investors who actually request it. There should be a mail-in card for you to do this. Unless this stuff really puts you to sleep, ask to have the six-month report mailed to you. You'll be reminding the fund company that you take your money seriously.

Getting worked up about the financial details in the statements is pointless, but some important items to check include the following:

✔ The report must show the complete portfolio for the fund, not just the top holdings. It's worth it, and interesting, to glance down the list to see if the manager has any funny-looking stuff that may be an attempt to jazz up performance while taking on more risk. The full portfolio listing will also show how much the fund paid for each stock and bond and what it's worth now: It's always fun to see which investment has proved to be a disaster for the fund, although managers often "window dress" by dumping a turkey so it doesn't show up in the report.

✔ The statements often contain a commentary by the manager or fund company on what went right or wrong for the fund. As usual with mutual fund handouts, these tend to be bland and boring descriptions of the market or economic outlook, rather than an honest discussion of the manager's good and bad moves. But look for some important clues. If the portfolio manager has been replaced or if the fund's strategy is being changed in a major way, it may be time to dump it. And keep an eye on the top holdings. If they look riskier than you want, or if they leave out major sectors of the economy, then the fund company may be rolling the dice in order to jack up returns and attract more investors.

Don't throw the book value at your manager

Be careful when comparing the book value of your investment in a fund with its market value. The book value is the total sum that's been put into the fund, so in that sense it represents your total investment. But it also includes the value of any distributions made by the fund in the form of new units, even though they weren't real investments that came out of your pocket. The reinvested distributions have the effect of increasing the book value, and they can make it grow larger than the market value — making it appear the fund has lost you money when it may have been a winner. For example, say you originally invest $10,000 in a fund that produces a return of 20 percent, leaving you with a market value of $12,000. But say the manager is an active trader and she pays out $4,000 in capital gains distributions along the way. Then your fund could have a book value of $14,000, or $2,000 more than its market value on your statement, even though the manager has done a good job.

Chapter 4

Building Your Very Own Financial Plan

*M*utual funds, when selected carefully, are great for almost everyone and work best as part of an overall financial plan. You need to consider some important factors before jumping right in, however. The most important is taking a frank look at your financial health. Good financial planning isn't rocket science and doesn't have to be scary. It starts with getting your debt under control and buying enough insurance. Still, for those who have their act together and want to save and invest money, funds are a powerful ally.

Mutual funds are ideal for building retirement savings. Make sure you buy plenty of funds that invest in high-quality shares and bonds, and you will have found a simple and painless way of taking advantage of the high returns earned by most professional investors. Yes, share and bond prices drop from time to time, but if you don't need the money for years, you have enough time to ride it out.

Funds aren't just for retirement savings, however: They're also ideal if your life is in a holding pattern — trying to find someone special or figuring out whether to move to another country for a while. In that case, you simply buy a less-volatile set of mutual funds and sit tight. Funds are also just the ticket for building your short-term savings in order to make a big purchase, maybe your first home. In that case, you want no risk and a nice steady return. Whatever you're chasing in life, funds are a valuable ally above all for their convenience and ease of recordkeeping — just always keep an eye on your statement.

Mutual funds are also perfect if you're working toward early retirement but haven't yet made up your mind when to quit — that's because they can be shuffled and changed around with ease as your plans change. Funds are perfect for almost any financial plan because they're such a maintenance-free and relatively low-cost way of storing and accumulating wealth. Running your own business or buying real estate properties might produce higher returns and lucrative tax write-offs, but being self-employed represents a 24-hour commitment — and whining tenants who call about the drains at 4 a.m. get annoying after a while. Funds are problem-free and easy to monitor, and they produce excellent returns if you keep management fees and costs down.

In short, funds are for dealing with your savings, the money you have left over after feeding, housing, and clothing your family and taking care of your own bloated desires. Most people want to do one of three things with their savings, or at least a mixture of these three: Grow a big nest egg for retiring, put money in safekeeping with a reasonable return because they don't know what their ultimate plans will be, or, finally, save money for a short-term purpose like buying a first home.

In other words, they want funds to grow their money over the long term, for several years or more; to give them a reasonable rate of return while avoiding big losses; or to simply hold their money safely with a modest annual payoff. In this chapter, we walk you through using funds to achieve each of the three goals. We outline the best way to set your objectives, help you identify what kind of investor you are, and show you how to start building a suitable portfolio of funds.

Looking at Your Long-Term Financial Future

Your first step is to relax, grab a giant plate of poutine, and remember you live in the best country in the world. If you're working and paying into the Canada Pension Plan (CPP) — and have a reasonable prospect of doing so until you're 60 or so — then you're unlikely to end up in absolute poverty. If you're in a pension plan sponsored by a company, union, or professional association, so much the better. If you can build even some modest savings on top of that — a lump sum equivalent to your final year's income, say — then you really shouldn't have any problems getting by in retirement. But you're no doubt planning to buy something nice near the water or take some agreeable cruises, and, for that stuff, just "getting by" won't cut it. So even if you have a good pension and full government benefits coming your way, you'll need cash to kick-start things. And if you're not in a pension plan, you certainly want to be accumulating your own rainy-day fund.

No clear-cut science exists for determining how much you need to save for retirement, but you don't want to find out that you hugely underestimated your needs. Don't panic: The government may reduce benefits, but seniors are a powerful, organized lobby and, most of all, they vote. So it's a near-certainty that the government will provide some kind of pension when you retire. The greying baby boomers will see to it. But unless you want to spend a lot of time kicking around the local mall, like you do now, then a lump sum will come in handy.

Many experts claim that you should try to generate an after-tax income — including all pensions and government benefits — equal to about 70 percent of your present net income.

And the conventional assumption for many planners is that you ignore the value of your home (if you own it, of course) when calculating your wealth in retirement. That's because planners often treat the value of an investor's home as an insurance policy that might be needed for medical expenses and so on.

Mind you, those guidelines are pretty extreme. Many people get by on much less than 70 percent of their former net income when they quit work. And a lot of people will be able to sell their family home for a tidy sum, leaving them with a healthy tax-free profit when they move into something smaller. Still, the rules represent an ideal to aim for.

Just about everybody in Canada with a paying job, including the self-employed, is covered by the CPP. That's the federal government–sponsored pension plan, which you pay for by making contributions throughout your working life. The very similar Quebec Pension Plan exists for those working in Quebec.

For 2008, the maximum monthly benefit payable under the CPP for those aged 65 was $884.58, payable for life and increasing in line with inflation.

On top of that is Old Age Security, a pension provided to all Canadians over 65 who've lived in this country long enough. As of July 2002 it was $505.83 a month. Finally, the Guaranteed Income Supplement is for low-income seniors, which is something you won't have to worry about if you heed the advice in this book and become a successful mutual fund investor.

Now, obviously, you'd be hard-pressed to live off those amounts from the government. But look at seniors all around you. Especially at your parents, relatives, and friends. Notice how they seem to be, well, comfortable? That's largely because, when they retired, their expenses were significantly reduced. More specifically:

- ✔ When you stop working, your house will almost certainly have been paid for, leaving you free of accommodation costs apart from utilities and maintenance.

✔ Your employment expenses, including transportation, parking, and clothing, will fall to nothing.

✔ Sure you'll want to travel, but now you can take advantage of off-peak discounts and other special reductions. And, let's face it, you'll be slowing down.

✔ Your kids will almost certainly have flown the nest and their education will be just about paid for. No more pimple-faced, sullen . . . well, you know.

In other words, before you assume you face an old age of penury — meaning you think you automatically have to put the very maximum into your wretched registered retirement savings plan — remember that you'll have spent a lifetime living frugally already, earning enough to pay your taxes and mortgage and bankroll the kids' hockey skates and education. That said, the best way to ensure you'll be free of financial worries in the years to come is to plan carefully and pay attention to your finances. By using investment options like mutual funds, you can make your retirement a better experience. You'll feel more flush with cash and be able to travel, shop, and generally relax in high style. Plus, investing isn't all about your day in the sun; sound investments can help you meet many of your life goals, like educating yourself and your children, buying your dream home, starting your own business, and much, much more.

Start saving now, today, because the younger you are the more powerful the effect of buying mutual funds. Yes, you'll probably get by in retirement, but starting a regular contribution plan to a fund at an early age can earn you thousands of dollars. Let's say you'd put $100 monthly into Scotia Global Growth Fund for five straight years, from June 2003 to June 2008: You'd have ended up with more than $6,000. But if you'd started five years earlier, in June 1998, you'd be sitting on a lot more — $11,000 or so.

Meet the Cleavers: Last-minute savers who did just fine

Actuaries — pension and life insurance experts who work on cheerful questions such as when you can expect to die — get a lot of ribbing for being dull. Even accountants, not exactly known for their excess of personality, like to make jokes about them. But some actuaries are a lot of fun. Especially Malcolm Hamilton, a retirement expert with the consulting firm William M. Mercer Ltd. in Toronto. He accuses the investment and savings industries of scare tactics, especially with their pious assertion that you'll need 70 percent (or even 80 percent) of your pre-retirement income when you retire. Mr. Hamilton says that's a load of bull, and that people get by on as little as one-third of their gross working income. That's because many living costs — such as employment expenses, kids, mortgage, and, most of all, taxes — disappear. Here's an example of what he means, adapted from his description of a typical Canadian couple.

Take the Cleavers, a couple who just got married at 25. They have a combined income of $60,000, roughly in the middle for Canadians. Of that, $20,000 goes in taxes, employment expenses, and savings for their first home. This leaves the Cleavers with $40,000 to spend on themselves.

Ten years later, the Cleavers have two kids and a $300,000 home. They now make $100,000 each year, of which taxes, employment expenses, RESP contributions, and mortgage payments eat up $45,000. The kids cost them another $15,000. That leaves the Cleavers with the same $40,000 to spend on themselves. They save nothing for retirement. Ten more years later, in their mid-forties, they can finally begin diverting money to their RRSPs, accelerating the pace when the children go to college. And all of those RRSP contributions generate huge tax savings. By age 54, the Cleavers are earning $120,000 annually, of which $65,000 goes to RRSPs (they're able to put such large quantities into their plans because they have years of unused contributions). Taxes and employment expenses consume $15,000. On themselves, the Cleavers spend the same old $40,000. So at 55, with a house and $600,000 of retirement savings, the Cleavers retire. They reckon that their savings, the CPP, and Old Age Security will give them an inflation-protected income of $44,000 per annum. Does that mean they're living in poverty? No, says Mr. Hamilton, and here's where he starts having fun.

In his words, "Financial planners warn that the same fate awaits others who don't save millions. 'Look at the feckless Cleavers,' they say. 'They used to earn $120,000 per annum; now they subsist on $44,000.'

"For the record, the Cleavers' finances . . . are remarkably simple after retirement: $44,000 of income, less $4,000 of income tax, leaves $40,000 for the Cleavers to spend on themselves, just as they always have — just as they always will. The Cleavers' version of Freedom 55 is not the one you see on television. They will not winter in the Caribbean, nor will they enjoy that sunset view of the Pacific. Their riches are measured in leisure time, not dollars. And since the government hasn't found a way to tax leisure, the Cleavers live well and pay little or no tax."

The moral of the story: Your costs will fall off a cliff when you retire, so don't get spooked into diverting every spare penny into your RRSP. Sure, saving is good — and it'll get easier as the kids leave and the house is paid off. But always question the assumption that you'll need 70 percent of your pre-retirement income.

Setting Your Financial Priorities

Pick up any of the piles of unwanted personal finance books in the store and they all begin by saying the same thing, mainly because it's true: Pay your debts.

I gave at the office: Making a contribution at work

If you're working for a large company or for the government, and they offer a traditional defined benefit plan, it's usually a good idea to sign on for it. These plans usually provide a significant pension income, and they are becoming harder and harder to find as many employers stop offering them in favour of less expensive defined contribution plans and group RRSPs. A defined benefit plan is a pension that promises to pay a percentage of your salary when you leave. A typical generous scheme might offer 2 percent times years of service times the average of your best (or last) 5 years of income. So if you worked for 35 years, with the best 5 years averaging $50,000 each, your annual pension would be 2 percent times 35 times $50,000, which works out at $35,000 a year. When you're negotiating with a new employer, look for a pension that's at least this good — or seek compensation for not getting it.

Sure, you might do better investing on your own rather than making contributions to the pension scheme — and being in a pension plan reduces the amount you can put into your own RRSP — but for people who are poor savers, a pension scheme is a wonderful backup. It's especially important to get into a pension plan if you're over 40, and certainly if you plan to stay with the employer after age 50. That's because the actual value of being in a defined-benefit plan shoots up exponentially as soon as you reach middle age (because your quitting date is drawing closer).

If you're leaving a job early, it's frequently a good idea to stay in the plan rather than take a lump sum. Pension benefits are often increased in line with inflation, either formally or by way of goodwill payments, and pension schemes also may bring you health benefits. At least ask the human resources people to explain how much you'll get in dollar terms if you leave your accrued contributions in the scheme and then collect a reduced pension later at 55, 60, or 65. If you can, show the projections to an accountant who's knowledgeable about pensions or, better yet, call up a firm of actuaries. See if you can persuade one to give you an hour or two of advice for an agreed fee of, say, $300 or $400. It'll be money well spent. Just as it's wise to always have your lawyer by your side before you talk to the cops, it's good to have your own expert looking out for you when dealing with something as complicated as a pension. A corporation is happy to see you take a lump sum and stumble off into the night, with no more claim on them. But it could be a lot better for you to stay in line for a pension down the road, at 55, for example. So ask the other old codgers at work what they're doing (they're usually pretty savvy) and stick around in the scheme if you can.

That's the first step for anyone, and often the most difficult. Remember that if you're shelling out $100 in credit card interest each month and you're in a 50 percent tax and deductions bracket on your uppermost income, then it takes $200 in earnings to pay for that sucker.

Building wealth with debt bleeding you dry is impossible, so — with the exception of your home mortgage — becoming borrowing-free is the first move. That's difficult, but it's the first step toward freedom.

Fund salespeople and even banks will often suggest you borrow money to buy mutual funds. This is known as leveraging your investment and it works out fine as long as the funds go up in value. But remember that if the funds drop, you'll still be on the hook for every penny you borrowed to buy them. So think long and hard before taking out a loan in order to buy mutual funds that invest in stocks and bonds.

Here, roughly in order, are the priorities to set on your road to fiscal responsibility:

1. **Pay off your debts:** Start with the high-interest and non–tax-deductible kind.

2. **Get life insurance:** Buy enough insurance to provide for your loved ones if they lose you, and buy fire and theft coverage for your home and property.

   Get quotes on disability insurance. This insurance will provide at least some income if you can't work. If your job doesn't provide any coverage, then it's a must, especially if your household has only one wage earner.

3. **Set up an emergency fund:** Make sure you have access to some cash if an emergency hits. Traditionally, experts advise six months' income.

4. **Have a will drawn up:** Save everybody a lot of hassle and delay (at a horrible time) by biting the bullet and getting this done. If you have a very straightforward situation, a lawyer (or in Quebec, alternatively, a notary) might be able to prepare a will for about $300 to $500.

5. **Hire an accountant or other fee-charging expert:** For a charge that can be as low as $200 or $300 they will look over your tax situation. If you do any kind of freelance work or earn any sort of self-employment income, this step is essential (unless your income is so low you can't afford it).

Only when you've completed those steps should you think about saving and investing money, including buying mutual funds. And here you'll run into one of the main problems with the way mutual funds are sold: They're a wonderful product, but financial planners and other advisers who earn commissions from funds don't get paid for telling clients to cut their debts and buy insurance. So they see buying funds as the solution to just about everybody's problem, at the risk of leaving customers underinsured or paying far too much in interest on their debts. That's why we recommend you remember that anyone who sells mutual funds for a living has a natural in-built bias. It's also why in Part II of this book, where we take a close look at financial planners, we recommend you think strongly about going to a fee-charging financial planner or accountant who doesn't get commissions for selling products.

Understanding What Type of Investor You Are

So you've decided to build some capital. Mutual funds are the most convenient way to do it. The next question is what you'll need the money for. And here's where you can build funds into your financial plan. After your debts and spending are under control, and you've bought adequate insurance and tax advice, the next step is to set goals. Most people have financial objectives that fall into one of these three groups. Chances are your situation fits one of the following descriptions, or it's a blend of two of them:

- ✔ **Growth investors** are building a portfolio of long-term savings that are supposed to last through retirement or through an extended and far-off period of not working. In that case, it doesn't really matter if the stock market goes into long slumps — it can even be to your advantage if you're steadily investing all the while, because you get to buy stocks cheaply. The real danger is having your money eroded by inflation. So the goal is maximum growth, and that means lots of equity funds with a relatively small proportion of the portfolio in bonds in order to spread your risk. Growth investors are the greediest of all: They typically chase annual returns of 8 percent or more, and are willing to expose their portfolio to danger in order to get it.

- ✔ **Balanced investors** aren't sure what's likely to happen in their life, but it could include buying a home, moving to an exotic locale, or starting a family. But whatever the eventual goal is, it's definitely going to require a few thousand dollars. In that case, caution is the watchword. You might need the money soon, and it would be awful to have to sell your mutual funds straight after the stock market collapsed, scything into their value. So the best formula is lots of money market funds and bond funds, with a modest equity component if you're comfortable taking on some risk. Balanced investors are generally happy with returns of 4 to 7 percent annually.

- ✔ **Savers** are amassing a pile of money to buy a home or car within the next few years, or building a war-chest so they can stop working for a while, perhaps to go back to school or to dig for ancient pornographic mosaics in old Thrace. If you're one of these people then you want to keep risk to a minimum, because this is money you'll be needing very soon. That means no stocks, or hardly any, and lots of short-term bonds and money market securities. Savers traditionally will settle for annual rates of return of 4 percent or less, as long as their money isn't at risk.

For all three types of investor, mutual funds are a wonderful tool. They're cheap or free to buy, flexible, and convenient. The fund company handles all the recordkeeping, which means funds require little or no thought or attention from the investor (but do check your statement carefully). And funds offer attractive rates of return. So decide which goal matches yours, and then look at the suggested sample portfolios at the end of this chapter for some ideas.

Understanding That Investing Is an Inexact Science

Okay, so we're going to give you the straight goods. Even reporting on financial markets daily doesn't shield us from the inevitable hits and misses every investor encounters when he or she throws his or her hat in the ring. Andrew's investing career began in the mid-1990s, when he opened a self-directed RRSP at Toronto-Dominion's discount brokerage, then called Green Line Investor Services but now known as TD Waterhouse. We'll spare you all the details of his expensive education, but here are a few lowlights:

- ✔ Andrew thought a company called Pallet Pallet — which was trying to consolidate the vibrant and exciting market for wooden warehouse pallets — was a turnaround possibility. The company's stock had plunged to pennies after it tried to grow too fast and ran into soaring costs. Needless to say, the pallet industry turned out to be fragmented into tiny mom-and-pop operations for some very good reasons. (Andrew never really found out what they are, though. He's sure a sitcom is in there somewhere.) And he ended up selling his Pallet Pallet shares at a loss.

- ✔ He decided that flying basket-case Canadian Airlines was another recovery candidate — but being the greatest market strategist of the late 20th century, he was too clever to bother with the company's boring common stock. No, he bought warrants, a speculative sort of certificate that gains real value only if the underlying shares climb. Climb a lot, that is. They didn't and he lost more money.

TIP

Dealing with documents

What about all that mail, both paper and electronic, you receive from your broker and fund company. What should you keep? All you really need to keep are brokerage statements and transaction slips. Retain them for several years, especially if taxable transactions are involved. The mailings are easy to clip together with a big bulldog clip, in order by date. Use one clip for the current year and then attach all the previous years together using another.

If you're fortunate enough to be able to avoid paper statements and transaction slips altogether and pick them up by logging on to the broker's or fund company's Web site, make sure you will have ongoing access to these documents. If not, save them as PDF files and set up a logical filing system on your computer — and back it up regularly. If electronic storage scares the wits out of you, then throw in the towel and print them. You'll have to live with the fact that you're using up paper and filing space — and letting the broker or fund company escape postage and paper costs.

✔ Andrew reckoned Asia was in for a major bounce back from its sell-off of 1994, when the average Asian fund dropped 11 percent. So he plunged into madcap Asian mutual funds. Asian markets promptly went into a four-year slump, culminating in the near economic meltdown of 1998. After a while, he stopped looking at his returns.

Okay, Andrew had a couple of successes in technology stocks that actually popped up like they were supposed to. But he has found that funds are the way to go, for him anyway. His mainstream Canadian equity funds — which he once despised as ballast in his scheme for world financial control — have proved to be his best investment. And even Andrew's speculative resource and Asian funds have finally bounced back to something like the price at which he bought them — after he stopped looking at them. Andrew wishes he'd bought dull global equity funds instead; he would have made a lot more money.

For some reason, Andrew's portfolio seems to thrive when he ignores it and just gets on with his life. When he attempts to fiddle and fuss and apply his master strategies, it all goes wrong again. So now he does what most Canadians do: He just checks the statement and files it in a drawer. Periodically, Andrew looks at his funds' performance and main holdings, but otherwise he lets the pros get on with their jobs. After all, why hire a plumber and then go around yourself with droopy pants hanging off your backside? The moral of this story: Prepare yourself for the fact that your best-laid plans, including can't-miss investments, can suddenly go awry. Prepare yourself for this probability and you'll not only sleep better, but also be able to afford a more expensive mattress.

Borrowing for RRSPs

Borrowing to invest can be a good idea if you plan to put the money into your RRSP — that's because contributions to an RRSP can be used to reduce your taxable income, generating lucrative tax savings for you. You can then use the tax refund you get to pay off some of the loan: Banks even have RRSP loan-marketing schemes based on this strategy. And remember that when it's in the RRSP, the money grows tax-free.

Still, even though taking out an RRSP loan offers advantages, experts often advise that you limit your borrowing to an amount you can pay off in one or two years. If you're borrowing money to invest outside an RRSP, then the interest you pay on the loan can be written off as an expense for tax purposes, even if your investments tank. But because the government considers RRSPs to be such a generous tax break, interest you pay on a loan taken out for an RRSP contribution can't be used as a tax deduction. Don't let the tax sweetener blind you to the fact that playing with other people's money in this way, by borrowing money to invest, is a risky strategy: you still have to pay them back. See Chapter 22 for more on RRSPs.

Investigating How Various Investments Have Performed

Always remember that when you're saving and investing money, you have a fundamental choice. You can settle for low risk and low return by buying things like bonds or guaranteed deposits. The returns are thin, but the fluctuations in the value of your holdings tend to be small. Or you can gamble on high risk plus (you hope) high return. That involves buying stocks. They can make a lot more for investors, but the price swings are wild. There just ain't no such animal as a low-risk, high-return investment. Sorry. But low-return investments carry their own special risk: the danger that you'll see the value of your savings devoured by *inflation,* which is the long-term decline in the value of money. It all gets a bit confusing, but here are some examples to help you figure out your choices.

Have a look at Figures 4-1 through 4-4, which show the rate of return from four different sorts of investments over two decades. We picked four indices to get an idea of what your options are:

- ✔ **Canadian stocks:** The S&P/TSX composite stock index
- ✔ **Canadian balanced:** A blend of 60 percent Canadian stocks and 40 percent Canadian bonds (as represented by Morningstar's balanced Canadian index)
- ✔ **World stocks:** The Morgan Stanley Capital International (MCSI) world index
- ✔ **Global balanced:** A blend of 60 percent global stocks (MSCI World Index) and 40 percent global bonds (Morningstar's global balanced index)

Each case is expressed in Canadian dollars, and assumes an investment of $100 was made each month from mid-1988 to the end of June 2008.

Figure 4-1: How a Canadian stock portfolio based on the S&P/TSX composite index fared over 20 years.

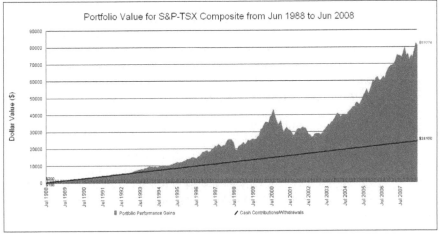

Portfolio Value for S&P-TSX Composite from Jun 1988 to Jun 2008

■ Portfolio Performance Gains   ✔ Cash Contributions/Withdrawals

Source: Morningstar

Figure 4-2:
How a
Canadian
balanced
portfolio
based
on the
Morningstar
Canadian
balanced
index (60
percent
stocks, 40
percent
bonds) per-
formed over
20 years.

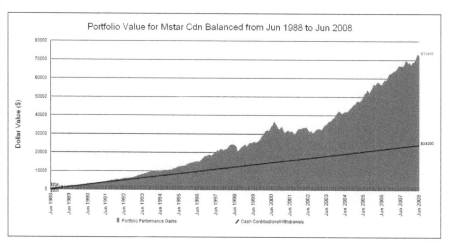

Source: Morningstar

Canadian stocks

Of the four strategies, the biggest return for Canadians came from staying at home and buying only Canadian stocks. Now, that's a switch from what used to be the tedious out-performance of foreign stocks against our piddly little market on Bay Street. But rising prices for oil and other commodities — our traditional national strength — accompanied by a Canadian dollar that has skyrocketed to be worth more than its U.S. counterpart, have put the S&P/TSX composite index on steroids.

When this book last went to press, in 2002, the TSX had lagged global stocks — as measured by the performance of the Morgan Stanley Capital International (MSCI) World Index, which tracks the performance of every major stock market on the planet — by more than two percentage points over a ten-year period. Six years later, it was a completely different story, with our market outpacing the global competition by an embarrassing six percentage points over ten years.

Anyway, Canadian stocks, as represented by the S&P/TSX composite index, were the top performer among the four portfolios, with a 10-percent compound annual return over the 20 years ended June 2008. It outperformed in four out of the five calendar years ended 2007, as well as in a number of years during the 1990s. An investor who put $100 each month into this portfolio during that span would have ended up with more than $81,000 at the end of June 2008.

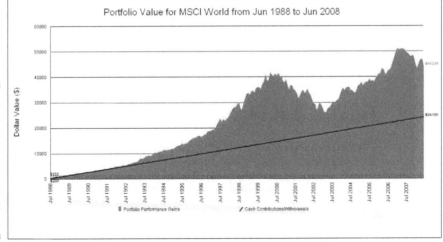

Figure 4-3:
How a global stock portfolio based on the MSCI World Index fared over 20 years.

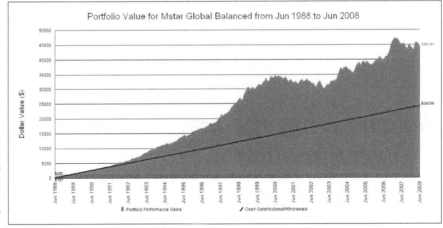

Figure 4-4:
How a global balanced portfolio based on the Morningstar global balanced index (60 percent stocks, 40 percent bonds) performed over 20 years.

Canadian balanced index

Snapping at the heels of the TSX index fund was the Canadian balanced index, with a 9.7-percent, 20-year compound annual return as of June 2008. This portfolio is a blend of stocks and bonds — the sort of thing just about every investor should own. (We've used Morningstar's balanced fund indices to represent this and the global balanced investment.) The Canadian balanced index has a cautious, stay-at-home mix of 60 percent in the S&P/TSX composite and 40 percent in the S&P/TSX Canadian Bond Market Index. The strong showing of this balanced investment demonstrates that Canadian bonds as well as stocks have done well over the years. If you had put $100 a month over ten years into this portfolio, you would have been nearly $72,500 richer.

Global balanced

There was a big gap in performance between the Canadian and global indices. The global balanced fund managed a 7.2-percent, 20-year compound annual return, producing $44,300 from $100 per month investments during that span. This index has 60 percent of its assets in the MSCI World stock index and the rest in the Citigroup World Bond Index.

World stocks

Owning the blue-chip stocks that make up the MSCI World Index from June 1988 to June 2008 produced a 7.2-percent compound annual return in Canadian-dollar terms. That would have produced a relatively unimpressive $44,200 nest egg for an investor who put in $100 each month. (It was a tad less than the global balanced fund because the 7.2 percent annualized return was rounded up to a single decimal point.)

Remembering the Importance of Diversification

Investing over two decades, as the portfolio examples in the previous section demonstrate, makes the stock market look like a pretty good place to be. Well, certainly the Canadian stock market, anyway. But you might also have noticed that the road to riches looks somewhat smoother with bonds added to the mix. Indeed, the graphs for the balanced portfolios resemble a gentler hike up the Quebec's Laurentians, compared to the Rocky Mountain image presented by the stock-only portfolios. So despite the potentially better returns from stocks, your nerves will probably have an easier time of it with a balanced portfolio.

When Andrew wrote the first edition of this book in 2000 — when the stock market was only beginning to turn bad — the 20-year return on the MSCI World Index was a huge 17.1 percent, and a $100-a-month investor would have ended up with more than $168,000 over 20 years, or twice as much money. Stocks may be a great long-term investment, but it depends whose long term we're talking about — in other words, which period you use for measuring. The bottom line is you may get lucky with stocks if you cash out at the right time, when the market is surging. But who's that lucky? (Not he, Andrew will tell you.)

The sensible course is to own lots of bonds (loans to companies and governments) as well as shares — that way your portfolio has a chance to produce the steady returns that retirement saving is all about. Remember, too, that prior to 2006–2007 a good chunk of the gains from foreign investments came from currency changes, mainly because the Canadian dollar slumped against the U.S. dollar in the late 1990s. That produced a bonus for Canadian investors: the value of overseas holdings grew steadily because they were denominated in foreign currencies. The opposite, of course, has been the case during the loonie's recent surge.

So, for those building a mutual fund portfolio, here are some general observations drawn from the analysis of the four portfolios:

✔ Over the two decades, portfolios with lots of bonds performed nearly as well as 100-percent equity portfolios. Admittedly, that was against a backdrop of falling inflation and interest rates worldwide, always great for bond prices. But cautious investors who took the balanced approach kept up nicely with the ears-pinned-back, all-stocks-or-be-damned gamblers. So, own some bonds.

✔ The two balanced indices suffered much smaller price plunges than the stock-only barometers during most of the 20 years. For example, in 2001 and 2002, the balanced Canadian index fell 4.2 percent each year, compared with tumbles of about 12.5 percent each year by the S&P/TSX. In 2007, bonds did little to protect the global investor, however, as the balanced global index fell 6.5 percent, only about half a percentage point better than the MSCI World Index.

✔ Canadian stocks have, for the most part over the long term, underperformed overseas shares, in part because Canada doesn't have many of the giant global companies that made so many investors so rich in the 1980s and 1990s. That means a portfolio that has most of its assets in Canada is exposed to a small market that may be less likely to produce big winners. Although Bay Street's recent strength might make many of us question the necessity of foreign investing, remember that these gains have come largely on the back of strong oil and commodity prices, and, of course, have been bolstered significantly by the soaring loonie. Canada still represents only a fraction of the world's stock market value. (On the other hand, at least some of your long-term savings should remain in Canada if you plan to retire in this country. That's because in retirement you'll need Canadian dollars to draw on. Plus, as we've all seen, when the loonie climbs a lot versus other currencies, it reduces the value of your foreign investments.)

Portfolios for Your Type of Investing

In this section we look at three suggested mutual fund portfolios that offer a good prospect of achieving the different goals of a short-term saver, a balanced investor, and a growth investor. Are these the very best portfolios that could ever be designed? No, because the future can't be predicted with complete accuracy. Distrust any financial professional who says he or she can tell you what the markets will be up to, or down to, in the years to come. These portfolios represent a cautious guess as to what the global economy will do, and they amount to a forecast that the world isn't likely to slide into either hyperinflation or bitter deflation (a prolonged fall in prices).

As you become more knowledgeable about and interested in investing, you may want to start adding to or altering these suggestions. But they're a good place to start when you're adding the power of mutual funds to your financial plan.

The portfolios include lots of so-called index funds — funds that simply track a stock or bond market average or index by essentially buying every stock in the market. For example, most Canadian equity index funds are designed to produce a return in line with the S&P/TSX index. Index funds offer huge advantages to investors, such as low costs (less than 1 percent of your money each year, compared with well over 2 percent for traditional equity funds) and the reassurance that your fund won't badly underperform the market. (If you opt for exchange-traded funds, or ETFs, instead of index mutual funds, you'll save even more in annual expenses.) But as the new millennium neared, market indexes in most parts of the world were taken over by a few highly priced glamour stocks, many of them technology companies. In Canada it was Nortel; in the U.S. it was stocks like Cisco. That meant index investing itself had become something of a risky proposition. Stock index proprietors introduced capped versions of their indices to offset the effect of these dominant stocks, and some fund companies launched capped index funds based on these new barometers. Most of Barclays Canada's iShares Canadian equity exchange-traded funds track the corresponding S&P/TSX capped indices. However, most index funds remain true to the basic, uncapped indices. Thus, half the stock market money in our portfolios has been allocated to traditional-style, "actively managed" funds, which have managers who attempt to predict which stocks will go up and which will drop. For more on index funds and ETFs, see Chapter 15.

Note that international equity funds usually invest in stocks outside of North America, so the international index funds mentioned here don't track the U.S. market. That's why we've also included U.S. index funds. However, global equity funds buy stocks everywhere, including the United States. The actively managed funds in these portfolios are global, so you needn't include separate U.S. equity funds.

Some experts will look at these suggested portfolios and complain that we haven't included any specialized funds that invest in small companies. In the past, shares in small companies have occasionally produced huge returns, and evidence suggests they sometimes do well when big-company stocks are languishing. Traditionally, that has happened in very hot stock markets, when investors are willing to buy risky little stocks in pursuit of big gains. In other words, buying shares in lesser-known companies provides something called diversification — the strategy of spreading an investor's risk among different investments. But small-company shares also have a nasty habit of stagnating for years, and their returns tend to be highly volatile: big gains one year and then nothing for several years. So to keep things simple, we've left small-company funds out of these sample portfolios. You might miss out on a percentage point or two of returns every few years, but you'll be avoiding a lot of risk. As you get more comfortable with investing, you may decide to add some small-stock funds to your portfolio. Just make sure you buy at least two, because different types of small stocks tend to thrive at different times. It's frustrating to find yourself stuck with a manager who bought just the wrong sort of small-company shares.

Part III contains chapters on each type of fund, explaining the advantages and drawbacks of each in detail.

A penny earned is a penny saved

The first portfolio, shown in Table 4-1, is ideal for savers. The savers' portfolio consists mostly of Canadian assets (no point speculating on currency changes if you're just saving for a Volvo), so it can be held both within and outside an RRSP. It includes small quantities of regular bonds, even though their prices can be volatile, to increase its interest income. And the global bonds provide a small amount of protection against a possible drop in the value of the Canadian dollar because they're bought and sold in foreign currencies.

You could make this portfolio even simpler by just putting half the money into a money market fund and the rest into a short-term bond fund. Money market funds are very unlikely ever to lose money for their unitholders (it would probably take a major financial dislocation before one did). Short-term bond funds are a little more dangerous, but they're also slightly more lucrative to own than money market funds. The median short-term bond fund produced an average annual return of 3.7 percent during the ten years ended June 2008, compared with an even 3 percent for the median Canadian money market fund.

Table 4-1	Suggested Portfolio for Savings (20% Money Market and 80% Bonds)
Fund Type	**Percentage of Total Portfolio**
Money market fund	20%
Canadian short-term bond or short-term bond index fund	50%
Canadian bond or bond index fund	20%
Global bond or global bond index fund	10%

Balancing act

The next portfolio, Table 4-2, for balanced investors, is truly one you can just buy and forget. Yes, it will go into a slump if inflation returns and interest rates surge. But that's true of virtually any investment except for cash (usually held in the form of bonds and other debt instruments with less than a year to go before they mature).

With its large 30-percent proportion of cash and cash-like, short-term bonds, this portfolio is unlikely to lose more than 10 percent in a single year, unless a sharp uptick occurs in inflation, the economy slides into a recession, or some national or global mishap sends the bond market into a downward spiral.

Table 4-2	Suggested Portfolio for Balanced Investors (55% Bonds and 45% Stocks)
Fund Type	**Percentage of Total Portfolio**
Money market fund	5%
Canadian short-term bond or short-term bond index fund	25%
Canadian bond or bond index fund	15%
Global bond or global bond index fund	10%
Canadian equity index fund	8%
Conservative Canadian equity fund A	4%
Conservative Canadian equity fund B	3%
Conservative global equity fund A	7%
Conservative global equity fund B	8%
International equity index fund	10%
U.S. equity index fund	5%

One for the risk-takers

Then there's the Ferrari of the stock market, for those who relish the cold taste of fear, the brutal snapping, and the terrible slashing. Check out Table 4-3. You could easily make this portfolio more exciting and dangerous by reducing the bond weighting even more, or by buying emerging-markets funds and narrow regional funds that invest in Asia or Europe.

Arguably, every aggressive portfolio should contain a small weighting in developing countries (because of their huge growth prospects), but we've left out emerging-markets funds to keep the portfolio as simple as possible. In any case, at least one of your conservative global equity funds is certain to own a few companies in emerging nations. You could also step on the gas by going into volatile sector funds that track just one type of company, such as technology outfits or oil and gas producers. However, once again, your index funds and actively managed funds are almost certain to own these companies and industries anyway.

A portfolio like this is certain to do well as long as stock markets stay strong. It's very broadly diversified, and its big index fund component means you'll end up owning lots of huge, well-run companies.

Table 4-3	Suggested Portfolio for Growth Investors (25% Bonds and 75% Stocks)
Fund Type	*Percentage of Total Portfolio*
Canadian bond fund or bond index fund	15%
Global bond fund	10%
Canadian equity index fund	10%
Conservative Canadian equity fund A	5%
Conservative Canadian equity fund B	5%
International index fund	20%
U.S. equity index fund	10%
Conservative global equity fund A	13%
Conservative global equity fund B	12%

Chapter 5

Beyond Mutual Funds

. . . .

In This Chapter

▶ Considering Canada Savings Bonds

▶ Checking out old, reliable, guaranteed investment certificates

▶ Looking at regular bonds and strip bonds

▶ Taking stock of stocks

▶ Sniffing out income trusts

▶ Investigating managed products

. . . .

So you've got your debt under control and your insurance taken care of. Time to start saving money. But what are you going to do with those vast piles of cash? Think of this chapter as an investment primer, a rundown on the drawbacks and attractions of the different types of financial assets you can buy with your savings. If you're certain by now that funds are the way to go for you, then feel free to skip to Part II, where we explain where you can go to buy them. But it's useful to know about the other investment choices you have — including Canada Savings Bonds and guaranteed investment certificates, which can't be bought through mutual funds at all.

Don't worry, though. The decisions you need to make are fairly simple when you come down to it. The investment business is an incredibly conservative industry. For all the dot-com flash and techno-trading systems, your basic investment options are the same as they were in the 1920s or even the 1820s — stocks, bonds, or cash. Here's what's out there: everything from the mundane to the manic. In this chapter, we take you for a stroll down Risk Road, moving from the very safest choices to the most unpredictable. Along the way, we point out some of the dangers and delights of each investment — so that even if you end up handing your money over to a fund company to manage, you'll at least have an idea of what they're going to do with it.

Canada Savings Bonds: Dull Yet Dependable

Every fall, Ottawa starts running ads in the newspapers and on television touting the wonders of lending money to the government by buying Canada Savings Bonds (CSBs) and their flashier-sounding cousins, Canada Premium Bonds. (CPBs). Some provinces sell their own versions. Actually, these things aren't really bonds at all, because their market value never fluctuates in line with prevailing interest rates. That's because they can be cashed in at virtually any time by simply selling them back to the government at the purchase price plus accumulated interest. With most normal bonds, you have to find a buyer to take them off your hands and no certainty exists as to the price you get. If interest rates have gone up, making other bonds more attractive, you'll have to accept a lower price than the one you paid.

Five series of each type of bond are sold from November through March, with new interest rates announced for each series at the start of each sales month. They can be bought at nearly all banks, credit unions, stockbrokers, and trust companies. Or you can buy them from the government itself: Go to the Web site at www.csb.gc.ca or call 1-888-996-8899, Monday through Friday from 8 a.m. to 8 p.m. Eastern time. Thousands of employers across Canada offer them to their staff by way of direct deductions from their pay.

The interest rates paid on the bonds are announced at the time of sale, but the government is free to increase the rate above those minimums if interest rates in the broad market have increased enough (if the rate is too low, the public has an annoying habit of cashing in all of their CSBs). Canada Premium Bonds pay slightly more interest but carry more limitations on when you can cash them in.

Canada Savings Bonds can be sold back to the government at any time (although you get no interest if you cash them in within the first 90 days), but Canada Premium Bonds are redeemable once a year, on the anniversary of the issue date or during the 30 days afterward. CSBs and CPBs currently have a term to maturity of ten years — that is, you have to take your money back after that time or roll it into another set of bonds.

Looking at the upside of CSBs and CPBs

Apart from the ability to get your investment back easily (a wonderful convenience), CSBs and CPBs come with some major advantages for investors. They're

✔ **Easy to buy:** You can make small investments of as little as $100, or $500 when the bonds are bought under the "RSP option" for inclusion in a registered retirement savings plan. You can put the bonds in your own "self-directed RRSP" — an account you run yourself at a stockbroker or discount broker — or in a special RRSP for Canada Savings Bonds and Canada Premium Bonds. It's called the Canada RSP.

✔ **Available in two appealing types:** These bonds can be purchased in regular interest form, with the annual interest payments going directly into your bank account. Or you can buy no-brainer compound interest bonds, where the income is added to your investment and thus starts generating interest of its own.

✔ **Safe and secure:** The money is safe as long as the federal government's credit remains good. And you always know exactly how much your principal — the money you have tied up in an investment — is worth. That's not the case with a stock, bond, or mutual fund, whose value may have slumped by the time you go to sell it.

The ability to get your cash back easily makes CSBs and CPBs like a sort of savings voucher, entitling the holder to a stream of interest payments and the return of his or her capital on demand. That flexibility is one of the great virtues of Canada Savings Bonds, and it's a good reason to consider buying them for your short-term savings needs — but the low interest rates on offer mean they're unsuitable for the lion's share of your savings. Meantime, the reassuring government guarantee makes CSBs suitable for the "cash" or no-risk portion of your investment portfolio.

Weighing the downside of CSBs and CPBs

CSBs and CPBs do have some major drawbacks, such as the following:

✔ **Low returns:** The price of security and convenience is a return that's a lot lower than the potential payback from bonds or stocks. For example, the Canada Savings Bonds that went on sale from March 2 to April 1, 2008, carry an interest rate of 2.45 percent. The rates paid on that date's Canada Premium Bond issue are 2.75 percent for the first year, 2.90 percent for the second, and 3.05 percent for the third year, for an annual compound rate of return of 2.90 percent over three years.

As you can see from Figure 5-1, an investor who invested $10,000 in Canada Savings Bonds and left it there from mid-1988 to mid-2008 ended up with about $25,600, or a tad more than what he or she would have gained by buying one-year guaranteed investment certificates (GICs) at a bank ($24,300). However, an investor who took on more risk and put his or her money into AGF Management Ltd.'s AGF Canadian Balanced Fund, a huge and fairly cautious balanced portfolio of stocks and high-quality bonds, would have finished with nearly twice as much money — about $48,000.

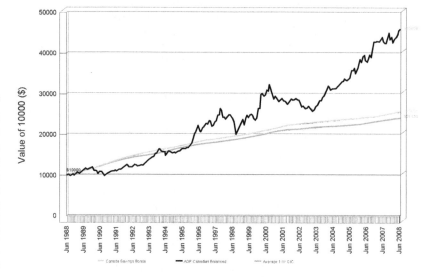

Source: Morningstar

Figure 5-1:
How
Canada
Savings
Bonds and
GICs stack
up against
a balanced
fund
investment.

✔ **Lack of long-term projections:** Because the rates on CSBs and CPBs are periodically re-set to keep them in line with competing interest rates, you can't know exactly what you'll earn over the life of the bond beyond the announced years. By contrast, if you buy a GIC or ordinary bond and hold it until it matures, you know exactly what you're getting.

CSBs and CPBs are really more of a savings vehicle than a true investment. Nothing's wrong with that — but the price you pay for simplicity and peace of mind is a low return.

Go ahead and buy them if you want a safe investment that you can choose and then forget about. CSBs are great for people who want simplicity and security. The government takes care of the recordkeeping, and the return you get is usually slightly better than that of a bank account. But the interest rate on CSBs and CPBs is so low that with a little homework it's easy to find investments that will make your money work harder.

The Good Old GIC: You Know Where You Sleep

You've no doubt noticed that most banks offer miserable rates of interest — 1 percent if you're lucky — on money dumped in a "savings" account. You may be able to get more if you keep a very high balance in the account, or if you opt for an account with a higher rate but exorbitant transaction fees. And some "e-savings" accounts pay a decent rate with low fees if you abide by certain transaction rules. But without getting bogged down in bank-account research, you can do better if you put the cash in a guaranteed investment certificate (GIC) with a bank, insurance company, or trust company for a fixed period.

A *GIC* is a deposit that a financial institution accepts on the understanding that the money, plus a guaranteed amount of interest, will be returned after a set number of years. The interest is calculated on an annual basis and each year's interest is usually added or "compounded" onto the total for the purpose of calculating the next year's interest — so you earn interest on interest. Using the above 20-year investment example, $10,000 invested in June 1988 in five-year GICs (with interest compounded annually) would have grown to $30,300 in mid-2008 — considerably more than with a CSB or one-year GICs. A drawback is that you may not be able to get the deposit back before the term is up, or, if you can, you might have to forfeit the interest earned. In other words, these deposits aren't as liquid — cashable — as you might think. That means GICs are less flexible than Canada Savings Bonds. The great beauty of GICs, though, is that you know exactly where you stand: For example, a five-year deposit of $10,000 at a rate of 3 percent compounded annually will give you $11,592.74 after 60 months — no more and no less.

For years, generations even, the GIC was Canada's favourite investment, and it's still the number-one choice of many Europeans. And why not? As recently as 1990, when interest rates were high and prices for food and shelter were rising fast, you could leave money on deposit at a big, safe bank and come back a year later to collect a lump sum that had magically grown by 12 percent. Well, it wasn't magic, actually. Banks had to offer those kinds of rates to attract any money because inflation was rising. But as you can see from Figure 5-2, a steady drop in the rate of inflation during the 1990s meant a remorseless decline in GIC rates. And after rates slumped below the 7- to 8-percent mark in the early part of the decade, the stage was set for a flood of hundreds of billions of dollars into mutual funds as Canadians demanded a decent return on their money.

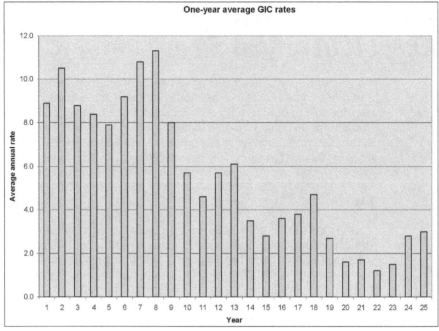

Figure 5-2:
One-year
average
GIC rates,
1983–2007.

The recession of the early 1980s and fears of a recurrence around 1990 kept interest rates high until 1992, when the economy strengthened and rates began their plummet to historic lows before rising ever so slightly the past few years. So, no bonanza.

Types of GICs

GICs come in a sometimes-bewildering range of shapes and flavours, so always make sure you understand all of the mechanics before you buy one. Get an employee of the financial institution to write down the value of the deposit when it matures (except in the case of index-linked GICs, whose returns are tied to the stock market).

Here are some common variations above and beyond the traditional non-cashable GIC (even more specific types exist):

✔ **Cashable GICs:** Traditional GICs tie your money up or at least reduce the interest you get if you cash out early. But cashable GICs let you take all or part of your money out early with no penalty. Expect to get a lower annual rate, though. It can be a full percentage point lower than the return on a normal non-cashable GIC.

✔ **Index-linked GICs:** These pay you little or no fixed interest but they promise to return your initial investment and pay a return that's linked to the performance of a stock market index — always a bit watered-down, though, in order to pay for the guaranteed return of capital and leave a profit margin for the bank. In other words, your money is safe from loss but your potential return isn't as good as it would have been investing directly in stocks. For example, a typical GIC linked to the Canadian stock market might pay no guaranteed interest but give the investor a return identical to the change in the Standard & Poor's/ Toronto Stock Exchange 60 index — subject to some limitations.

Index GICs are popular when interest rates on ordinary GICs are low. The problem with these products is that their rules and terms are so complicated it can be difficult or impossible to know how well you're doing as you go along. Yes, they offer some stock market action for investors who would otherwise be too nervous to go into equities, but most investors will do better with an index fund and a couple of con-servative equity funds, especially if they can ride out downturns in the market over a few years.

At least one bank, CIBC, has a GIC linked to a diversified "portfolio" of market indices. Its Market Mix GIC attaches the return to performance of the S&P/TSX 60 index (20 percent); S&P 500 composite index (40 percent); FTSE (*Financial Times*) Eurotop 100 index (17 percent); and Japan's Nikkei 225 index (13 percent) — as well as 5 percent Merrill Lynch Canada Broad Market (bond) index. An additional 5 percent of the product's return is based on a three- or five-year CIBC GIC rate.

Some institutions have rolled out GICs linked to the performance of a specific mutual fund. Royal Bank has one linked to its RBC O'Shaughnessy International Equity Fund. Bank of Montreal links one of its "Progressive GICs" to returns of its BMO Dividend Fund.

✔ **Convertible GICs:** RRSP marketing season is the first 60 days of the calendar year, when money put into your RRSP can be used to reduce taxable income for the previous year. For example, if you earned $50,000 during 2007 but managed to put $5,000 into a plan by March 1, 2008, then you'd have to pay tax on income of only $45,000 for 2007. During that two-month period, institutions offer flexible GICs that let you invest your money at the one-year rate, but then allow you to switch to a longer-term deposit or to the company's mutual funds.

✔ **Escalating-rate GICs:** These GICs also don't lock you in. You can cash out without penalty after one or two years, but if you stay on, the interest rate gets higher. The design of these GICs varies among institutions, and some, like TD Canada Trust, offer more than one type. For example, a TD Triple Value GIC taken out in mid-2008 paid 3.1 percent during the first year, 4.3 percent in year two, and 5.5 percent in year three, for an effective annual yield of about 4.3 percent. A three-year cashable GIC at TD, by compari-son, paid 2.3 percent. Like index-linked GICs, the returns offered by some of these "escalator" GICs are based on some pretty complex formulas.

Finding the best rates

A quick way to find out the various GIC rates on offer from a wide variety of institutions is to check Web sites like Canoe Money (`money.canoe.ca`), which is run by Quebecor Inc., publisher of the Sun daily newspapers. If you prefer to pore over printed tables, most major daily newspapers publish consumer interest rate tables in their weekend or Monday editions. Both online and print tables list rates at a range of lenders and deposit takers, from the biggest bank to the most obscure trust company. (You'll also be able to check rates for mortgages and bank accounts while you're at it.)

You often can get a higher rate by going to a smaller company, but dealing with the little outfit may be more troublesome because it won't have the same branch network and resources. (Wherever you go, make sure the institution is a member of the Canada Deposit Insurance Corp. See below for more on the deposit insurance protection provided by this government agency.)

Checking out the benefits of GICs

Don't spurn the humble GIC out of hand. They never lose money. Remember bad-news years for the stock market, such as 2001 and 2002, when the median Canadian equity fund lost 8 percent and 14 percent, respectively? Sticking to one-year GICs would have kept you in the black those years, gaining an average 2.7 percent and 1.6 percent, respectively. GICs offer other advantages:

- **Simplicity:** They're simple and quick to buy, with no extra fees or complicated forms to fill out. Just about any bank, insurance company, or stockbroker will sell you one.

- **Income generating:** They're a useful planning tool if you need your portfolio to throw off a regular stream of income. That can be done by "laddering" GICs — putting the money into deposits with separate terms, each maturing on a different date to match your spending needs. Even if you don't need the money for income, having your GICs come due at different times is also handy for reducing "reinvestment risk." That's the problem of getting a pile of money to reinvest from a maturing bond or deposit just as interest rates are low. If the money comes up for re-investment at different times, you can re-invest it at a variety of interest rates.

- **Safe and secure:** If you buy a GIC from a bank, trust company, or loan company, as long as the GIC's term to maturity doesn't exceed five years, your money is protected by insurance provided by the federal government's Canada Deposit Insurance Corporation. If the financial institution fails, CDIC will cover an individual for up to $100,000 in deposits (including chequing accounts and the like but not mutual funds) at that institution.

When buying a GIC, always make sure the company you're dealing with has CDIC coverage. Go to the Web site at www.cdic.ca for more information, including the "Quiz on Deposit Insurance" — at last, a fun activity for guests at one of your interminable soirees.

Watching out for inflation

Before you abandon all thoughts of buying mutual funds and plunge into GICs instead, remember that fixed-rate deposits are a dangerous investment in one important sense. Their rates of return can be so low that they do little to protect you against inflation. As Table 5-1 shows, even quite modest rates of inflation eat away alarmingly quickly at the real value of your savings. The U.S. dollar, still the world's main store of wealth, lost its value at an average of about 5 percent during the 1980s and 1990s — in other words, prices in the United States rose by about 5 percent per year. The inflation rate has been much lower in recent years, dipping to less than 2 percent in Canada, before inching back up thanks to rising commodity prices. Inflation of just 3 percent a year wipes out about one-fifth of the value of your money in five years.

The curse of inflation means that, as an investor, you're constantly clambering up a slippery, moving staircase covered in rotting mackerel and parts of Scotsmen. Stand still or go forward too slowly, and you end up sliding backward.

Table 5-1	How Inflation Destroys Money over Time
Time Elapsed	*Approx. Value of $10,000 at 3-percent Inflation*
Initial amount	$10,000
One year	$9,700
Two years	$9,215
Three years	$8,754
Four years	$8,317
Five years	$7,901
Six years	$7,506
Seven years	$7,130
Eight years	$6,774
Nine years	$6,435
Ten years	$6,113

Bonds and Strip Bonds

Bonds are loans to governments or corporations that have been packaged into certificates that trade on the open market. They usually pay a fixed rate of interest, often twice a year. And they "mature" or come due after a set number of years, when the holder of the bond gets back the value of the original loan, known as the "principal." But don't bother buying individual bonds until you've got $10,000 or so to spend, because the cost of buying a cheap bond index mutual fund is so low. Index funds, which just earn a return in line with an entire bond market or index, are particularly suitable for the bond market because normal human managers find it very difficult to earn much more than their rivals without taking risks.

The median Canadian fixed income fund has annual expenses of about 1.8 percent, but many bond funds can be held for less than 1 percent a year. That's less than $100 out of a $10,000 investment, so you're doing fine.

Considering bond alternatives

If you're comfortable buying and selling on the stock exchange, it's worth thinking about buying a bond exchange-traded fund — bond ETFs are units in a simple trust that give you ownership of bonds but trade on the exchange like a share. We talk lots more on exchange-traded funds — which are perhaps the best deal of all for small investors — in Chapter 15. The big advantage to buying bonds or a bond ETF is that you save on fees. The biggest domestic bond ETF, iShares Canadian DEX Universe Bond Fund, charges just 0.3 percent.

You can also consider bond funds. The annual fund expenses will cut into your yield, yes — but you may just decide the cost is worth it. In Chapter 14, we single out some bond funds that have relatively low expenses — and whose mannagers have done a good job investing, too, by the way!

Don't forget, though, that with a bond fund you are essentially playing the bond market without the backup security of being able to hold a bond to its maturity date, and thus recover your original investment, or principal, in addition to the periodic interest payments. Bond fund managers buy and sell bonds on the market, and thus you are signing on to a pretty aggressive form of investing. No, you won't exactly be a "master of the universe," as in Tom Wolfe's *The Bonfire of the Vanities,* but you will be participating in a fairly active market.

Investing directly in bonds

You can obtain a far better yield than bond funds by investing directly in bonds. However, the bond market is not always the friendliest place for small investors — it can be difficult to get information or do trades. It's just not a popular product, and profit margins for the dealer are thin.

Finding bond prices and yield quotes on the Internet is not as easy as looking up stock prices. One source of this information is globeinvestorgold. com, *The Globe and Mail*'s premium Web site for investors, which charges a subscription fee.

The trouble with bonds is that, unlike stocks, they don't trade in a central marketplace where the prices are posted. If you buy stocks, your broker usually just acts as an "agent" who connects you with the seller's broker, collecting a commission for the service. But your broker generally buys and sells bonds as a "principal" — that is, the firm actually owns the bonds it trades, holding them in "inventory" like a store. That means when you're trading bonds, you generally have to ask your broker what the firm's price quote is for a bond you want to buy or sell. And then you more or less have to accept the price that's offered.

Even bigger problems can occur in buying and selling strip bonds, which are bonds that have been modified by brokers to reflect the fact that many long-term buyers who hold bonds until maturity aren't interested in collecting periodic interest payments. In fact, such dribs and drabs of interest are a liability because they must constantly be reinvested. So strip bonds pay no interest until they mature — the interest payments have been "stripped" away. Instead, they're bought at a deep discount to their face value, maturing at full value or "par" like a normal bond. For example, you might pay your broker 50 cents on the dollar for a strip bond maturing in ten years. That will give you an annual compound yield of about 7.2 percent. In other words, an investment of $5,000 becomes $10,000 after a decade. Because strip bondholders are prepared to wait until they get any of their money back, they're rewarded with a higher yield to maturity. It's often 0.5 to 1 percentage point of extra yield yearly compared with a regular bond with a similar term to maturity.

Strip bonds can be difficult to unload. They're volatile, losing their market value quickly when interest rates rise. That's because higher rates offer better interest-earning opportunities in the here and now, so they rapidly devalue money you don't get for a long time. And strip bonds are all about waiting for a faraway payoff. Because strip bonds are often sold as a retail product, your broker may be reluctant to buy one back from you at a decent price if the firm has no demand for strips from other clients. So if you're buying a strip, plan on holding it to maturity.

You can put through a regular bond order at discount broker TD Waterhouse for as little as $5,000, but the yield you get won't be as good as the one you see listed in the newspapers. Table 5-2 shows a typical listing for a government bond and for a big blue-chip corporation in mid-2008. These are approximate rates for large trades of bonds, and you could expect to pay a higher price, and get a smaller yield, with a small order. Notice how in each case the bond was producing an annual yield lower than its annual stated interest rate, or coupon. That's because, with interest rates so low, investors hungry for income were trading the bonds at a premium to their face value. When the bonds mature, at their face value, the buyers who paid a premium will take a small loss on the extra they paid. Notice also how the Bank of Montreal bond offers a higher yield than the federal government issue: Corporate bonds yield more than government bonds because they're slightly more risky (the government can print its own money, after all). But it's harder to trade corporate bonds because the market is smaller, and if you want to get out of a bond you could find it hard to sell the thing at a decent price.

Table 5-2	Yield on Ten-Year Canadian Government and Bank of Montreal Bonds			
Issue	*Interest Rate*	*Maturity Date*	*Price per $100 Face Value*	*AnnualYield (to maturity)*
Gov't of Canada	4.00%	June 2017	$100.82	3.89%
Bank of Montreal	5.45	July 2017	101.21	5.28

So if you have at least $10,000 to play with, buy bonds and hold them to maturity by all means. You know exactly what yield you're getting and how much money you'll have when the bonds mature. With a bond mutual fund, which is constantly rolling over its holdings, you won't have nearly that much certainty.

If you plan to try trading bonds, remember that making money in this market ("going forward," an annoying expression Bay Street types like to use a dozen times before breakfast) will be tougher in the long run. That's because bond prices usually only go up when interest rates and the rate of inflation fall — if inflation stays unchanged, then all you're likely to get from a bond is its yield to maturity at the time of purchase.

Stocks: Thrills, Spills, and Twisted Wreckage

The stock market is insane. Although you can spot stocks trading at crazy prices and make money buying those individual shares, it's hard — so hard as to be damned near impossible.

Going with index funds

Unless you plan to spend quite a bit of time tracking stocks and reading the financial press, you're probably best off in equity funds. The easiest strategy of all: Just climb aboard the madness by putting a chunk of your money into stock index funds — which track the whole stock market — and you'll be doing what a lot of smart pros do. The indexes themselves go crazy from time to time, as they did in 2005 and 2006 when investors rushed to buy income trusts and then rushed even more quickly to sell them off when the government removed income trusts' tax advantages in late 2006. More recently, skyrocketing crude-oil prices sent the S&P/TSX composite index on a wild ride, while U.S. and other markets slumped. Perhaps the most spectacular example of abrupt stock market activity was in 1999 and 2000, when technology and telecommunications stocks dominated the market benchmarks. It might all seem too much to stomach, but when you look at the long-term record of stock market performance, particularly in North America, it's hard to stay away from the index-investing party. You're only alive three times, after all, and the last two times you come back as something in the sea, so why not have fun now?

As Figure 5-3 shows, an investment of $10,000 in Canadian dollars in stocks outside Canada and the United States grew at a compound annual rate of 5.7 percent to about $30,400 between mid-1988 and mid-2008. The same $10,000 put into U.S. stocks grew to about $62,000 — a 9.5-percent, 25-year compound annual return — while Canadian stocks left you with more than $67,100, or a 10-percent growth rate.

If we've whet your appetite with this brief glimpse into the world of index funds, head over to Chapter 15, where we discuss them in greater detail.

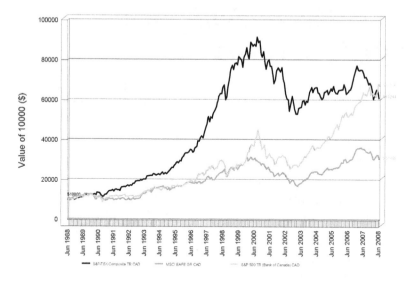

Figure 5-3:
$10,000
initial
investment,
held from
mid-1983 to
mid-2008.

Buying individual stocks

Think you can beat the market? Go ahead and dive into the shark . . . er, whatever . . . water where loads of sharks are swimming around. Picking good stocks consistently is really, really hard. You also need a broker to put through your trades. Your shares get held in the brokerage's computer system under an account in your name. Always check your statement and transaction confirmation slips carefully, because mistakes happen.

If you want to buy individual stocks, you will need a bit of money to make it worth the trouble and expense — say, at least $10,000 — unless you're just throwing a few thousand at the market for laughs (and it is enjoyable, so try it when you get a chance). Most trades go through in "board lots" of 100 shares at a time, for efficiency. If you're dealing in blue-chip companies, buying 100 shares can add up — it costs $2,500 for 100 shares trading at $25 each. Buying fewer than 100 shares at a time is generally inefficient because it means dealing in an "odd" or "broken" lot of less than 100. If you deal in odd lots, you'll often get a lower price when you sell and have to pay more per share when you buy.

And, as usual in investing, you must make a choice between having a sales-person take care of all the humdrum stuff at a cost, or doing it yourself at less expense. The price of buying stock through a full-service traditional stock-broker is usually shrouded in black curtains and dry ice. Establishing com-mission rates can be like bargaining in a grim, sweaty bazaar on the edge of a poisoned desert — in other words, full-service brokerage commissions are completely negotiable. A small trade typically might cost 4 percent of a transaction's value. That's quite a haircut to take when you buy and again when you sell, but most frequent traders could haggle for much less. But don't expect a full-service broker to be too thrilled about your business unless you've got at least $50,000 or even $100,000 to throw into the market, because with any less than that you're more of an annoyance than a revenue stream. And it's not unusual for an experienced and acclaimed broker to accept only "high-net-worth accounts" of $1 million or more.

So investors with modest means are left with a discount broker, which may impose no minimum account size at all but also provides little or no advice or help. Their commission rates vary, but discounters' minimum commissions typically run from $5 to $20, depending on whether you use the Internet or a live human to do your trade. We talk plenty more on discount brokers in Chapter 6.

Buying and selling stocks profitably and reliably is difficult — perhaps impossible — but evidence indicates that ordinary investors can do well by investing in a few well-run, growing companies and simply holding them for years. Mind you, that's emotionally tough to do. Take Bombardier Inc., a Montreal company that sells planes, trains, and other transportation equipment all over the world. If you'd bought Bombardier shares in the summer of 2003, you'd have roughly doubled your money in five years. But it would have been a tough buy-and-hold experience, with the share price moving from about $4.50 a share at the end of June 2003 to above $7 in the winter of 2004, thanks to strong sales, then tumbling to below $2 at the end of 2004, at which point the company's retired chief executive, Laurent Beaudoin, returned to the executive suite. Investors clearly embraced this move, and the shares soared to the $7 neighbourhood by mid-2007. Industry challenges caused the stock to fall back to nearly $4 by the winter of 2008 before rallying big-time to around $9 by mid-2008, largely on the back of strong business-jet sales. Have a look at Figure 5-4 to see the rises and falls of Bombardier stock. The area graph along the bottom of the chart shows monthly trading volume, which indicates how much attention a stock is attracting in the market. High volumes often accompany a significant rise or fall in price.

Figure 5-4: Bombardier's share price over five years.

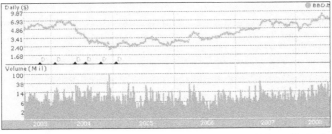

Source: Morningstar

Taking a wilder ride with stock alternatives

For those who find even stocks too staid, options, warrants, futures, and rights are the wonder drug of investing — volatile ways to play or speculate on a share, market, or commodity. They're structured to offer faster price changes than the underlying asset itself. The general principle is that for a little money you get to "buy risk" from someone who doesn't want it. But the downside is that your wild party has a time limit, because the speculative instrument always expires after a set period. That's a huge drawback: Many a market veteran will testify that picking the right investment is tough enough, without having the clock ticking against you. Buy these things only with money you don't care about. For more about the stock market, see Chapter 10.

Income Trusts — No Longer the Taxpayer's Best Friend

Income trusts are businesses that have been turned into a sort of fund that pays out regular — usually monthly — distributions to holders of their units. Say an income trust's yield, or yearly payout to investors per dollar invested, is 8 percent. On a $10,000 investment, you could expect $800 in income payments, or one-tenth annually, versus the less than $300 you could expect in mid-2008 on a government bond.

Income trusts trade on the stock exchange like an ordinary share, so they're simple to buy and sell. Look for them under "trust units" in daily newspapers' stock market listings, and on stock-quote Web sites.

Remembering income-trust mania

Canadians initially took to the income trusts with wild enthusiasm. Financiers took regular publicly traded companies and essentially turned them inside out. As an income trust, the cash generated by the business is paid directly to investors in the form of a frequent cheque. That replaced the regular corporate system, in which businesses generate a profit that is then taxed before they can pay out a dividend to their owners.

In addition to the generous tax treatment, investors welcomed the prospect of a healthy alternative to low-interest fixed income investments. In an era of rates below 2 percent, any investment that produced regular income was welcome.

Oil and real estate companies were the first to use this type of financing vehicle, and by 2006 almost half of the long and growing list of income trusts were oil and gas, electricity, and pipelines companies. But as the boom approached new heights, income trusts began to pop up in unexpected places. One fund paid out cash flow from an international sardine producer, two frozen-food warehouse funds, a pet food fund, and another fund that paid income from a burger chain.

Income trusts' popularity as a substitute for common shares had become so great that by mid-2006 it was common to see a horde of income trusts mentioned in daily stock market summaries in the news media.

Clamping down on income trusts

However, the wheels fell off the income trust bandwagon in late 2006, when the federal government pulled the plug on the favourable tax treatment this type of investment had enjoyed. As trusts, they had provided a considerable tax-deferral on income paid out. But income trusts were in danger of replacing traditional stocks as the main product traded on the Toronto Stock Exchange (we could just see it: the Toronto Income Trust Exchange), and Ottawa acted suddenly to level the fiscal playing field. Income trust income is now taxed in the same way as dividend income.

While most existing income trusts survived the loss of their tax advantages, based on their investment fundamentals, the parade of stock-issuing companies heading to the trust conversion machine has slowed to a small line of stragglers.

Considering investing in income trusts

Most income trusts generally kept their distributions flowing as promised (oil and gas trusts have had to cut theirs when commodity prices fell, but that was obvious to investors all along). Yields have remained quite generous, at anywhere from 6 to 13 percent. Those are pretty generous income streams, but income trusts are riskier than a bond — particularly now that they're no longer the taxpayer's best friend. The bottom line? Evaluate an investment in an income trust in exactly the same way as you would a stock. Just as no certainty exists that a company's share price will go up or it will be able to continually pay dividends, no guarantee exists that an income trust's underlying business will indeed be able to keep up the profits or revenue needed for the distributions. The trusts' structures tend to be horrendously tangled, with corporate diagrams that would make your hair stand on end — complexity is always a red flag in investing. And the danger exists that the necessity to pay out cash will in fact bleed some of the businesses dry.

But the small investor who buys a trust has one thing on his or her side: Mutual funds are also investing in trusts. Anxious to get in on the act, mutual fund companies have started funds that buy the trusts. We're a little skeptical here: When you combine the trusts' management fees with the fees on the new funds (the median Canadian income trust equity mutual fund has an annual management expense ratio of 2.5 percent), you end up paying a lot of money to a lot of people. But at least professional investors are keeping an eye on the folks running the trusts.

The bottom line here is that income trusts are too new and potentially volatile to go overboard on, but the generous yield means they're a reasonable bet for many investors. As with any investment area, make sure you buy more than one to spread your risk. Better yet, you can invest in an income trust fund — we look at those in Chapter 18.

Managed Products: A Fee Circus

Every year, the investment industry comes up with warehouses full of glittering, new, nougat-flavoured, candy-coloured, "managed" investment products, each holding out the prospect of riches and implying your savings will be exposed to only the barest smidgeon of risk. And pretty well every year, a lot of these exciting innovations fail to deliver the golden eggs. The problem is that when investments are done up in such fancy packages, somebody has to pay for all the frills and gorgeous ribbons — and it's always the retail buyer. The investment may be called a *unit trust*, a *structured* or *hybrid fund*, a *royalty trust*, a *closed-end fund*, a *partnership*, or an *income trust* — whatever the name and no matter how wonderful the sales spiel, never forget that if someone's trying to sell the thing to you, they are collecting a fee somewhere down the line.

A number of complex investment vehicles are best left to sophisticated, experienced investors. Although they can be difficult to understand, it should be noted that some are, however, well managed, underpriced, and lucrative to own. But all carry disadvantages:

- **Limited partnerships:** These things are so complicated you need to have a lawyer look them over for you, and even then you're vulnerable. They usually produce tax breaks for the buyers by investing in risky things such as movies or natural resources, but unless you have money to burn, don't consider these highly speculative investments.

- **Hedge funds:** These began as privately run funds for the very rich, but are now sold to the small investor, often through hedge "funds of funds." Hedging is the practice of protecting your investments against loss — by selling borrowed shares at the same time as you buy others, for example. And that's what the rich are mostly interested in when it comes to investing: protecting what they have. Hedge funds are no longer all about avoiding losses, though. Some, although not all, use exotic or risky techniques to chase high returns. Hedge funds used to require a minimum investment of $25,000, but they now can be had for as little as $1,000. But absolutely make sure you get professional advice before putting any serious money into this type of product.

✔ **"Structured" or "hybrid" funds:** These things don't represent Bay Street's finest hour. Investors plowed hundreds of millions of dollars into the funds in 2001, attracted by their promise of a high yield plus the guaranteed return of capital after ten years. The typical fund sold units at $25 each with the pledge to refund that purchase price at the end of a decade — while also trying to pay a rich yield in the range of 8 to 10 percent annually. The funds planned to pull off the neat trick with financial engineering — it involved a risk-free strategy of selling options to other investors that gave *them* the right to buy the fund's stock holdings. Didn't work. The market for options turned tail, which forced many of the funds to reduce their hoped-for distributions to unitholders. The promise to repay investors' purchase price still looks safe because it's generally bankrolled by a major bank. But investors expecting a stream of fat cheques have been disappointed.

In your investing career, stick to the things the professionals buy — bonds and stocks and simple mutual funds that invest in bonds and stocks. Buying a fancy, managed product adds a level of cost and complexity that can only reduce your returns. Buying a stock or a royalty or income trust at the issue price when it's first sold to the public is risky, too, even though you traditionally get it commission-free. Grab it later when the price has fallen, which it likely will eventually. The issue price has often been inflated to pay for brokerage commissions and other marketing expenses, not to mention general hype — so let some other poor investor pay for all those shiny new Mercedes and BMW automobiles you see parked in Bay Street garages.

Part II
Buying Options: Looking for a Helping Hand

The 5th Wave   By Rich Tennant

"You may want to talk to Phil — he's one of our more aggressive financial planners."

In this part . . .

We list and describe the different companies and people you can go to for advice on selecting funds . . . or simply to have your purchase orders carried out. We point out a few of the advantages and drawbacks of each method of buying funds and discuss the selection of funds that each salesperson or company will offer.

Chapter 6

Discount Brokers: Cheap Thrills

Discount brokers are about the closest you can get, as yet, to investing heaven — they're cheap and simple. A discount brokerage account is a great place to build wealth for the long term because you can put almost any kind of investment into it — including mutual funds, shares, bonds, Canada Savings Bonds, or even your own mortgage. Next to the invention of the mutual fund itself, discount brokers have done more than any other financial innovation to open up the stock and bond markets to ordinary people. Best of all, discount brokers are great for keeping costs down, which is one of the most important determinants of investment success. Discounters are firms set up simply to carry out your buy-and-sell orders — charging low commission rates — and provide an account in which you can hold your investments. They sometimes purport to offer lots of flashy services and information, some of which can actually be useful. But, essentially, a discounter is just a bare-bones, order-taking service.

Picking a discount broker can be tricky. In this chapter, we give you the whole story — how discounters work, how they can save you more of your hard-won cash, how to pick the right one for you, and, finally, a few warnings about problems some discount brokerage customers have run into.

What Are Discount Brokers?

A discount broker is a true broker in the sense that it's a firm set up simply to act as an agent. It collects a commission — that is, a transaction fee — when you buy or sell stocks, bonds, funds, and other investments. Yes, financial planners, insurance agents, and traditional stockbrokers also take your orders in this way, but they also bill themselves as advisers and experts who get a fee for helping out. Nothing wrong with that as such — but their fees eat into your returns. A Canadian discount brokerage firm is nearly always an arm of a big bank, taking most orders over the Internet or over the telephone. In the United States, discounters execute your share-buying transactions for as little as US$10. In Canada, minimum charges for a single trade are generally $20 and up for smaller accounts and $10 for larger ones, although you can trade for as little as $5 through at least one independent online broker.

If you're absolutely certain you're going to want personal advice from someone when you pick your funds, then skip this chapter and jump to Chapter 7, where we talk in detail about banks and the services they provide. Discount brokers don't provide much advice, so if you feel you need help picking funds, you won't enjoy using one.

A discounter is like a toothless dealer at a seedy Romanian horse market — an evasive, mildewed character with bushy eyebrows, smelling faintly of cheap plum brandy. You wouldn't expect him to hold your hand (you wouldn't really want to touch him, in fact — just sell you a horse and go away!). In the same way, a discount broker offers little or no advice or financial planning. Just a bare-bones account to hold your investments, and rock-bottom fees to buy and sell. Discounters may offer to sell you fancy packages of pre-selected funds, but won't provide much personal advice about your situation.

Discounters, then, essentially offer a commodity. They employ a bunch of youngsters who are paid a wage for covering the phone and who don't traditionally get extra pay for persuading customers to buy things. In return for charging low commissions, discounters hope to attract enough business to turn a profit. That's why they're so keen to turn as much of their business as possible over to the Internet, where it can be automated.

In the past, discounters were subject to the provincial securities rule that obliges brokers to ensure trades are suitable for the client. Like other people in the investment business who accept your money, they were supposed to follow the Know Your Client rule. (See Chapter 3 for more.) However, in recent years, securities regulators in Canada have relaxed the requirement that trades through a discount broker be vetted to see if they fit with the customer's risk tolerance and investment knowledge. That was after lobbying by the discounters, who claimed that having a human being check every trade slowed up the process too much. The message, for those who may have missed it, is this: When investing through a discounter, you're on your own.

Looking into Canadian discounters

This is an industry where you have to be large to make money. That's why the big banks dominate the discount brokerage sector in Canada, because they already have vast customer bases. Each of the big banks has a discount brokerage arm, giving the banks a lock on the business, but they do have at least one formidable competitor — E*TRADE Canada, the Canadian unit of giant U.S. discount broker E*TRADE Group. Toronto-Dominion Bank's discount broker, TD Waterhouse, dominates the market. This means that other banks don't earn huge profits from their discount brokerage arms, but banks usually feel obliged to push into every business they can.

Considering the savings

How much cheaper are the discounters? Well, their commissions for trading stocks are usually a small fraction of the fees levied by traditional stockbrokers, or even less, for trades of all sizes. And, unlike full-service brokerages, discounters publish their rates openly. For example:

- ✔ At a bank-owned, full-service brokerage, trading 100 shares priced at $25 each could cost as much as $150, the minimum fee, but in many cases this would be discounted to $100 or less.

- ✔ The same trade at that bank's discount brokerage arm would cost less than $30 if the trade were placed online, and approximately $60 if placed over the phone with one of the discounter's agents.

In both cases, more active traders and individual large transactions would be eligible for much lower commissions.

Getting set up with a discounter

Setting up an account with a discount broker is simplicity itself. You don't have to sit through a sales spiel or show that you have thousands to invest — just go online or telephone them, complete a few forms, open an account, and put in some money. Here's more about how to get set up:

- ✔ Visit the Web site of the discount broker you picked and print out an account application form or an RRSP application form. (Chapter 3 has more details on account paperwork. Or go to the TD Waterhouse site at www.tdwaterhouse.ca for an example.)

- ✔ Notice the dense pages of conditions they make you sign. Guess what? They're not in your favour. But just about all discount brokers impose these convoluted terms — which essentially say that in the event of a disagreement the broker is always right — so you can't really escape.

✔ A discounter will pretty well accept your business no matter how poor you are. But you'll have to have the necessary cash in your account, Jack, before you make the first trade. For a fund, the minimum buy is nearly always $1,000.

✔ You never have to meet anyone face to face. The anonymity is relaxing, although you'll almost certainly get put on hold for a good stretch when problems occur in your account. And you'll get used to shouting at dazed employees in a harsh barking tone.

✔ After that, just enter your orders at the firm's Web site, or phone them in. Ensure you have fast access to the trade-confirmation slip, and check it against the order you placed.

You can access your password-protected, discount-brokerage account on the Internet. You also can opt to receive periodic statements by mail. Either way, check the account information against your own records.

Using a discount broker is investing for grownups. No one is around to hold your tiny hand or coo into your tight little rosebud of an ear that "the market always comes back." In return for the low commissions they charge, discounters are geared to provide little or no personal service.

Why Discount Brokers Are a Great Place to Buy Funds

If you're confident about making investment decisions yourself, a discount broker is the best place to buy and hold mutual funds. Discounters let you buy certain mutual funds for no upfront charge when other brokers would demand a commission. They also carry a vast selection of hundreds of mutual funds (more than any broker does), lots of bonds, and just about any stock you care to name. That means you can hold funds from a multitude of different companies — including some low-cost, no-load funds that are hard to buy from a broker or financial planner. And a discount brokerage account also lets you combine funds with your other investments, such as stocks or guaranteed investment certificates, so that all your holdings show up on one convenient statement.

Discounters are the perfect source for mutual funds because the choice is so huge and the charges are so low. Here's a rundown of the other main reasons to strongly consider leaving your money with a discounter.

Your one-stop shop — Convenience

Discount brokers are just extremely convenient. You can be on top of a mountain in Nepal, or in a jail cell in Ballydehob (say hello to Liam but don't let him "arm wrestle" you), but as long as you can get access to the Internet or a telephone you should be able to sell or buy funds, stocks, and bonds in your discount brokerage account. By contrast, a full-service broker may be out of the office, ill, or busy, creating a delay if the backup person is slow.

Another reason to love discounters: They've embraced the Internet whole-heartedly, with many letting you look at your account, and place orders, at any time over the Web. So if you enjoy surfing the Web, then a discounter is the place for you. With a discounter, you have control over what happens in your account. No salespeople are there to interfere or offer advice that may be tainted by the desire to earn sales commissions or — by orders from higher-up, brutal Stalinist-style commands that blare from a cracked loudspeaker inches from the poor broker's ear — to push a particular stock or fund.

Access to a broad selection of options

Wide selection is a powerful reason to go with a discount broker, because discounters sell just about everything. A bank branch or no-load fund company can generally sell you only its own funds, and a broker is likely to have a "select list" of funds with which he or she is most familiar. But a discount broker will let you buy hundreds of funds, as well as thousands of stocks and bonds, in North America and often on overseas markets as well. That means you can have the luxury of just one central portfolio that holds all your investments, instead of spreading them all around town.

Discounters have to carry every major fund because otherwise their competitors will beat them on selection. Having every fund available can be very useful for you if you want to leave an underperforming fund. It means you have somewhere to move the money. If you're with a broker who doesn't sell the funds you want to switch to, however, you're in trouble.

Many firms proclaim that they carry hundreds of funds, and in fact they probably do. But you'll find that some low-cost funds from independent providers come with high minimum purchases of $5,000 and up. Always ask if the fund you're interested in is available and find out about any conditions.

A wealth of investing information

Finally, discount brokers can be useful channels for getting hold of investing information. Check out their Web sites and you'll find fee calculators and other useful online tools. Some may have offers of investment newsletters and books at cut-rate prices. A few discounters sell research reports from stock analysts at full-service brokerages — usually the brokerage owned by the discounter's parent.

Research shows that most investment newsletters fail to beat the market over time. And brokerage analysts are notorious for seeing the world through rose-coloured glasses; they rarely say a stock is a Sell because that's certain to enrage the company's management. Angry corporate managers are likely to cut the critical analyst off from information and may even blacklist his or her firm in the future when it comes to picking brokers to handle a stock issue or other deal.

At Last — A Break on Costs

One of the big pluses with discounters is the fact that most let you buy funds on a front-load basis at no initial cost to you. Front-load means that the fund buyer pays an upfront commission directly to the broker or financial planner at the time of purchase — the exact rate is negotiable, but it's usually 3 percent or less these days, and sometimes as little as 1 percent. The advantage to paying a front load is that the funds can then be sold at any time with no further charges.

The discounters aren't being particularly generous with their zero-load offer on front-load funds, mind you. Fund companies love it when their wares are sold front-load because they don't have to pay any commission to the broker. So they pay an especially generous annual trailer commission — typically 1 percent of the client's holding in an equity fund — to the broker that sold the fund when it was bought on a front-load basis. Trailer commissions are ongoing commissions that a salesperson or his or her firm gets as long as the client stays in the fund or funds sold by the manager. Paid by the fund company itself, trailer commissions ultimately come out of the management fee your fund is charged. Big fat trailers on mutual funds sold on a front-load basis (even if the investor actually paid no load) are the reason why discounters are happy to let you have front-load funds at what looks like no charge — they're often indirectly collecting 1 percent of your money each year from the fund company.

A word on commissions

Table 6-1 lists the major discounters, their Web sites, and their toll-free telephone numbers. Going online is the best way to check out commissions, which change as discounters jostle for market share. By the time you read this, they'll no doubt have come up with new special offers and dancing kittens in little kilts. Check out the Web sites listed for all the latest and greatest. Discounters need to recruit new clients because this is a volume-driven industry: If you're not No. 1 or No. 2, you're really an also-ran, limping down the home stretch with the glue-factory van waiting beside the stables....

When looking at these prices, keep a few things in mind:

✔ Bank-owned discounters usually levy no fees at all if you're buying or selling funds managed by their parent banks (and most outside funds as well). So, for example, if you're dealing with Royal Bank of Canada's discounter, RBC Direct Investing, you can sell Royal Bank's no-load funds for free.

✔ Discounters generally require a $500 to $1,000 minimum investment if you're buying mutual funds. It's a low-margin business, after all, and tiny orders are just more trouble than they're worth for the firm.

✔ Higher commission rates often apply if you place your order by talking to a person over the phone. For Internet and automated-telephone orders, the commissions are considerably lower. Note that some brokers have fees for buying and selling certain funds, and fees for short-term trading may also apply.

Table 6-1	How to Contact the Discounters	
Discount Broker	*Contact Information*	
BMO InvestorLine	www.bmoinvestorline.com	1-888-776-6886
CIBC Investor's Edge	www.investorsedge.cibc.com	1-800-567-3343
Credential Direct	www.credentialdirect.com	1-877-742-2900
Disnat Online	www.disnat.com	1-877-842-0582
E*TRADE Canada	www.canada.etrade.com	1-888-872-3388
HSBC InvestDirect	www.investdirect.hsbc.ca	1-866-865-4722
National Bank Discount Brokerage	w3.nbdb.ca	1-800-363-3511
QTrade	www.qtrade.ca	1-877-787-2330
Questrade	www.questrade.com	1-888-783-7866
RBC Direct Investing	www.rbcdirectinvesting.com	1-800-769-2560
ScotiaMcLeod Direct Investing	www.scotiamcleoddirect.com	1-800-263-3430
TD Waterhouse	www.tdwaterhouse.ca	1-800-465-5463

In Chapter 2 we discuss the other type of mutual fund sales commission — the redemption charge, or back-end load. Funds sold on that basis charge you nothing upfront, but levy a commission if you sell the fund within six or seven years. Most discounters simply treat back-end loads like regular brokers do. When a client buys an equity fund on a redemption-charge basis, the broker collects a 5-percent commission directly from the fund company (not from the client). The firm then extracts any applicable redemption charges from the proceeds if the customer sells the fund early. Some discount brokers have tried "rebating" a portion of that 5-percent commission back to clients who buy deferred-load funds. It's a nice little bonus, but it also makes the whole exercise more complicated. You'll do fine without it if you just buy front-load funds.

Back-end-load rebates and bonuses: As if life wasn't complicated enough

We're sorry to keep burdening you with all this commission stuff. And by now you're probably wondering: Why is everyone in the fund industry obsessed with sales charges? Why do they create myriad different classes of the same fund, each sold with a different commission, and drape them with incomprehensible conditions, rules, and names? Well, the bottom line is that selling expenses — particularly the cost of paying commissions to brokers and financial planners — are an enormous cost of business for mutual fund companies. Let's look at this example: Equity-fund salespeople, as a general rule, get 1 percent of the client's assets each year, either upfront or payable as an annual "trailer" commission. Well, the median Canadian equity fund charges an annual MER of 2.5 percent, so more than a third of the management fee revenue is going to the broker or financial planner who sold the fund.

Just one more commission complication before we leave the subject. Some discount brokers have tried taking the 5-percent commission they get from the company for selling a deferred-load fund and "rebating" some of it to the customer in the form of a bonus. For example, if you invest $10,000 in a fund on a back-end-load basis, and the discounter pays you a 2-percent bonus,

then $10,200 would immediately show up in your account. Seems like you're getting money for nothing. These rear-load rebates have ranged from 2 to almost 3 percent depending on which broker you're dealing with — as long as you meet their many conditions.

Getting a bonus straight off the top like that sounds like a great deal, but it hasn't proved popular with discount brokerage customers. That's because with a deferred-load fund, you're "locked in" by the commission you must pay to the fund company if you cash out within about six years. Discount brokerage customers are independent souls who don't like having their hands tied in any way. So they have steered clear of rear-end-load funds carrying rebates, even if the funds looked like a real bargain at first glance.

The bottom line? Sure, take advantage of a rebate if you're certain you want to stay in the fund for several years (until the deferred load no longer applies), but don't lose dollars just to save cents. If you think a possibility exists that you'll want to sell the fund again while the back-end load is still in effect, then go with the front-load version to keep life simple and your investment strategy unencumbered.

How to Pick a Discounter

Don't get in a lather comparing the discounters' commissions and totting up their special offers. Seeing people in the investment business offering to cut their prices is wonderful, but over the long term, saving $100 on a one-off basis doesn't amount to much. If you plan to simply buy and hold high-quality funds and stocks, it doesn't make a lot of difference if you've spent $100 or $200 in commissions building the portfolio. Yes, cheaper is always better, but fast and polite responses to your orders or questions, and investments that suit your needs, are just as important as low rates.

Getting a feel for the service

The important thing is efficient, accurate, and prompt service — something that, sadly, discounters seem to have had a problem providing in the past. After a debacle in the hectic stock market of early 2000, when some clients said they were left on the phone for up to a week, the discount firms embarked on a hiring frenzy aimed at ensuring they had enough staff to handle soaring demand. Service levels are better now — although lots of the credit goes to the fact that much of discount trading happens online nowadays, with no human intervention required.

Forget the personal touch

Select a discount broker carefully. Until a few years ago, service at too many of the firms tended to be spotty, with orders and requests sometimes going through incorrectly or after long delays. But those days happily appear to be behind us — and, of course, traditional "full-service" brokers and financial planners can get orders wrong too.

Nonetheless, if you're worried about getting trades executed on very busy market days, you might be more comfortable with one of the large bank-owned brokers, which are likely to have more people available to handle your calls, and which may have more robust Web sites for standing up to heavy traffic.

Generally, when dealing with a discounter, remember that the people answering the phone don't know you (unless you're a high roller who's given special attention), so you can forget about getting much personalized help. Yes, some discounters are offering more research and information, but they'll always be the port-of-call for resolute independent souls who want to make all their investing decisions for themselves.

If you've got the time and energy, you could pick a firm by first opening two or even three separate accounts at different discounters — signing up as a client generally doesn't cost a cent. After a year or so, you'll get a good feel for which discounter is most reliable and the easiest to use and you can transfer all your assets there. Be sure to ask your family, friends, and work mates about their experience with discounters. If you keep coming across horror stories about a particular firm, then shop elsewhere.

Apart from commissions, the fee you're most likely to face at a discount broker is an annual administration fee of roughly $40 to $100, although some no-charge brokerages do exist. In any event, some firms will waive RRSP fees if you have assets of $15,000 to $25,000 or more in the account.

Don't worry too much about picking the right discounter. If you make the wrong choice, you can switch later at the cost of a few weeks' wait and a fee of about $100. It's messy — and watch out for mistakes while they transfer your investments — but you have a right to move.

Finding the right discounter for you

A good source of information on discount brokers (and low-cost investing in general) is the Stingy Investor Web site, at www.stingyinvestor.com. Run by avid number-cruncher Norman Rothery of Toronto, it offers a rundown of discounters' rates. (Before deciding to use a particular firm, however, be sure to double-check fees with the brokerages you are considering.)

Don't become obsessed with commission rates when choosing a discounter. Some have decided to market themselves as cut-price providers, offering minimum commissions for a stock trade that can run $25 or even less. That's a tremendous deal for investors, but remember that if you don't plan to trade stocks frequently, it's only of limited value. Look at the whole picture — including mutual fund commissions, service standards, and special options — before you make your choice.

Try calling the company a couple of times with questions. If you can't seem to get decent answers, then consider going somewhere else.

Some experts advise using a discount broker not owned by your usual bank. That way, if a dispute over a trade ever occurs, the broker can't just dip into your bank account and extract money.

Considering a mutual fund discount broker

Apart from the true discount brokers, which are licensed to deal in stocks and bonds as well as funds, investors also can choose from among dozens of "no-load" or "discount" mutual fund dealers that sell only mutual funds. These companies, which are often happy to buy and sell funds over the telephone, usually charge no commission on front-load funds, living off the rich trailer payment instead. Individual stockbrokers and financial planners also frequently offer to sell funds with no load.

Discount fund dealers will clearly save you money, and if you're happy with the level of service available and the selection of funds, then go with one. But, once again, don't let cost be the only deciding factor. Saving yourself a one-off expense of 2 percent is pointless if the dealer subsequently doesn't give you enough advice and choice of products.

 From our perspective, if we were looking to save money we'd stick to a regular discount broker who's able to sell us shares and bonds as well as funds while also offering low commissions. Call us scaredy-cats, but we'd rather deal with a discounter that's a large multi-billion-dollar organization. That way, we know the systems are in place to administer our accounts properly.

What's Wrong with Discount Brokers?

The major problem with discounters, especially for investors who are just getting going, is that they do not provide advice on your personal financial situation or help you create a financial plan. A discounter is essentially a tool for doing transactions — but buying and selling investments is only part of getting rich. A good planner or full-service stockbroker will also provide tips on tax and wealth management — using life insurance, for example — that you won't get from a discounter.

Getting seduced and abandoned

Discounters leave you on your own to make all the decisions, but freedom can bring problems. Some research seems to show that retail investors who work without an adviser don't do well because they're prone to buying high and selling low. That is, they euphorically buy shares and equity funds when the market has soared and then dump them when prices have already crashed. That may be true or just a self-serving myth fostered by the brokerage industry. But a good fund salesperson can impose valuable discipline in two ways: by getting you to save money in the first place and by persuading you to hang on when things look bleak.

So if you're a nervous or impulsive type, holding your stocks and funds at a discount broker might be a recipe for panic selling and hysterical buying. Perhaps you'd be better off with a planner or old-style broker.

Knowing when to stay away

Although the lure of cheap trades and special offers may be pretty hard to resist, discounters aren't for every Canadian, not even close. Some investors should probably stay away from discounters. For example:

- ✔ Nervous investors who are just starting out might be happier opening a mutual fund account at a bank first. They can get at least some personalized help while they learn the basics of investing, before venturing into the discount world.

- ✔ Those who plan to trade frequently in and out of the stock market might be better off going with a competent traditional stockbroker who'll give them a break on commissions. Full-service brokers are more expensive, but they can often provide better "execution" of your orders — that is, they can buy and sell stocks at more attractive prices.

Chapter 7

Banks: The Fast Food of Funds

. . . .

In This Chapter

▷ Discovering why banks are the simplest place to buy mutual funds

▷ Dealing with your bank

▷ Bank funds to consider for your portfolio

. . . .

A decade ago, the banks didn't seem to be able to run a decent equity fund. Those days are long gone. The banks' equity funds have been strong performers in recent years. Plus they have reduced the costs charged to mutual fund investors, thanks in some part to their lineups of index funds, which simply track the entire market (we take a closer look at index funds in Chapter 15). Expenses also have been kept down thanks to Internet sales, which are cheap to process. In most cases, a bank-fund purchase is no farther than a mouse-click away from your online bank account statement page. So, perks to keeping your investments where you keep your cash do exist. No meddlesome salespeople are involved.

In this chapter, we explain why banks are a great place to buy mutual funds, especially if you just want a simple option that's also an okay value. This chapter shows why you can just go ahead and use your local bank branch for mutual funds if you want a quick solution. You might not get the best bargain going or make the most money, but it'll do the job.

Buying Where You Bank

Banks are the very simplest place to buy mutual funds: Just walk in (virtually or to a branch) and put your money into a selection of the house brands. But don't assume they're the best choice. A bank is a great place to start out buying funds, but certainly do take a long, hard look at what they can and can't offer.

Hey, you're busy, what with training your cat to play the xylophone ("No, the left paw!") and getting into the Guinness Book of Records for growing the longest nose hairs ever officially recorded (that old fool in Sinkiang-Uigar glued them in). So why not just make things easy on yourself and simply grab your mutual funds at the bank? Mutual fund buyers, especially rookies, can do well at the bank for a number of reasons.

Providing one-stop shopping

Even if you don't have an account with a bank, you can still walk into a branch, hand over a cheque, and sign up for a mutual fund account. Okay, it might take a couple of days to arrange an appointment with a registered representative, a bank employee who is licensed to sell funds, but after that the process should be painless. Most banks have telephone services for buying and selling funds after you've opened a fund account, and nearly all offer telephone and Internet services that let you check your account balance and recent transactions. In fact, most banks will let you open a mutual fund investing account online, as part of your banking account access. (In some cases you might have to set up an online account in person at a branch.)

Banks sell their own funds on a no-load basis — no commissions or sales loads. That means all your money goes to work for you right away, and you can cash out at any time with no penalty (although companies impose a short-term trading penalty, typically 2 percent, on those who sell a fund within 30 to 90 days, depending on the specific fund).

You can set up a fairly decent mutual fund *registered retirement savings plan* — a tax-sheltered account of retirement money — at a bank in half an hour flat by simply buying one of their pre-selected fund packages. Staff are trained to sell these mixtures, and questionnaires are designed to slot you into the right one so you're likely to get a reasonable fit. See Chapter 20 on fund packages for more about this type of product.

Keeping it together

Most likely you have your mortgage, line of credit, and chequing account at a bank. So buying mutual funds from the company that already holds the mortgage on your house means you can take care of everything in one place, be it a branch, at the bank's Internet site, or on the phone.

Offering to move your mutual fund business to a bank can radically improve your bargaining power when seeking a loan or mortgage. Bank employees get little chocolate soccer balls as rewards when their customers bring their investment portfolios to the branch. Use this to your advantage when looking to extend your credit, take a plunge into the real estate market, or buy a car. In today's competitive banking environment, an investor with a portfolio is a sought-after prize.

Offering appealing options

The employees you deal with at a bank branch or on the telephone are paid wages, so they're not commission-driven jackals. But they usually sell only the house brand. And yes, they receive incentives to attract business, and yes, the banks tend to be vague on exactly what bonuses are paid.

For the most part, you'll find that banks are happy to sell you index funds — low-expense funds that simply track the stock- or bond-market index or benchmark. Index funds are such a good deal they should be part of every investor's arsenal, although we suggest you also have between one-third and one-half of your stock market investments in traditional actively managed funds, featuring a person who buys and sells investments in search of trading profits.

Banks, unlike mutual fund companies that market their products through commission-paid salespeople, are able to make money from running index funds because they don't have to pay out those big commissions. Most offer index funds with low expenses — around 1 percent or less — compared with 2.3 to 2.4 percent on, for example, the median Canadian equity mutual fund. If you were to simply walk into a branch and open up a mutual fund account full of index funds like that, chances are you'd do better than millions of mutual fund investors. For that matter, almost all of the banks' actively managed (non-index-based) mutual funds have expenses that are less than the category medians.

Fighting for the right to serve you

The banks are hungry for your mutual fund business and they're willing to cut prices and improve service to get it. The fantastic growth of the Canadian mutual fund industry, with assets soaring to more than $700 billion in mid-2008 from less than $30 billion in 1990, has represented a migration of cash from bank savings accounts and guaranteed investment certificates into funds. The banks have been working very hard to hold on to as much of that money as they can.

Another reason why the banks are fund-mad: Mutual funds are a wonderfully profitable and low-risk business. The management company just keeps raking in those fees no matter how well or badly the fund does. That must be a great comfort to Canadians invested in U.S. equity funds; the median U.S. stock fund lost nearly 11 percent during 2007.

Lending money, banks' traditional way of making a profit, is more risky than selling mutual funds because borrowers can default and interest rates can jump, leaving the banks stuck with a pile of underpriced loans. So the banks have reinvented themselves as "wealth management" companies, and mutual funds are key players in that ballgame.

Buyer Beware: Shortfalls in Bank Offerings

Nobody's perfect, and buying funds at a bank — online, on the phone, or in person — has its drawbacks. Here, for your viewing pleasure, are the drawbacks of lining the pockets of nasal, power-hungry guys from Quebec and New Brunswick, the sort who become bank chairmen.

Few options

The big problem is lack of choice: The banks have been in no hurry to market other companies' funds because a banker likes sharing fees like a lobster enjoys taking a hot bath. That means customers are often stuck with the bank's line of products, which isn't always the strongest. More and more bank employees have personal finance training, but most aren't specialists in the field. To get a full analysis of your situation, you may still have to go to a planner working for an independent firm.

The narrow selection of funds at many branches is the biggest problem with buying from a bank. Most of the big banks offer a full range of funds under their own brand name, but that doesn't necessarily mean that their Canadian equity or global equity funds will be any good. And even if you try to build a diversified fund portfolio by buying the bank's index funds and actively managed funds as well, you run a risk you're leaving too much money with just one investment team. Let's say a particular coterie usually tends to get excited about flashy technology stocks — then you're likely to lose money when other investors get tired of such high-priced, science fiction tales. You can get around this lack of diversification — the annoying word for spreading out your investments — by opening an account elsewhere as well, perhaps with another bank. Or you can at least increase your diversification by buying several of the bank's actively managed funds.

Overworked and underpaid: Not just you, some bankers too

With the rapid growth in online banking and investing, it's getting harder and harder to talk to an actual human being unless you've got a whopping balance in your account. That's a drag, and it's a disadvantage of going to a bank if you'd rather deal with a person than peck at the keyboard of a machine (what's wrong with you, anyway?). Banks may be losing their traditional advantage of owning huge networks of physical branches, because all their competitors are as easily accessed online as they are. Well, almost, because you likely visit your banking Web site every week anyway.

Lack of pressure to perform

Customers who buy funds from a bank are isolated in the sense that the fund managers don't have brokers and other salespeople breathing in a damp, hot way down their necks, insisting on good returns. If a broker-sold fund's performance goes into the tank, salespeople get angry and embarrassed because they have to face the clients they put into the loser. That's never a fun session. The sales force demands explanations from the manager. So the presence of salespeople probably serves to impose some discipline on fund companies. With bank funds where no brokers are involved, terrible performance used to drag on for years with little publicity or outcry.

Banks now take funds more seriously, meaning that problems get fixed fairly quickly, but bank fund unitholders arguably still don't have anyone looking out for their interests. Yes, nearly all mutual funds have "trustees" who theoretically are on the side of investors, but we've yet to hear of a fund trustee saying a single critical word about a fund's management or expenses. Most unitholders wouldn't know where to look for the trustees' names and no wonder — you have to dig deep into a financial report to find them. However, this search is less onerous now that fund companies are obligated to produce a management report of fund performance twice a year (see Chapter 3 for more on MRFPs). You no longer have to plow through a fund's obscure "annual information form" to identify the trustees.

Another problem with buying funds from your bank is that, well, you're forced to deal with a bank. The Internet has made this a lot easier, but if you need to reach them by phone, your calls may get routed to on-hold hell or voice-mail purgatory before they end up in the bottomless pit of general delivery, with Tats in shipping. Increasingly, bank customers are being asked to telephone a central information line (1-800-PLS-HOLD) or go to an Internet site (which saves the bank a packet). This is intended to relieve some of the pressure on branch staff, who usually have to deal with all the other services and products the bank delivers and then face the whining, puking, and foot-stamping at home (not to mention the kids). So you might not get the sort of personal attention and time that a good financial planner or even stockbroker delivers.

How Banks Pulled Up Their Socks

Performance of bank-run equity funds has greatly improved during the past decade, although the banks still haven't built much of a record in global equity funds. (Their fixed-income funds have long been okay.) In the past, bank stock funds lagged the competition by a wide margin. They seemed to have difficulty attracting and keeping gifted fund managers (if such a thing as stock-picking talent exists, as opposed to sheer luck). Explanations varied, but one problem seemed to be that hot fund managers demand lavish paycheques and bonuses — but if the banks were to pay such huge amounts to a few individuals, managers elsewhere in their vast dreary bureaucracies would get jealous in a grey, whining way. To some extent, though, the banks seemed to have fixed their performance problems, in some cases by spinning off their portfolio management operations into separate companies.

But that has changed. Some bank fund managers have achieved prominence and turned up on portfolio manager round tables at conferences and in print. More important, the funds' numbers are quite strong. Table 7-1 shows the three biggest bank funds in the Canadian equity funds as of mid-2008. As you can see, over five years these giants (with a combined $11 billion in assets) all beat — or stacked up well against — the median fund return and the S&P/TSX composite index. Over ten years all three outpaced both the median and the index. Mind you, the people running bank funds arguably had an advantage in recent years because, wow, bank stocks have done so well they're just the sort of stuff that conservative bank funds tend to hold.

Mutual funds have now become such an important business for the banks that it's very unlikely an equity fund would be allowed to drift along with poor numbers for very long before the manager was reassigned . . . to checking mortgage applications . . . in Tuktoyaktuk.

Table 7-1	**Getting So Much Better: Bank Funds Are Catching Up**	
Fund Name	*Five-Year Return*	*Ten-Year Return*
RBC Canadian Equity	17.1%	9.5%
BMO Equity	15.8	9.4%
TD Canadian Equity	22.1%	11.8%
Median Canadian equity fund	16.3%	9.3%
S&P/TSX	16.3%	8.5%

Improving your choice of funds

Banks branches now have staff who are registered to sell other companies' funds (known in the jargon as third-party funds). However, don't expect to be able to buy any fund you want at a bank branch; it seems in-branch reps are most keen on training their staff to talk about funds from companies such as AGF Management Ltd., AIM Funds Management Inc., CI Funds Inc., Fidelity Investments Canada Ltd., Mackenzie Financial Corp., and Franklin Templeton Investments. Those are all honourable companies, but they also happen to be commission-paying fund sponsors that sell their products through brokers and planners — which means that the banks are in line for a gush of commission income in return for selling their wares.

Stretching the rules with bank offerings

You can create a widely diversified portfolio from the funds of just one bank by using a bit of ingenuity. In Chapter 4, we recommend portfolios whose equity portion is made up of a Canadian index fund and an international and U.S. index fund, plus a couple of actively managed Canadian and two global actively managed funds. (Global equity funds buy shares everywhere, but international funds stay out of North America.) Achieving that kind of broad mix used to take a good bit of work, but the banks, along with most large fund companies, now offer a wide selection of packaged portfolios. (We explain these "fund packages" in Chapter 20.) Table 7-2 shows one such package, the Scotia Selected Balanced Income & Growth Portfolio (a balanced portfolio consisting of Bank of Nova Scotia funds) in mid-2008. This is a traditional, cautious mix, with 54 percent of the assets in stocks and 46 percent in fixed income. Half of the equity exposure is to U.S. and other foreign stocks. (This holdings information was as of the end of 2007.)

Table 7-2   A Conservative Portfolio Using Just Scotiabank Funds

Fund Name	Percentage of Portfolio
Scotia Canadian Income	35.6%
Scotia Canadian Growth	13.0
Scotia Canadian Dividend	11.0
Scotia Global Growth	10.2
Scotia Mortgage Income	10.1
Scotia Canadian Small Cap	5.1
Scotia Global Small Cap	4.3
Scotia U.S. Value	3.9
Scotia International Value	3.8
Scotia Global Opportunities	2.9

A Few Gems from the Banks

Below we discuss three bank funds (as selected for us by Morningstar's fund-analysis team) that have produced solid returns in recent years. Will their good performance continue? Impossible to tell. However, Morningstar's analysts favour funds with strong management, good long-term performance, and relatively low expenses. (Modest costs always load the dice in favour of the investor.) Check out these three funds:

✔ **Renaissance Global Markets:** Long term is the name of the game for this CIBC fund, which invests for the long term and holds only companies that have solid long-term track records. Ironically, the fund's own long-term performance is unimpressive. But the fund got a new manager in late 2006 and has been transformed from a stodgy index hugger to an exciting, actively managed portfolio. The result has been promising, as the new manager — David Winters, formerly with Franklin Templeton — outperformed the MSCI World Index during his first year and a half on the job. What's more, this has been achieved at a lower cost; the fund's annual expenses have come down since his arrival.

✔ **RBC Global Precious Metals:** Why buy a precious metals fund if the price of gold has shot through the roof in recent years? This fund is much more than a holder of gold-mining companies. Unlike in some precious metals funds, this fund's manager, Chris Beer, has a mandate to invest as much as 20 percent of the fund's portfolio in silver and platinum producers. Better still, he is known for his talent at identifying companies that are able to efficiently mine metals and have a good record of delivering and financing an exploration project. But be aware that precious metals funds aren't for the faint of heart and should represent only a small part of your investment portfolio. This fund is also a good bet because it sports the lowest annual expenses in the precious metals category, at 2.07 percent.

✔ **TD Entertainment and Communications:** Now here we have something unusual: A truly unique bank-run fund. Its mandate allows it to invest in stocks of all sizes in such sectors as telecom, media, IT services, Internet, advertising, and broadcasting. And it does so with a lower risk profile than many other funds in its category (global equity). This comes partly from a fund mandate that allows the manager to hold up to one-fifth of the fund's value outside its core investment areas of media and telecom. That's not to say considerable risks don't exist if you buy this fund, so hold it only as a small dose. View it as the entertaining corner of your portfolio. However, with annual expenses of 2.7 percent, the price of admission is a little high.

Chapter 8

Stockbrokers, Financial Planners, and Advisers Aplenty

Civilization may run out of water, out of brain surgeons, out of Vancouver Island marmots, and out of braying, self-important, financial journalists. But it'll never run out of mutual fund salespeople. At least 50,000 Canadians hold themselves out as financial advisers or planners in one way or another, and most of them are licensed to sell you mutual funds. They come in a bewildering range of guises, from Boss-suited executives in the downtown core of big cities to down-home types wolfing down the free sandwiches at fund company lunches. And they give themselves a galaxy of names: financial consultant, investment counsellor, estate planner, financial adviser, investment executive, personal financial planner. Don't get worked up trying to figure out the differences among them. Financial planning remains a mostly self-regulated industry, if at all, although a few national industry groups like Advocis and the Financial Planners Standards Council do exist.

In this chapter, we describe the main types of fund salespeople and tell you about the advantages of using financial planners who charge only an upfront or annual fee, rather than collect commissions on the products they sell you. We also provide some basic tips on the right and wrong ways to pick an adviser.

Alphabet Soup: Figuring Out All those Titles

You could spend a good month or two crafting a long list of all the elaborate titles financial advisers give themselves. You could then have a couple of gloomy women in leotards read it out on a darkened stage at the Toronto Fringe Festival, to the accompaniment of randomly played cymbals and flutes. Probably be a huge hit — better than the usual dreary one-person show about a failed actor, anyway — but it wouldn't help people much with their financial planning. So how do you wade through all the options and get down to what's best for you and your money? That's the key — your first challenge should be figuring out exactly what kind of financial planning you want rather than trying to decode their titles. In other words, do you need a fast once-over or a harrowing session of soul-searching?

After you've decided you need some help drawing up a financial plan and picking the right mutual funds, ask yourself two questions:

- ✔ **Do I want just a quick solution or a complete financial plan?** If you're reasonably comfortable with your money arrangements as they stand and you just want someone who'll suggest a few funds, then you can keep things simple by going to a storefront mutual fund dealer, a stockbroker, or a bank. They can recommend a package of funds and set up the account for you. If, however, you want help planning your fiscal future, make sure you deal with someone who has had some formal financial planning training (more on that later) and is also genuinely interested in the subject. And the best choice of all is to go with an unbiased planner who charges you a separate fee for his or her expertise, instead of selling you mutual funds that pay them a commission.

- ✔ **How much money will I be investing?** Don't expect miracles. If you're planning to put $5,000 a year into your fund portfolio, the chairman of CIBC Wood Gundy Inc. won't be asking you out to golf. It can be a good idea to tell the adviser upfront how much you think you're likely to save each year. You'll often be able to tell from his or her reaction whether you're likely to get much in the way of attention or advice.

Here's a great way to find out if a fund salesperson is likely to be of much use in drawing up a financial plan: Don't just ask about investing. Also bring up subjects such as buying disability and life insurance, estate planning, and minimizing taxes. If the answers are superficial or unsatisfactory, then this person probably isn't the best adviser to help you build a successful plan.

Drawing up a comprehensive financial plan is a complicated process, covering the client's taxes, income, spending, and retirement plans. Choosing investments is only a small part of that, but many advisers are paid just for selling life insurance or mutual funds, so saving and investing become all they want to talk about. In fact, as we outline in Chapter 4, every competent financial planner worth his or her salt should emphasize getting rid of high-interest debt as your first step toward sound money management. If they don't look at your whole financial picture, look elsewhere for help. So beware of commission-paid salespeople who encourage you to go ahead and buy funds even though you already have big credit card debts. This is no way to build a sound financial plan or invest for profit.

Be sure a financial planner is qualified. The Institute of Advanced Financial Planners (IAFP) has some good guidelines. Check out the Consumer Guide section of the IAFP Web site at www.iafp.ca. Advocis also has excellent information in its Consumer Info section at www.advocis.ca.

Advisers can be divided into several main groups according to how they earn their living: You'll find advisers who

- ✔ Get paid a commission for selling you investments.
- ✔ Charge a one-time fee for producing a financial plan, without specific investment advice.
- ✔ Charge you a separate fee for designing an investment portfolio.
- ✔ Earn a salary from an organization such as a bank that markets its own line of investments.

Commissioned advisers

The vast majority of Canadians choose to go with a financial adviser who gets paid by a mutual fund company or insurance company for selling investment "products." In part that could be a reflection of the nation's thrifty Scottish psyche. Unlike many Americans, Canadians seem to prefer having the expense of investing advice hidden from them, buried in the fee of a mutual fund or the cost of insurance. That way, it seems so much less painful than having to cut the adviser a cheque.

An obvious example of a commission-paid salesperson is the traditional stockbroker, who makes money when you buy stocks, bonds, or funds. The broker gets a transaction fee, or commission, each time you put an order through.

✔ With stocks, the commission is added onto the cost when you buy or is deducted from the proceeds when you sell — and your transaction confirmation should clearly show how much was charged. For example, when you buy or sell $10,000 worth of shares, you can expect to pay a sales commission of about $300.

✔ With bonds, the "commission" is normally a profit margin that's hidden in the price, just like buying a pair of jeans at the Gap. That's because brokers usually sell to their clients bonds that they already own themselves. No separate commission is charged or shown on your confirmation slip because the broker has already taken a markup.

✔ With funds, things get more complicated. But the essence of the system is that the broker (or financial planner or insurance salesperson) is paid by the fund company. The fund company, remember, charges an annual management fee — which is deducted from the assets of the fund — and pays roughly half of that out to the salesperson.

Commission-paid salespeople also include life insurance salespeople, whether independent or tied to a particular insurance company. In addition to life insurance, these agents are often licensed to sell mutual funds or the insurance industry's version of mutual funds, which are known as segregated funds. Segregated funds — so-called because their assets must be kept separate from those of the insurance company — carry guarantees to refund up to 100 percent of an investor's initial outlay. More on those in Chapter 19.

Finally, Canada is home to thousands of *financial* planners, either in franchises, chains of stores, or small independent offices, whose bread and butter is the mutual fund.

Fee-only financial planners

The next group is far smaller but represents an excellent choice for those who don't mind signing a cheque to get advice. They're fee-only financial planners who aren't interested in selling products. In fact, they are not licensed to sell products. Fee-only planners will draw up a financial plan that addresses your entire money situation and sets personal financial goals, both near term and far. A good financial plan helps you set broad investing goals but does not discuss specific investments, or even market sectors. Rather, it points you in the right investing direction based on your present lifestyle needs, tax situation, insurance needs, and estate planning goals, among other factors. You must go to a licensed investment adviser, commissioned or fee-based, to construct and maintain an investment portfolio.

A properly executed, custom financial plan will cost $1,000 or more, although some acceptable — but less customized — financial plans are available for a few hundred dollars. These plans are created by planners who use off-the-shelf computer software.

A fee-only financial planner might produce a plan and then refer you to a commission-charging dealer — or even collect commissions on funds you buy under the table. First, such practices are illegal. Second, that kind of double-charging adds another layer of complexity and fees, and it might not be the best deal for you. If the adviser is simply putting you into funds that pay commissions to salespeople, then why did you pay a fee for advice?

Fee-based investment advisers

Unlike fee-only financial planners, fee-based investment advisers are licensed investment salespeople who can be affiliated with a traditional stockbroker-age firm, a mutual fund dealer, or a financial planning firm. The drawback of going with a fee-based adviser is the pain of paying the freight, which can be substantial. It might be a fee based on assets under management — a percentage of your investments (typically 1 or 2 percent) — or it can be a charge that ranges from $100 an hour to a few hundred, depending on the complexity of your affairs.

With a fee-charging planner, you may have to make more choices about the investments you buy and the strategy you adopt. That's because the financial plan produced for each client is different, reflecting individual needs and wants, whereas commission-paid salespeople are often happiest suggesting a predesigned and relatively fixed package of funds that leaves you with few decisions to make.

Investors with substantial assets — say, approaching $1 million — should strongly consider going with a fee-charging planner. Your accountant or lawyer may offer the service or may be willing to recommend someone. The fee will often run into several hundred dollars, but that's a bargain compared with the hidden cost of high mutual fund management fees levied by fund companies that sell through commissioned advisers.

Salaried advisers

Thousands of financial advisers are being trained by the banks to take over the "wealth-management" needs of the aging baby boomers. They're generally on salary — plus bonuses if they can persuade you to put your savings into one of the bank's products, usually mutual funds or some other kind of managed-money program.

As we explain in Chapter 7, these bank employees are often limited in the products they can offer, and their training may not be as full as that of brokers or specialized financial planners. That means their advice should always be taken with a pinch of salt: They're employed to push the bank's products or sell funds that pay the bank a fat commission. Still, especially for investors with relatively simple needs and clear financial goals, the bank can be a great place to start off investing. Compared with the hard-driving world of brokers or financial planners, little sales pressure occurs. The product choices are simple, and having all your money in one place makes for easy recordkeeping.

But don't forget you're doing the bank a favour by handing over your savings. That means you're entitled to a helpful and experienced bank employee, not some rookie or sleepyhead. And don't get railroaded into buying one of the fixed arrangements of funds the banks love to pitch (it makes their administration much easier, for one thing). If you feel that none of the pre-selected packages meets your needs, insist on a custom mixture of funds.

In general, the bank is the perfect first stop for starting-out investors who have only a few thousand dollars at their disposal. The banks are equipped to deal with small accounts and they have handy automated systems that allow you to check your account balance and transactions without waiting for someone to get back to you.

And banks' employee training in investment advice is getting better all the time as the wealth-management business becomes vital to their future profit growth. Some banks even have qualified brokers available in the branch who can sell you a range of stocks and bonds or funds from nearly every company.

The blurred distinctions among all these types of commission-paid advisers make the whole business of looking for help confusing. But at least you have one thing going for you: Remember that if you buy mutual funds, your money is reasonably safe because it goes to the fund company instead of staying with the broker or dealer. So if you decide to dump your salesperson and his or her firm, you can simply shift the account elsewhere, after some whingeing and delays on the part of the old salesperson. Your money is doubly safe because even the fund company itself has to leave the fund's assets with a separate custodian for safekeeping.

Make sure you'll be receiving a statement at least twice a year from the fund company (ask to see a sample) so you can be certain you're on the fund company's books. And make your cheque out to the fund company, not to the salesperson. Finally, get transaction confirmations for your purchases from the company — alternatively, you can call the fund company itself to double-check that they have a record of your investment.

Deciding Whether to Pay a Fee or a Commission

Your first decision when selecting an adviser is this: Do you want to pay a fee to a fee-based adviser, or are you happy with a commission-collecting salesperson? Don't rush your decision and refuse to pay a fee upfront. For example, the first time Andrew went to a tax accountant, he agreed to pay a couple of hundred dollars to have the accountant look over his taxes and file his return. He got back a much bigger refund than he would have on his own, and it felt great to have a professional working for him. And because he was paying the accountant a fee, he knew what was motivating him.

Paying fees

The first step in hiring an adviser is to look for fee transparency. A fee-only planner or fee-based adviser charges by the hour or by the project (say, producing a financial plan). A fee-based adviser is licensed and may charge by the hour or by assets under management, and/or earn commission for product sales. A commissioned adviser depends entirely on product sales to cover the cost of doing planning work.

In any case, insist on an "engagement letter" stating what the adviser will be doing for you and how you will be paying for it. That way, you've separated or "unbundled" the advice from the sale of the investment product.

Be realistic. If you have only a few thousand dollars to invest, the commissions are not going to cover much. If you want planning, you'll have to pay extra. Competent professionals don't come cheap. Fee-only planners and accountants will almost certainly charge from several hundred to several thousand dollars to produce anything more than a "quickie" plan. Be aware that a fee-only adviser is not licensed to provide specific investment advice, so you still have to find someone to help purchase and manage your investments.

Going with a commission-paid adviser

You often indirectly pay hundreds of dollars to invest in mutual funds. Frequently, commissioned advisers are able and willing to provide significant planning in return for your investment business.

Follow the money

Here's a breakdown of how you pay the adviser and his or her firm hundreds of dollars, directly or indirectly, when you buy broker-sold funds.

Say you have a total of $10,000 to invest in a mutual fund. You usually have two choices:

✔ **Buy the fund with a "front load" or "sales charge."** If you purchase this way, the sales charge — usually 0 to 2 percent, depending on what you can negotiate — is deducted from your investment and the balance is used to purchase the mutual fund. Under this option, you may sell your mutual fund at any time with no further sales charges.

✔ **Buy the funds with a "redemption charge"** (also called "deferred sales charge" or "back-end load"). In this case, the fund company pays the adviser's firm a commission, but no deduction is taken from your purchase amount and all your money goes into the investment. However, you're on the fee hook if you sell within a specified period, typically seven years. The size of the redemption fee declines as time goes by, and you will not have to pay the fee if you keep your investment within the fund's "family." Some back-end load funds are called "low-load" and have a two-year redemption charge period.

How much is the adviser paid? If you buy the funds with a front load and pay a 1 percent upfront commission, the adviser's firm is immediately paid $100. The adviser gets a portion of this, generally 40 to 70 percent. If we assume a 60 percent split, he or she makes $60 on your $10,000 investment. If you buy the fund on a redemption-charge basis, the adviser's firm is paid a commission from the fund company — usually 5 percent of the amount invested, or $500. Again, if the split is 60 percent, your adviser will be paid $300.

The adviser's firm is also paid a "trailer" commission from the fund company, usually 1 percent per year on equity funds (less on balanced or bond funds) purchased on a front-load basis. The trailer is half that amount if the fund is purchased with a redemption charge. The trailer fee remunerates the adviser for providing ongoing service to you. Assuming a $10,000 investment, the trailer will vary from $25 to $100 per year, depending on the fund purchased. The trailer is part of the fund management fee and is based on the market value of your funds. If your fund increases in value, the trailer will be higher; if it decreases, it will be lower. So if you prosper, so does your adviser, and vice versa.

Fee-charging advisers who'll also help with investing are easier to find in Canada than was the case a few years ago, although you'll have to ask around to find one. Canadians by the millions use commission-paid salespeople. After all, such advisers offer a handy one-stop solution: a financial roadmap of sorts and the glitz and comfort of a mutual fund from a familiar name — all backed up by gorgeous brochures and torrents of advertising in the press and on television, and increasingly on Internet sites. Most of them do a reasonable job for clients, putting them into solid (if overpriced) funds and getting them to save money, the first step in wealth accumulation.

Imagine a confusing, tangled jungle where every plant, animal, and weird fungus is grey. Well, that's kind of like the financial planning scene in Canada, where investors are confronted by competing trade associations, duelling regulators, and rival professional qualifications. Except in Quebec and British Columbia, just about anyone can call himself or herself a financial planner — even with no training.

Progress has occurred on the self-regulatory front, however. Many financial planners are members of Advocis, a national umbrella group formed in 2002 through the merger of the Canadian Association of Insurance and Financial Advisors (CAIFA) and the Canadian Association of Financial Planners (CAFP). The much smaller Institute of Advanced Financial Planners (IAFP) was formed by a group of financial planners who saw a need to promote the former CAFP's professional designation, the RFP or Registered Financial Planner. Also significant was the creation of the Financial Planners Standards Council (FPSC) in 1995 by Advocis, groups representing the three accounting professions, and the credit unions. The FPSC is the official administrator of the Certified Financial Planner (CFP) designation in Canada. Although not legally required, the CFP is regarded as the minimum qualification for a Canadian financial planner. The IAFP believes its RFP designation is superior, but of course that falls into the category of debate.

Commission-paid salespeople and advisers usually fit into one of these three groups:

- **Stockbrokers:** They often like to be known by more touchy-feely names such as "investment adviser" and are at the top of the food chain. They work for fairly tightly regulated traditional brokerage firms, the biggest of which are owned by the major banks. Examples include RBC Dominion Securities, CIBC Wood Gundy, and BMO Nesbitt Burns. Because brokerage firms generally are geared to dealing with relatively wealthy clients, a broker usually won't give you too much time unless you have $100,000 or so to invest. He or she may take you on as a client if you have less money than that, but don't expect fawning attention, just a meeting or two per year at most. For those with enough money, brokers can be an excellent choice because they can sell anything — including stocks, bonds, funds, and a range of more exotic investments. Another plus: Their training and in-house support are fairly good.

On the negative side, be aware that many brokers are obligated to promote stocks and other securities that are underwritten by their firm's investment bankers.

Stockbrokerages are self-regulated by the Investment Dealers Association of Canada (IDA), and are members of one or more stock exchanges. Find out more about the IDA online at www.ida.ca, or contact them at 121 King Street West, Suite 1600, Toronto, ON M5H 3T9.

✔ **Financial planners:** They are usually licensed to deal only in mutual funds or guaranteed investment certificates. They may work independently or as part of a large chain, and their quality varies greatly. Some are professional, smart, and dedicated, and some are little more than part-timers who can sell you a fund and that's about it. To deal in funds, they must register with the provincial securities commission, but regulation of the profession has been patchy. The creation of the Mutual Fund Dealers Association of Canada (MFDA) in 2001 has provided a self-regulatory framework for fund dealers. It was set up to catch mutual fund dealers who "fall through the cracks" with no industry-run body to keep an eye on them. The MFDA is affiliated with the IDA and governs all mutual fund dealers who aren't already covered by the IDA or a similar body. It will admit members, check that they're complying with the rules, and publicly discipline offenders, imposing fines, suspension, or termination of membership. Learn more about the MFDA online at www.mfda.ca, or contact them at 121 King Street West, Suite 1000, Toronto, ON M5H 3T9.

✔ **Insurance agents and brokers:** Both will sell you insurance, but a broker usually deals with numerous insurance companies while an agent generally has a relationship with just one. The lines have blurred to an extent between financial institutions, due to ownership of fund companies by insurance companies and other relationships between the two. As a result, some insurance salespeople now are registered to sell mutual funds. Moreover, life insurers, which once had a lock on the retirement planning market, in some cases have launched their own mutual fund families to hang on to customers' money. They've also made their traditional segregated funds more innovative and have spruced up their marketing. Seg funds are mutual fund–like products that usually promise to refund your invested capital if you hold them long enough (see Chapter 19). In general, pick an insurance agent or broker to help you with financial planning if they are able to sell mutual funds as well as insurance products. If the salesperson is limited to insurance, you're narrowing your options.

The Advantages of Using a Salesperson

We've all got hectic lives, so it can be a nice feeling to have someone take us by the hand and deal with our investing dilemmas. The stock and bond markets are confusing, scary places, and millions of people find it reassuring to have an ally looking out for them.

Brokers or planners, especially if they're experienced, will usually know some neat tricks and handy shortcuts when it comes to investing. For example, they may suggest ways of minimizing your tax liability by setting up a simple trust for your children or grandchildren.

A good adviser imposes discipline on his or her clients by inducing them to save money — and should prevent them from making rash decisions, such as selling after the market turns down sharply. Without an arm's-length person imposing some sort of structure on your finances, it's easy to let debts mount up and your money problems drift.

Finding the Right Professional

To fix yourself up with a well-trained and professional planner, make sure he or she meets one of the following tests:

- ✔ **Membership in Advocis:** This national association and lobby group for financial planners, also known as the Financial Advisors Association of Canada, had 12,000 members as of early 2008. To join, a planner must complete some fairly tough planning courses or have a professional designation such as Chartered Accountant. The requirement to take courses probably discourages complete incompetents from becoming members of Advocis. The group has a code of ethics — although no guarantee exists you won't end up with a bad apple — and it imposes follow-up "education" on members each year. Contact Advocis at www.advocis.ca or 390 Queen's Quay West, Suite 209, Toronto, ON M5V 3A2.

- ✔ **Membership in the Institute of Advanced Financial Planners:** The IAFP was set up in 2002 by a group of RFPs to promote, as the organization's name suggests, a higher level of financial planning than is promised by the FPSC and its presumably more basic CFP designation. The group claims its requirements for admission (including the RFP exam) and continuing education are more stringent. Contact IAFP at www.iafp.ca or P.O. Box 19055, RPO #16, Delta, BC V4L 2P8.

- ✔ **Completion of a recognized industry course:** These include courses that lead to the Certified Financial Planner (CFP) and Registered Financial Planner (RFP) designations. You can confirm that an individual has one of these designations by contacting the FPSC or IAFP, respectively; both organizations' Web sites have look-up tools.

- ✔ **Employment by a chartered bank or by a stockbroker who is a member of the Investment Dealers Association of Canada:** If the person works for a bank, you can be sure of some supervision, although take nothing for granted. The banks have set up their own personal finance training system, but no guarantee exists the person you get is particularly knowledgeable. If the broker works for an IDA brokerage firm, he or she could be incompetent or greedy, but at least you know he or she has passed the courses required to become an Investment Adviser, the official term that describes an IDA-member broker.

The core IDA-qualifying course is the Canadian Securities Course, which covers an impressive range of investing and industry-related information. Members of the public are also welcome to take this and other excellent courses offered by the IDA's educational arm, Canadian Securities Institute (CSI). Contact the CSI at www.csi.ca or 200 Wellington St. West, 15th Floor, Toronto, ON M5V 3C7. The IDA is a lobby group and disciplinary body for stockbrokers. If the person who wants to sell you mutual funds doesn't work for an IDA firm, then check the Mutual Fund Dealers Association.

✔ **Employment by a member of the Mutual Fund Dealers Association (MFDA):** This provides protection to mutual fund investors similar to that offered by its affiliate, the IDA. See the section "Going with a commission-paid adviser" in this chapter for MFDA contact information.

✔ **In Quebec, membership in the Institut québécois de planification financière:** Quebec regulates financial planners based in that province, requiring an exam and offering its own designation, the Financial Planner (F.Pl., or *planificateur financier* in French). A financial planner practising in Quebec also must either have a certificate issued by the Autorité des marchés financiers, the Quebec government body that regulates securities markets in that province, or hold one of several professional designations. Contact the IQFP at www.iqpf.org or 4 place du Commerce, bureau 420, Verdun, QC H3E 1J4.

✔ **In British Columbia:** A financial planner must be a Certified Financial Planner (CFP), or be licensed by one of a number of professional groups as laid out by the B.C. Securities Commission.

Unfortunately, you can easily come across bad planners, brokers, and advisers who have impressive qualifications or reputable employers. But at least you know that if they've gone to the trouble of getting trained, or they're under some kind of supervision from a large organization, you're less likely to be stuck with a complete turkey.

The right way to pick an adviser

Finding an adviser is like picking a building contractor or nanny: Word of mouth and your own gut instincts are among the best methods to use. So your first move should be to ask friends and relatives what they've done and whether they're happy with their advisers. Then go see several candidates. Apart from qualifications and membership in a professional association, also check out a few more things.

Does the adviser seem curious about you and willing to answer questions frankly?

A good adviser will ask you questions about your income, life history, assets, financial goals, health, marital status, pension, and investment knowledge. If that doesn't happen, you could be dealing with a sales-driven hotshot who's just looking to make commissions quickly. Shop elsewhere. And ask about sales commissions as well as the adviser's experience and training. Vague answers are a bad sign.

Does the adviser work for a firm with an adequate back office for client recordkeeping and supervision?

Jargon alert — having an adequate "back office" is just a fancy way of saying they are set up to administer clients' accounts and orders. Ask to see a typical client statement and ensure that the firm has a compliance officer, an employee who keeps an eye on the salespeople and the way they treat clients.

Does the adviser sell a broad range of products?

A planner who wants to talk about funds from just one or two companies is probably lazy. Nobody can be familiar with the products from every company, but you want someone with a good idea of what's out there. You also want an adviser who's knowledgeable about life insurance, or who can at least hook you up with an insurance expert.

Are the adviser's office, grooming, and general image professional?

Nobody's looking for Armani or marble halls, but sloppy-looking premises or a scruffy appearance are signs of someone who hasn't been able to attract many clients.

Check out Chapter 24 for some tough questions to ask any adviser before hiring them. We talk more about warning signs in Chapter 25, which includes ten sure signs it's time for you and your adviser to part ways.

The wrong way to pick an adviser

Unfortunately, a lot of what passes for investor education is just a giant sales pitch. So-called "seminars" that purport to enlighten you on a particular topic such as preparing a will or taking early retirement are really just a way of getting lots of sales targets into a room. Wandering around a glitzy "exhibition" or "forum" for investors may be fun and even informative, but these events are also a lure for getting "prospects" — potential customers — into a nice concentrated bunch where they can be picked off easily. In fact, be careful about attending seminars if you're the excitable or gullible type. The colourful celebrity speakers who work the investment circuit are often masters of making their audience both greedy and afraid — and easy targets for the inevitable sales spiel from the salespeople who paid for the event.

If the phone rings with a broker, adviser, or planner offering to help, decline politely and hang up. Always. Such "cold calls" are a time-honoured method of drumming up business for brokers. The salesperson calling may be perfectly legitimate, but responding to a random phone call out of the blue is an awful way of picking someone who's supposed to help you manage your money — such an important aspect of your life.

The telephone is still a favourite tool of those creatures that occasionally crawl out from under the rocks — the dishonest salespeople pushing "unlisted" and "over-the-counter" stocks or other "unregistered" investments that promise fantastic returns. Do yourself a favour and have some fun. Rent two wonderful movies about these crooked sales reptiles: Glengarry Glen Ross, based on David Mamet's play about sleazy real estate marketers, and Boiler Room, which tells the tale of some Long Island junk-stock pushers. After watching those two great films, you'll be better equipped to deal with telephone sales pitches.

Minding your ABCs — And T's

Glance down the mutual fund listings and you'll notice that quite a few broker-sold fund families market their funds in different classes or series, often listed as A or B and even C through F. Not to mention I's and T's. Alternatively, some, such as Guardian Group of Funds, sell funds labelled "classic mutual" or "adviser."

What do these labels mean to you, the potential unitholder? In most cases, the difference is in the management expense ratio (MER) — the fee charged to the fund to cover sales commissions, portfolio management, and other management costs. In most cases, the MER difference is purely due to the type of sales loads (front- or back-end). Sometimes it is because investors in that class of units have paid the sales charge themselves or because they bought the fund directly from the company, bypassing the salesperson. The difference in annual expenses is usually between 0.5 percent and 1 percent per year. We offer a few examples here:

✔ AIM Trimark has for years sold its funds in two basic versions. Its original funds, such as the Trimark Fund SC and the Trimark Canadian Fund SC, can be bought only on a front-load or "sales charge" basis (hence the SC). Its "Select" versions can be bought with a back-end load. The back-end load is expensive for the company to finance — because it must dish out the sales commissions to the salespeople itself — so the Select funds carry higher expenses. Just to make things even more confusing, the original SC funds can also be bought with a back-end load — and higher expenses for the investor.

✔ Guardian sells its funds in two basic classes, classic and mutual. The classic units must be bought with a front-end load, whereas the mutual units, which carry a higher management fee, are available with a deferred load.

✔ Several fund companies, including RBC, have introduced T-class funds, in which the T stands for "tax." These funds pay distributions to unitholders in the form of return of investment capital rather than dividends, interest, or capital gains. The latter remain within your fund investment, while the return on capital is paid out to you tax-free. As part of your original investment capital, it is not taxable income.

✔ Many F-class funds now exist. These have very small MERs, as they are sold only through advisers who charge management fees directly to their clients. In effect, the MER represents only the fund's portfolio management fee.

It's all pretty bewildering, but treating investors differently according to how they buy a fund is arguably fair. That's because the front-load buyers have saved the company a lot of money by paying the load themselves, so they deserve a break on the management fee.

If you're buying a fund that comes in more than one class, do everything you can to get the one with the lowest management fee, especially if you plan to invest for a long time. Sometimes even paying a small sales load is a good idea — but remember that with a front-load fund your adviser often gets a bigger trailer, so don't put up with any whining at the bargaining table. Over the years, a difference of only 0.5 percent in management fees really adds up. For example, say you put $10,000 into a deferred-load fund that produced an average annual compound return of 10 percent over a decade: You'd end up with $25,937. But say the fund was also available in a front-load version with a management fee that was 0.5 percentage points lower. The fund would be likely to give you an annual return of 10.5 percent instead of 10 percent. If you managed to buy that version of the fund with no sales load, your $10,000 would grow to $27,141 — or $1,200 more! Even if you had to pay an upfront sales load of 2 percent, reducing your initial investment to only $9,800, you would still end up with $26,598, or $661 more than an investor who chose the rear-load version.

Chapter 9

Buying Direct: Six Independents that Sell to the Public

In This Chapter

▶ How to find and assess independent no-load companies

▶ Checking out the advantages of dealing with these firms

▶ Weighing the cost of going direct

▶ Investigating the changing landscape of independents in Canada

▶ Comparing the direct-sales companies

*Y*ou may think that being independent is an admirable thing — footloose and fancy free, with no strings attached, right? Unfortunately, in the mutual fund world, that's not always the case. Canada's mutual fund sellers are often referred to as being either bank-owned or "independents." A second, important form of fund-seller categorization is load or no-load. Banks' products are no-load, for the most part, meaning they don't levy sales charges or loads to increase your expenses. The independents, on the other hand, almost all sell on a load basis. That's a steep price to pay for independence.

Until fairly recently, independent no-load sellers held a reasonable chunk of assets, but bank acquisitions of the two biggest independents in recent years have relegated this fund-sales type to a tiny corner of the fund industry. You no longer have much to choose from among independent no-load funds in Canada.

So why even bother to seek out an independent no-load fund, you might ask, when the banks now have some pretty impressive no-load offerings? (Go to Chapter 7 to see what we mean.) Well, the remaining players in this selling category are respected money managers who run interesting and innovative funds. What's more, dealing directly with an independent is one of the more enjoyable and profitable ways of investing in funds. The company is directly answerable to you when you call or e-mail, and you can pull out your money with no strings attached if the managers don't make the fund go up. In this chapter, we look at getting rolling with buying direct, go through the pros and cons of this style of investing, and take you through a list of the top no-load players.

Note that a lot of the advice in this chapter also applies if you're investing in the funds sold by banks or their subsidiaries. In those cases, you also are buying no-load funds directly from the "manufacturer." The missing ingredient — an important one — is independence. The independent no-load sellers mentioned in this chapter are a unique breed of specialized money managers.

Getting Started with Direct Sellers

Setting yourself up with an independent no-load company is easy:

1. **Check out the investing philosophy and fund lineups of the independent no-load companies on the Internet.** You can consult both the companies' own Web sites (which we list in Table 9-1) and third-party information sources such as Globefund.com and Morningstar.ca.

2. **Download the company's application forms (if available online) and then call them to open an account.**

Table 9-1 lists the biggest no-load fund companies on the Canadian scene, their Web site addresses, and their phone numbers.

Table 9-1	No-Load Direct Sellers in Canada	
Company	*Web Site*	*Toll-free Phone*
Beutel Goodman	www.beutel-can.com	1-800-461-4551
GBC	www.gbc.ca	1-800-668-7383
Leith Wheeler	www.leithwheeler.com	1-888-292-1122
Mawer	www.mawer.com	1-800-889-6248
McLean Budden	www.mcleanbudden.com	1-800-884-0436
Sceptre	www.sceptre.ca	1-800-265-1888

No-load fund managers treat you rather like discount brokers do. They have an accessible telephone-answering staff that will handle your orders, but they don't know much about you. All you have to do to invest is call their number (often toll-free) and transfer some money or send a cheque. Some companies have forms on their Web sites that you can download and fill out in advance, before you call to set up the account. You won't face any wheedling, pawing salesperson in the shape of a broker, planner, or insurance agent, which means you needn't worry about any fiddly and costly commissions.

No-load companies are generally fairly big businesses, and they can usually be relied on to send pretty reliable statements of your account. Sounds perfect, doesn't it? It is — except you'll have to put up with a narrow selection and a higher minimum investment.

Paying to play

Expect to face stiff minimum investments of $5,000 or more with some companies that sell directly to the public. The fees they charge are low, so they can't afford to fool around with tiny accounts. By contrast, most banks and fund companies that sell through advisers let you invest as little as $100.

Direct sellers impose these high minimum purchases because they have pretty small mutual fund operations. Their main business is usually managing money for institutions such as pension funds. These companies are not equipped to deal with thousands of unitholders, so to avoid attracting lots of small and unprofitable accounts, they often impose the required minimum investments.

Take Calgary-based Mawer Investment Management Ltd., for example. It sells its no-load funds directly to the public in several provinces, although they also can be purchased through salespeople such as financial planners. Mawer requires a minimum investment of $5,000 in its funds if acquired through an adviser, and $50,000 minimum if bought directly. So an investor who wants to buy direct but is just getting started may have to build up a pile of cash elsewhere before transferring money to the company.

Considering whether a direct seller is right for you

Many Canadians are still in love with their banks and brokers, not independent no-load fund companies. They continue to seek out the reassurance of a salesperson or the comforting embrace of a giant institution. That means no-load direct sellers have yet to really catch on in this country. That said, direct sellers are an excellent choice for investors who like to follow their investments closely or seek out funds with low costs.

If you can belly up to the bar with the minimum required investment and don't mind the lack of a personal touch, take a good look at this chapter to see if you're really a fit with this type of investing. Direct sellers of no-load funds are best suited for:

✔ **Investors looking for simplicity:** People who are very keen to get a simple solution, with all of their investments on one clear account statement. Direct sellers are easy to deal with because you can simply call up and ask questions or make changes to your account without having to go through a broker or other adviser. The same advantages apply to holding your funds at a bank — but direct sellers are much smaller than banks, so they're easier to talk to.

✔ **Savvy market trackers:** People who are interested in investing and want to follow the process closely. Such savvy investors love the low annual expenses and often excellent performance that no-load fund sellers offer. Many choose to leave a portion of their money in an account with a direct seller while investing the rest elsewhere. People who enjoy watching the markets often find that the information given to investors in direct-sold funds is more complete — that's because no-load companies deal directly with the investor and see him or her as the customer; fund salespeople won't muddy the picture. And the simplicity of a no-load account held at a fund company, instead of through an adviser, makes it easy to move money from fund to fund. Active investors who closely track the markets often do more switching around.

The Advantages of Dealing with an Independent No-Load Company

Using a no-load company that sells to the public is a halfway house between the lonely course of picking your own funds at a discount broker on the one hand and the comfy warm blanket of getting help from a bank employee or a salesperson who earns commissions on the other. When you go to such a salesperson (the option we deal with in Chapter 8) or a bank (see Chapter 7), you get lots of help — but you usually pay for the advice in the form of higher annual costs imposed on your fund. And the selection that a bank or commission-paid salesperson carries is often limited to only a few dozen funds. At a no-load company, the people answering the phone will offer some advice, and the expenses on their funds may be low. But the selection of funds on offer is once again limited to the company's own products, and that might be just a handful of funds. Discount brokers (Chapter 6), whoopee, have lots of funds on their sales lists. They're the amusement park of funds. But you'll be riding that roller coaster alone, because you'll get hardly any help.

When you contact any fund company, no matter how it sells its products, ignore all of the marketing blather and ask for an application form and prospectus. In many cases, these are available online. Those two usually set out the stuff you need to know, such as minimum investment and annual costs. You can always slip 'em in the recycling bin later. Or toss them in that old rusty oil drum you use to burn garbage. (Don't the people next door complain about the choking greasy plume of smoke, by the way?)

If you want a hassle-free solution to buying your mutual funds, going with a no-load, direct fund seller offers some important advantages. In this section, we discuss the main ones.

Putting more money in your pocket

The biggest plus of buying from a no-load company is the fact that you cut out the intermediary. No-load companies can charge you lower fees — although they don't always choose to do so. Because they don't have to pay an army of brokers — or cover the expense of running a sprawling network of bank branches — some direct sellers' domestic equity funds have annual expenses of 1.3 percent or less. That's much cheaper than most domestic equity mutual funds, which have total annual costs and fees closer to 2.3 percent. The more expensive fund is taking an extra 1 percent annually out of your mottled hide — over ten years, that difference adds up to 10 percent of your money.

If you were to invest $10,000 and earn a tax-free average annual return of 9 percent for a decade, you'd end up with $23,674. But the same $10,000 invested at a 10-percent rate of return, because the expenses were one percentage point lower, would grow to nearly $26,000 (see Table 9-2). That's why it's better to have a fund with a significantly lower annual expense ratio.

Table 9-2	Think One Percent Doesn't Matter? That'll Be $2,263, Please	
Year	*Value at 9-Percent Return*	*Value at 10-Percent Return*
Initial investment	$10,000	$10,000
1st	$10,900	$11,000
2nd	$11,881	$12,100
3rd	$12,950	$3,310
4th	$14,116	$14,641
5th	$15,386	$16,105
6th	$16,771	$17,716
7th	$18,280	$19,487
8th	$19,926	$21,436
9th	$21,719	$23,579
10th	$23,674	$25,937

Offering advice for adults

Another advantage of going directly to a fund company is that you're treated like an adult rather than simply as a faceless consumer of the fund product. In other words, the company's Web site and mailings to investors often are more candid about performance. That's because many of the investors who use no-load companies tend to be independent souls who relish the low costs and are happy with the lower level of advice. They're the sort to demand complete reporting of performance.

If you're not satisfied with the performance of your no-load funds, or if you have queries, it's simple to just pick up the phone and call. You may not get the errant fund manager or a senior executive, but the representative who answers the phone will probably be able to give you some answers.

And, best of all, buying no-load doesn't mean you have to give up getting advice altogether. Unlike discount brokerages, for a fee, most direct sellers have staff who can advise you on choosing funds and even help you shape your overall investment strategy.

Keeping things simple

Dealing with a fund company directly is simpler than buying a fund through a salesperson. You're not forced to relay your order or request via someone else, potentially causing confusion or delay. You can call up the company and buy and sell funds in your account right over the phone, as well as ask for forms or other administrative help. Your relationship as a customer is clearly with the fund seller, not with an intermediary like a broker. That's great for you because

- ✔ You have just one company to deal with and complain to if a mistake occurs in your account. Or did you say you enjoyed muttering endlessly into voice mail?
- ✔ You get just one annual and quarterly statement of account.
- ✔ If you own several funds, it's handy to be able to check on their performance if they're all included in one company's mailings.
- ✔ You can switch money easily from fund to fund as your needs or assets change.

Allowing frequent trades

Moving your money frequently from fund to fund in an attempt to catch rising stock markets and avoid falling ones is often tempting. Naturally, frequent traders love using no-load companies because they don't charge investors to switch their money in and out. That makes a no-load fund company the perfect choice if you fancy yourself someone with the ability to time movements in stock and bond prices — for example, every time the Canadian stock market goes up 20 percent in a year, you might decide to pull out of stocks. But no-load fund companies don't appreciate it when customers move their money around constantly, because it greatly increases the company's administration costs (all of those transfers must be accounted for). So they'll eventually crack down on you by limiting your trades. And you'll often get slapped with a charge of 2 percent of your money if you switch out of a fund within three months of buying it.

Still, if you want to try to outguess the markets and trade some money around every few months (even though it's often a bad idea), then direct and no-load may be the way to go. Here's why:

- The companies have people on staff to move your money from fund to fund quickly and easily.

- You won't face any sales charges to complicate the transfer of money or add to your costs.

- Buying the fund directly from the no-load fund company rather than through a discount broker or commission-paid adviser means your sale orders go directly into the fund company's system instead of through a discount brokerage employee. That speeds up the process and reduces the probability of mistakes in your order.

- You get an account statement and transaction confirmation slip in the mail directly from the no-load company and not through the discounter. That's simpler and more convenient for investors who are closely tracking their own performance.

Switching into and out of no-load funds through a discount broker can in fact cost you commissions, because discounters often impose small fees of $25 or more each time you sell a no-load fund. A conventional broker won't welcome your business if you plan to chop and change your portfolio all the time, because of all the troublesome paperwork you create. (In fact, if you bring a portfolio containing no-load funds to a full-service broker, expect these funds to be sold fairly quickly because they pay no fees or commissions.)

Heavy and constant trading won't thrill even a no-load fund company. That's because trading raises administrative and mailing costs, which have to be paid by other investors. So, with many companies, expect to pay a 2-percent penalty when you move money out of a fund within three months of buying it. And if you really go over the top, you may be banned from switching your money around or limited to a certain number of trades — say, one a month.

No firm rules constitute what counts as heavy trading, but here are a few guidelines:

- ✔ An investor who moves some of his or her money from fund to fund twice a year or less would count as a light or infrequent trader.

- ✔ Someone who made between 2 and 12 trades a year would count as a medium trader.

- ✔ More than a dozen trades a year indicates the investor is a heavy trader who thinks he or she can outguess the market.

A fund company is unlikely to cut off your buying and selling privileges unless you're trading very frequently — making changes to your portfolio every few days or every week. If you do get cut off and you can't resolve the situation, you may have to move your money to a discount broker that allows constant trading. But even if you buy through a discounter, the funds you're buying may well levy that 2-percent penalty if you sell a holding that was bought fewer than three months ago.

The 2-percent penalty for trading early seems small, but it reduces your return. Imagine you invest in the Canadian stock market ahead of an oil boom. (As the past few years have reminded us, foreign investors see us as resource producers in toques, so they tend to buy into our market when prices for commodities, such as lumber, energy, and metals, are going up.) Say you put $10,000 into a no-load company's Canadian *equity fund,* a fund that invests in stocks and shares (which in turn are a tiny slice of ownership of companies). The Canadian market goes up 10 percent in two weeks and your fund matches the rise in the broad market, boosting your investment to $11,000 — at which point you sell half of your holding in the fund, or $5,500. If the company slaps a 2-percent fee on investors who leave a fund after less than 90 days, then you'll receive a cheque for just $5,390, which is $5,500 minus 2 percent. Of course, your other $5,500 is still sitting in the fund.

Knowing when to hold 'em

How many trades are too many? Well, research seems to show that almost any level of chopping and changing reduces overall returns because most investors let emotion distort their judgment, leading them to do things at the wrong time. People sell when the market has slumped and is about to bounce back. And they buy after it has already shot up and is about to go on the slide.

Over time, share prices may tend to rise remorselessly as good companies thrive and the world economy grows, but the stock market also advances in sudden starts. If, following the dictates of your brilliant, can't-lose trading strategy, you happen to have sold your equity funds just before one of those days, then you miss out on the profits.

Knowing when to walk away

Moving money out of a fund can be sensible at times, and holding the fund directly at a no-load company makes the process easier. Good times to move money include when

- ✔ The fund has gone up so much that it now represents a huge portion of your portfolio. For example, if you've decided to keep just half of your money in shares, but one or more of your equity funds have produced a 100-percent return over the past year, then you probably have too much money riding on equities. Time to sell some of those stock funds.

- ✔ You've been foolhardy enough to bet on a specialty fund that invests in just one narrow section of the market, such as South Korea or financial-services shares, and were lucky enough to score a big profit. Such one-flavour funds tend to post huge crashes soon after their big wins — as investors go cool on the kind of stocks they hold. So think strongly about selling at least some of your units in a specialty fund as soon as it has a good year. No, don't just think about it: Pick up the phone and do it immediately.

- ✔ Your reason for holding the fund no longer applies. For example, a fund manager you like may have quit, or the fund may have changed its investment style.

Check your portfolio once or twice a year, and if it's out of line with your ideal mix of investments, then readjust it by moving money from one fund to another. For example, say you've decided you want one-third of your $10,000 mutual fund collection in sure-and-steady government bonds — certificates issued by the government that pay interest and can be cashed in again at the issue price after a set number of years. The other two-thirds is in lucrative-but-dangerous stocks, those tiny pieces of ownership in companies. See Chapter 5 for more on bonds and stocks.

So your setup is:

$3,300 bond funds	33 percent of portfolio
$6,700 stock funds	67 percent of portfolio
$10,000 total portfolio	100 percent of portfolio

Say the bonds hold their value over the next year, remaining at $3,300, but the stocks rise 30 percent to $8,710, which gives you a mix of:

$3,300 bond funds	27 percent of portfolio
$8,710 stock funds	73 percent of portfolio
$12,010 total portfolio	100 percent of portfolio

This means you have too much riding on the stock market in relation to your original plan — almost three-quarters of the total pile. You can fix it easily by moving $663 out of stock funds and into bond funds, leaving you with a portfolio that looks like this:

$3,963 bond funds	33 percent of portfolio
$8,047 stock funds	67 percent of portfolio
$12,010 total portfolio	100 percent of portfolio

If you hold a super-volatile fund that invests in a narrow sector or region, such as a technology company or Latin America, it's a good strategy to move some money out of the fund if it shoots up in value. That way, you lock some profits before the inevitable crash. Holding such funds forever is of dubious benefit because they're at risk of losing money for long periods, as explained in Chapter 12.

Weighing the Drawbacks of Going Direct

Most no-load mutual fund companies offer too few funds to really give you a diversified portfolio — that means an account with many different types of investment. Here are the main drawbacks to using a direct seller.

Significant levels of cash required

As we mention at the beginning of this chapter, not everyone can go direct. As attractive as it seems to investors who are serious minimalists in terms of their need for guidance and their interest in paying fees to invest, you need a minimum amount of cash to play — in one case, as much as $100,000. This is obviously not the case with novice investors, or those in the process of building their portfolio. Although this type of investing may not be the right choice for you now, it is something to keep an eye on as your investing savvy and your portfolio grow.

Lack of choice

The main problem with direct purchase of funds is the narrow selection. Few direct sellers have more than one or two funds, so if you leave all your money with one company, you're at risk of seeing the market turn against that particular investment style.

A typical no-load fund company sells just a couple of funds of each type. Generally, the company will offer the following:

- ✔ One or two stock funds
- ✔ One or two bond funds
- ✔ One or two global equity funds
- ✔ Perhaps a few specialty funds, such as one that buys only U.S. stocks

That's a small selection compared to buying from a broker, insurance sales-person, or financial planner, who can often sell you at least a dozen funds in each category. At a discount broker, you can buy hundreds of each.

You can avoid this lack-of-choice drawback by buying the direct seller's funds through a discount broker instead, if they're available. That lets you use the no-load seller's funds, with their nice low expenses, in combination with index funds or funds from other companies. However, your discount broker may not even carry a low-expense company's funds (because the discounter gets little or nothing in sales commissions).

Doing it through a discounter

Yes, you can often buy no-load mutual funds through your full-service broker and discount broker, instead of going directly to the fund company. But brokers often hit you with a commission or "transaction fee" to let you buy or sell low-expense, no-load funds.

That's because these funds often don't pay the brokers much of anything in ongoing annual commissions — known as trailers in the colourful argot of the fund world. But the low costs and fees charged to unitholders in many no-load funds usually make it worthwhile to buy them despite the small charge imposed by the broker, especially if you plan to hang on to the funds for a few years.

Be warned, though: If you buy the funds through a broker, discount or full-service, the fund company probably won't have any record of your investment, so you lose the advantage of being able to deal directly with the company.

Direct Sellers' Struggle in Canada

No-load funds from independent companies are a huge business in the United States, with companies such as Janus Capital, T. Rowe Price, and Vanguard Group attracting tens of billions of dollars. But Canadians have never really fallen in love with the concept.

When Fidelity Investments came to Canada in the 1980s, it eschewed the no-load approach that brought it great success in the U.S. market; in this country, it sells only through advisers. Fidelity Canada hardly even looked over its shoulder at its parent company's no-load approach.

Two other U.S. no-load giants, Scudder and Charles Schwab, ventured north of the border in the 1990s, but lasted only a few years before crying uncle. Scudder came north in 1995, but dismal sales prompted the company to call it quits in 1999 when it sold its funds to IG Financial, which soon funneled the funds into the Mackenzie Financial lineup. Apparently undaunted by the failure of its home-market rival, Schwab set up shop here that same year, only to throw in the towel less than four years later when it sold out to Scotiabank.

Vanguard, the U.S., no-load, index-fund powerhouse, has taken heed of our inhospitable climate, reviewing the possibilities in our market from time to time but always deciding against it.

The two homegrown no-load independents to have achieved success in terms of amassing significant assets — Phillips, Hager & North and Altamira — were summarily gobbled up by big banks. And in mid-2008, Saxon Investment Management, a small but highly regarded independent, was gobbled up by Investor's Group's Mackenzie Financial division.

Sizing Up the Six Independents

Although the remaining independent no-load pickings are slim, they're still well worth a look. This group of six has some interesting funds, many with great performance.

The problem with buying from these low-cost, no-load sellers is that they don't offer enough funds to give you a truly diversified portfolio. They might argue the point, but we can't help feeling that just one Canadian equity fund or one global equity fund isn't enough to spread your risk adequately — relying on a single manager, management team, or style of investing means a fund can go into a prolonged and nasty slump.

In this section, we take a look at some of the best known sales policies and products from direct no-load sellers.

Beutel Goodman

The biggest among our group of six independent no-load sellers, Toronto-based Beutel is a big name in institutional investing. The primary function of its 13 funds, as with most of the six, is to provide portfolio management to its individual clients.

Its flagship Canadian Equity Fund, a consistent top performer, is known to fare better than most during bear markets. Its other big funds, income and balanced, also have been strong long-term performers. And 1.19 percent is about as cheap as it gets for a balanced fund's annual expenses. The other funds are similarly inexpensive, in the 1.3-percent neighbourhood.

The minimum investment in a Beutel Goodman mutual fund account is $10,000. Contact the company to obtain an application form and to set up an account.

GBC

This Montreal-based, private-client money manager sells its funds to anyone who can handle the $100,000 account minimum. Its six funds serve primarily as portfolio building blocks for its high-net-worth private clients, most of whom pay the firm to manage their portfolios. GBC is a specialist in small- to medium-capitalized companies — so if you want big blue-chips, go elsewhere.

It has seven funds, the largest being GBC International Growth Fund. It carries Morningstar's five-star rating, an accolade it managed to retain despite a gruesome record in 2007. No matter — GBC's focus, besides market capitalization, is long-term. Although smaller-cap investing can bring instant gratification, thanks to volatile stocks of smaller companies it can also bring instant disaster — but only if you sell.

The firm has a good reputation for being conservative in the risk-plagued, small/mid-cap market. As a no-load independent, its funds' annual expenses are lower than those of the load firms and the banks, although they tend to be on the high side when compared with independent direct sellers.

GBC has by far the highest minimum investment requirement: $100,000. While that figure might seem exorbitant, it is not excessive for the calibre of investor that typically invests in the group-of-seven funds. You can download application forms from the firm's Web site, and set up an account by speaking to a GBC rep over the phone.

Leith Wheeler

The vast majority of Leith Wheeler's more than $6 billion in assets are managed privately for pension plans, foundations, and high-net-worth people. In terms of mutual fund assets, this Vancouver-based company is by far the smallest among our group of six. Its five mutual funds have achieved above-average returns without taking on undue risk.

As a value-style manager, recent markets have not been hospitable. However, the firm has hung in with its funds achieving performance close to their category medians. Its Canadian Equity Fund had a one-year loss of 0.3 percent midway through 2008, but it had a stellar 18.3-percent return over 10 years. Its MER is among the lowest in its category, at 1.5 percent.

Minimum investment is $25,000. The funds are available only to residents of British Columbia, Alberta, Saskatchewan, Manitoba, and Ontario. You have to telephone the company to obtain forms to set up an account.

Mawer

This Calgary-based company's nine funds are all strong performers. But the big star is its World Investment Fund, run by 20-year-veteran Gerald Cooper-Key. This well-diversified fund always shows up at the top of performance lists — and all for annual expenses of 1.46 percent; the median international equity fund's MER is 2.6 percent. Its one-year return at mid-2008 was a 5 percent loss — but that was better than most other funds in the international equity category, in which only seven of nearly 300 funds broke even over that period. Mawer's main domestic equity fund has been a middle-of-the-pack performer, although it was among the best over 10 years as of mid-2008.

You can buy direct from Mawer only if you live in Alberta, British Columbia, Saskatchewan, or Ontario, and the minimum investment is $50,000. Residents of these provinces can download an application form from the Web site and then complete it with the assistance of a Mawer representative. If you do not live in one of those provinces — or if the $50,000 minimum is a problem — you must go through a discount broker or full-service dealer, in which case the minimum purchase is only $5,000.

McLean Budden

Toronto-based McLean Budden is a big institutional money manager that also has a stable of 11 mutual funds. Its biggest fund by far is a U.S. equity offering, with an experienced team of managers who have made it a consistent top performer. The fund's conservative growth strategy has held it back when markets are roaring, but depend on it to outperform when the chips are down. It has one of the lowest MERs among U.S. equity funds, at 1.25 percent.

The minimum investment in McLean Budden funds is $10,000. To open an account, download the application form from the Web site, complete it, and mail it in, and a representative will follow up to complete the process.

Sceptre

This long-established Toronto investment management firm's biggest fund is a small-cap equity offering. Sceptre Equity Growth has produced top returns over the long term, although it has been among the many value-oriented portfolios to suffer of late. But a 15-year compound annual return of nearly 18 percent from a small-cap portfolio is mighty enticing. One problem, though: That impressive number was largely the work of Allan Jacobs, who left the fund in 2007 to join Sprott Asset Management, a high-achieving hedge fund manager. However, Jacobs has competent replacements in the form of co-managers, and fund critics including analysts at Morningstar are confident the fund has good fortunes ahead. Sceptre Equity Growth's MER is a bargain at 1.58 percent.

Sceptre's minimum investment is just $5,000. You can download an account application but must telephone the company to set up an account.

Investors Group: A special case

Investors Group Inc. of Winnipeg is Canada's second biggest fund company. It had a huge $108 billion in assets as of mid-2008, $3 billion short of the Royal Bank of Canada. Nearly one-third of those assets are held within its Mackenzie Financial Corp. subsidiary, which IG runs as a separate operation.

Giant Investors Group got to be that size by giving about a million investors exactly what they want: An all-in-one solution to their financial planning needs.

The company sells directly to the public, but it does so through dedicated salespeople who work exclusively for Investors Group. That means it is rather like a regular "broker-sold" company, such as Mackenzie or Fidelity Investments Canada Ltd., that markets its funds via advisers. If you buy into an Investors Group fund, you face sales commissions, although they're buried in the management fee charged by the fund.

Investors Group is unique on the Canadian scene because its army of more than 3,000 salespeople is tied to the company. That makes it a hybrid of broker-sold fund companies that market through independent salespeople and no-load companies that sell directly to customers. Investors Group representatives are also trained and equipped to provide other financial services and products, offering a cradle-to-grave, money-management plan for the customer.

(continued)

(continued)

The company levies annual costs that are in line with or slightly higher than fund industry averages. For example, the enormous $13-billion Investors Dividend Fund has annual costs of 2.69 percent, substantially higher than the 2.6 percent levied by the median Canadian equity balanced fund.

Investors Group funds are generally middle-of-the-pack performers. Investors Dividend had an 8.1-percent, five-year, compound annual return as of mid-2008, compared with the median Canadian equity balanced fund's 9.4 percent. Its category-mate Investors Balanced achieved 9.1 percent during the same period. Over in the Canadian dividend and income equity category, Investors Canadian Equity returned 15 percent during the period, while Investors Canadian Large Cap Value gained 13.6 percent — the same as the category median.

The company has a truly bewildering selection of offerings. As of mid-2008, it included nearly 900 different funds and versions of funds on its shelf, including its Mackenzie and Counsel subsidiaries. Some of that number includes funds run by other mutual fund companies and external money management firms — including 22 funds sold under the specific Investors brand that are managed supposedly externally by Mackenzie! But a big gap exists in the lineup: No sign of any index funds. That's because it's impossible for an index fund to be profitable if you're paying commissions to salespeople.

The company's enormous financial clout and partnership with sister company Great-West Life Assurance (which itself has more than 100 segregated funds) allow it to offer a wide range of non-fund products and services. But dealing with Investors Group is essentially the same as buying funds from other broker-sold fund companies that market through commissioned salespeople — in other words, the expenses on its fund are higher than those imposed by the cheaper independent no-load companies.

Part III

The Fund Stuff: Building a Strong Portfolio

The 5th Wave   By Rich Tennant

"I like the value stocks too, but right now we're looking into a more aggressive growth fund."

In this part . . .

We talk about the different categories of funds you can buy. We recommend the funds to concentrate on — only about six types — and warn you against the dozen or so types of risky, expensive, or confusing funds to avoid. We also dig into the bewildering varieties and wrappers in which funds are sold, separating out the useful features from the gimmicks and hype.

Chapter 10

Equity Funds: The Road to Riches

*E*quity mutual funds, which buy stocks and shares of companies, are perhaps the best route to riches you will ever find. Okay, marrying a 95-year-old, hang-gliding, suicidal millionaire in poor health might be quicker, but then you have to fend off all those whining rival heirs. Equity funds are a wonderful invention because they hold shares in a huge variety of (usually) great companies. So wide is the selection of holdings in most equity funds that if some of the businesses fail or stagnate, the fund nearly always has enough winners to pull you through.

Equity funds should be the core of just about anybody's investment portfolio, assuming he or she is investing for at least five years. Because the economy and well-run companies are almost certain to grow over time, stocks and shares can be the engine of growth for your money. If you want to earn decent returns on your cash over the long term, and you've decided to buy mutual funds, you're pretty well forced to buy equity funds. That's because they're the only type of fund likely to produce big returns, possibly 8 to 10 percent or more annually, over the long haul. And those are the types of returns you need to defy inflation and build a substantial nest egg.

Yes, the stock market and the funds that invest in it can drop sharply, sometimes for years — we provide some scary examples in this chapter. So make sure you have a good chunk of bond funds in your holdings as well. But strong evidence exists that equity markets pretty well always rise over periods of ten years or more, so equity funds are a relatively safe bet for buyers who are sure they can hold on for a long time without needing the money back at short notice.

In this chapter we give you a crash course on how the stock market works and explain why funds are a great way to profit from it. We show why you're best off buying equity funds that invest in big and stable companies, especially businesses that sell their wares all over the world. We also make clear why it's a good idea to hold six or seven equity funds — three Canadian and three or four global — and we give you simple tips for selecting great funds.

Why Investing in Stocks Is Simple

Believe it or not, making money in the stock market is easy — in theory. You just buy shares — tiny slices of ownership — in well-managed companies and then hold on to them for years. As the businesses you've invested in thrive, so do their owners, and that includes you as a shareholder. But when you actually try to select wonderful companies, things get complicated. For one thing, it's hard to tell which companies have genuinely bright prospects, because the managers of just about every corporation do a great job of blowing their little brass horns and making everything look wonderful in their garden. And, like everything else, the stock market is subject to the whims of fashion. When investors decide they love a particular company or industry, the shares usually go to fantastic heights. At that point, buying stocks turns into a risky game — no point buying a great business if you pay four times what it's really worth.

Being fallible human beings, we constantly sabotage ourselves in the stock market. When everything is going well and shares are climbing to record highs, we feel all warm, fuzzy, and enthusiastic — and we stumble into the market just in time for the crash. And when the economy or the stock market is slumping, we get all depressed and sell our shares at bargain-basement prices — just when we should be grabbing more. But perhaps the biggest problem with investors is our innate belief that we're smarter than everybody else. Everybody thinks the same thing, which means that lots of us are going to end up losers. Don't let us stop you: You can try to make pots of money buying speculative technology companies or penny mining stocks or companies consolidating the pallet industry (don't laugh, Andrew did), but that's really gambling. True investing in stock markets is simply buying well-established, well-run businesses and holding the shares, ideally for years.

Mutual funds are one of the very best and easiest ways to make money from the stock market. That's because they

- ✔ Are run by professionals who are trained in the art of checking out businesses.

- ✔ Are set up to make it easy to put your money in and get it back out.

- ✔ Hold a wide variety of companies, spreading your risk and giving you the chance to benefit from growth in a huge range of industries.

By handing your money over to a mutual fund company, you're saving yourself from yourself — if you aren't making the decisions, then you can't risk your savings on wild bets or crazy dreams.

The real kicker in stock market investing is figuring out whether a company is genuinely good — a quality outfit worth putting money into — and whether the price you're being asked to pay for shares is too high. Unfortunately, though, there may be no such thing as a true value for a company, because the numbers all vary so wildly according to the assumptions you make about the future. In that case, a stock is simply worth what people decide to pay for it on any given day. And that may not be very much: Stocks can dive for no apparent reason. But ordinary people saving for the future should care about the crazy volatile stock market for one reason: Good companies thrive, their profits go up, and their stocks gain value over the long term.

Sometimes selecting a good company to invest in can be almost embarrassingly simple. Take everybody's favourite telecommunications toy — sorry, tool — the BlackBerry. From the day these minuscule but versatile little computers appeared in cellphone company boutiques, they seemed a must-have addition to daily life. Innovation, good design, and clever marketing is no accident — it requires talented people, and they don't stay long with badly run companies. Sure enough, an investor who bought shares of Research In Motion — or RIM, the manufacturer of the BlackBerry — soon after the company first issued shares to the public in 1999, multiplied their money more than twentyfold over the next nine years. That's a spectacular case, but once in a while RIM-like success stories come along.

In for the long haul

Based on experience in the past century, you almost always win in the stock market over periods of at least ten years provided you stick to big, high-quality companies and you spread your risk by owning at least a dozen of them in different industries. Most equity mutual funds play it even safer by holding at least 50 different stocks (many hold 100 or more) so they can be sure of buying and selling their holdings easily.

Remember, too: It's hard to lose money in the stock market as long as you buy well-run, large companies and hold them for long enough. Studies that looked at every ten-year period in the market during the 20th century found that stocks produced a profit in 99 percent of the periods, although that falls to 86 percent if you take inflation into account. So while 20 to 1 might be a stretch, with diversification and patience a RIM-like 5 to 1 is doable.

Why do most mutual funds hold so many different stocks? Why doesn't the manager just buy his or her favourite half-dozen shares and run with that? One reason is that when the market turns sour on a company its stock tends to drop like a rock. So exposing a huge proportion of your fund to a single company is a bad idea. Getting stuck with a stock nobody else wants is a fund manager's most ghastly nightmare. Whenever he or she offers the shares for sale, rival investment managers make sympathetic faces and gentle cooing noises — and then refuse to buy the garbage at anything but sub-bargain prices. To protect investors, under provincial securities law a mutual fund can have a maximum of 10 percent of its assets in a single stock. And most funds limit their exposure to single shares to 5 percent or less.

A test case for capitalism: Meet Angus and Bronwyn

Take an equity fund apart and figure out just what it's made of. The "equity" in equity funds is just a fancy word for stocks and shares — two words that mean the same thing. Just like stocks, shares are tiny portions of ownership of a company, imaginary certificates that represent ownership of the business. (Long gone are the days when investors hoarded elaborately printed stock certificates in their safety-deposit boxes; it's all done electronically now.)

Consider a grossly simplified example to see how the stock market works. Suppose you and your Welsh sister-in-law Bronwyn start a dry cleaning business and you each invest $5,000, while your Scottish boyfriend Angus puts up $10,000. That means the store has three shareholders, or owners, and a total of four shares: One each for you and Bronwyn (in return for your $5,000 each), and two shares for Angus, because he put up twice as much. Now, say people's silk blouses get wrecked and the business doesn't do well. Bronwyn realizes that Angus wants to get out of this mess, even if he has to take a loss. So she buys both of his shares at only $3,000 each, giving her ownership of three shares, or three-quarters of the business. The important point here is that the price of the shares has fallen because the prospects of the business are poor. But the fact that Angus sold the shares to Bronwyn has no direct effect on the store itself. People are still coming and going, beefing about their spoiled clothes, while the stock trading takes place entirely separately — behind the scenes, as it were.

A real-life example of equity investing

Now, mutual funds usually aren't allowed to buy dry cleaning stores (don't laugh, we know some wild-eyed fund managers who probably would if they could), because investments in tiny companies are too risky. Instead, they trade stocks on the stock market, a vast organized exchange system.

To see how this works, consider Canada's now-fallen stock market star Nortel Networks Corp., a giant global maker of equipment for sending signals over the Internet, phone lines, and just about anything else you care to name. In late 2000, Nortel had about 3 billion shares — that's 3,000 times 1 million — outstanding (that is, in the hands of investors), and they were trading in Toronto at about $70 each. That means the stock market placed a value on the company of about $210 billion — 210,000 times $1 million.

The significant thing in this snapshot, though, was that Nortel shares had soared more than threefold over the previous year. Does that mean Nortel's real value had increased by $140 billion in just a year? Probably not, but Nortel shares climbed because investors went crazy for technology stocks, sending the stock ever higher. In other words, investors kept bidding, or offering high prices for Nortel, and as the mania to own the company's shares grew, the stock price continued to rise. But don't forget that the opposite is true, as Nortel investors discovered to their detriment in 2001 and 2002. If investors turn sour on a company, the stock normally drops like a dead donkey. During the summer and early autumn of 2000, Nortel shares had climbed as high as $122, but they slumped to the $70 range by the fall as investors went cool on the Internet.

You might think Nortel was a great value at that point, with the shares down 40 percent from their peak. Many investors did. Wrong. Nortel just kept dropping as the market for telecommunications gear imploded and fears for the company's very solvency increased. By summer 2002, the shares had collapsed to less than $2, dragging down the whole Canadian stock market with them. Nortel since has rebounded and fallen again, so thousands of investors remain out of pocket — unless of course they swallowed their losses, bailed out of their Nortel investment, and made their money back elsewhere by buying and selling other stocks.

"Equity" sounds nice and rich — But what does it mean?

The term equity means "fairness" or "equal treatment," and it's used as a shorthand for stock to indicate that each share is as good as another (in the real world, controlling shareholders sometimes run companies for their own private benefit, but that's another story). In other words, if a friend owns 100 shares in a company and you own 1,000, then you're supposed to get ten times as much say in choosing the directors and you're also supposed to get ten times as much in dividends — no more and no less. Basically, it comes down to who picks the directors, because they call the shots. "Who cares?" you ask. Well, that little fact — the rule that holders of shares get exactly the same treatment in proportion to how many they own — is one of the great things about the stock market. If you hold 100 shares and a mysterious Cayman Islands trust owns 1 million, you both get exactly the same dividends per share and potential increase in share price. The stock market is often rigged or brutal, but it's also a very democratic and fair place — you either sell or buy, your call, with no sort-ofs or might-dos.

Deciding How Much to Bet on Equity Funds

How many of your loonies are you going to dedicate to equity funds? Finding the right balance here is critical. As we mention elsewhere, stocks, in the form of quality equity funds, are the place for the lion's share of your long-term savings. But not everyone has the time or nerve to be a long-term investor.

Equity funds are not a good place to hold money you're going to need in the next couple of years. And stocks and equity funds are not suitable investments when you can't afford to suffer any short-term losses. That's because even though stock markets rise over time as the economy expands, share prices can go into vicious slumps for a year or more. For example, as of the spring of 2008, the median global stock market fund had gained 2.9 percent over three years. Over five years, it was up more than 7 percent, but up less than 1 percent over ten years.

The *median* return is the midpoint between the highest and lowest values of the members of a group — in this case, a fund category. We refer to median returns in this book instead of average returns because they are regarded as more useful measures of how well a group of funds have performed as a group. A category's *average* return is the sum of the returns for all funds within the category, divided by the number of funds — thus giving equal weighting to each fund, regardless of how big or small it is in terms of assets.

Anyway, back to global equity funds. Despite all the diversification provided by a global equity fund, you can't count on it being there absolutely whenever you need it. So the money you allocate to equity funds should be cash you can let ride for several years — that way your funds have time to bounce back from one of the market's periodic funks.

Knowing your investment style

In Chapter 4, which is all about using mutual funds in your financial plan, we suggest three basic portfolios, depending on what sort of investor you are. The allocation of stocks and bonds in these packages is based on professional portfolios designed by banks and fund companies, but it's not infallible. That's because nobody knows what will happen to the world economy and interest rates in years to come. And besides, everybody's different: If you have a fat pension from your job, you can afford to take far more risks with your mutual fund portfolio in search of higher returns. If the funds lose money, at least the regular pension cheque will keep you fed.

By contrast, if your mutual funds have to supply all your retirement income, then risking the whole wad in equity funds would be reckless. For example, the S&P/TSX composite index — a collection of Canada's biggest companies — plunged 25 percent in 2001–2002. For someone who had his or her entire savings tied up in the stock market, that would have been a hair-raising experience.

Investors can logically be divided into three types, each with a very different need and desire for equity funds. Chances are you don't fit neatly into any of the categories, but you'll almost certainly feel closest to one of them:

- ✔ **Savers** are people for whom investment losses are either unacceptable or unbearable. Typically, a saver is someone who will be using his or her money to make a major purchase, such as a home, within the next couple of years. So all that savers want is a steady and guaranteed return, even if it's less than 5 percent a year. The group also includes people of modest means who will need every penny they've saved to live on, and thus can't afford to take any risks. Investors like this probably shouldn't own any equity funds because the risk of loss is just too great.

- ✔ **Balanced investors** are like most of us — we just want a steady return year after year, without too many stomach-turning drops along the way. After all, life plans change, and we may find it necessary to dip into our savings long before retirement. Avoiding huge losses means owning lots of bonds, which are loans to governments and investors that have been packaged into tiny slices so investors can trade them. In Chapter 4, we suggest that investors in this balanced group limit equity funds to only 45 percent of their portfolio. Only 45 percent in stocks is a very cautious mixture, but remember that as you chase higher returns your risk of loss climbs.

- ✔ **Growth investors** are the aggressive or "long-term" types who don't mind double-digit losses in their portfolios as long as they, ideally, earn 10 percent or more over the long term. In other words, they're investing for at least five years. In Chapter 4, we suggest a portfolio for growth investors that's 75 percent in stocks. If you have many years to go before you'll need the money in the portfolio — that is, you can tie the money up for a decade or more — then you may be happy putting even more of your money into pure stock funds. But before you decide to roll the dice on equities with compete abandon, remember that nearly all professional investors make sure they own a good dollop of guaranteed investments, in the form of cash and government bonds, in the portfolios they run.

Learning from history

For most of the second half of the 20th century, no other type of investment performed as well as stocks. Real estate went into big slumps. Cash or bonds were safer, but they generally pay much less, meaning their returns are often wiped out by inflation.

How good have stocks been in the long run? Well, sorry to give you a weasel-like answer, but it depends on what period you want to look at. For example, consider three recent 10-year periods and then a 20-year span:

- ✔ **1987–1997:** U.S. stocks were way ahead of global and Canadian stocks. The S&P 500 composite index rose a cumulative 477 percent over this ten-year period, more than twice as much as the MSCI world stock index, which rose 216 percent. Canadian bonds, measured by the TSX DEX universe bond index, outperformed the S&P/TSX composite, 200 percent versus 184 percent.

- ✔ **1992–2002:** Roll ahead to another ten-year span, and U.S. stocks are still well ahead of the pack, up a cumulative 203 percent compared with around 135 percent for Canadian stocks and Canadian bonds.

- ✔ **1997–2007:** More recently, it's a very different story. Canadian stocks, propelled by an explosion in the price of oil, gained 147 percent during this period. A distant second was Canadian bonds, up 84 percent, followed by global stocks, up a so-so 41 percent. U.S. stocks trailed badly at 23 percent — thanks in large part to Wall Street's miserable 2007.

- ✔ **1987–2007:** Longer term, stocks were the clear winners, with both Canadian and U.S. stocks producing cumulative returns in excess of 600 percent. Global stocks fared fine, too, gaining nearly 350 percent. But Canadian bonds, aided more recently by a strong loonie, rose 450 percent.

These numbers demonstrate a couple of vital lessons:

- ✔ To get really big growth in your money over many years, you almost certainly have to own at least some stocks — but as the time approaches when you need to dip into your savings, sell your equity funds to protect against a market slump.

- ✔ Despite Bay Street's recent outperformance, you also have to keep lots of your money outside Canada and in big global companies to realize real long-term growth.

Remember, the time period you choose to compare investment returns can make all the difference. Global stock markets made huge gains during the last quarter of the 20th century, although a few serious bumps happened along the way. The 21st century has started out more tentatively, although markets still have made huge gains. As we preach earlier, there will be years or even strings of years when the markets will lose you money. In fact, stock markets can produce losses over many years, so it's unwise to risk every penny of your retirement savings there.

Take a great-grandma out to lunch — And ask what deflation was like

The big hope is that inflation remains under control, despite volatile markets, and that we won't return to the days of double-digit price increases, last seen in the 1960s and 1970s. Runaway inflation means money itself is losing value at a brisk pace, and that's scary news for investors — who depend on their financial assets growing in value, not shrinking.

From 1970 onward we had a recession about every ten years that was sparked in part by overheating in the economy and the resulting inflation. Oil price increases also hurt. But inflation hit only 8 percent during its 1990s bout, and as of mid-2002 it was still a benign 2 percent or so in Canada and the U.S. In fact, there was even talk of deflation — falling prices for goods and services because of global oversupply. Very few adults alive today have lived through that, but the resulting despair and relentless contraction in the economy could make inflation look like a walk in the park.

The last time prices fell in Canada in a sustained way was the late 1930s. Lots of people had outdoor washrooms then, and lots of kids in Canada didn't get enough to eat. Not a good time to own stocks. If you know someone who was an adult in the 1930s, take the old girl or boy out to lunch. Ask them what they remember about falling prices — but also look them in the eye and ask them about the poverty and stagnation of those times.

Investors in the late 1960s and early 1970s saw the entire stock market in the United States and Canada stagnate for a decade as inflation and recession sapped confidence in the future of equity investing itself. The inflation-racked period from 1967 to 1977 presented the worst possible conditions for stocks because interest rates that soared above 20 percent simply tempted investors to put their money into guaranteed deposits. No mutual fund, and practically no type of investment, will be able to get through catastrophic inflationary times like those without losing money. However, central bankers seem to have figured out how to run the economy without slipping into inflationary spirals. Or so it seems.

The point of all of these dire warnings about stock declines is that most of the people who are running and selling mutual funds don't remember the grim 1960s and 1970s either. Many of them hadn't been born, even. So they'll often spin you a cheerful yarn along the lines of "the stock market always goes up over the long term." Maybe it does, but they won't be around to refund your money if the market goes into a 1970s-style collapse, either. That said, equity salespeople had much to chirp about in recent years; the S&P/TSX rolled up four straight years of double-digit gains before settling for a modest 9.8 percent in 2007. It fell for anyone who made a big bet on U.S. stocks, though. The S&P 500 composite index, Wall Street's principal benchmark, achieved much more modest gains during that span and then lost more than 10 percent in 2007.

Splitting between index and actively managed funds

The best plan is to take the money you've set aside for equity funds and simply buy an index fund that tracks the Canadian stock market, another that tracks the U.S. market, and yet another that tracks stock markets in the rest of the world. Or you may someday simply be able to buy a Canadian index fund and a global index fund that follows markets everywhere, including the United States.

Put between one-half and two-thirds of your equity money into those two or three index funds. Then, with the rest of your stock market money, buy two high-quality "normal" or "actively managed" Canadian equity funds and two high-quality global stock funds. By normal or actively managed, we mean funds whose managers actually buy and sell stocks in pursuit of extra profits — instead of, as an index fund does, simply buying every stock in the market and giving you returns in line with an index or benchmark, such as the S&P/TSX composite index or the MSCI world index. (We offer tips on selecting the best actively managed funds in the section "The ABCs of Picking a Fund," later in this chapter.)

Knowing What Return to Expect from Your Funds

Should you have confidence in the Canadian stock market to make more than 10 percent consistently in the future? Are U.S. stocks sure to return to their heady days of the 1990s, when the S&P 500 achieved an astounding 150 percent cumulative return during the second half of that decade? Can you count on 10-percent-plus returns in the future? No, no, and no. And no again. (Although yes, you might be able to earn that sort of return over the long term if you take big risks in volatile markets, such as during the 1990s in Asian markets, which registered huge gains followed by massive losses almost in alternating years.)

If you look for about 6 to 8 percent a year, you may achieve your goal by buying shares in large and stable companies, but you're still stuck with a lot of your money at risk in the ever-choppy stock market. If you settle for a 4- to 6-percent annual return, you're being pretty conservative, meaning you can afford to hold less volatile investments such as bonds and cash; only a major recession or a triumphant return of the dark forces of inflation are likely to give you major losses.

The ABCs of Picking a Fund

If you've been worrying about which equity fund among the 3,000-plus on sale in Canada has the best chance of beating the market, forget it. You're better off looking for UFOs in the evening sky (at least you'll be out in the fresh air and you might meet a fellow Space Cadet to start a new life together and bring little Star Pups into the world). No point trying to pick a fund that'll beat the market, because only a tiny group of managers are likely to do so consistently, based on experience over several decades.

Even if a brochure, ad, or salesperson tells you (or at least implies) a fund is the sure road to riches, always make sure you kick the tires yourself. (We explain just how to kick those tires later in this section.) The people who design and run mutual funds are master marketers and they often sincerely believe their fund is a magic lamp that will reliably outperform the market. If you go to a broker, financial planner, or insurance agent to buy your funds, they too will trot out the same line.

These people are salesmen and saleswomen and, to do a good job, they have almost certainly convinced themselves the fund they're selling you is a world-beater. They'll use reassuring phrases and labels such as "conservative" or "growth at a reasonable price" to convince you their fund is a way to achieve that impossible dream: Big returns at almost no risk. They'll even talk about the fund's "black box" (a cynical expression used in the investment industry) in the shape of some impressive-sounding formula or method that purports to maximize returns while reducing the danger of losses. Think of witch doctors brandishing painted bones and you'll get the idea. Yes, you might get lucky and seize on a manager who outperforms the pack for a while, but they always fall to earth.

Of the nearly 800 funds broadly classified as Canadian equity with a five-year track record as of June 2008, only 68 managed to beat the 18.2-percent return from the S&P/TSX index during that period. It was even worse for the three-year period, when a paltry 102 among the more than 1,000 funds that had been in existence for three years on that date beat the benchmark. And 193 out of nearly 1,500 funds managed this feat for the one-year period. It's tough to beat the index, apparently.

So instead of using complicated criteria to choose a fund you hope will be a world-beater, we recommend that you follow three basic rules, what we call the ABCs of selecting a great equity fund:

1. Look for a fund that's full of companies from **A**ll industries — and, in the case of global funds, **A**ll major regions of the world.

2. Insist that your fund holds lots of big, stable, and conservative companies — the type that investors call Blue-chip (because the blue chip is traditionally the most valuable in poker).

3. Look for a fund that has a habit of producing Consistent returns over the years that aren't out of line with the market or with its rival funds. Later in this chapter, we show you how to do that.

Select from all industries

A fund should hold companies from all, or nearly all, major industries, in order to spread risk — and to give unitholders a chance to profit if the stock market suddenly falls in love with a particular type of company. Here is one way to break down the industry groups:

✔ Banks and other financial companies, such as Citigroup, Royal Bank of Canada, or Deutsche Bank.

✔ Natural resource processors, such as Imperial Oil, Alcan, or Slocan Forest Products.

✔ Technology companies, such as Microsoft, Intel, or Research In Motion; cable-TV companies like Shaw Communications also fit in this group because they're battling the phone companies for control of the retail telecommunications market, including telephone service, Internet access, and television.

✔ Manufacturers of industrial and consumer products, such as drug maker Pfizer or General Electric.

✔ Dull but steady utility and pipeline companies such as Alberta power generator TransAlta or pipeline system TransCanada PipeLines; telephone companies such as Telus and AT&T also officially fit into this group.

✔ Retail and consumer service companies such as Canadian Tire and Wal-Mart.

Not every group has to be represented in the top holdings of every fund, but a portfolio without at least one resource stock, financial services giant, or technology player among its biggest ten investments might represent a dangerous gamble. Why? Because of the ever-present chance that share prices in that missing sector will suddenly and unpredictably take off, leaving your fund in the dust. Avoid funds making bets like that.

Hold blue-chip winners

Glossy mutual fund brochures often promise the sun, moon, and stars . . . but just look at the fund's top holdings. Whether the fund is Canadian, U.S., or international, at least two-thirds of its ten biggest investments should be big, blue-chip companies that you or someone you trust has at least heard of. A list of the top stocks in any fund is readily available on the Internet — see Chapter 21 for details of what the data-company Web sites as well as those of individual fund companies offer. Look in the fund's marketing material or in the reports and documents given to unitholders (see Chapter 3). What you're looking for are big and stable firms, the type that offer the best prospect of increasing their shareholders' wealth over the years.

Talk is cheap and fund managers love to drone on about how conservative they are. But managers of supposedly careful funds can sometimes quietly take risks: They put big portions of the fund into weird stuff like resource stocks or Latin America to jazz up their returns and attract more investors. The list of top holdings is one of the most valuable pieces of information an investor has about a fund because it can't be faked or fudged (ruling out pure fraudulent reporting). If you don't see at least a few giant names — companies like Thomson Corp., Bombardier Inc., Coca-Cola Corp., Bank of Montreal, New York Times Co., General Motors Corp., GlaxoSmithKline PLC, or Toyota Motor Corp. — in the fund's list of its biggest holdings, then the fund manager may be taking undue risks, fooling around with small or obscure companies.

Check out past performance, with caution

After you've satisfied the first two of these conditions, look at the fund's past performance. Begin by filtering out funds that have been around for fewer than five years, unless it's quite clear someone with a record you can check has been running the money. Then look for consistent returns that aren't too much above or below the market. We all want to make lots of money, so leaving past returns until last may seem crazy, and exactly opposite to one's natural inclination. But it's the way sophisticated professionals do it. If the people in charge of a multi-billion-dollar pension fund are interviewing new money-management firms, for example, they'll ask first about the expenses and fees the money managers charge and also about the style and method the firms use to select stocks and bonds (more on that topic later). Only then do the pros examine the past record of the managers — it's just assumed they'll be near the average.

Measuring past performance is almost as impossible as determining the true value of a company's stock — it depends entirely on complex and varying assumptions and conditions. Here's an example: Legendary money manager Frank Mersch of Altamira Investment Services thrashed his competition for most of the early 1990s, playing resource stocks masterfully. He was a journalist's delight, always returning phone calls and providing pithy quotes. Everybody loved him, especially people with money in his fund. It soared more than 30 percent each year from 1990 through 1992, far ahead of the average Canadian stock fund. Who could blame you for deciding Mersch was good — and for putting money into his fund? But then resource stocks slid when commodity prices fell, and Mersch missed out completely on the climb in financial stocks, which rose more than 50 percent in 1997 and again in 1998. The market and his once-beetle-like rivals left him behind, and by 1999 he had departed as manager of the fund. What happened? Did Mersch suddenly become dumb, or did the market turn against him through no fault of his own — or was it simply that his luck changed? Such questions probably can't be answered accurately, so let's not bother debating them. But let us repeat, yet again: Betting too heavily on yesterday's hot performers, hoping they'll outrun the pack again tomorrow, is a good way to end up in a dud fund.

Don't get too hung up about hot results in the past. Mutual fund companies like to offer lots of funds so they can have a few big performers to bray about in the ads, but those returns are always partly a result of luck. And mutual funds, incidentally, are managed more recklessly than pension funds. The temptation always exists to jack up the risk and returns a little to get the money pouring in. With a pension fund, a manager is expected to stick to a certain set of goals and investing style, and the penalties are severe for taking unauthorized flyers. That's because you have a bunch of actuaries, pension experts with thin lips and no sense of humour, keeping a watery eye on a pension fund's portfolio. But retail investors usually don't have the knowledge or resources to check or worry whether a manager is sticking to the fund's prescribed style — say, lots of fast-growing companies with high-flying stocks.

Find out what a fund's past performance has been and, above all, compare it with that of rival funds and the market as a whole. *The Globe and Mail* and the *National Post* used to publish vast monthly reports providing a plethora of rate of return data, but no longer do so because the Internet has almost completely taken over as the objective source of comparative fund performance information. The leading Internet sites for Canadian mutual fund investors and investment advisers are Morningstar.ca and Globefund.com. Morningstar.ca is run by the Canadian unit of Chicago-based Morningstar, Inc., and Globefund.com is part of *The Globe and Mail*'s substantial Internet network, which also includes Globeinvestor.com. (Advisers also rely on desktop computer software sold by these organizations.)

Who's running your fund? Managers on the move

Equity funds offer endless sources of amusement. One of the fun games you can play with a fund is figuring out who exactly is running it. This is often so difficult that investors shouldn't get too worried about it when they start buying funds. It's impossible with some companies that use a vague "team" to pick stocks. And remember that a superstar manager is extra likely to go cold because he or she gets too much money run. Remember that what is actually in the portfolio is far more important than any amount of talk of wizards running your money.

If you get more interested in mutual funds, you'll no doubt start wondering: Why not just put my money with guys and gals who have been successful in the past? One problem is that managers move around so much. As soon as a stock picker builds a strong reputation, all too often he or she jumps ship to another fund that offers a fat signing bonus. And remember the warning that we've been repeating endlessly, in a smug nasal drone: Star managers invariably fall to earth. Sometimes, they go inside themselves and sometimes they seem to . . . well, they always go inside themselves. Don't get excited about the past history of the manager running your fund. And pay even less attention to fawning newspaper articles proclaiming them a genius. Just look at the fund's main holdings and its track record. If these meet the ABC tests outlined above, then it's probably a high-quality fund.

You can find much more on how to use the Internet for fund research in Chapter 21, but for now just remember to stick to funds that have been around for at least five years. Compare a fund's numbers against those of its peers — those within the same category — and also against the median returns for all funds in the category. (Refer to Chapter 2 for more on medians, averages, and other performance measures.)

Globefund.com and Morningstar.ca supply the annual compound returns for every fund as well as for the average fund in its category and for the market as a whole. If you're interested in a fund, its compound returns should be above the average for its group, but if they're way above — for example, an annual return of 15 percent over five years while the average fund made less than 10 percent — then the manager is probably a risk-taker. Above all, though, be wary of funds whose returns over five and ten years are below those of the average fund: Such pooches have a dispiriting habit of continuing to bark and dig holes in the garden.

Also check whether the fund has been near the top or bottom in each individual calendar year, to detect big swings in performance over time.

What's in a name?

A fund's name may not tell you much about what it invests in. Look up the fund online and check what category it's in. You might be surprised to see what you assumed was a growth-oriented equity fund is actually a conservative balanced fund. Or check the top holdings of a global equity fund and wonder why it's missing "U.S. Equity" from its name.

If a fund isn't guided by a responsible-sounding name, it in fact might be a volatile fund that's suitable only for aggressive risk-takers or those who don't mind riding out losses. At the very least, it will be ignoring important areas of the stock market. For example, "international" funds, which stay out of the Canadian and U.S. stock markets, are intended only for those who already have plenty of money invested at home and in the U.S.

Avoiding Being Bitten by a Dog

Stocks generally go up over time, as the economy grows and companies become more efficient at creating wealth for their owners (which means the people who own their shares, remember). Does this mean that any equity fund you get your hands on will line your pockets over the long haul? Not so fast — for mutual fund buyers, the problem is that individual funds can go into long slumps if the fund manager gets it wrong.

Remembering the importance of diversification

As a mutual fund buyer, you can really miss out on returns if you're stuck with a hound. We can't emphasize this point enough: Spread your holdings among half a dozen funds — including two or three index funds, funds that track the entire stock market, instead of trying to pick individual shares (and possibly getting it wrong) — to help ensure they don't all rot away in something that never really comes back to life.

At all costs, avoid having more than one-third of your money in any one stock market fund. That way you won't expose too much of your capital to a pig of a fund. Fund companies and planners might tell you differently, but we really can't think of an exception.

Looking at the big picture and knowing when to bail

Fund companies and brokers (with some justification) argue endlessly that buying stocks and shares is a long-term game because the market can drop for no good reason. (Of course, that doesn't prevent them from taking out huge ads trumpeting their short-term numbers, but we'll let that go for the moment.)

In fact, an old joke in investing goes like this: Everybody says he's a long-term investor as soon as his stock goes down.

The fund industry says you should ride out losses and that the market always turns, meaning you should be happy leaving money in an equity fund for at least five years. And the industry advises against selling a fund when it becomes a dog, arguing that it's simply having an off year. Well, perhaps, but a fund can take an awfully long time to recover. And it's impossible to tell whether its slump is temporary or long term.

For example, investors in AIC Advantage, a powerhouse fund in the 1990s, have not enjoyed the 21st century so far. The fund has a seemingly inbred approach to investing: It focuses on the stocks of mutual fund companies. This approach served well during the fund's spectacular 547-percent gain from 1991 through 1997. Returns have been uneven since then, however, and investors soon grew tired of AIC's pleas for patience and began leaving the fund in droves. The fund seemed to break out of its funk in 2006, when it produced a 24-percent return, but the bad times resumed in 2007 with a 3-percent loss. Is AIC Advantage now a bad fund? Probably not. After all, its mandate clearly states it uses a long-term, buy-and-hold strategy. As they say: Time will tell.

In some cases, a brief period of bad returns is not the manager's fault. The market just hates the type of companies the manager likes to buy.

Take a look at the ups and downs over the years at AIM Trimark Investments, which was Canada's sixth-biggest mutual fund company in mid-2008 with about $38.2 billion in assets.

AIM Trimark's managers use a distinctive style of picking a few companies that they get to know intimately (pipe down there at the back of the hall) and hold for years (stop it). Besides, they also often buy lesser-known names. That's all fine — we'll show you how it has produced big returns — but the eccentric style sometimes means the company's funds go in a different direction from most others. That's because most other managers like to thunder herd-like into the same globally famous shares. Really, how hard is it to grunt "1 million Coke"?

A manager with a distinctive style — as long as it isn't too, ahem, weird — is a great person to invest with. That's because he or she often makes lots of money on a violent turnaround in the market when other managers are losing their pricey embroidered shirts. But when the odd stocks the manager likes fall out of favour themselves, unitholders in the fund miss out.

Here's how the up–down syndrome worked with AIM Trimark. The company's funds sold their bank stocks in the late 1990s after financial shares climbed to record highs because the managers reckoned the shares were trading at inflated prices. Turned out they were right — but they sold too soon. This, after all, was one of Canada's biggest fund companies, boasting an excellent long-term record in both Canadian and global equities. But the market went against the Trimark team in 1997, and bank stocks went on climbing (although they finally slumped in 1999). That meant Trimark underperformed the broad market and its rivals, and investors pulled more than $1 billion out of its funds. The Trimark saga included another humorous pie in the face — the fund giant missed out on the upside of the insanity in tech stocks. The huge Trimark Fund, normally a nice way to invest in global equities, made only 6.4 percent in 1998 while most global equity managers were up 17 percent or more. But then, for two and a half years straight from 2000 through summer 2002, Trimark ruled the earth. Its funds, featuring established solid companies instead of telecom companies run by head-banging greedy executives, took off as the tech scene turned into shabby figures huddled around a fire in an oil drum. By mid-2002, Trimark Fund had made its unitholders richer by a wondrous 15.4 percent annually over ten years, among the best return for any fund of any type at that time.

But perhaps an oil drum — a full one, that is — wasn't such a bad place to be, as Trimark's managers found out a few years later. The company's refusal to invest in oil companies and other energy stocks has once again sent its equity funds into the performance dumpster. Its biggest Canadian equity fund, Trimark Canadian Endeavour, was one of the worst one-year performers in mid-2008 among its 1,400 competitors, with a loss of nearly 30 percent. Of course, as we've already said ad nauseam, time will tell if Trimark's hardheaded consistency will once again pay off. Our bet is that it will, thanks to the power of long-term, buy-and-hold equity investing.

The moral of the story: If possible, try to make sure the funds you buy are run by managers with a clearly stated style or method of picking stocks. Then try to choose managers with different styles. That way, when one manager is doing badly the other could be doing well, smoothing out your returns.

But what if your manager, who was good in the past, keeps posting bad returns year after year? Unfortunately, no quick answer exists for the question of when to dump a good manager. Just follow your gut. And ask a few questions if your salesperson seems all puppyish and keen to do a switch. She or he could be indirectly getting a cut of 5 percent of the money you switch to another firm's funds because the new firm pays sales commissions.

Chapter 11

Heirloom Equity Funds: The Dull Stuff that Will Make You Wealthy

*T*his is the most important chapter in this book if you're a long-term investor who's able to commit money to mutual funds for at least five years. That's because equity funds — funds that buy stocks and shares in companies — are such powerful investing tools, offering the potential to grow your money many times over. If you pick a sensibly varied portfolio of high-quality funds, and this chapter will show you how, then you're almost certain to do well as an investor.

We refer to these funds as "heirloom" funds because that's what they should be — treasured possessions you can hang on to indefinitely. Sorry if you find these funds a little dull. This chapter isn't about crazy technology funds that soar 80 percent in a year and then crash just as quickly. And it isn't about finding somewhere safe and predictable to hold the cash you're saving up for a car. It's about the "core" mutual funds that account for most of your long-term money, funds you can buy and hold forever if necessary. Yes, they may have bad years, perhaps several in a row, but over time their top-quality stocks and varied holdings are almost sure to pay off. In Chapter 10, we outline the basic steps you need to take to identify a good equity fund. In this chapter, we provide more details of the things to check, we suggest some excellent funds, and we show you how to select your own mixture of mutual funds.

How Many Equity Funds Do You Need?

Building a great portfolio of mutual funds is simple. All you have to do is make two decisions:

✔ How much risk you want to take — in other words, how much you want riding on equity funds.

✔ How much you like Canada's long-term economic prospects.

We wish we could tell you to simply buy a single stock market fund, using the techniques we suggest, and forget about it. Some salespeople will even insist you're safe with a single wonderful fund. But that course is just too dangerous.

Putting all your money into just one equity fund, even if it's a great one, can lead to periods of harrowing underperformance if that fund goes into a slump — and nearly all funds do from time to time. Consider, for example, the fate of investors in Trimark Select Growth Fund, which in mid-2008 was AIM Trimark's biggest fund with $3.7 billion in assets. The fund, which gave investors a glittering return of 8.5 percent annually from its launch in May 1989 to the middle of 2008, might have done even better had it not been for a catastrophic 2007. The fund lost 16 percent, as it was hit harder than many other global equity funds by a rapidly rising Canadian dollar. It was Trimark Select Growth's first negative year since 1990, when the young fund lost 7.2 percent in a year when almost all of its peers also were firmly in the red.

Own more than one equity fund. That way, if one of your funds sags, you have a shot at doing well with the others.

But how many funds should you buy to ensure you've assembled an adequately varied collection? Before we answer that, look at the only two types of funds to consider for your serious long-term money:

✔ **Global equity funds** buy stocks and shares everywhere, from Taiwan to Tupelo. In practice, they usually end up investing in large companies in the rich economies of the world because, to paraphrase the bank robber, that's where the money is. In other words, giant corporations have proven to be just about the most profitable and most stable investments you can make.

✔ **Canadian equity funds, not surprisingly,** buy Canadian stocks. A number of individual categories exist under the Canadian equity umbrella. Some funds concentrate on the very largest corporations, such as the big banks or other blue-chip companies like communications giant Telus Corp., and others are more specialized, such as *small-cap funds,* which buy only smaller companies with supposedly bigger growth prospects. In practice, Canadian equity funds end up holding pretty well the same companies because the Canadian market offers a limited selection, although it offers a little more variety among small-cap funds.

Ruling out specialty funds

In Chapter 12, we look at the host of dancing unicorns and dogs in tutus the fund industry has come up with to entice money from investors. By that we mean the "specialty" or "regional" equity funds that hold only a certain type of shares or shares in only some countries, the idea being that a concentrated fund will produce huge profits when share prices in that particular industry or part of the world take off like little rockets.

These riskier funds include technology funds, small-company funds, developing-country funds, resource funds, U.S. equity funds, and Asian funds. Some have produced great returns and many hold excellent stocks. But they all suffer from one insurmountable handicap: Because they can invest in only a small section of the world's stock markets, they don't give you the variety and stability your long-term money requires.

So, the only two types of funds you truly need for the portion of your money you've decided to have in equity funds are global equity funds and Canadian equity/large-cap equity funds. Go ahead and buy some of the risky specialty and regional funds if you must, but limit them to just 10 percent of your total portfolio. No hard-and-fast rule applies here, but that's the advice you'll get from many pros.

Deciding how much to put into equity funds

In Chapters 4 and 10, which deal with using equity mutual funds in your financial plan, we state that all of us as investors fall into one of these three groups:

- ✔ **Savers,** who need to use their money in the next couple of years, shouldn't own any equity funds. The risk of loss in the short term is too great, so savers should just buy investments that pay regular interest.

- ✔ **Balanced investors,** who want only modest drops in the value of their funds in any one year, often put 45 percent or slightly more (up to about 60 percent) into equity funds. With the rest they buy bond funds, which invest in loans to governments and corporations, leaving a small portion of their money sitting in cash or cash-like investments. Or they buy special balanced funds, which consist of a mixture of stocks and bonds.

- ✔ **Growth investors,** who want the maximum return on their money and plan to let it ride the ups and downs of funds for five years or more, often put about 75 percent of their money into equity funds. If you're investing for periods of ten years or more, and definitely don't mind big slumps in the value of your mutual fund portfolio along the way, you might want to put even more into the stock market with its allure of higher returns.

Dividing your money between Canadian and foreign equity funds

Should you be patriotic and keep your money in Canada, or look abroad for your investments? No definite answer exists, but the prevailing advice has been to keep the majority of your stock market money outside Canada. The world offers many wonderful opportunities and the Canadian stock market represents a tiny fraction of the world's overall stock market value. For example, few Canadian companies have the might of Japan's Sony Corp., Royal Dutch Shell of the Netherlands, or U.S.-based Microsoft Corp.

However, most experts would also advise keeping at least some of your money in Canada if you plan to go on living in this country, because you'll need to have assets in Canadian dollars to pay for your expenses here. Plus our market has fared pretty well during the past decade or so. But if you're convinced that Canada's in trouble, then you may want to move 80 percent or more of your mutual fund money, including equity funds, into non-Canadian stocks and bonds.

How do you split your money among equity funds?

In Chapter 4 we describe a method of dividing your money among equity funds. Put one-half to two-thirds of your stock market money into index funds or exchange-traded funds, funds that simply track the entire market at low cost to the investor instead of trying to pick the stocks that will go up the most. For much more on index funds and ETFs, check out Chapter 15. Their reliability and low expenses make them one of the very best deals out there for investors.

Canadian stock market index funds and ETFs track the Standard & Poor's/Toronto Stock Exchange composite index or the S&P/TSX 60 index (a more focused collection of the biggest companies listed on the TSX). Global index funds are rare, so you usually have to buy a combo: a U.S. index fund, such as one that gives you the same return each year as the giant U.S. companies that make up the Standard & Poor's 500-stock index, and an international index fund that tracks all the major global markets except for the United States and Canada. Put a U.S. index fund and an international index fund together, and you've got a pretty good global equity index fund. So all you need to buy is a Canadian, a U.S., and an international index fund.

Two categories of funds invest broadly in foreign stock markets:

- ✔ Global equity
- ✔ International equity

Here's the difference. Global equity funds are free to invest anywhere, including the United States, but international equity funds stay outside Canada and the United States. The idea behind international funds is that many investors already have plenty of money in the States by owning stocks or other funds, so some fund companies offer funds that stay out of the U.S. market. That's logical thinking, but in keeping with the ABC rules, we believe that when picking your non-Canadian stock funds you're better off sticking with a fund that's free to go anywhere the manager anticipates getting the best return.

With the rest of your equity fund money, buy just four equity funds — two global and two Canadian — that have a person or team trying to select winning shares. Those are called actively managed funds because they buy and sell holdings in an attempt to beat the market and other fund managers instead of just trying to keep up with a market benchmark. The managers, in other words, are trying to pick the few stocks that go up the most.

Often, though, managers fail. But at least if you buy a few actively managed funds as well as index funds, you have a portfolio that isn't tied to just one market benchmark. It has enough variety to ensure that at least one of your funds is probably doing relatively well, even if the others are sagging — as long as the whole stock market isn't crashing. In the event of a wholesale decline in stocks, just about all equity funds — both Canadian and global — will be losers anyway.

Global Equity Funds: Meet Faraway People and Exploit Them

Global equities are the Boeing 747s of the mutual fund world, huge magic carpets that offer the best chance of steady, high returns on your savings over many years. They should make up about two-thirds of the money you're putting into the stock market — unless you're convinced the Canadian stock market's out-performance is a long-term event.

Global equity funds have earned steady, attractive returns over the years, which makes them the very best type of fund to own. Put most of your money here because

- ✔ They tend to own multinational blue-chip companies, the best growth asset of all.

- ✔ They invest all over the world, spreading your risk and smoothing out your ups and downs — when one country is up, another is often down.

- ✔ The executives running multinational corporations sometimes foul up (remember "new Coke"?), but the companies are usually large enough and sufficiently sophisticated to recover from errors.

✔ Your mutual fund company is just one of dozens of big international money managers owning shares in these firms — between them, all those sharp lassies wearing Prada and those lads in Armani keep an eye on the companies. When their hangovers aren't too bad, that is.

Many of Canada's biggest mutual funds fall into the global equity class, and some large ones have produced excellent results over the years. Global equity funds are hugely profitable for the companies that run them, so the managers are intensely motivated not to let the performance slip too much. Most global equity funds hold high-quality, blue-chip companies and they spread their risk over numerous industries and countries, so they also meet our ABC test.

Buy at least two global equity funds, because an individual fund can go into a slump for a year or more. Different managers are hot and cold at different times.

Applying the ABC rules to your global equity funds

Be sure to apply the ABC rules we describe in Chapter 10 when selecting a global equity fund:

✔ Make sure the fund invests in **All industries** and **Anywhere** in the world. All of the important economic regions (that is, North America, Europe, and Asia) should show up in the top-ten holdings.

✔ Insist on **Blue-chip** companies, some of which you've at least heard of.

✔ Demand **Consistent** performance that isn't wildly out of line with the other funds in the group.

Investors who just go to a bank branch to buy their funds or who deal with another company that sells funds directly to the public will have a problem: The bank or company may offer just one suitable global equity fund. And you may not be able to buy index funds. No easy way around this problem exists. If you can't or don't want to go somewhere with a wider selection of funds, just buy the global fund with half of the money you've earmarked for global stocks and then hedge your bets by putting the rest into one or two narrower funds that invest in a single region, such as Europe or Asia.

Check any global equity fund you buy to make sure it offers plenty of variety. If the top holdings contain no European stocks, for example, or they seem to be all technology companies, then look elsewhere.

Investment styles: Bargain hunter or Champagne Charlie?

The following is detailed stuff that's likely to interest only investors who enjoy peering into mutual funds. It talks about the different styles of investing that managers use. You really don't need to know about this if you simply remember to buy two or three funds. That way, when one manager's style isn't working, you'll probably have money with another manager who's having a better year.

Value investors like stocks that are out of favour with the market, maybe because the company, its country of origin, or its industry has run into a temporary setback. So they look for shares that are a good value and are trading at cheap prices, and they hope to hold them until the shares bounce back.

Growth investors argue that the real way to make money in the market is by buying businesses that are already doing well, so they concentrate on buying shares in companies whose sales and profits are growing fast, even if their shares have already gone up. Growth investors believe that so-called value shares are cheap for a reason, because the company is a pooch.

No evidence shows that one style is superior. Until the mid-1990s, value managers had the upper hand, posting stronger long-term returns. Then soaring technology and telecom stocks — just the sort of shares that value managers hate — brought growth stocks into fashion until those sectors collapsed in 2001–2002.

Checking out three global equity winners

Here are three conservative and well-run global equity funds that Morningstar's analysts see as good bets in today's increasingly challenging global marketplace:

- ✔ **Mackenzie Ivy Foreign Equity** is a well-known global fund run by a well-known manager, Jerry Javasky. Global investing means diversification and long-term gains, and this fund is a good bet to deliver just that. True, the past few years have not been kind to this fund, thanks to outperformance of specific sectors, prompting some investors to take their global investing business elsewhere. But Javasky is an industry veteran who has produced excellent long-term results. And although his fund typically underperforms in hot markets, it usually outperforms on the downside. If you're patient, chances are you'll be well rewarded over the long haul in this fund. This fund's annual expenses are slightly higher than the category median, but the cost might be justified.

- ✓ **PH&N Global Equity** is a good fund from longtime, no-load specialist Phillips, Hager & North. As a value fund, it hasn't fared well in recent years. But it has a reputation of avoiding large losses when markets tank. For example, the fund has been spared some downside by the reluctance of its managers to invest in financial markets, thus escaping some of the losses brought on by the credit crisis. However, its mandate requires it to not deviate too far from sector weightings of its benchmark, the MSCI World Index. The fund is among the least expensive global equity funds, with annual expenses of just 1.56 percent — nearly a full percentage point below that of the median global equity mutual fund.

- ✓ **Mutual Discovery,** offered by Franklin Templeton, is a go-anywhere global equity fund run by experienced value managers. Unlike many value funds, it has done quite well in recent years, due to broad diversification through more than 100 individual stock holdings. Its performance also has been helped by its ability to invest in bonds of troubled companies — investments that can offer the opportunity for high returns and whose prices often behave a lot like those of stocks. The fund also will move well into cash if stocks or high-yield bonds aren't to the managers' liking.

Canadian Equity Funds: Making Maple-Syrup-Flavoured Money

As we explain in Chapter 10, your first move when picking Canadian equity funds for the core of your portfolio is to make sure they're classified in one of the Canadian equity categories. These include:

- ✓ **Canadian equity:** These funds must have 90 percent of their holdings in Canadian-based companies; the fund's average market capitalization must be more than $3.8 billion (for 2008).

- ✓ **Canadian focused equity:** The criteria are identical to the Canadian equity category, except funds need be only 50 percent or more in Canada.

- ✓ **Canadian small/mid-cap equity:** These funds must be 90 percent in Canadian stocks with an average market cap below $3.8 billion (again, for 2008).

- ✓ **Canadian focused small/mid-cap equity:** The same as Canadian small/mid-cap equity, except funds need be only 50 percent or more in Canada.

- ✓ **Canadian dividend and income equity:** These funds must have a stated mandate to invest primarily in income-generating securities, and 90 percent of their equity holdings must be Canadian. The average market cap must be above $3.8 billion.

✔ **Canadian income trust equity:** These must keep at least 90 percent of their equity holdings in income trust securities issued by Canadian entities (we talk about income trusts in Chapter 5).

If the company where you hold your mutual fund account offers only one conventional actively managed Canadian stock fund, then use it for half of your Canadian stock money and put the rest into a Canadian index fund. If no index fund is available (and one should be), then open an account elsewhere for at least part of your money.

Keep it simple and don't worry about which equity fund manager is going to thrash the competition, because such an outcome is impossible — or at least very, very difficult — to predict. Canada's tiny stock market, which accounts for just 3 percent of the world's publicly traded shares, offers a limited number of companies. In fact, for a big-company fund, only a few suitable names exist outside of the S&P/TSX 60 index. So most Canadian equity funds tend to be pretty similar.

Applying the ABC rules to your Canadian equity funds

Applying the ABC rules when you buy Canadian equity funds is simple:

✔ Check that the fund invests in **All of Canada's** major industrial sectors, including technology, natural resources, and financial services.

✔ Make sure that most of the top-ten holdings are **Blue-chip** companies that you've at least heard of.

✔ Demand **Consistent** performance that doesn't lag or wildly outpace the other Canadian equity funds.

Looking at three winners in Canadian equities

Here are three Canadian equity funds selected by Morningstar analysts on the basis of solid long-term performance and strong fund managers:

✔ **Mawer Canadian Equity** is a solid offering from an innovative and independent no-load company. Its annual expenses of 1.24 percent make it one of the least expensive Canadian equity funds. Manager Jim Hall has a knack for limiting losses, which has helped the fund produce solid long-term results. It's a great choice as a conservative core Canadian equity fund around which to build a portfolio. The manager's wary approach steered the fund clear of investing in CIBC, which suffered mightily from the credit crisis. On the other hand, his avoidance of the resources sector caused it to miss out on recent big gains. The manager is down on these companies because they are too susceptible to cyclical volatility. So if you see resource stocks as being forever strong, it might not be your cup of tea.

✔ **Saxon Stock** has experienced recent struggles in a growth/momentum market environment, but its managers, Richard Howson and Suzann Pennington, have continued to stay true to the fund's value-investing philosophy. Their investment approach has produced one of the best track records in the category over the long run. Risk management is a major focus and the fund is well diversified in terms of both sectors and individual stocks. With annual expenses of just 1.86 percent, it is one of the least expensive Canadian equity funds — thanks in part to its low portfolio turnover rate of about 12 percent. The combination of low expenses and experienced management — Howson has been in charge for nearly two decades — makes this fund a solid long-term bet.

✔ **Brandes Sionna Canadian Equity** has the advantage of being run by Kim Shannon, widely recognized as one of the top Canadian value managers. Her relative value approach to investing has produced a mandate with an excellent track record (mostly with her previous fund, CI Canadian Investment) and has historically fared well during most market conditions. The fund is relatively conservative and may lag the market over shorter periods. Shannon typically keeps her portfolio's sector weights fairly close to those of the index, although she does have the flexibility to deviate substantially. She completely escaped the tech stock collapse, despite those stocks' heavy weighting in the benchmark index. The fund remains underweight in this sector. All this comes at a price, though; the fund's annual expenses are 2.49 percent, well above the category median.

Beware of overwhelming hype

An incredible amount of hype and hot air surround the people running equity funds. Fund companies take the managers on cross-country tours as though they were rock stars. But ignore all the sound and fury.

The people who sell equity funds make a lot of noise about them because this product is their bread and butter as well as their caviar and champagne and bloated drunken evenings

(actually, they're quite a sober lot nowadays). A good Canadian equity fund is a fund company's showpiece asset, drumming up business across the board. The six Canadian equity categories account for about one-quarter of the industry's total assets, or nearly $178 billion. Canadian equity funds generate a tidal wave of fees — about $4 billion per year — for the people who run and sell them.

Chapter 12

Las Vegas–Style Equity Funds: Trips You Don't Need

*W*e know it's boring and glib, but it's also true: Slow and steady really does win the equity fund race. In other words, you'll almost certainly do best over the long haul with the conservative equity funds we describe in Chapter 11, the ones that buy established companies in all industries and in all parts of the world. But you're only human, and the temptation to chase the really hot returns always exists. It wasn't that long ago — 1999 — that the median science and technology mutual fund gained 100 percent. Well, help yourself — but get ready to be bitten. Those funds went on to lose 108 percent of their value over the following three years. Mutual funds are a wonderfully convenient and relatively cheap way of playing, say, the Chinese market. But with this type of narrow investing, focusing on specific areas like small/mid-cap stocks, an individual geographic region, or a particular industry sector is essentially gambling. In a nutshell, it's probably a waste of time because of what Nobel Prize–winning economists call "rational expectations."

Crudely put, here's how the theory applies to these specialty funds. By the time you realize something might be a good investment, everyone else — or at least everyone who matters — will have cottoned on to it too. By the time you decide that telecommunications is the fuel of the future and load up on a telecom fund, professional investors all over the world have concluded the same thing and have already bid telecom stocks up to high prices. Yes, you might do well in a technology fund — just ask anyone who invested in Northwest Specialty Innovations in mid-2003. After five years, they had enjoyed a 16-percent compound annual return. But we're really talking about slot machines here, and the flood of coins dries up eventually. Someone who had owned only that fund for a year would lose 8.5 percent as of mid-2008.

Still, hope springs eternal and all that . . . so here's a roundup of the more dangerous types of funds. In this chapter we refrain from suggesting candidates when it comes to these wild funds because returns from this gang are largely a matter of luck — a manager looks like a genius when his or her favourite type of company or market is in favour, and a loser when that type of investment goes out of fashion.

Small and Mid-Sized Company Funds: Spotty Little Fellows

On the face of it, funds in the Canadian small/mid-cap equity category look mighty enticing. The median Canadian small/mid-cap equity fund had produced an impressive 20-year compound annual return of 10.5 percent as of mid-2008. But these funds have benefitted enormously from the success of the Canadian resource industry, in which much of the big money is made when a small resource player strikes it rich. Actually attaining that return, though, is entirely another matter. Small/mid-cap equity funds are a volatile bunch of funds.

Hitting highs and lows

If you had bought Northwest Specialty Equity in mid-1988 and still owned it 20 years later, you would have been bragging about owning the top-performing Canadian small/mid-cap fund. The fund achieved an impressive 16.5-percent compound annual return over that period. But "if" is the operative term here. Even more impressive than your profit — more than $213,000 if you'd invested $10,000 back then — would have been your staying power. You'd have weathered some pretty big swings during the early going, including the 14.5-percent loss in 1990 that followed a 27-percent gain the previous year. Or how about rolling to an astounding 103-percent return in 1993 and then being handed a 6.7-percent loss the very next year? Most investors would have figured, absolutely, that a triple-digit return was completely too good to be true and sell out. But then they would have missed a rebound of nearly 100 percent in the next two years.

Who's to know, though? The important thing to note here is that, had you taken the much, much safer middle ground and invested in large-cap Canadian equity funds, you'd have done almost as well. The median fund in the Canadian equity category achieved a 9.3-percent compound annual return over those same 20 years. (We're focusing on Canadian funds here because relatively few U.S. and global small-cap funds exist. And, for the record, these funds have fared nowhere near as well as their Canadian counterparts.)

Picking a winning fund

Long before you worry about having the nerve to stick with a winning small-cap fund, the first challenge is to pick that fund in the first place. The problem is similar to what confronts the guy who's investing directly in small-cap stocks. Guessing which ones are going to "pop" — market talk for getting their stocks to go up — is a tough game. But never fear; investors have a willing ally in the executives and main shareholders of a company. In fact, they're sometimes only too happy for their share price to shoot up. Cling! — is that an option bulb lighting up? (Options are shares that company management can buy at a fixed low price — and that become nicer and nicer to have when the market price of the shares goes up.) But what's left in a hot stock for everybody else after the corporate management and the investment bankers have torn off their giant hunk often wouldn't fill a small McDonald's pop cup that's been lying for days on the ground beside a gasoline pump.

First, a vital bit of terminology — a company's stock market capitalization is the value in money terms that investors are applying to the business. For example, a company with 50 million shares in the hands of its shareholders and a stock price of $5 has a market value, or "market cap," of only $250 million (or 50 million shares times $5), which still makes it quite a small company.

The three most important things to remember about investing in small and medium-sized companies are that:

- ✔ Shares in small companies move in their own strange cycles, sometimes sliding when blue-chip stocks go up, which can make them a sort of insurance policy for a portfolio.

- ✔ And yes, when they're hot, small caps can produce rich returns. Of all the wacky fund categories, small-cap funds can best justify their existence. But you don't really need them, either.

- ✔ Small-company funds can go into long slumps, leaving you with "dead money" that just stagnates — or, worse, saddles you with heavy losses. Most people are better off putting their savings into regular equity funds that buy big companies, a strategy that offers steadier returns.

Understanding the disadvantages

Take any recommendation to buy a small-cap fund with a hefty dose of salt. These are volatile investments best suited to investors who keep a close eye on their holdings. Unpredictable rallies and collapses are the way that small-cap stocks work. Yes, Canadian small/mid-cap funds have put together a string of consecutive gains in recent years. But over the longer haul, most investors have had to wait through lean and hungry years for the good times, and disappointments are all too frequent.

So remember that small-company funds are marked by moves upward that happen only too rarely, a disadvantage that makes them unsuitable for much of your serious money. The numbers show that small-cap stocks may have their good long-term record only because of periodic crazy bull markets in small-company shares — typically at the end of a great period in the stock market, when investors feel clever and brave enough to start chasing riskier stuff. Investors in small-cap funds didn't get any compensatory extra return as a reward for taking on the risk of buying into smaller companies.

If you insist on buying small-company funds, buy at least two or three. That's because the managers of small-cap funds tend to be eccentric individuals who love poring over obscure little businesses and developing their own methods. It's very personality-driven. Even an excellent manager can do terribly if his or her favourite type of stock is out of fashion. And don't forget that the small-cap sector has plenty of walking dead.

Regional Equity Funds: Welcome to Bangkok — Or Hong Kong?

Funds that invest in limited areas of the world may sound like they're a good way to speculate. After all, the median emerging markets fund had a five-year compound annual return of about 20 percent as of mid-2008. Regional funds are exciting investments, however, and that brings both the good and the bad. Although emerging markets mutual funds somehow produced double-digit returns during each of the five calendar years through 2007, before that investors had a pretty uneven ride. Uneven as in a 19-percent loss in 1998, a 61-percent gain in 1999, and a 27-percent loss in 2000.

Funds that specialize in a particular area suffer from the curse of all narrow investments, whether they invest in European, Asian, or emerging markets, or in individual countries. These markets usually go into slumps, which was amply demonstrated by Japan in 2000–2002, when the median Japanese equity mutual fund suffered losses of 30, 26, and 13 percent during those calendar years. Things haven't been too good lately for these funds, either. The median Japanese equity mutual fund lost about 6 percent during the first half of 2008, resulting in a ten-year compound annual loss of 1.7 percent. (Oh, that pared-down Zen aesthetic! We'll have our brown rice and twig now, please.) Investors in the broader region fared better, as Asia–Pacific Rim mutual funds — which are free to lose money anywhere in the region — eked out a small profit of 3.3 percent over those ten years, despite the Japan market's woes.

If you must go regional, you might try European funds, with their giant blue-chip companies, and then perhaps Asia–Pacific Rim. But you're probably better off with two or three global equity funds that hold assets in countries just about everywhere. Look at the holdings of nearly any big global equity fund and you'll see European and Asian stocks as well as U.S. names.

The pros aren't infallible, though, and they can easily get the mix of countries wrong. That's why it's important with global equity funds to avoid managers who make big bets on a particular region or country, such as China or India.

The following is a quick rundown of the main types of regional foreign equity funds. We won't spend too much time on them — although we have to admit these narrow, specialized funds can be lots of fun.

European funds: Why are all these people so well dressed?

European funds invest almost entirely in major companies in big, stable European countries, so they're a sensible choice compared with most specialty funds. However, after a fairly steady run of profits during the 1990s, these funds have produced uneven returns. This is partly due to the global technology stock fallout of the early 1990s. The tech–telecom millennium stock party turned out to be just as deranged and overpriced as North America's. The median European equity fund dropped almost 7 percent in 2000, 18 percent in 2001, and 11 percent in 2002. Things subsequently improved, and returns have been steady since 2002, including a handsome 31-percent gain in 2006. The euro's strength against the U.S. dollar (and our high-flying loonie as well) has been a boon for funds that invest on this continent.

Don't bother trying to wager on currencies when you buy mutual funds — stick to rock climbing at night. The individual investor has little chance of predicting foreign exchange movements; even the experts in the forex trading pits are challenged!

As always, if you do go into Europe, buy more than one fund so that a dog doesn't chew up your portfolio too badly. A simple way to do this is to buy one of the half-dozen European index funds available, as opposed to one of the hundred or so actively managed European equity funds. *Index funds* buy every stock in a recognized market index or benchmark so that they earn returns in line with the broad stock market. An *actively managed fund,* which is the most common type of fund, buys and sells stocks in an attempt to select the best ones — but it runs the risk of making the wrong choices. European index funds track the Morgan Stanley Capital International European Index, a well-recognized benchmark for Europe's biggest stocks.

Asian funds: The dream that died

This is it — the biggest rollercoaster at the amusement park. A chart of the Asia–Pacific equity category's calendar-year returns since 1990 is littered with double-digit gains and double-digit losses. But things have been mostly positive since the millennium; the category's median five-year compound annual return was 9.5 percent as of mid-2008.

On the face of it, Asia presents a pretty enticing investment pitch. The success of many Asian countries in escaping their post-colonial poverty and building modern economies has been a genuine miracle, one of humanity's greatest achievements (that and chocolate-chip ice cream). The region has a young population, pro-business governments (although often repressive), and an apparently insatiable desire to become as fat and self-satisfied as the West.

The region's two established stock markets, Tokyo and Hong Kong, are being upstaged by the up-and-coming Shanghai exchange. You may have a hard time considering China a "developing" country — but it certainly is developing, and fast. As a trip to most any North American shopping mall will remind you, China quickly has become a global economic powerhouse.

Economics and politics aside, it's hard to ignore Asia when investing outside Canada. But remember the last time you felt queasy on a rollercoaster? Investing in Asia likely will continue to be a wild ride, so tread lightly when considering an Asian fund investment. Or, again, consider doing so through a diversified global equity or international equity fund.

If you buy into Asia, your first choice is whether you want a fund that includes Japan or treats it as a completely separate market. No right or wrong answer exists here. Asian funds that also hold Japanese stocks represent a sort of handy one-stop-shopping investment in the Far East, much of which is an economic suburb of Japan anyway despite China's recent economic surge. But, arguably, a specialized manager located in Tokyo has a better chance of getting it right in such a distinctive country, as Japan marches to its own very strange Kodo drumbeat. In 2007, the median Asia–Pacific ex-Japan fund (the category representing funds in the region that do not invest in Japan) jumped more than 18 percent in 2007. Meantime, the median Japanese equity fund fell more than 21 percent. So it's hard to believe a manager sitting in Hong Kong or London can hope to become as knowledgeable about the Tokyo scene as someone right on the spot. That suggests you're better off buying a specialized Japanese fund (more about them below) plus an Asia ex-Japan fund that stays out of the Japanese market.

A handful of "country" funds invest only in China, or India, or even a combination of the two. China's economy, of course, has taken off in recent years, and six China funds were available to Canadian investors. India is essentially a continent in its own right, with a potentially giant stock market that moves to its own rhythm. As of mid-2008, but one India-only mutual fund existed. That fund, Excel India, had an unfathomable 202-percent return in 1999, its first full calendar year. Its top holdings included Bharat Heavy Electricals Ltd. and United Phosphorus Ltd. — a bit more exciting and exotic than good old Royal Bank of Canada or Canadian Tire. Excel India went on to post huge losses the next two years, dropping 47 percent in 2000 and 34 percent in 2001. It has been on a tear in recent years, with one-year gains ranging from 24 to 83 percent from 2002 to 2007, but then it lost nearly 39 percent during the first half of 2008.

Japanese, please: Once hot, now not

Japan, land of fast trains, paper walls, and coffin hotels. And, oddly, a place where Wall Street's crash also happened, but ten years earlier. At the end of the 1980s, foreign investors in the then-red-hot Tokyo market reckoned that any price they paid for a stock was okay because the Japanese economy had moved to a new way of valuing assets. So, Nippon Telegraph traded at 100 times its profits in 1989 and people weren't worried — a bit like the way U.S. investors argued in early 2000 that they were being all prudent and careful when they paid 50 times earnings for a telephone-company stock because they were getting an "earnings yield" of 2 percent, which isn't far short of the one-year deposit rate. See "U.S. equity funds: Land of the fat" in this chapter for an explanation of earnings yield and similar magic incantations.

But Japan crashed, as insane stock markets always do. By 1992, the Nikkei average of 225 big Japanese stocks had fallen by half from its highs of the late 1980s and it went nowhere for the rest of the decade. The market made the occasional nice bounce off the bottom, but over the ten years from 1990 to 2000 the median Japanese fund produced a miserable median annual return of 5.3 percent. By mid-2008, the ten-year annual "return" had turned into an exciting annual loss of 1.7 percent.

Nonetheless, Japan still is one of the world's biggest economies, a powerhouse of ingenuity and brilliant design. Any country that has people who devote their lives to mastering the art of tea-pouring has to have something going for it. Everybody should have a small portion of their assets in the great Japanese global companies, such as Sony, Hitachi, and Fujitsu. We suggest you do it by buying a couple of conservative global equity funds. As with other major economic regions of the world, most good global stock funds put at least some of their portfolio in Japan.

How Andrew blew it in mutual funds — And how you can do better

The good news is that the only truly hot mutual fund Andrew ever owned, Altamira Japanese Opportunity, went up 123 percent in 1999. The bad news is that he invested a miserable $200 in it. His failure at picking shoot-the-lights-out mutual funds pretty well convinced him it's a crapshoot trying to figure out which volatile specialty funds will do well and which will bark. If you buy a few quality conservative funds from the start, you'll do fine. Or better than he did, anyway. Around 1994, Andrew decided it would be a good source of newspaper stories if he opened accounts with as many fund companies as he could, including banks and direct sellers such as Altamira. So he opened about ten small accounts, putting only about $1,000 in each or opening a $50 monthly pre-authorized contribution plan. That's the industry's beloved PAC, where they go into your bank account each month and take out the money. It's actually something the fund companies often lose money on, because the investments are small and administration costs are high, so he reckoned there could be something in it for him.

Andrew will admit he's a gambler by nature, so he went for pitbull-aggressive funds. He reckoned there was no gain without pain, stocks always go up, rah rah rah. Altamira Equity (then under the legendary heavy trader Frank Mersch) was his most conservative choice. Otherwise, it was frothy Asian and emerging markets funds, not to mention small-company nightmares and other stuff he prefers to forget. Needless to say, Andrew took some serious hits. The average emerging markets fund lost 7 percent in 1995 and went down in a fairly straight line from there. Japanese funds delivered three straight years of losses — until the carnage of 2000 to 2002, no asset class had probably inflicted that kind of damage since the stock market died in the 1930s. He also bought an energy fund and a precious metals fund, both of which crawled along the bottom until he dumped them around 1998 and switched to regular equity funds.

Even Andrew's Altamira Equity stumbled and fell as resource stocks wore out and financial stocks went up for three years straight. But what was up with old Frank? After all, he had the hottest numbers in the industry. That's why Andrew bought the fund. He remembers once being at a presentation by some pension fund suits who presented the results of a survey that showed a single unnamed manager way out in front. Andrew asked who it was and was told: "That was Mersch." But Frank didn't like banks so he and Andrew missed the party. The lesson is this: Forget about small-cap junk, weird foreign markets, and managers who abandon large sections of the market — at least for the bulk of your savings. Buy funds that invest in a wide range of companies and countries that are familiar to you.

U.S. equity funds: Land of the fat

Back in early 2000, the U.S. stock market looked like a very beautiful thing indeed — but we were standing on the slopes of a mountain, looking back at a gorgeous landscape that was a decade of strong performance. Then the millennium came and Wall Street fell onto hard times. From 2000 through

2007, the median U.S. equity fund posted four calendar-year losses and only one double-digit gain. The other years saw slim gains. The credit crunch of 2007–2008 made things even worse, and the median U.S. equity mutual fund had lost an additional 10 percent by mid-2008.

Maybe the good times will come back — or maybe U.S. stocks will become the greatest horror show in the history of investing as U.S. shares go on falling list-lessly to earth with all the grace of crashing Boeing 747s. Unfortunately, you can't tell what will happen. Nonetheless, America is the engine of the world's economy, a magic lamp of creativity and intellect. So you must have at least some of your savings there. But you don't have to buy regular U.S. equity funds that try to pick winning American stocks. Any sensible global equity fund will own plenty of U.S. companies, so owning a couple of those will give you American content. Add a U.S. equity index fund — one that tracks the entire U.S. market, usually by mimicking the famous Standard & Poor's index of 500 giant U.S. stocks — and you'll have collected plenty of Americana.

In the U.S. market, you must own an index fund because the managers of U.S. equity funds sold in Canada have done a particularly pathetic job of keeping up with the S&P 500. The index produced an average annual loss of 0.8 per-cent in Canadian-dollar terms over the ten years ended June 2008, better than the 2.5-percent loss from the median U.S. equity mutual fund. Nearly all U.S. index funds track the S&P 500 — but, as investors have discovered, the S&P 500 is no perpetual motion machine that always goes up.

One of the reasons why the debacle of the new millennium has been so severe was that by the end of the 1990s the Standard & Poor's index had established a virtuous but insane cycle in which the stocks that made up the index kept going higher simply because they were in the index, which induced investors to buy the stocks in the index at ever-higher prices because it was such a good index to invest in, if you get our drift. Now that's all dandy while it works, but it's also a bit like a Ponzi scheme, a fraud in which late arrivals to the scam pay off the first lucky investors.

 If you want the most diversification in a U.S. index fund, have a look at the **CIBC U.S. Index Fund,** which tracks the Russell 5000 index, a massively broad measure that includes just about every stock that matters in the United States. The idea is that if a long-term decline occurs in the huge blue-chip stocks such as Microsoft Corp. and General Electric Inc. that dominate the S&P 500, then you'll be hedging your bets by owning lots of smaller companies. Speaking of blue-chips, it doesn't get much bluer than the Dow Jones industrial average of 30 industrial stocks — even your aging Aunt Betty in North Bay has heard of "the Dow." While the S&P 500 is a much better barometer of large U.S. stocks, the Dow Jones industrial aver-age is still the most-quoted U.S. index. If you like the familiarity, you can buy an index fund that tracks it, such as the imaginatively named TD Dow Jones Industrial Average Index.

Don't forget that U.S. equity funds are like any type of regional or otherwise overly focused fund: You don't really have to own them. Any well-run global fund will contain a large number of U.S. stocks, because America is just too dynamic to ignore.

Emerging markets funds: And you thought you were corrupt

Emerging markets or developing countries — we'll drop the euphemisms and call these nations what they are: poor. At least two-thirds of the world's population lives in places such as Ghana and Malaysia, where industrial society and all of its plush comforts have yet to fully take root. But why invest there? The theory is that these economies are growing fast from a low level of activity, as opposed to the "mature" economies of the West. Fast growth means corporate profits that are rising quickly — and that's good for stocks, remember?

So these markets are supposed to give you higher long-term returns, at the cost of bigger price swings because shares in these strange places are relatively unstable and prone to dangers such as currency collapse (which nearly always happens, don't kid yourself).

Emerging markets have outperformed many other markets in recent years. The median emerging markets equity mutual fund gained nearly 20 percent during the five years to June 2008, compounded annually, compared with 5.4 percent for global equity mutual funds. However, emerging markets are small and thus far more volatile than North American and other developed markets. That means one or two foreign lads with MBAs — fund managers from the rich world — can make the whole index go up and down. Emerging markets will move independently from developed markets. If your Wall Street shares are tanking, your investment in a Brazilian sewer digger might be doing just fine.

Although the performance numbers have been attractive, you need to ask yourself if you can put up with the volatility. Prior to the recent run-up, an emerging markets fund's returns for the most part were up one year, down the next. As brokers are reputed to say about a junk stock, "It's for trading, not for owning."

Bear in mind other complications with emerging markets, too. One minor difficulty: Managers don't agree on what constitutes a developing market. Some funds have a broad definition of what constitutes a developing market. For example, many emerging markets funds will invest in Hong Kong–listed stocks — needless to say, a well developed market — in addition to emerging markets in the region like Thailand and Vietnam. That produces a more conservative mixture of investments that can protect investors from some of the nasty drops in emerging markets. But it also could mean missing out on big rallies.

The big problem for investors in emerging markets funds is the tendency of nervous managers to slavishly buy the same few stocks around the world, usually the local phone company, in whatever emerging markets they like. So buying two or even three emerging markets funds may not spread your risk as much as you might think — the portfolios often contain the same stuff. In fairness to managers, they're often forced to stick to one or two big stocks in a lot of developing countries because at least they know some sort of professional supervision of the corporate executives is happening, supplied by the other foreign investment managers who own the stock. Many developing countries, like the United States 100 years ago, are still at a stage of cowboy capitalism in which corruption and sharp dealing are rampant.

What ever happened to Latin American funds?

One obvious emerging markets zone is Latin America. These funds at one time were numerous enough to justify a separate category. But investors were reluctant to put all their emerging markets eggs into one geographic basket. By mid-2002, many Latin American equity funds were showing double-digit losses on a ten-year compound annual basis. Fund companies, tired of the poor sales, began to shut down their Latin funds, rolling them into their existing emerging markets funds.

Wouldn't you know it: Latin American markets have produced strong gains since then. The four remaining Latin funds — now lumped into the oddball "specialty" category, which we cover in Chapter 18 — all had five-year compound annual gains near 30 percent or more as of mid-2008. You don't necessarily have to own one of these three — they're offered by Fidelity, Scotia, and TD — to invest in the region, because most emerging markets funds have sizeable positions there.

Latin American markets are about as dangerous as they come. The main justification for investing in Latin America, as with Asia or emerging markets in general, is that these countries are still in the early stages of their economic growth, which means companies there have lots of room to expand. In practice, most managers in the group end up with nearly all of their assets in Mexico and Brazil because the other countries in the region are too small or too impoverished to offer many opportunities. Yes, Latin America has managed a wonderful transition to pretty good democracy, leaving its brutal military regimes of the 1980s behind. However, some exceptions exist — including, much to the frustration of the U.S. government, oil-rich Venezuela. And Latin American politicians still have an unpleasant habit of papering over the cracks in their economies until after they have been elected. At that point, they announce the bad news, sending their currency and stock market sliding. Fresh-faced foreign portfolio managers are inevitably brought along for the ride. Sorry, *gringo*.

Don't get us wrong — we love emerging markets funds, but only as a form of amusement. We enjoy the exotic names, the strange companies, and the potential for huge returns. But the evidence seems to be that as the world's markets become linked ever more closely, shares in developing markets are simply going to track those of rich countries. And most well-run global equity funds hold at least a few big companies in developing markets anyway, which further reduces your need to bother with a specialized emerging markets fund. Sure, put a small portion of your portfolio, at most a few percent, in these funds. But don't go banking on double-digit returns — they come along all too rarely.

Sector Funds: Limitations Galore

Funds that buy stocks in just one industry or sector of the economy — for example, technology or resource funds — are bucking broncos, producing wild leaps and sickening plunges. That's because investors have a long-standing habit, as we've seen, of suddenly falling in love with a particular type of stock and then bidding those companies' shares to ridiculous prices.

The most recent biotech rally was in 2000, when it wasn't unusual to see obscure biotech stocks in Toronto jumping fourfold in a couple of weeks. The median healthcare fund jumped 38 percent that year. Then somebody dropped a jar and biotechs went squelch, and the category fell nearly 35 percent over the next two years.

Specialized funds are far more volatile than high-quality diversified equity funds that hold all industries, the first of our ABC rules in Chapter 10.

The volatility of these funds means they're essentially a gimmick, and not the place for your serious money. Still, they can be fun. Those who enjoy trading can use no-load sector funds as a cheap vehicle for jumping aboard a trend (or what they fondly hope is a trend). And some of the ideas that fund sellers have come up with are impressive: At the end of this section, we talk about some of the weirder sector and specialty funds.

But investors should consider only two types of sector funds:

- Resource and precious metals funds may arguably have a place in the portfolios of those who are very worried about inflation.

- Technology funds, despite their difficulties in recent years, may be good long-term holdings because at least the companies they own are doing something new (although all too often lately it's dreaming up new ways to entice money out of investors).

Resource funds: Pouring money down a hole

Resource funds buy companies that used to be the backbone of Canada's economy: macho, doughnut-eating types that sell oil, forest products, minerals, and basic commodities like aluminum. For complicated reasons to do with oversupply and shifty men meeting in damp hotel rooms in Belgium, the prices for these commodities tend to be extremely volatile, often doubling or falling by half in a matter of months. That means the shares of resource companies are incredibly prone to swings.

Investors in resource companies must get used to living like teenage girls in their first week in junior high. One day they're up, everyone loves them and their shares, and profits are rolling in as commodity prices rock. The next day, prices are down and suddenly everyone in the class thinks you're a freak.

Take oil, for example. Periodically since the 1970s — and most spectacularly in the past few years — the producers have been able to get together in one of those Belgian hotel rooms, sip warm beer, and rig prices for a while. Oil company stocks duly rise accordingly. But it's pretty well a mug's game trying to predict when oil booms will come and go, and oil exploration companies have been abysmal at creating long-term wealth for their shareholders. When their shares rise, they tend to flood new share issues into the hot market to grab as much cash from investors as possible while the going is good — sorry, to raise capital for developing new reserves. Eventually, existing shareholders realize that, thanks a lot, they now must give some of the company's profits and dividends to all those scruffy new shareholders. Then oil prices tank again and, presto, oil stocks collapse. No wonder investors in Canada have largely favoured oil and gas income trusts, which at least pay out a steady stream of cash. (Refer to Chapter 5 for more on income trusts.)

Although natural resource funds have been on a roll since the millennium, if you look farther back in time you'll be reminded of how uneven this market can be. In the second half of the 1990s, resource funds were a rough place to invest, with the average fund in the group posting back-to-back losses in 1997 and 1998, in an era when consecutive yearly losses were still rare. Resource funds delivered an abysmal annual return of just 3.1 percent during the 1990s. But when the tech became long in the tooth, investors began to look elsewhere and turned to natural resources. Many commodity stocks took off — especially in oil and gold, which were lifted by soaring prices for energy and bullion — and resource funds posted strong gains in 1999 and 2000. Their gains cooled somewhat in 2002, but then took off again. As of mid-2008, the median natural resource mutual fund had posted a five-year compound annual return of nearly 29 percent.

The rise in precious metals funds, which buy mostly gold miners' stocks (the easiest way to bet on gold), also has been spectacular. The price of gold bullion prices rose from less than US$260 an ounce in early 2001 to nearly US$1,000 by mid-2008. Despite a money-losing 2004, the median precious metals mutual fund had a five-year compound annual return of more than 20 percent as of mid-2008.

Why has the price of gold shot up? Well, conspiracy theories abound when it comes to precious metals prices (dark mutterings abound of a plot to keep gold down to protect the U.S. dollar), but the simple answer is that gold tends to rise when the world loses confidence in its paper money as a store of value. And the U.S. greenback certainly has had its woes of late, thanks to the policies of the Bush administration and the credit crisis. Gold is the world's oldest form of money. It soared back in 1980, when investors around the world were scared that geopolitics was spinning out of control (Jimmy Carter had just stumbled through the Iranian hostage situation and the Soviet Union had invaded Afghanistan). Inflation is also great for gold prices because it means paper money is losing its value, which makes timeless and readily portable bullion more valuable. But gold slid during the 1990s, after Communism collapsed and America basked in a low-inflation golden age. The latest rally in gold began as a partial recovery from bullion's slump in the late 1990s — for most of that decade, the yellow metal traded well above $325 before heading south.

Very conservative investors may wish to put small amounts into a couple of diversified resource funds, perhaps a couple of percent of one's portfolio in each fund, or even a couple of gold funds. That's because resource stocks can act as portfolio insurance — commodity prices move in their own weird cycles, and sometimes in the opposite direction to stocks in general.

Before you rush to buy into resource stocks along with everybody else, or catch the gold bug a little too late, consider a much simpler and somewhat less risky way to invest in these markets: Just buy a Canadian equity fund, large-cap or small (see Chapters 10 and 11). If you do decide to buy resource funds, try to buy two with very different portfolio mixtures of forestry, energy, mining, and other commodities. That way, if one manager crashes and burns, the other might make it. And if you buy into gold funds, make sure you hold at least two, because managers can easily miss out on the very hottest mining stocks that are leading the whole group higher. Remember, with most precious metals funds you are buying mining companies, not bullion.

Science and technology funds: But how will you control it, Professor?

Technology funds can buy virtually anything as long as it has something to do with computers, telecommunications, biotechnology, or research. But they're really just super-high-growth equity funds that hold fancy companies trading at Versace-type prices.

Back in 1994, Canada had about five science and technology funds. By the end of the decade at least 35 existed, and by mid-2002 more than 100 were kicking around. Incredible returns on technology stocks during the 1990s, which reached a hysterical climax of greed and speculation by 2000, produced 100-percent-plus returns for investors in technology funds who were brave enough to hang on for the whole ride. Then the technology market collapsed. The median science and technology fund posted massive losses from 2000 through 2002, then recovered somewhat in 2003. Since then the category has stumbled along, posting small gains or losses each year. The typical investor who didn't get out in time lost all the profits he or she made during the run-up in tech stocks, and then some.

We'll spare you a dull sermon about the danger of investing in wild tech funds. Back in 1999 and 2000, people just had to look at the sort of returns these things had posted, and a shifty, greedy look came into their eyes. And, for all we know, technology stocks might start climbing again, to as-yet-undreamed-of heights. Doesn't seem likely, though. So if you think the party's going to continue, go ahead and buy these funds.

If you decide to buy a science and technology fund — and we advise against it for most investors because of the excessive risk — limit your investment to less than 5 percent of your total fund holdings.

Some people reckon they've got a pretty sharp tooth when it comes to technology, which lets them predict which industries will do best next. In that case, you could select more specialized types of tech funds, such as a telecommunications fund, which gives you "exposure" (money management slang for a chance to profit from something) to telephone, Internet, and wireless companies that continue to revolutionize communications — and that drive consumers crazy with incomprehensible telecommunications "bundles" and little hand-held devices that presented frightening challenges to our thumbs and necks and have created a whole new treatment-specialty area for physiotherapists and orthopedic surgeons. Or you could consider investing in a biotechnology fund, which buys into obscure companies selling strange new drugs and bits of protein in jars.

Technology fund managers like to put on statesmanlike, long-term faces and predict that the companies in their portfolios today will be the giant household names of tomorrow, as though the kids will be pestering you to take them out to look at the new network routers from Cisco Systems or log on to Sun Microsystems' latest servers.

The high priests and priestesses of tech-forever may have a point, and these companies could have many years of exponential growth ahead of them. So there could be a good case for holding a tech fund if you're investing for long periods of, say, ten years or more. But a few good global and Canadian equity funds, including index funds, will own plenty of the big tech stocks that show up in specialized technology funds — so, once again, you'll probably be well covered by simply sticking with your core equity funds. As with so many other specialty funds, buy these only for fun. And get ready to take some spills along the way.

Beware of markets in which people buy for trading, not for owning. They have a nasty habit of collapsing.

Financial services funds: Buying the banks doesn't always pay

Everybody hates the banks — except as investments, it seems. The Canadian financial services sector is dominated by the huge Big Five banks and several mammoth life insurance companies. Indeed, these institutions are almost as big a driver of the Canadian stock market as resource companies. However, most funds in the financial services category invest globally, so you are buying into not just Canadian institutions but U.S. and overseas ones as well. So if you want to buy Canadian financials, stick to the Canadian equity category — which, as we keep preaching, is a better place to be anyway.

The median financial services fund produced five- and ten-year compound annual returns in the range of 1 to 2 percent as of mid-2008, well below the returns posted by the median Canadian equity fund. Funds in this sector fared better, more or less, than global and U.S. equity funds, though, which strengthens the case to buy Canadian in this sector.

If you insist on focusing on the Canadian financials rather than participating in this sector through a diversified Canadian equity fund, you can buy the iShares Canadian Financial Sector Index ETF. Its five-year compound annual return at mid-2008 was 11.5 percent.

Chapter 13

Balanced Funds: Boring Can Be Good

*E*ver have a really good roti — a West Indian treat packed with extra spices, tasty meat, and East Indian–style stuff like chickpeas? Remember the wonderful numb feeling of fullness afterward? Balanced funds are supposed to be a satisfying all-in-one meal like that. You hand your money over to the fund company or bank, and they make all the decisions. A balanced fund is a nice broad mixture of many types of investment — the idea being that it'll never lose too much money. The manager usually invests the fund in a cautious blend of stocks, which are tiny pieces of ownership of companies, and long-term and short-term bonds, which are debts owed by governments and companies.

Balanced funds are investment products you buy when you want nice steady returns of around 4 to 7 percent per year while avoiding losses as much as possible. They're one of the mutual fund industry's most useful inventions and an excellent place for the nervous beginner to get going. In this chapter, we introduce you to the main types of balanced funds, explain why they're a great way to start off in investing, and warn you about the problems you may encounter.

Understanding Balanced Funds

Balanced funds are for busy people who want a one-decision product they can buy and forget about. Imagine your family had a trusted lawyer or accountant who took care of all of your investing needs — the professional, if he or she were at all prudent, would end up putting the money into a judicious blend of bonds and stocks, with a healthy cushion of cash to further reduce risk. That's the essence of a balanced fund — it includes a little bit of everything so that losses can be kept to a minimum if one type of investment falls in value.

Balanced funds, which have been around since the dawn of the fund industry in the 1920s in one form or another, have attracted billions of dollars in recent years as confused investors decide to let someone else pick the right mix for their savings. As of June 2008, more than $250 billion in total assets were in some sort of balanced fund. That's a lot of coin when you consider it's not too far off the equity fund total of $311 billion. (These figures are from the Investment Funds Institute of Canada, which represents most mutual fund sponsors.)

Reviewing the asset mix of balanced funds

For most investors, a balanced fund should be a ready-made cautious investment portfolio. Yes, it might lose money — nothing is absolutely safe in investing — but it's unlikely to drop as much as 10 percent in a year. Just check the fund's mix of assets at the fund company's Web site or in its handouts. If the fund holds plenty of bonds and cash, it's probably safe enough to buy.

Happily, the knowledgeable and practical folks who supervise the classification of Canadian investment funds into various asset categories, the Canadian Investment Funds Standards Committee, several years ago split the unwieldy Canadian balanced and global balanced categories each into three subsets. The following categories help investors immediately identify a fund's asset mix:

- **Equity balanced funds** have at least 60 percent of their portfolio in equities.
- **Fixed-income balanced funds** have no more than 40 percent of their portfolio in equities.
- **Neutral balanced funds** have between 40 and 60 percent of their portfolio in equities.

To keep things simple, in this chapter we primarily refer to the middle-of-the-road Canadian neutral balanced category.

Remember the old rule that your portfolio's weighting in bonds plus cash should equal your age? If we assume the average Canadian balanced fund has 54 percent in stocks and 46 percent in guaranteed investments like bonds and cash, then most neutral balanced funds are suitable for investors aged about 46. So if you're younger, look for a slightly more aggressive mix in an equity balanced fund, and if you're older, try to find a fixed income balanced fund that appeals to you.

Plodding along profitably

The good news is that Canadian balanced funds have done a pretty good job of avoiding — or at least limiting — losses. In 2002, the last calendar year in which Canadian equity funds lost money, with the median fund falling nearly 13 percent, the median Canadian neutral balanced fund fell about 6 percent. Of course, balanced funds do a decent job of limiting gains, too. As of mid-2008, the median Canadian equity fund did more than twice as well as the median Canadian neutral balanced fund in terms of five-year compound annual return: 16.3 percent versus 7.9 percent.

In terms of a global balanced fund — a type of fund we really like because it provides as much diversification as possible within a single fund — it's even better. In 2002, the median global equity fund plummeted more than 20 percent while the median global neutral balanced fund fell just 4.4 percent. Yet despite the more hospitable years for stock markets that followed, the balanced funds managed to match the five-year compound annual return of the equity funds, at 5.4 percent. Part of this is due to 2007, when global equities were dragged down by the debacle in the U.S. stock market, while Canadian stocks shone.

Now, we know that, over the years, a few weak balanced funds got lost in the shuffle after they were merged into better funds, but that's not a bad showing. The fund industry, always remember, has a habit of quietly folding under-performers into its stars, cancelling the dogs' years of terrible returns. For example, Fidelity in the mid-1990s took a weak balanced fund and popped it inside its huge Fidelity Canadian Asset Allocation Fund. The old fund's poor returns vanished forever. It's always possible that you'll find yourself stuck in a similar underperformer. To minimize that risk, the best solution of all is to hold two balanced funds so that your entire portfolio doesn't suffer from weakness in one fund. (Morningstar calculates rates of return that overcome this data weakness — known to data geeks and analysts as *survivorship bias* — with its Morningstar fund indices; for more about these indices, see Chapter 21.)

Don't worry: Despite the broad licence many fund managers have taken in their definition, balanced funds are all about simplicity. Until you make up your mind about your long-term investing plans, you'll almost certainly do fine over three to five years by simply buying a regular balanced fund, or two for more safety, and then forgetting about them.

Retiring with balanced funds

If you really want to adopt a simple approach, use balanced funds in your *registered retirement savings plan* — a special account in which investment gains add up without being taxed until you take them out, usually at retirement (see Chapter 22). Balanced funds are a nice cautious mix, just the thing you want for your life savings. Younger investors can be more aggressive, putting nearly all of their money into stocks, but above the age of 35 it's a wise idea to own bonds as well. Nothing is forever. If you decide later that you want something else in your RRSP, maybe because the balanced fund you picked turned out to be a dog, then it should be a simple matter to shift the money to another fund or funds within the same RRSP or to another RRSP account without incurring taxes.

So if you just want a simple investment to buy and forget, go for one or two balanced funds. A balanced fund has a single unit value that's published daily in the newspapers and on the Internet, making the value of your holdings easy to check. Its return appears in the papers every month and on the Internet every day. And the performance is also published clearly by the fund company, or should be. As with any regular mutual fund, if you've bought a pooch the whole world can see, the fund manager will be under pressure to improve it.

Steering clear of potholes: Consistently strong returns

Balanced fund managers' scaredy-cat caution has served investors well. As stocks slid in the first half of 2002, the average balanced fund escaped with a modest loss of 5.9 percent, less than half as bad as the median Canadian equity fund.

During the last 25 years, the only year in which Canadian equity funds posted a loss that was less severe than that of Canadian neutral balanced funds was in 1994, when the equity funds lost 2.6 percent while the balanced group fell 3.1 percent. But that wasn't really the fault of the balanced fund managers. Interest rates jumped suddenly that year, slashing the value of the bonds they held.

Otherwise, balanced funds have generated nice steady returns, just as they're supposed to. But remember that balanced funds — and all other investors who own bonds — have had a gale at their backs since the early 1990s, because the drop in inflation has made bonds steadily more valuable. (See Chapter 14 for more on bonds.) Then the inflation rate spiked in mid-2008, precipitating a reminder that bonds easily can under-perform stocks. The Canadian consumer price index doubled to 3.4 percent during the second quarter of 2008. During that period, the median Canadian fixed-income fund fell nearly a percentage point, while Canadian Equity funds jumped more than 7 percent. Thanks to the sagging bond market, Canadian neutral balanced mutual funds were held to a modest 1.4 percent return during the quarter.

If we move into an era of deflation (that is, falling prices), bonds will almost certainly become increasingly more valuable because the value of their steady payouts of cash rises consistently. In that case, which unfortunately could involve a very painful recession, balanced funds could easily outperform stock funds. But whatever happens, the point remains: A balanced fund is a safe spot for your money, leaving you to get on with your life.

Taking a look at one balanced biggie

Take a look at the biggest Canadian neutral balanced fund, Royal Bank of Canada's RBC Balanced Fund, to get an idea of how a traditional balanced fund works. In mid-2008, this fund had just over $9 billion in assets. Remember, that's more than a million dollars 9,000 times over — so obviously the bank has been delivering something that Mr. and Ms. Canada want: an attractive rate of return with minimal losses.

Here's a breakdown of the fund's assets:

- 30 percent in Canadian stocks
- 16 percent in shares outside Canada
- Just under one-third in bonds
- About 10 percent in cash

The fund has a one-year loss of 0.4 percent as of mid-2008, performing slightly better than the 0.8-percent loss posted by the median Canadian neutral balanced fund. At 5.4 percent, its ten-year compound annual return was a tad better than the median fund's 5 percent. In other words, it was a typical balanced fund: a solid investment that's fine for your portfolio if one of your key objectives is security.

Reviewing the Problems with Balanced Funds

Balanced funds, both Canadian and global, have their problems. Their fees and expenses are far too lavish, which scythes into investors' already modest returns. Fund companies have come up with their usual bewildering variety of products and combinations of products, waving magic wands and muttering incantations that invoke the gods of portfolio theory and the "efficient frontier." It may all be true, but one thing's for sure: You're paying for it. All balanced products are basically porridge. Returns from their different investments are mixed together in a gooey mess, so judging exactly how well the manager did on which asset is hard.

High fees and expenses

The costs and fees charged to balanced fund unitholders are just too high. Fund companies already run big equity and bond funds, paying the salaries and expenses of the people who manage them, and they usually get those people to help select the stuff in their balanced funds. How much extra work is involved in that? The bond manager basically just does the same job again with his or her portion of the balanced fund, and the equity manager does the same. Some geezer in a huge black robe and cone-shaped hat decides what the asset mix will be and you're away to the races. As Table 13-1 shows, the median Canadian neutral balanced fund vacuums up 2.5 percent of its investors' money each year, almost as bad as the 2.6 percent charged by the average Canadian equity fund.

Table 13-1	Balanced Fund MERs
Category (Mutual Funds Only)	*Median MER*
Canadian equity balanced	2.29
Canadian neutral balanced	2.30
Canadian fixed income balanced	1.99
Global equity balanced	2.44
Global neutral balanced	2.36
Global fixed income balanced	2.09

The long-term annual return from balanced funds may be only about 7 percent, or even less. The long term, incidentally, means the rest of our lives, as economists like to say (it's the only joke they know). So, say inflation and taxes combined take 4 percent out of your annual 6 percent — then your real return is down to around 3 percent. So, for a tax-paying account, most of your real return from a balanced fund like Royal Bank's giant may go into fund expenses and fees.

Bewildering brews of assets

Fund companies know that many of their customers just want simple solutions they can buy and never look at again. So they've come up with a bewildering array of balanced combinations in which you can buy their wares. See Chapter 20 on fund packages for more. Many of these arrangements, such as Mackenzie Financial Corp.'s "Star" and AGF's "Elements" packages, have their own unit values, making them look very much like mutual funds themselves. By mid-2008, more than 2,200 Canadian and global balanced funds existed, counting different "classes" of fund units as separate funds.

Difficulty judging fund manager performance

A big difficulty with balanced funds, or any kind of casserole that you buy from a fund company, is that you may have a hard time knowing just what the manager did right or wrong. He or she may have blown it in bonds, or struck out in stocks, but you can't work it out from the comfortable-looking (you hope) overall return number that the company publishes. Some fund companies provide a commentary that at least gives you a clue as to what went right and what exploded in the manager's shiny little face. For many customers that's fine, because they couldn't care less what went on inside the fund as long as the return is reasonably good. And that's a perfectly sensible approach to take if you don't have the time or interest to look further into mutual funds. But balanced funds are opaque and mysterious, violating one of the huge virtues of mutual funds — the ability to check on performance easily.

Because checking where balanced funds' profits came from is difficult, picking the right fund is harder than it is to pick funds in other categories. In other words, you won't get a clear answer to this crucial question: How much risk did the manager take? Here's an extreme example of two imaginary funds to help illustrate the point.

Say you're trying to choose between two balanced funds:

- ✔ The Tasmanian Devil Fund, which made an average 11 percent over the past ten years, enough to turn $10,000 into $28,394

- ✔ The Mellow Llama Fund, which made 9 percent a year and turned $10,000 into $23,674, or almost $5,000 less than the Tasmanian Devil

What if the Devil Fund made its bigger profits by buying bonds and shares issued by risky little technology companies, whereas the Llama Fund owned shares and bonds from big and stable companies and governments? Most balanced fund investors would choose the second fund, because the danger of it crashing and losing, say, half of its value in a year is so much less.

The Devil Fund, with its volatile but high-profit-potential stocks, may be suitable for an investor who doesn't need the money for years and can afford to take risks now. But it's not the right fund for an investor who may need the money at any time.

A Simple Plan for Picking the Right Canadian Balanced Fund

When selecting a balanced fund, you needn't get all worked up about picking the right one. Like money market and bond funds, many balanced funds resemble one another. They're run cautiously, remember, so you're unlikely to go too far wrong.

Too many investors make one classic mistake that has cost millions of dollars: Failing to think twice before buying a balanced fund run by the people who also manage your stock fund. First, it will almost certainly be skewed toward equities. Second, within the fund's equity section, you'll likely be putting too many eggs in one basket within the fund's equity section. Naturally, the managers will tend to select the same shares for both funds, and if they get that wrong, then both of your funds will be poor performers.

We frequently refer to the neutral categories in this chapter because we feel these represent the only true, traditional balanced funds — the type that provide the uninspiring but steady performance making these funds so popular and fundamental to the average Canadian investor.

Figure 13-1 compares the three categories' returns over 25 years.

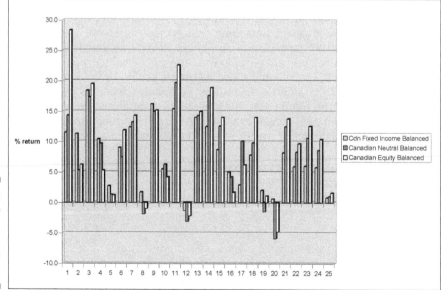

Figure 13-1: How Canadian balanced fund returns compare.

Source: Morningstar

Knowing what to avoid

Be careful with balanced funds that don't include just about every industry in their list of stock holdings. After all, if they are truly "balanced," the balance should extend across industry sectors (and, in the case of bonds, maturity dates). Consider the fate of investors in the Ivy Growth & Income Fund — with assets of about $2.3 billion, one of the biggest Canadian balanced funds as of mid-2008. The fund was very overweight in consumer staples stocks, which took a beating during the first half of 2008. ("Overweight" refers to its position relative to that of the benchmark index, the S&P/TSX composite, which had just 2.2 percent of its constituent stocks in the consumer staples group as of mid-2008.) As a result, the fund lost 4 percent during that period, while the median Canadian equity balanced fund slipped 0.4 percent.

Identifying the best funds

Relax: Picking a good-quality Canadian balanced fund is surprisingly easy. Easier, anyway, than getting a cranky, tired child into a snowsuit at 7 a.m. Look for the following:

- **A wide asset mix to reduce the fund's risk of loss:** Under the industry's agreed definition, a middle-of-the-road (that is, neutral) balanced fund should have at least 40 percent of its portfolio anchored in cash or bonds or other liquid short-term securities. (*Liquidity* is a measure of how easy it is to sell an investment without suffering a significant loss.)

- **Low expenses:** This is important because returns are relatively modest with this type of fund. Try to choose a fund or funds with annual expenses lower than the median 2.3 percent for Canadian neutral balanced funds.

Looking at some high-quality balanced funds

In this section, we list the picks of the litter in Canadian balanced funds. Because being obsessive about costs is essential when buying this type of fund, we've limited the sample to funds with modest annual fees and expenses. Remember, though, if inflation and/or interest rates rise abruptly, then even the most boring of Canadian balanced funds will probably lose money. That's because the value of both their stock and bond portfolios will almost certainly go on the slide at the same time. Here are a few high-quality Canadian balanced funds, chosen with the help of analysts at Morningstar:

- ✔ **TD Dividend Income** is an example of why you can't judge a fund's content by its name. This fund is actually a balanced fund; its sibling TD Dividend Growth is classified as a dividend income fund. Anyway, TD Dividend Income is a little more aggressive than most balanced funds because it invests heavily in banking and other financial services stocks. Before you dismiss it as being too volatile for your balanced fund tastes, realize it has an excellent management team at its helm. The equity portion of the fund has more individual holdings than the typical balanced fund and they tend to be more conservative picks, helping to offset some of the risk. On the fixed-income side, the portfolio has more corporate bonds than most other balanced funds, but this extra credit risk is tempered by a very conservative duration stance. (Bond investing can be complicated; see Chapter 14.)

  The managers are part of a team that looks after TD's top-rated income-oriented fund lineup. These funds are a good example of how the banks have become extremely competitive in the mutual fund industry. We discuss the banks' role in the industry in Chapter 7.

- ✔ **CI Signature High Income** is a balanced fund that provides a good income stream. Its blend of common equities, income trusts, and high-yield debt has historically given it an asset mix unlike any other fund in the Canadian equity balanced category. Although this fund brings some risks to the balanced-fund table — it generally does not invest in government debt or even investment-grade bonds, preferring higher-yield corporate issues — it mitigates this risk by moving into cash when market storm clouds gather. It also has been known to invest in *floating-rate notes,* which offer partial protection against rising interest rates because their coupons adjust to rate fluctuations. Eric Bushell, the fund's lead manager, has a terrific track record on this and other CI funds. And you get top management for a very reasonable 1.55 percent in annual fund expenses.

- ✔ **PH&N Balanced** is a more traditional balanced fund with an asset allocation of 60 percent equities, 35 percent bonds, and 5 percent cash. Unlike many of its peers, it has the ability to invest anywhere in the world, although as of mid-2008 it was classified in the Canadian neutral balanced category. The fund's Canadian, U.S., international, and bond managers all have excellent track records, and it is another fund that offers solid management at a bargain. Its annual expenses are just 0.86 percent — way below the 2.3 percent charged by the median fund in the category.

Global Balanced Funds — As Good as It Gets?

Those who want to chase (possibly) higher returns outside Canada while spreading their wealth over a huge range of investments may want to explore global balanced funds, which, like Canadian balanced funds, come in three varieties: equity balanced, neutral balanced, and fixed-income balanced. (For definitions of each of those categories, see "Understanding Balanced Funds" in this chapter.)

As always, check the top holdings in the portfolio of a global balanced fund. If they're not mostly stocks and bonds issued by giant companies that you've already heard of, plus bonds from countries such as the United States, Germany, and Japan, then look elsewhere. Why take a risk on low-quality investments?

Like their Canadian counterparts, global balanced funds pull off the trick of buying a bit of everything, but the fact that they do it globally gives you even more diversification and the potential for higher returns. Very few have been around for even ten years, but the median global neutral balanced mutual fund's five-year annualized return as of June 2008 was 5.4 percent, well behind Canadian equity funds dragged down by fixed-income investments. Figure 13-2 compares performance of the three global balanced categories.

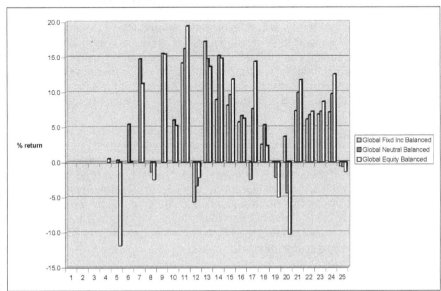

Figure 13-2: How global balanced fund returns compare.

Source: Morningstar

Insisting on low costs is important with any balanced fund, Canadian or global, because so much of the portfolio is made up of steady-but-dull bonds and cash, and that keeps annual gains down. So if you want to be left with a decent return, you can't pay too much.

The median global neutral balanced fund hits its investors for 2.36 percent in expenses each year. That MER works out to $118 annually on a $5,000 investment. Some global balanced funds charge well above that, in excess of 3 percent. These include funds with fancy features, such as *segregated funds* — funds that provide guarantees to refund some or all of your original investment after ten years or to pay at least that much to your heirs (those snivelling jellyfish), even if the fund has in fact produced a loss. These guaranteed or "segregated" funds may give you enormous satisfaction in knowing your money is protected. For that reason, thousands of people buy them. But, like the overpriced extended warranty that pushy electronics salespeople try to get you to buy, such guarantees are usually not worth paying for on something as stable as a balanced fund, which rarely loses money. (We tell the whole story on segregated funds in Chapter 19.)

Few funds of any sort lose money over ten years (except for the speculative gamblers' funds we look at in Chapter 12), and that means the guarantee is of limited value. So to keep costs down and returns up, look for a global balanced fund with an MER lower than the median 2.36 percent.

Going global: A near-perfect investment?

If you had to invest money in a single fund for 100 years without ever moving it or looking at it, some kind of global balanced fund with low expenses would make sense. The global balanced fund has finally caught the imagination of Canadian investors, with the number of these funds nearly tripling between mid-2003 and mid-2008, with $90 billion in total assets. The majority of these assets, happily, are in the global neutral balanced category.

In some ways, the dull old global balanced fund is the perfect mutual fund. Look at the portfolio of any sophisticated, wealthy investor and it'll almost certainly contain stocks all over the world plus bonds, with the safety cushion of a little cash. That's what a global balanced fund provides for the average person. It offers instant access to a professionally chosen mixture of investments that should produce a consistent return on their money while staying clear of market gambles. Nearly every major fund seller sells some sort of global balanced fund, and it's a simple matter of dumping your money in and forgetting about it.

Where did all the income balanced funds go?

As inflation and interest rates tumbled in the 1990s and stayed near historic lows for many years, older people who were trying to live off their savings have had to cope with an unpleasant reality. With inflation below 3 percent, the rates seniors got on their GICs and other accounts were at a subsistence level of no more than 4 percent — and, as interest income, it's fully taxable. That's one of the drawbacks of low inflation: It leaves those who live on a fixed income high and dry. While inflation rose rapidly during the first part of 2008, few deposit rates were above 3 percent as of mid-2008.

The mutual fund industry has benefited from a huge invasion of "GIC refugees" since the mid-1990s. The companies' little elves figured out a way to deliver one of the things these people held dear: a nice regular cheque in the mail. The problem was that mutual funds aren't really designed for producing a predictable spinoff of cash — or, at least, enough cash to satisfy investors, especially when companies take out MERs of up to 2 percent to pay the managers and provide forage for brokers. Finding top-quality bonds or shares that had a high enough yield to satisfy everyone was hard. All the good stuff had been driven up to such high prices by other investors hungry for a stream of cash.

Thus was born the *income balanced fund,* an odd hybrid that's usually designed not only to throw off plenty of interest and dividends, but also to gain or at least hold its value over the long term. For example, an income balanced fund might try to generate monthly payments of $50, or $600 a year, for an investor who held $10,000 worth of the fund. That's a yield of 6 percent annually, but some funds chase even higher rates of up to 9 or 10 percent. To produce this income while also holding its value in the face of inflation, the fund buys a mixture of bonds, shares, and other sorts of investments that pay out cash. The new fund managers were turned loose like hungry bears to grab and eat anything in the world — animal, vegetable, or mineral — that threw off a decent stream of interest or dividend payments. The shortage of good-quality investments producing a decent yield became so acute that many of these managers have been obliged to move down the food chain. They've had to buy *income trusts* as well as *real estate trusts* and similar funds that invest in other stuff. These trusts are sort of like mutual funds themselves, but they hold a narrow collection of properties, such as a few power stations, gas wells, or other relatively dull and predictable businesses.

But as income balanced funds snowballed in number, they eventually needed to be classified in different ways. They're now scattered across a number of categories, including Canadian dividend and income, Canadian income trusts, and the two fixed income balanced categories. See Chapter 16 for more on dividend and income funds, and income trust funds.

Over the short term — particularly in recent years — relying on a global balanced fund to address all your investing needs might not seem so shrewd. A big risk attached to a global balanced fund, as with any foreign fund, is the possibility that Canada's economy, and with it the loonie, will prosper relative to the United States and other countries. Well, guess what happened during the past few years. Right. A climbing loonie relative to foreign currencies slashed the value of your foreign holdings in Canadian-dollar terms, an unpleasant prospect for those who plan to retire in this country. That's why it's almost certainly a good idea to own Canadian assets, too.

Examining a couple of world-beaters

In this section we highlight a couple of high-quality investments that are unlikely to lead you far astray. But bear in mind that any fund can go into a slump because the manager made a bad call. And buying a global balanced fund is always a compromise, because you cannot know exactly what sort of assets you'll end up owning or how precisely the manager produced his or her returns. A balanced fund is for investors who just want a quick, instant solution.

Here are a couple of global balanced funds with low MERs favoured by Morningstar:

- ✔ **PH&N Balanced** is a traditional balanced fund, currently classified as a Canadian neutral balanced fund, but would be more at home in the global balanced category depending on management's outlook on foreign versus domestic markets. The Canadian, U.S., international, and bond teams are all strong and experienced, with excellent track records to back them up. The offering's MER of 0.86 percent is lower than nearly all of its competitors and is less than the weighted-average of its component funds.

- ✔ **Trimark Global Balanced** has managed to escape fallout from the many highly publicized manager departures and lagging performance that have put a cloud over many of Trimark's fund offerings. But with lead manager Bruce Harrop still making the calls, and long-time fixed income manager Rex Chong riding shotgun, this fund remains in good hands. It's a tad pricey though, with an MER of 2.34 percent.

Tactical Balanced Funds: Pay Me to Lose Your Money

Tactical balanced funds, also known as asset allocation funds, are the unruly younger brothers of balanced funds — given the freedom to raise hell by dumping all their bonds or stocks, and to chase hot returns with lopsided portfolios. ("Tactical" simply means that the fund makes short-term bets on moves in the different asset classes every few months. The conventional balanced fund categories, on the other hand, contain funds with *strategic* portfolios, which usually means a manager adheres to a rigid asset-allocation mandate over the years as required by the fund's stated investment mandate.)

These are funds that move between different types of investments and take bigger risks than regular balanced funds, all in an attempt to earn fatter returns. For example, a fund of this type may sell nearly all of its bonds and seek big profits with a portfolio that's made up almost entirely of shares. Or it might even move heavily into a volatile area of the stock market such as technology stocks. The idea is that the manager is smart and lucky enough to anticipate big swings in the prices of financial assets — history shows, though, that very few people can pull off that trick consistently.

All flash and no pan: Looking at asset allocation returns and management styles

The median Canadian tactical asset allocation fund posted a ten-year compound annual return of only 3.3 percent as of mid-2008. That was not as good as the 5-percent return from the median Canadian neutral balanced fund, supposedly a sedate compromise between low risk and steady appreciation. Over five years, the tactical group put in a better showing, with a compound annual return of 7.1 percent at June 2008 compared with 7.9 percent for Canadian neutral balanced funds.

A few star performers shine among tactical balanced funds run by managers who have managed to consistently generate returns in the top half of the pack — including the $7-billion Fidelity Canadian Asset Allocation Fund, which was the top performer on a five-year compound annual basis at mid-2008, up 11.5 percent. Other strong five-year performers include

- Investors Group's Counsel Funds
- Empire Life Insurance Co.
- CI Funds

Ultimately, these funds basically represent an opportunity to watch someone mess around with your money. That's fine if you trust the company and the warty old wizard or witch mixing up the ingredients in the cauldron, but remember that the less balanced a portfolio, the greater the exposure to loss if the main asset class goes into a slump.

Who's running this crazy show?

Much as we'd love to portray tactical balanced fund managers as wild, blonde, Finnish women dressed in leather and thundering down the highway of life on bucking portfolios full of junk bonds and Internet stocks, in reality they're pretty similar to balanced fund managers. Unassuming folk in conservative business attire, that is. A major fund seller is unlikely to let an asset allocation fund slide off the road completely because the manager took crazy bets.

In fact, the typical tactical balanced fund's asset allocation isn't that different from what you'd find in a neutral balanced fund. In mid-2008, the weighted average tactical balanced fund was 61 percent stocks, 25 percent bonds, and 13 percent cash, and the Canadian neutral balanced fund mix was 53:34:11. So the tactical fund was not exactly providing a night of passion beside a cooling Harley. Moreover, the median tactical fund comes with a higher MER than its staid cousin — 2.47 percent versus 2.3 percent.

The bottom line on asset allocation funds: Put your money in one if you find regular balanced funds too boring, but get ready to pay more in fees — and be prepared to lose if the manager gets it wrong.

Chapter 14

Bond Funds: Boring Can Be Sexy, Too

*B*uying a bond means you're lending money to the government or company that issued the thing. The word "bond" means promise, indicating the borrowers have given their word they'll be around to pay interest and refund the loan. All you're really entitled to get back are the periodic interest payments plus the return of all your money when the debt comes due.

Dull, huh? Bond funds simply hold a bunch of these loans, collecting the interest cheques and cashing in the bonds when they mature. That means bond funds tend to plod along with modest returns, while stocks fly and crash from year to year. Equity (or stock market) funds, with their promise of apparently limitless growth, just seem so much more exciting. But remember that bonds along with stocks represent the two main financial assets you can invest in for the long term — while a little bit of cash on the side is an essential safety valve for nearly any portfolio.

In this chapter we explain why it's wise to own at least one bond fund, show you how to pick a good one, and help you work out how much you need to invest in bonds.

Some Great Reasons to Choose Bonds

Almost any sophisticated investor's holdings should include a good leavening of bonds, because betting the whole wad on shares is just too crazy. That's because it bares your entire savings to nasty losses if the stock market turns down. Some fund salespeople and diehard stock market players used to strut and boast that "I've never owned a bond," but they miss out on the advantages bonds offer.

Offering greater security than equities

Although stocks are generally acknowledged to have better long-term performance than bonds, surprisingly, Canadian stocks have an edge of less than a percentage point over domestic bonds over 25 years. The Standard & Poor's/Toronto Stock Exchange composite index's 25-year compound annual return was 10.1 percent as of mid-2008, compared with the DEX universe bond index's 9.5 percent.

The *DEX index* tracks a combination of investment-grade Canadian bonds, including federal, provincial, municipal, and investment-grade corporate bonds that mature in more than one year. Until 2007, the DEX fixed income indices formerly were known as the Scotia Capital indices. The indices' owner, the Toronto Stock Exchange, changed the name after it began taking fixed-income data from multiple dealers, not just Scotia. DEX is a new derivatives exchange being launched by the TSX and an international partner.

Bonds have done particularly well in recent years, aided by falling inflation and the declining interest rates that come with it. What's more, bonds can provide a steadier performance. The DEX index lost money only twice during that 25-year span, and provided healthy returns in the each of the six years the S&P/TSX was in the red (see Figure 14-1).

But, numbers aside, here's why you must own some bonds or bond funds: Lending your money short-term, by popping it into a bank deposit or account, doesn't pay you enough. Okay, so you can invest most of your money in the stock market, but that's a recipe for losing most of your pile if the market goes into a huge dive. So we all should leave a portion on long-term loan to big, secure governments and companies. And the way to do that is to buy their bonds, which are essentially certificates representing interest-paying loans to the corporations or governments that issued the bonds.

But with inflation and interest rates still with mostly nowhere to go but up (as of mid-2008), bonds may have trouble doing as well in the coming years. If inflation and rates rise, then bond prices will drop, dragging down bond funds.

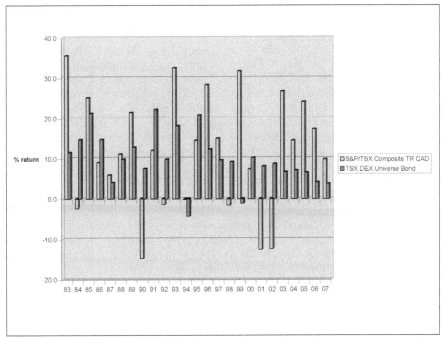

Source: Morningstar

Figure 14-1:
Domestic stocks versus bonds.

Sure, equities have always bounced back in the past. But stocks can go into a slump for years, just as they did in the inflation-and-recession-prone 1970s. From February 1966 to August 1982, a stretch of 16 long years, the Dow Jones industrial average of blue-chip U.S. stocks fell 22 percent. Yes, America's blue-chip companies paid regular dividends during the period, reducing investors' losses. But it was still a horrible time to be in the market, a depressing and endless era of new lows.

Remember Japan and the way its market hit a euphoric peak in 1989 (just as technology and communication stocks all over the world did in 2000)? A decade and a half later, the Japanese market is still a volatile, unprofitable place, unless you get extremely lucky playing the dangerous game of market timing. (Refer to Chapter 12 for more about Japan's market woes.)

Or you might lose your job, have legal troubles, or run into some disaster right in the middle of a periodic stock market slump. It would be ugly to be forced to tap into your serious money just after it's been carved up by a stock sell-off. So own some bonds. They serve as a giant, reassuring outrigger for your canoe, producing steady returns while holding their value.

Increasing their value against deflation

Companies and individuals all over the world are getting smarter and more efficient all the time and are producing goods and services at ever-lower prices. Inflation in most wealthy countries fell to less than 2 percent in recent years from double figures in the 1980s. While inflation has been on the rise lately, aided in large part by rapidly rising commodities prices, for a while there was genuine concern that we might enter an era of actual falling prices, or deflation. If that happened, bonds and cash would be likely to hold their value or even rise in price because the value of money will be rising (inflation, the opposite scenario, simply means that money is losing its purchasing power). In other words, deflation is a weird Through the Looking Glass world in which cash under the mattress becomes a solid investment that produces a real return.

Does a world of falling prices sound incredible? It's been happening all around us for years in computers, where prices drop and processing power increases every few months. Natural resource prices were in a slump for most of the 1990s as Russia and other poor countries flooded the market in a desperate bid to get U.S. dollars. Granted, an economy-wide slump in prices hasn't happened since the Depression of the 1930s, so nobody knows what it would be like — or what would happen to equity markets. But falling prices squeeze corporate profit margins like a vice, and declining profits are like rat poison for stocks. From September 1929 to July 1932, as the Depression got going, the Dow fell by almost 90 percent. We wish that was a typographical error, but it's not. The Dow dropped to 41 from 381. So own some bonds.

How Much Do I Need in Bonds?

Take the old rule — that your weighting in cash and bonds should equal your age — as a starting point. Sure, leaving a big 40 percent of one's savings in such dull fixed-income stuff will seem pathetically craven to all you racy 40-year-olds out there. So bring it down to 30 percent, or even 25 percent if you insist. But any lower than that and the volatility of your portfolio — a fancy word for the yearly up-and-down changes in the market value of your holdings — starts going off the scale. In other words, if you own only stocks, you're betting a lot of your wealth on swings in just one asset.

Now, all this will probably fall on deaf ears for people like Andrew, who weren't playing the market in the grim days and blacker months and years of the 1970s. If you haven't lived through a grinding decade-long bear market in stocks, you may be hazy on the value of a bond and think that stocks will always pull you through. But the risk of a long-term slump in equities means that if you're in your 20s, it's probably safe to hold one-fifth of your portfolio in bonds; in your 30s, hold one-third or less in fixed income; in your 40s, hold 40 percent in bonds; in your 50s, hold half your dough in cash and bonds; and in your 60s go toward two-thirds of your portfolio in bonds.

Do I need all this boring bonds-versus-stocks stuff?

Financial planning and structuring a portfolio are not clear-cut techniques that you can just learn and use. Folks in the investment game make the whole thing even more confusing. They like to conjure up arcane lore and mutter magic spells as they unveil their latest gizmo. Salespeople must have something to sell, after all. But investment theories can't be proved or disproved, in part because they depend on the future. And the future is always unknowable. So investment "research" is more like folk legend or articles of faith.

That means no "right" proportion of your wealth to have in bonds exists — if stocks surge, then almost any amount will seem too much because you'll miss out on returns. But when stocks sink, you'll get a toasty warm feeling from your bonds. If the inflation rate rises, then bonds and cash assets will steadily lose their real value. But if the opposite happens, and deflation hits, bonds may be about the only things that go up in price, because money will steadily gain value. Once again, just remember to buy a bit of every asset class and buy quality, and you'll be fine.

Begin with the age rule and then take the cash-plus-bonds weighting up or down depending on your personality.

If you already have or will have another source of income, such as a company pension fund, then you can afford to be more aggressive with your independent RRSP money because it doesn't represent your only hope. In other words, own more stocks.

Bonds are a guaranteed source of income, a mighty comforting port in the gale if equity markets collapse. If you're a self-employed professional and you definitely have to generate your entire retirement income from your RRSPs and other savings, then the asset mix in your portfolio is of life or death importance for you. You almost certainly already have an accountant helping with your taxes, so get her or him to help you choose the amount of bonds in your portfolio or refer you to another fee-charging professional who's knowledgeable about financial planning (see Chapter 8).

Just about any commission-paid broker or financial planner will have an off-the-shelf system or software package to help you choose the amount of bonds to hold. Remember, as always, that the results are only as valid as the assumptions the program makes about inflation, interest rates, and the economy. Professional investors routinely get those conditions wrong, so no reason exists why salespeople or their systems should do any better. But just about everybody will tell you to put a portion of your savings into a bond fund. Even the aggressive Canadian Maximum Long-Term Growth package in Mackenzie Financial Corp.'s Star series (Star is a bunch of pre-mixed cocktails of Mackenzie funds) had nearly 20 percent of its assets in fixed-income investments in mid-2008. And that's supposed to be a volatile mixture for somebody who's sure they won't need the money for a long time — for example, investors in their 30s without much left to pay on their home.

Picking a Good Bond Fund in 30 Seconds

Selecting a superior bond fund boils down to two simple rules: It should hold plenty of high-quality long-term bonds, and it must have low expenses. And, as always, favour funds with low MERs.

Here's more good news: Own at least two Canadian and two global stock funds, because any equity manager can go into a slump for years. But you'll almost certainly do fine with just one bond fund, as long as it has a low MER and is full of quality bonds. No big fund seller would allow its managers to make weird bets with a mainstream bond fund, such as buying 20-year paper issued by a bankrupt tin mine. The backlash from investors, the media, and possibly even regulators would be too great.

Insisting on affordability

In general, look only at bond funds with MERs of 1 percent or less. The funds with low expenses will almost all turn out to be no-load products that you buy directly from a bank or direct-selling fund company. That's because fund companies that sell through brokers, financial planners, and other advisers have to add on extra charges in order to have something left over to pay the salespeople; expect to pay an extra 0.5 to 0.75 percent annually on most broker-sold bond funds.

Looking for quality in provincial and federal bonds

Buy a fund with plenty of high-quality, long-term federal government and provincial bonds. A few super-blue-chip company bonds are okay, but remember that with business changing at the speed of Bill Gates's rubbery mind, today's corporate grande-dame could be tomorrow's bag lady. So go easy on the IBMs. If you're a bit nervous that inflation might come back, you want a middle-of-the road solution when it comes to bonds. So just get a bond fund that matches the DEX universe bond index — which pretty well represents the entire Canadian bond market.

If you want a compromise, buy a plain-vanilla bond fund whose average term to maturity is close to the DEX universe index, which includes both short- and long-term bonds. Many fund companies and bond investors use the index as the benchmark with which they compare the performance and holdings of their funds.

Checking out two beautiful bond funds

Here are two bond fund picks from Morningstar. Although not quite vanilla, both have high-quality holdings, flexible mandates that may enable them to beat the index, and relatively low expenses:

- **Beutel Goodman Income** is one of the few options in the fixed income category that has a chance at beating the benchmark over the long run, according to analysts at Morningstar. The fund's low fees and excellent manager give it a leg up on most of its peers. More recently, the fund has performed well through the credit crunch as manager Bruce Corneil adeptly steered the fund away from bank-issued bonds because of their lack of transparency. The fund's MER is 0.69 percent.

- **PH&N Total Return Bond Fund** benefits hugely from the expertise of Phillips, Hager & North, a company known as a strong fixed-income manager. PH&N has more than 20 managers and analysts assigned to this asset management area. With its flexible mandate and very low fees, this fund is one of the best fixed income funds in Canada. Other than investing in core bonds, management can use derivatives to capture value and add a small allocation to high-yield bonds when opportunity knocks. And the fund's MER is a modest 0.58 percent.

Understanding How Inflation Affects Bonds

Although bonds are generally a stable investment, they do have a pair of mortal enemies: rising inflation and his evil henchman, rising interest rates. National banks generally raise interest rates when an economy starts to overheat, or become inflated. Those higher interest rates tend to cool things off. Unfortunately, they also tend to reduce the value of bonds.

Rising interest rates, falling bond prices

A bond falls in value when interest rates rise, because investors are willing to pay less for it. To take a simple example, say you hold an 8-percent bond but interest rates increase so that other comparable investments, with the same term to maturity, are yielding 9 percent. If you try to sell your old 8-percent bond, you'll have to cut the price to get anyone interested. For example, you might have to mark it down to 95 cents per $1 of face value (bonds always mature at face value or "par," which is 100 cents on the dollar). When you offer the bond at 5 percent off, the buyer of your cut-price bond will get the regular 8-percent interest payment but they'll also make an extra kick because they've bought it at the 5-percent discount. When the bond matures at its full face value of $1 per $1 face value, that'll be enough to bring its annual yield up to 9 percent.

In 1999, interest rates increased sharply, mainly because the U.S. Federal Reserve was worried about inflation, and rising interest rates always reduce the market value of bonds that are out in the hands of investors. Bond funds were thus obliged to mark down the value of their holdings accordingly. That year, Canadian bond funds produced a modest average loss of 2.5 percent.

Rising inflation makes bondholders and other lenders very, very afraid because they become petrified of seeing the real value of their money wither away. So they demand higher interest rates and bond yields. That means they refuse to buy bonds without getting big discounts, so bond prices fall and you'll make less money on your bond funds.

Falling interest rates, rising bond prices

When interest rates fall, as they've been doing pretty well without a break since the early 1980s, the picture looks brighter for bonds. If rates in the market drop to 7 percent, then your 8-percent bond becomes a hotcake and investors will be willing to buy it from you at a premium.

Interest rates fall when inflation drops because lenders become confident that their money won't lose its value too fast while it's in the hands of the borrowers. So they're prepared to accept lower interest rates. About the only thing that's likely to send bond prices sharply higher in coming years, giving bond funds more good times, will be an era of falling prices or at least growing confidence among investors that inflation is dead for the foreseeable future. In that case, bond buyers are likely to bid bonds up even higher.

Lower inflation makes bond buyers and other lenders feel more comfortable about tying up their money for years, so they'll accept lower interest rates and bond yields. Lower rates and yields mean higher bond prices, which mean extra profits for your bond funds.

The bottom line, though, is that predicting changes in interest rates is a futile exercise akin to forecasting the weather. Just buy a good bond fund and view it as an insurance policy for your entire savings.

Index Funds and Bonds: A Marriage Made in Heaven

A bond fund should be like a holiday in upstate New York. Cheap and dull. So index funds with their low expenses and dreary habit of tracking the whole market are just the ticket. In the United States, index bond funds that simply match the market are by far the most common method of investing in bonds. Index funds, you'll recall, are funds that match a well-known market benchmark. In Canada, index bond funds usually track the DEX index. In the United States, index fund giant Vanguard sells funds whose annual expenses go down as low as 0.2 percent — that's only one-fifth of a percent. The median Canadian fixed income fund, by contrast, charges nearly 1.5 percent. Alas, a Canadian resident cannot buy U.S.–based mutual funds, although some investors have been known to open an account from a U.S. address and/or using a U.S. discount broker to do this.

You can, however, buy a low-fee Canadian bond index fund from a bank. Better still, consider iShares' fixed-income ETFs. The iShares Universe Bond Index's MER is just 0.3 percent. The cheapest bank-sponsored bond fund is Toronto-Dominion Bank's TD Canadian Bond E class, at 0.48 percent. See more on exchange-traded and index funds in Chapter 15; also check out www. shares.com.

Long Bonds: Grabbing the Lion by the Tail

Long-term bonds are those with maturity dates five years or more in the future. They are generally regarded as being more risky than short-term fixed-income securities because of the uncertainty of the future direction of interest rates. In exchange for this risk, they tend to provide a better long-term rate of return.

Unfortunately, no clear rules force managers to disclose to the public how long-term their bond portfolios are, but many companies voluntarily compare their holdings to the DEX universe index. Bond managers revel in bizarre formulas, and one of their favourites is "duration," which measures how much a bond or portfolio of bonds will drop when interest rates rise. A duration of six years and higher is generally aggressive, while five and down is conservative.

Aggressive bond managers are betting that interest rates will fall or at least stay stable. So if you're really worried that inflation will come back, seek out a manager who holds lots of short bonds.

Why you may want to rule out long-term bond funds

Short-term bonds, those with five or fewer years to run, are less vulnerable to rises in interest rates and inflation. Why? Because the time they have left is so brief that investors don't mind tying up their money in them. An instrument with 30 years left to run on it looks far worse when rates rise. (We look at short-term bond funds in the section "Playing It Safe with Short-Term Bond Funds" in this chapter.)

Managers of bond funds, like their flashier stock-picking colleagues, love to dress up their rather monotonous jobs with fancy-sounding strategies and jargon. But running a bond fund basically involves deciding how much risk you're going to take and then buying the bonds that suit that strategy. Bond managers buy as many long-dated bonds as they dare. Investors who can't handle that kind of risk should turn to the next type of fund, which concentrates on short-term bonds with fewer than five years to run before they retire. (Wouldn't it be nice to quit in five years!)

Why you may want to consider long-term bond funds

Why should you look for long-term bonds? If you have a home mortgage, you probably know that in recent years the best thing to do as a borrower has been to keep renewing your mortgage for short terms at low rates instead of "locking in" for a longer term at a higher rate. But for lenders, such as buyers of a bond fund, the opposite strategy has been better. Lending long, by buying long-term bonds with ten or more years to run before they mature, has been the most lucrative approach because short-term interest rates kept dropping. Now the next ten years may be different, but just buy a plain bond fund that's got plenty of long-term Canadian government bonds.

For the serious money portion of your portfolio, avoid risky "high-yield" bond funds or sleepwalking "short-term" bonds (more on those later in this chapter). The rule you apply should be this: Bet long-term as a lender because that's where the yield is. An old saying in the bond market is: Be long or be wrong. Longer-term bonds usually pay you more interest but they also drop the most when interest rates go up, and they gain in price more quickly when interest rates decline.

Playing It Safe with Short-Term Bond Funds

Funds in the short-term fixed income category are the funds to buy with money you'd like to have cruise along, earning steady single-digit returns and not being exposed to too much risk. The short-term fixed income category is defined as including funds that invest in investment-grade bonds and other debt securities with an average duration of 3.5 years or less. Most individual short-term funds' mandates specify they hold only securities with maturity dates no more than five years in the future. To be classified in this category, these funds must have less than 25 percent of their portfolios in high-yield bonds. Some funds in this category hold residential mortgages.

These are the sort of funds a church might buy with money being saved up for a new roof. Nice and stable (the fund, not the old roof), but flexible and offering higher returns than a money market fund at the cost of slightly more risk. (*Money market funds,* the safest type of all, are an excellent place to hold the cash portion of your savings. Usually they hold nothing but very short-term loans to the government and big companies. We offer more about them in Chapter 17.)

Getting to know short-term bond funds

Short-term, fixed-income funds are almost entirely invested in government bonds with fewer than five years left before maturity. Corporate bonds may show up in these funds, but they should be from big-brother companies that you've heard of, like Bell Canada. The main holdings should all be from the federal government and provinces. But not too much from smaller provinces — they're great places, but they tend to have lower credit ratings. Not that much risk of default exists in bonds to those provinces, but in the bond market, perception is everything. A lower credit rating becomes a leaden factor in itself, dragging a bond down to lower prices.

Funds that focus on residential mortgages are even more stable than short-term bond funds, so they fit in just next to money market funds. They hold huge quantities of mortgages that have been packaged by math nerds working at a bank in downtown Toronto, who then also calculate a fee to help keep the bank in the comfortable style to which it's accustomed. The disadvantage of these funds is that they lack the simplicity of funds that stick to bonds. A fund might not be able to find mortgages to buy at decent yields, but bonds are always for sale.

Comparing short-term fixed income funds to money market funds

In the ten years to mid-2008, the median fund in the Canadian short-term fixed income category produced an average annual return of 3.7 percent, slightly better than what you'd have with a money market fund. Mortgage funds have dwindled in number in recent years, and now are categorized in one of the fixed-income categories, mostly in short-term. No matter, as these funds, along with money market funds, tend to load up on short-term, high-quality debt investments.

Mortgage and short-term bond funds are different from money market funds in one important way: Mortgage and short-term bond funds are true mutual funds, meaning that their units can drop below a fixed price — in other words, you can lose money. Money market funds are more like a form of savings account than a real fund because they're pretty well eternally held at their $10 unit price. Your return from a money market fund comes only in the form of cash or extra units, whereas short-term bond funds or mortgage funds both pay out distributions — and mark their units up in value when interest rates fall, and mark them down when rates rise.

In reality, though, all three types of funds are pretty darn stable. Since the late 1980s, none of these funds has lost money over a full calendar year, although short-term fixed-income funds came close in 1994, when interest rates rose sharply and the median fund in this category merely broke even. That was much more palatable than the fate of the median Canadian long-term fixed-income fund, which fell more than 9 percent.

Checking out a couple short-term bond fund winners

Here are two short-term bond funds that Morningstar likes:

- ✔ **iShares CDN DEX Short Term Bond Index** is a passively managed ETF, which means it simply tracks the relevant index, with no active investment decisions made to try to better the index's return. It sports the lowest MER in the Canadian short-term bond category at 0.25 percent. The expected return of this conservative category is not very high, so fees play a much larger role in performance. This low fee makes it a tough option to beat.

- ✔ **PH&N Short Term Bond and Mortgage** is one of the least expensive options (next to the ETF) in the Canadian short-term fixed income category. Its MER is 0.61 percent. The fund also has the backing of one of the most highly regarded fixed-income managers in Canada.

High-Yield Bond Funds: Naked Bungee-Jumping

Brokers and investment managers like to call bonds issued by less-than-blue-chip companies in unstable industries such as media or minerals "high yield," because buyers demand fat interest rates before they'll touch them with a kilometre-long pole. "High yield" sounds nice and healthy, doesn't it? Sort of like it's full of fibre, dried fruit, and tasty bits of soy. But American investors have long used the correct term for such concoctions: "junk."

In other words, in the bond market you get what you pay for, and to achieve more yield you have to go down the quality scale. That involves buying riskier bonds from smaller companies — obscure stuff that's often hard to sell at any price if the bond market turns down sharply.

For example, during the global financial panic in the summer of 1998, bonds from even the biggest global corporations became difficult to trade as investors fled to the safety of government securities. Finding buyers for your junk bonds was like trying to sell lemon juice to hummingbirds.

Some funds in the junk group also hold safe-as-houses government bonds, but they're included in the high-yields because they're also free to juice their yields by grabbing riskier stuff as well.

Considering the strikes against high-yield bond funds

Junk bond funds are vulnerable in times of investor paranoia and economic jitters, when just about everyone seeks out government bonds and shares in big, relatively safe companies — a panicky rush for the exits known as a "flight to quality." When stock markets fall, junk bonds tend to do the same.

In other words, corporate and junk bonds have a habit of suffering just like stocks when recession threatens — unlike government bonds, which tend to go up because anxious investors reckon the government guarantee means they'll always get their money back. After all, bad economic times increase the pressure on small or debt-laden companies, making it more likely that they'll be forced to renege on their debts, including the hand-knit cozy junk bonds they issued.

Investigating high-yield bond funds in Canada

In the U.S., hundreds of billions of dollars have been invested in mutual funds that hold junk bonds, with generally good results and attractive returns. But in the U.S., investors can buy from a huge number of junk bonds, making it easy to build diversified funds full of the things. And a diversified fund, holding dozens of junk bonds from different issuers, spreads the risk of disastrous defaults in any one industry.

In Canada, publicly traded junk bonds are far rarer because our cautious pension funds and other investors usually insist on a high credit rating. In the past, riskier borrowers have been forced to sell their junk south of the border. A few mutual fund companies, though, have launched Canadian and foreign junk funds in recent years.

The record of the Canadian high-yield funds is too short to predict how well they'll do over the long term. But lately, junk bonds have shown their usual tendency to slip in price when speculative shares fall and investors get nervous. Add to that the impact of the credit crisis. The median high-yield bond fund lost 1.9 percent during the one-year period ended June 2008, compared with a 5.2-percent gain by the median Canadian fixed income fund.

Determining whether high-yield bond funds are for you

Deciding whether the bigger potential returns from high-yield funds compensate for the extra risk is up to you. But even the most fervent advocates of junk probably wouldn't advise you to risk all your bond money in high-yield debt. And your portfolio will do just fine if you shop elsewhere and simply stick to bond funds that hold only top-quality government and corporate bonds. After all, your stocks are risky enough, so why hold a bunch of dangerous bonds as well?

Buying Bonds Outside Canada

We'd love to tell you that your Canadian bond fund will provide the long-term stability and steady returns your portfolio requires, but we'd be wrong. A strong case exists for buying a fund that holds global bonds — a category that used to be called "U.S. bonds" because the funds so often end up investing in the almighty greenback. Most of these funds still have one-fifth of their portfolios in U.S. securities. It stands to reason that you need a U.S. bond fund in case a multi-year scenario occurs in which worldwide stock prices and the Canadian dollar both go down but bonds hold their value — in that case, foreign bonds will be the thing to own. So, unfortunately, for a complete portfolio you probably need to add a non-Canadian foreign bond as well. That's why we include them in the suggested portfolios in Chapter 4, but there we limit global bonds to just 10 percent of the total holdings.

If you're nervous about the prospects for Canada and the Canadian dollar, then switch money from the Canadian bond funds to the global bond funds to increase your insurance coverage. Yes, it's yet another asset class, so adding it to your holdings will reduce overall volatility. But it also adds more complexity, expense, and fiddly stuff to worry about. Bear in mind, though, that as of mid-2008 the median global fixed income fund had nearly half its portfolio in North American issues.

Fund sellers sometimes claim you need a foreign bond fund to give you currency diversification and protection against a collapse in the Canadian dollar. But you get the same sort of insurance from your global stock holdings, which, of course, are also priced in foreign currencies. That's why you need invest only a small portion of your portfolio in foreign bonds.

Diversification at a high cost

Holding global bonds instead of global stocks comes at a price, however. The median global fixed income fund sold in Canada has a hefty 2 percent MER, compared with less than 1.5 percent for a Canadian fixed income fund. That hefty price tag helps these funds underperform their Canadian counterparts. The median fund in the group had an unimpressive 1.3 percent compound annual return over the ten years to mid-2008. Canadian fixed income funds managed 4.6 percent.

Stinging losses posted by foreign bond funds in 1999 left the average fund down a spine-chilling 10.4 percent. That wasn't the fault of the managers: It was a lousy year for bonds worldwide as interest rates rose. Meanwhile, a slide in many European currencies relative to the Canadian dollar added to the losses.

A couple of recommended global bond funds

The analysts at Morningstar like a couple of global bond funds with annual expenses below the group average of 2.2 percent:

- ✔ **RBC Global Bond** has an intriguing mix of foreign government bonds, emerging markets debt, and high-yield securities. Its portfolio managers are free to make sector allocations, geographical shifts, and duration calls in an attempt to add value. They can also make currency overlay trades, but the fund's default policy is to have its foreign currency exposure fully hedged. The performance has been solid, and its 1.71 percent MER is well below the category median.

- ✔ **AGF Global Government Bond** invests in bonds issued or guaranteed by sovereign governments, with the management team actively managing the foreign currency exposure. Some manager turnover has dampened the fund's appeal, but it can still be a decent option for fixed income and currency diversification. It has a reasonable MER of 1.9 percent.

Chapter 15

Index Funds and Exchange-Traded Funds: The Lucrative Art of Owning Everything

*E*ver notice how things seem to be getting much larger? Monster mansions dot the landscape, movies last for hours, teenagers tower, and men's razors are as wide as shovels. Well, one of the most effective and profitable investing techniques to emerge in recent years is also a huge idea. It's indexing: buying a little of every single significant stock or bond in the market and just holding it, as opposed to trying to pick which one will go up and which will go down. The name comes from the fact that portfolios managed using this method aim to track a given market index or benchmark. To do that, they buy each stock or bond in the index. For example, a fund designed to follow the Standard & Poor's/Toronto Stock Exchange composite index will buy all (or virtually all) of the shares in Canada's main stock index. Mutual funds that use the technique are called index funds.

In this chapter we look at index funds and their doppelganger, exchange-traded funds (ETFs), discovering what they are, why they're a great place to put a lot (but not all) of your mutual fund money, and where to buy them.

Buying the Whole Enchilada: The Ups and Downs of Index Funds

The whole idea behind index and exchange-traded funds — giving up on trying to pick the best stocks and just betting on the whole market — runs counter to human nature, of course. We all want to believe in the hero fund manager, the Druid who can peer into the entrails of the market and decide which stocks will thrive. So the fund companies run huge ads and the news media produce fawning stories about how wonderfully perceptive and percipient these stock wizards are. But it's a myth: Managers who can be relied on to beat the market over many years are as rare as vegetarian leopards. And even if they do exist, determining in advance which ones will succeed is essentially impossible.

Exploring why index funds and ETFs are great for you

People who invest in index funds or ETFs are often passionate about their chosen vehicle, and will loudly espouse their many virtues.

They outperform most actively managed funds

Because few managers fail to beat the market over many years, index funds are an excellent way to go for ordinary investors. With an index or exchange-traded fund, you don't have to worry whether you made the right choice of manager, because all the fund tries to do is match the market. It doesn't buy and sell stocks or bonds in pursuit of profits, but simply buys the shares or bonds that make up a particular index and holds them forever. A computer could run the thing. These funds make stock-picking expertise irrelevant. That's great for busy people who don't have the time or knowledge to check a manager's credentials and find out whether his or her track record was achieved through luck or skill.

Making money in the stock market is a gamble. But it's a casino in which your long-term chances are excellent, because good companies grow their profits and share prices over the years. And you improve your odds even more by simply buying an index fund that tracks the whole market — because these big suckers, the successful companies like financial combine harvester Power Corp. of Canada or network empire Cisco Systems, actually become the whole market. And it's good to know that with an index fund, you own them.

They're low-cost

Index and exchange-traded funds have another shining virtue: They're cheap for an investor to own. No research is involved in just buying every stock in the market (although to hear some index funds types pontificate, you'd think it was the hardest thing in the world), so most index funds in Canada have a management expense ratio, or MER, of 1 percent or less. In other words, if you have $10,000 sitting in an index fund, you can expect to pay less than $100 (that is, 1 percent of your money) in fees and costs each year. If an index fund's MER is any higher than 1 percent, the concept starts to unravel, because it runs the risk of failing to keep up with the index that gives it its name.

Even cheaper are *exchange-traded funds* (ETFs), which are virtually the same as an index mutual fund except they're traded on a stock exchange rather than bought from and redeemed with a fund company. MERs range from a negligible 0.15 percent for iShares S&P 500 Fund to 1 percent for Claymore Financial Monthly Income Fund. We talk more about ETFs later in this chapter.

Normal non-index mutual funds — which do try to select particular stocks and bonds in an effort to turn a profit — are known as actively managed funds. They're far more expensive to own. The MER of the median Canadian equity mutual fund (active and passive funds included) is about 2.3 percent, which means the typical actively managed fund rakes off considerably more in fees and costs than an index fund. And that extra 1.3 percentage points is a lot — over 20 years, it adds up to nearly one-third of your money.

They're great for taxable accounts

Index funds expose you to very little in taxation until you cash them in, making them a great way to defer taxation.

Nearly all mutual funds pay distributions to their unitholders — cash payments that most people choose to take in the form of more units of the fund (so the investment continues to compound and grow). Funds make the distributions when they have trading profits or interest (and dividend) income that the manager wants to pay out to the fund's investors.

Say you hold 1,000 units of a fund at the end of the year and the unit value is $10, for a total investment of $10,000. The fund manager generated $1 of trading profits per unit during the year and pays this out to the unitholders. The value of each unit drops by $1, reflecting the payment that has been made. You now hold your original 1,000 units, which are worth $9 each, for a total of $9,000. But you've also received $1,000 in the distribution, which you can take in cash or new units, bringing you back to $10,000.

No matter how you receive the units, though, you're liable for tax on the distribution, just as if you had earned it trading stocks on your own. Some funds whose managers trade a lot can make very large distributions. Note, though, that getting distributions isn't a problem if you hold the fund in a tax-deferred account such as a registered retirement savings plan, which lets you delay paying taxes on the money you earn within the account. (We talk more about taxes in Chapter 23 and about RRSPs in Chapter 22.)

Index funds just buy and hold the stocks in the index and they do very little trading. So they tend to pay out very little in the way of distributions. That makes them especially suitable for taxable accounts — money that isn't held in an RRSP or other tax-deferred account.

Delving into the dark side of index funds and ETFs

No magic bullet exists in investing, and index and exchange-traded funds carry their own dangers. The big hazard is that the stock market indexes themselves — those seemingly logical benchmarks that these funds follow — often become dominated by just a few high-priced companies. In turn, that means the funds that track those benchmarks become risky investments because they're tied to the fortunes of just a few companies.

In recent years, stock market indexes have been dominated by high-priced growth stocks such as Nortel Networks Corp. or General Electric Corp. that left the rest of the market behind. *Growth stocks* are companies whose sales and profits are expanding rapidly. If investors decide that the companies can go on increasing their revenues and earnings for years, then they'll bid the shares up to high prices. But any sign of a slowdown in a company's growth is likely to make its stock price drop like a rock.

At one point Nortel represented more than 30 percent of the S&P/TSX composite index. That meant an investor in an S&P/TSX index or exchange-traded fund had one-third of his or her portfolio in a single stock — a very risky bet. The same was true, to a lesser extent, of the U.S. market, where a handful of companies such as GE made up a huge chunk of the market. So index and exchange-traded funds inevitably had a huge proportion of their assets in a few soaring giant companies. Many of the index funds, in other words, had turned into high-risk, high-priced investments as opposed to cautious mirrors of the whole market. Then came the tumble. Of course, the potential nightmare that a dominant stock might crash came true, as Nortel's share price collapsed. GE's shares also plummeted.

So, did index funds and ETFs crash and burn compared with regular funds? The short answer is that they often got whacked harder as growth stocks dropped, but their medium-term returns were still respectable. More important, the Nortel debacle prompted the Toronto Stock Exchange, in 2001, to produce *capped indexes,* which limit the impact of any one stock on an index by restricting a stock's percentage position in an index to 10 percent. One-fifth of a portfolio is not as dominant as one-third, true, but it's still quite a bit. So — no matter how good they may sound — don't put all your stock market money into one index fund or ETF. If the handful of giant stocks that dominate an index turn downward suddenly, your portfolio will take a beating.

The essence of wise investing is spreading your risk among a wide variety of holdings. Of the money you've set aside for equity funds, at most two-thirds should be in pure index funds or ETFs.

Fitting Index Funds into Your Portfolio

Treat index funds and ETFs as you would fruit and vegetables: They're great for you and they should make up most of your diet, but eat other stuff as well. In other words, these funds offer many advantages, so put lots in your portfolio — but consider keeping at least one-third of your stock market money in conventional actively managed funds.

The same caution doesn't apply to bond funds, however. "Growth" bonds don't exist — a bond is simply a loan, traded among investors, with a fixed rate of interest and period of time before it gets paid back. Because its terms and features are set in advance, a bond is known as a fixed-income invest-ment. And because bonds are so safe and stable, the average return you get from a bond or bond mutual fund will almost certainly be lower over sev-eral years than the return from a stock or equity fund. But every portfolio should include some bonds, in the interest of stability, and you can safely go ahead and put all the money you've set aside for bonds into two bond index funds, one for Canadian bonds and one for foreign bonds (although very few choices exist for the latter).

Bonds are ideally suited for index funds, mainly because low expenses are so vital in fixed-income investing.

Ideally, bonds and bond funds — including bond index funds — should be held inside an RRSP or tax-deferred plan because they throw off lots of interest income each year. As with an equity fund that pays lots of capital gains distribu-tions, if you have to pay tax on all those interest payouts, your after-tax return could be slashed. Better to let them pile up tax-free inside the RRSP. Most Canadian bond index funds simply match the entire bond market by tracking the DEX universe bond index. See Chapter 14 for much more on bond funds.

Evaluating Regular Mutual Fund and Index Fund Performance

But where's the evidence showing that regular mutual funds just can't beat the market? After all, those clever fund managers with shiny, well-scrubbed faces and expensive degrees can't be simply wasting their time, can they? The numbers seem to show that many of them are. As of mid-2008, only a dozen or so actively managed funds in the Canadian equity category had managed to outperform the S&P/TSX composite index in each of the three-, five- and ten-year periods, compounded annually. And just five earned that distinction over 20 years.

As you can see from Figures 15-1, 15-2, and 15-3, which compare calendar-year returns for the median Canadian, global, and U.S. equity funds and their respective indexes, actively managed funds have trouble keeping up in rising markets, although in down markets they sometimes come out ahead. U.S. equity managers have had a particularly tough time keeping up with their benchmark, the Standard & Poor's 500 composite index.

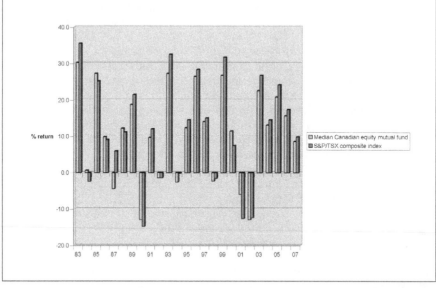

Figure 15-1:
The median Canadian equity fund can't keep up with the S&P/TSX composite index.

Source: Morningstar

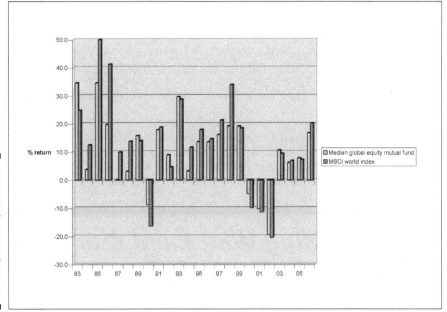

Source: Morningstar

Figure 15-2:
The MCSI world index generally outperforms the median actively managed equity fund.

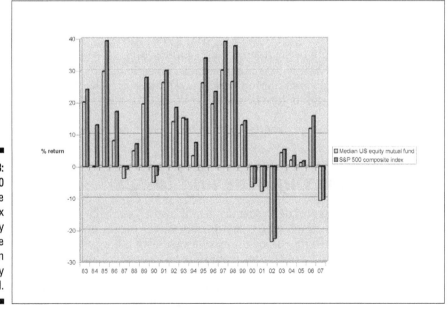

Source: Morningstar

Figure 15-3:
The S&P 500 composite index consistently beats the median U.S. equity mutual fund.

Unfortunately, it's almost impossible for index fund fans to keep things simple and just buy a global equity index fund. Fund companies usually already offer a U.S. index fund, so they normally sell an international equity index fund that tracks stocks in countries outside North America. That means you have to buy three stock market index funds: one for Canada, one for the U.S., and one for international stocks. (For the record, a number of European index funds exist as well, along with a handful of Asian and emerging markets index funds.)

Want an easy and fast place to buy index funds? Pop in to a bank branch and use the bank's index funds. The institution will be happy to deal in its own funds. You can hold your actively managed funds — which try to buy and sell stocks and bonds instead of tracking the whole market — in another account at a discount broker.

Understanding Why Fund Managers Seldom Beat the Market

Grasping the idea that no human being can develop the skill to consistently beat the stock market is tough. People naturally want to believe they'll improve their chances by handing the money over to an expert. History shows, however, that hardly anyone manages to stay ahead of the pack year after year.

Many people don't care about who will be running their money, and they simply put it in the first equity, balanced, and bond funds their salesperson suggests. Weirdly, it's possible these investors do better than those who assiduously hunt out top-performing managers — because the hot managers so often tend to flop the next year as their favourite stocks go out of fashion.

But why is it so difficult for most fund managers to beat the stock market?

Balancing wins and losses

Fund managers don't just trade in the stock market — they are the market. For every winner who beats the index and earns a profit, there has to be a loser to supply those profits. Yes, some of the losers may be small retail investors (or so the pros would like us to believe), but the institutional investors that dominate stock trading have their share of losers too. Economists argue endlessly on this point, but it seems clear that the stock market is ultimately a zero-sum game, or at least resembles one. It's sort of like a bunch of aging, flabby, boomer lads getting together to play poker on a Friday night. If Laurie walks away with $500, then Al or Rob or Justin is going to be down that much.

Why your fund manager isn't a monkey playing darts

The Wall Street Journal runs a famous stock-picking contest in which market experts are invited to compete with each other and with darts that are simply pitched at a list of shares. Folklore has it that the darts usually win, but in fact the Journal reports the experts actually have outperformed the darts. How come? We asked Burton Malkiel, professor of economics at Princeton University and author of A Random Walk Down Wall Street — and one of the godfathers of indexing. The courtly Professor Malkiel came up with two reasons for the darts' poor showings. First, the U.S. market contains thousands upon thousands of sad-sack, no-hope, tiny stocks. The darts, with nothing to guide them, often fell on one of those forgotten losers, whereas the human stock jockeys selected real companies with at least some prospects. His other explanation: When the Journal reported that a prominent expert had selected a stock in the contest, that news alone was enough to push the share price higher, giving the experts' stocks a leg up compared with the darts' selections. Incidentally, Professor Malkiel wrote in 1973 that a blindfolded monkey throwing darts at the stock page would do just as well as professional money managers. In its contest, the Journal got reporters to throw the darts. The paper considered using real monkeys, but, as reporter Georgette Jasen put it, "various hand-wringers have so far prevailed with concerns about things like liability insurance."

Money managers, believe it or not, are responsible souls who don't want their unitholders to be dragged over the hot coals unduly. So they often shy away from loading their funds to the gunwales with the extremely hot stocks that are driving the indexes higher. Remember the advice in the Monty Python sketch about the dirty fork in the restaurant? "Never kill a customer." It's just not good for business. History shows that the public will accept mediocre performance, sometimes for years, but it won't take kindly to losses. Increasingly in recent years, the stock market itself has become an insane place, and managers have had trouble keeping up with the index because they cautiously refused to go along with the madness.

Paying for active management

With the median Canadian equity mutual fund charging its unitholders 2.3 percent a year in fees and expenses, it's virtually impossible for managers to close the gap between them and the market. That MER is a yawning gap, especially when you're trying to compensate for it every year. That gives a natural advantage to index funds, with their MERs of typically 1 percent or less. (Some, from companies such as Toronto-Dominion Bank's E-class index funds, which are sold online only, are below 0.5 percent. And, of course, some exchange-traded funds charge even less. Now we're talking.)

Mutual funds have another hidden expense that's higher for actively managed funds: brokerage commissions. A fund that's constantly buying and selling stocks is naturally going to end up paying more to brokers.

Index funds: A good idea Canadians dislike

Only a few Canadians have purchased index funds, partly because the idea is so, well, strange. Ranking all the global, international, and domestic equity funds in Canada by size as of mid-2008 showed that the 250 or so biggest funds were all actively managed, with only one notable exception: the giant iShares Large Cap 60 Fund, Canada's oldest and by far largest exchange-traded fund, which had nearly $10 billion in assets in mid-2008. ETFs aside, the biggest traditionally structured index fund at that time was the $910-billion TD Canadian Index. That was smaller than a host of drab money market, balanced, and monthly income funds.

So why is the cherished notion of using a talented stock picker, a magician who knows which shares to buy, so hard to shake? Why do Canadians shy away from what seems like such a great investment opportunity? Maybe it's a cultural thing, but Canadians traditionally have been reluctant to pay for investment advice on an annual fee basis or in the form of an hourly fee. They would rather get hand-holding from a commission-paid mutual fund salesperson. But a problem exists right there: Such advisers have a powerful incentive to recommend actively managed funds rather than index funds. Index funds are sold almost exclusively by the banks, and as such are no-load products, which normally do not remunerate commissioned salespeople.

Why Most Salespeople Hate Index Funds and ETFs

Almost all brokers and planners don't like index funds because they don't pay them much or anything in the way of commissions. It's that simple. Well, that and the fact that an investment adviser traditionally has been expected to actually beat the market, which of course your basic index fund or ETF cannot do.

A guideline in the fund industry for equity and balanced funds is that the sales channel — that is, stockbrokers or financial planners — gets 1 percent of the client's money each year. They may get it through a commission paid by the investor or the fund company at the time of purchase. Or the salesperson may get this commission annually in the form of a regular "trailer fee," an annual sales commission paid by the fund company.

Index funds are an exception because, with their rock-bottom annual expense ratios of 1 percent or less, they can afford to pay little or nothing in commissions to salespeople. The fees just aren't high enough. So guess what? Be prepared if an adviser gives you a long speech explaining why index funds aren't that great after all. A fund salesperson is more likely to try to sell you on how you'll be better off buying an actively managed fund run by a reassuring-looking fellow who's known for his saint-like devotion to achieving high returns at low risk. The MER? Oh, never mind about that. It's the return that matters, silly.

Passive aggressive

Jargon abounds in the world of indexing. Because index funds aim to match the whole market, or an important benchmark, by simply buying and holding everything, the strategy is often called passive. In contrast, traditional funds, whose managers try to buy the stocks they think are going up and dump those they believe are dropping, are known as actively managed or active funds.

The debate between proponents of passive investing (who simply buy and hold the index) and active stock pickers will probably never be resolved. But we think indexing has enough clearly demonstrated advantages to make it a suitable strategy for your "core" equity money.

How's that for a fairly active recommendation of a passive investing style?

Yes, some fund marketers offer index funds through salespeople. But their expenses are generally high, at 2 percent and up. Or the index fund is sold in an F-class or other adviser-sold format, in which the MER is known but you pay the salesperson a separate fee, usually calculated as a percentage of your portfolio's dollar value. Of course, nothing's wrong with that — as long as you recognize you're paying more than if you simply bought a bank index fund, or perhaps an ETF through a discount brokerage.

 If your broker or financial planner refuses to sell you an index fund or an ETF, then strongly consider moving your account elsewhere. So much evidence suggests these funds are a great deal for retail investors. Any salesperson who refuses to carry them is being unfair to his or her clients.

Buying Index Funds and ETFs

Even though index funds supposedly simplify the experience of buying mutual funds, enabling you to skirt selecting the best fund manager, you do have some decisions to make. Which index should you follow? Should you buy an index fund or an ETF? And where should you buy? Read this section, and all will be revealed.

Selecting the right index

The problem of which index an index fund should use is thorny and difficult. On the one hand, if you start guessing which index is the best one to match, then you're getting close to picking stocks again, and this is the antithesis of passive investing. On the other hand, if you just let things go and blindly match a narrow index such as the S&P/TSX 60, which includes only Canadian stocks with very large market capitalizations, or one that's ruled by a few high-fliers, then your index fund has arguably become an aggressive and volatile fund. However, this problem doesn't have a simple answer: Just follow the advice in this book and keep index funds to a maximum of two-thirds of your equity funds. That way, if the big stocks in the index turn out to be bubbles that burst painfully, a good chunk of your money will be in regular funds as well.

In the U.S. market, the safest policy would be to buy a super-broad index fund, one that tracks the huge Dow Jones Wilshire 5000 Total Market Index, which contains just about every stock in America that's worth buying. CIBC's U.S. index fund tracks the Wilshire, so it would be a good choice. But it seems pretty certain that the better-known S&P 500, which is dominated by fewer and larger companies, will remain the main yardstick for the U.S. market for years to come. U.S. equity index funds are as cheap as Canadian ones, for the most part.

Most global equity index funds track the venerable MSCI world index, while international equity index funds track the MSCI Europe Australasia Far East (EAFE) index. You'd expect index funds based on overseas indexes to have higher MERs than their North American counterparts, but some in fact have very low MERs, such as TD's offerings.

Choosing between index funds and ETFs

ETFs are favoured by investors who want to work with an investment adviser and who tend to have larger portfolios. Index funds are better for do-it-yourselfers because they mostly are no-load funds and thus not normally within the adviser's product domain. ETFs are bought and sold like stocks, so commissions are payable on each transaction. Thus they're less suited than index funds to smaller investors who are building a portfolio and like to make frequent purchases. But the most significant difference between index funds and ETFs, of course, is the latter have lower MERs.

Knowing where to buy

If you want to buy an index fund with a truly low MER, you'll have to go to the banks. (They are also sold by life insurance companies in the segregated fund format, although many of these charge sales fees and, being seg funds, have higher MERs. We talk more about seg funds in Chapter 19.) Banks sell index funds on a no-load basis directly to the public. Every discount broker should carry at least one family of index funds, with no hassles.

ETFs are available only from investment dealers that are members of the stock exchange on which a particular ETF is listed. Although their MERs are extremely low, as exchange-traded securities, you must pay to buy and sell them. Many advisers include these transaction costs in an annual advisory fee based on the value of the investor's assets under administration.

If you're with a financial planner or broker who doesn't offer index funds or ETFs, nothing's stopping you from opening a separate index fund account at a bank and holding the rest of your money with your adviser. Each of the big bank-owned discount brokers has index funds available, usually from the bank that owns the firm. The simplicity and relatively clear account statements offered by discount brokers make them perfect for holding index funds, especially if you can avoid the fees that some discounters impose for buying and selling other companies' no-load funds. If the discounter is bank-owned, then the bank's own index funds will be free of fees.

Considering some winning index funds and ETFs

Here are three great low-cost funds that invest in Canadian stocks, Canadian bonds, and U.S. equities, as selected by analysts at Morningstar:

- ✔ **TD Canadian Index Class E** is one of Toronto-Dominion Bank's E-series low-cost index funds, which you purchase on the Internet. With an MER of only 0.31 percent, this is a cheap way to track the S&P/TSX composite index. Investors should keep in mind that, as with any fund that shadows this index, further diversification is recommended given its high concentration in resources and financials.

- ✔ **iShares Canadian DEX Real Return Bond Index** is an ETF that invests in real return bonds by mimicking the DEX (formerly Scotia Capital) real return bond index. It offers a safe and simple way to hedge against rising inflation. Given that the actively managed funds in this space tend to be expensive, investors looking to include this asset class in their portfolios will be well served by owning this ETF, with its attractive 0.35 percent MER.

- ✔ **iShares CDN S&P 500 Index** is a currency-neutral, exchange-traded fund (ETF) that tracks the S&P 500 composite index. Its modest 0.24 percent MER makes this one of the cheapest ways to invest in the U.S. stock market and gives the fund an instant leg up on the competition. Note, however, that even less expensive alternatives are available if you don't mind taking on foreign currency risk. For instance, the fund's U.S.–dollar version, iShares S&P 500, and its main rival, the SPDR S&P 500 (traded on New York's American Stock Exchange), can be had for less than half the price.

Cashing in or out?

Those sleek advisers who knock index funds sometimes claim these funds will plummet when stock markets are bad because index funds don't hold any cash reserves. Part of what they say is true — index funds are all about matching a market benchmark, instead of forecasting the direction of the market, so they nearly always simply hold the stocks in the index with barely any cash. By contrast, more than half of Canadian equity funds had at least 3 percent of their assets in safe-but-dull cash in mid-2008.

Although a fund with lots of cash will probably ride out a market downturn better than an index fund, stocks go up in the long term — which is really the point of the whole exercise. Sticking with cash-heavy investments means you're partly out of the game. And the index fund that drops first because it has no cash is also likely to bounce back to new highs sooner as the index itself recovers.

The fund industry speaks with a forked tongue on the question of cash in funds. On the one hand, fund companies say it's your time in the market that counts, not timing the market. Learn from history: Stay the course, hold on to your equity funds, and avoid jumping in and out of the market. On the other hand, managers are allowed to carry tens of millions of dollars in cash in their funds for long periods.

Not the Norm: Specialized Index Funds and ETFs

Although index funds and ETFs are most commonly used by investors to track the performance of the market as a whole, some specialized index funds and ETFs do exist. These funds are constructed to invest in certain types of stocks, or to track particular sectors.

Tilted funds: Indexing on steroids

Tilted funds have portfolios that are based on an index but adjusted to favour a certain investment style. Such adjustments are done according to a strict, consistent formula. For example, a tilted equity index fund might skew its portfolio slightly in favour of either growth or value stocks and/or toward either small- or large-cap shares. A tilted bond index fund might favour either debt issues with either short- or long-term maturities and/or a particular credit quality.

A well-known fund manager in this area in North America is Dimensional Fund Advisors, which sells nine DFA funds in Canada. Its DFA Core Canadian Equity Fund is based on the S&P/TSX composite index with what it describes as a "modest tilt toward small cap stocks and value stocks." Its investment gurus are Eugene Fama and Kenneth French, two U.S. professors and mathematicians whose research concluded that these types of stocks have a higher level of risk than large-cap and growth stocks and this contributes to higher expected rates of return. DFA Core Canadian Equity adjusts its portfolio to include small-cap stocks that are not in the composite index. The result is a weighted average market capitalization that, as of March 2008, was 20 percent lower than that of the index. (*Weighting* within a portfolio or index gives more emphasis to holdings that have higher values than to those with lower values, thus producing a more meaningful "average" figure, one that is not based purely on the sheer quantity of holdings.)

DFA Core Canadian Equity had more than 630 stocks in its portfolio at that time, compared with 250 or so in the index. So far, the strategy has produced lagging performance — although the fund has been around only a few years and thus has not had a chance to prove its mettle over the long term. As of mid-2008, it had a three-year compound annual return of 12.5 percent, compared with 23.6 percent for the S&P/TSX composite index.

Other ETF options

ETFs don't limit you to ownership of a broad market index. In Canada, for example, you can buy iShares funds that track several of the S&P/TSX subindexes — energy, financial, gold, materials, and technology industry sectors — as well as a small-cap fund. All have much lower MERs than the specialized mutual funds that invest in those areas.

A newcomer, Claymore Investments Inc. of Toronto, has 18 ETFs based on a variety of specific indexes. For example, one is based on Manulife's MFC Global Agriculture Index and another on the Sustainable Wealth Oil Sands Sector Index (created by Sustainable Wealth Management Ltd. of Calgary).

On the fixed-income side, six iShares ETFs are based on bond indexes that track various bond markets. These funds are designed to give you the same return as government of Canada five-year bonds and "iG10" units that give you ownership of ten-year bonds. Again, the MER is rock-bottom, at only 0.25 to 0.5 percent annually compared with about 1.5 percent for the median Canadian fixed-income fund.

Although the addition of any new cost-effective fund is welcome, ETFs tend to be bought as an inexpensive, simple means of investing in a broad index, minimizing the number and extent of investment decisions. However, when you buy ETFs that focus on specific sectors, in effect you're getting into market timing and making bets that stocks in, say, the technology industry — or long-term bonds — are going to do better than other sectors or the market as a whole. So tread carefully when building an ETF portfolio; you're probably better off sticking to those that track broad indexes.

Chapter 16

Dividend and Income Funds: Confusion Galore

....

In This Chapter

▹ Investigating dividend and income funds

▹ Deciding whether you need dividend and income funds

▹ Reviewing the tax implications of dividends

▹ Selecting a winning dividend fund

▹ Looking at endangered species: Preferred shares and income trusts

....

*W*e're afraid dividend and income funds exist in an area where the mutual fund industry has taken a great idea and turned it into a tangled mass of very different funds. The basic theory behind dividend funds is a good one — invest in blue-chip companies that pay a steady flow of increasing dividends, and you'll be off to the races. *Dividends* are the quarterly payments a company pays to its owners — the shareholders who own its shares. (Although this fund category includes both income and dividend funds, most of the funds in this group overwhelmingly invest in common stocks that pay dividends.)

Over the long term, buying into good-quality companies and growing rich as the dividends increase annually has been one of the best ways to build wealth. If you hold shares in successful companies for long enough, then your dividends will increase to the point where they represent a meaningful source of income. Seems simple, doesn't it? Don't count your earnings yet. This story has a lot more to it than that.

In this chapter we demystify the concept of the dividend and income fund, identify who should buy one, review the various types of dividend funds, and wrap up with some valuable tips on picking a winner. We also look at income trust funds, which sprung up early in this decade to give mutual fund buyers an opportunity to invest in the herd of *income trusts* — vehicles that pay the cash flow from a business directly to investors. We tell the whole sordid story of those once tax-effective investments and how they fell to Earth in late 2006.

What Are Dividend and Income Funds?

When a company earns a profit, it can do only two things with the money: re-invest it in the business or pay all or part of it out as dividends, actual cash paid to those who hold shares in the company. That's true for every company — from the dirtiest restaurant in Prince Rupert, B.C. (beware the chicken fricassee) to the swishest financial holding company in the fanciest marble-clad office tower in Toronto. Traditionally, established blue-chip corporations have lined their shareholders' pockets over the years by regularly paying a nice steady dividend.

A blue-chip company is a big and stable business, such as Toronto-Dominion Bank or supermarket giant Loblaw Cos. Ltd. The term blue chip comes from poker, where a blue betting chip usually has a high value.

We have some good news for you if you buy into a large blue-chip company. The other shareholders include big and assertive professional investors, horse-faced people with loud voices who usually keep management focused. So if you hold shares in big businesses, you can usually be sure the companies' managers and directors are under at least some pressure to look out for the interests of you and the other shareholders. By contrast, if you invest in small companies, they may not be big enough to attract professional investors, so management will find it easier to neglect shareholders' interests.

Many mutual fund companies sell conservative dividend and income funds that simply buy shares in a bunch of blue-chip mega-companies such as BCE Inc. or Royal Bank of Canada and then pass the dividends they collect straight through to their unitholders. This is investing in dividend funds at its very best — clean and simple.

Looking at the upside of dividend funds

Many big dividend and income funds perform well, producing a stream of ready cash for their investors. In other words, they collect the dividends from big companies and pay them out to you. Best of all, the money normally comes from the fund to you as a dividend payment for tax purposes that's lightly taxed (more on that under "The Appealing Tax Implications of Dividends").

Considering the downside

Sounds great so far, doesn't it? You're probably wondering why we're so cranky about dividend and income funds. The problem is that sometimes their complexity and lack of transparency (always a bad sign in the world of investing) make them next to impossible to wrap your brain around. In theory they're great; in action they can be horribly confusing.

It can be hard to tell whether a fund will actually pay you very much in the way of dividends, whether the distributions will actually be dividends or interest income, and whether the manager is really seeking dividend income or is in fact chasing stocks that will go up. But don't worry, in this section we show you a simple way to figure out what the flow of dividends from a dividend and income fund is likely to be — just look at the fund's main holdings and they'll tip you off as to what sort of job the fund will do for you.

Some dividend and income funds boost their flow of monthly payments to unitholders by holding riskier assets such as trusts that buy into oil wells. That'll increase the payments you get from the fund — but the stream of payments these investments dish out to the fund (and ultimately to you) could get cut drastically when business conditions turn down.

No matter how attractive those dividends might sound, over time there seems to be no substitute for good old capital gains. (*Capital gains* are trading profits a fund earns by buying assets at a low price and selling them at a better price.) As of mid-2008, on a median compound annual basis, Canadian equity mutual funds outperformed their dividend and income counterparts 16.3 percent to 12.1 percent over five years and 8.5 percent to 8 percent over ten years (see Figure 16-1).

Figure 16-1:
How Canadian dividend and income funds have performed relative to Canadian equity funds.

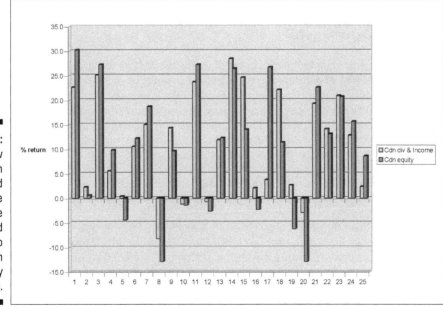

Source: Morningstar

Figuring out why companies pay, or don't pay, dividends

Companies pay dividends to their shareholders because that's how the owners of the business are rewarded. A large and well-established business, such as a bank, usually throws off enough profits each year to cover the cost of acquiring new equipment and other assets and still has money left over to pay out as dividends. But some companies — particularly fast-growing technology outfits with huge needs for cash to research and develop new products — don't earn enough cash each year to come up with a dividend. They offer such good prospects for growth in sales and profits over the medium to long term, however, that investors are happy to buy their shares even though little chance exists of getting a dividend for several years.

Slow-growing companies

Traditionally, boring businesses whose earnings grow slowly have had to pay out up to half of their profits each year in dividends in order to keep investors interested in their shares. Traditionally this has meant shares of one of the big five banks or utilities, such as pipeline operator TransCanada Corp., which as of mid-2008 paid a healthy dividend of $1.44 a share. That works out to a fat annual dividend yield of 3.6 percent. In other words, TransCanada's common shares traded at around $40 in mid-2008 and the annual dividend per share was $1.44; $1.44 represents 3.6 percent of $40, so the annual yield was 3.6 percent.

Banks are able to increase their profits faster than utilities, partly because they're expanding in profitable areas such as mutual funds. But banks are such big companies already they can't increase their profits as fast as, say, a software company can. So they occupy a sort of middle ground, made up of companies that are likely to increase their earnings at a respectable but not feverish pace in coming years. Banks also pay out a relatively large proportion of their profits as dividends to shareholders. As of mid-2008, most big bank stocks yielded between 4 and 6 percent. That might not sound generous, but it wasn't bad when you consider the stocks in the broad Standard & Poor's/Toronto Stock Exchange as a whole yielded just 2.3 percent.

Blue-chip companies are sometimes forced to cut their dividends when their profits fall unexpectedly. TransCanada did so, to great consternation and dismay among investors, at the end of 1999. Happily for its investors, the company has been raising its dividend ever since. And, for that matter, dividend cuts by established companies are rare because shareholders hate such reductions. They hate 'em like poison. Managers are unlikely to establish an annual dividend rate in the first place, if they know they'll have to take the humiliating step of reducing it. A portfolio that holds at least half a dozen blue-chip stocks — such as the typical dividend and income fund — will spread your risk, reducing the pain if one of them slashes a dividend.

Growth companies

So-called growth companies, whose profits are expected to increase rapidly, can get away with paying little or nothing in dividends, and investors still tend to throw their hat — and their cash — into the ring by buying the companies' shares. Investors are willing to forgo gratification today so the company can use the cash to build its business instead. The idea is that when the dividends do eventually come, they'll be bigger than if the company had paid out the cash to shareholders earlier in the game.

When the stock market bull is raging, dividend yield is the farthest thing from an investor's mind. In the techno-frenzy of the late 1990s and in 2000, you hardly heard a murmur about dividends. Dude, who cared? Don't-Care was made to care, in this case, as the Canadian stock market tumbled nearly 20 percent in 2001 and 2002. But the median dividend and income fund, typically with a heavy larding of stable stocks that pay dividends, managed to break even during that two-year period.

Hold at least some conservative dividend-paying stocks, even within an RRSP. Because as the popping of the tech stock balloon showed, it's nice to own something that doesn't depend on a weedy teenage software genius staying conscious. But don't worry. You don't have to take special vitamin pills if your diet is rich and varied, including plenty of herrings' backsides. And, by analogy, you don't need to worry about buying a special dividend fund if your portfolio includes some high-quality equity funds, like those we cover in Chapter 11. Those funds are bound to hold several dividend-type stocks — and that covers your daily requirement.

Those seemingly insignificant little quarterly dividend cheques are what capitalism and the stock market are all about. Under the law — in the Anglo-Saxon world, at least (and elsewhere, more and more, as the whole world becomes obsessed with investing in stocks à l'américaine) — dividends are about the only way that shareholders can legally get any money out of their company. Yes, they get a payoff if the company is taken over at a fat price or if they sell the shares after they've gone up or if the company "spins off" an asset to its shareholders in the form of a special restructuring. But receiving a dividend remains the only fundamental way in which you can actually extract cash from a business (apart from when an executive receives a bloated salary or options package). It's the thing that ultimately gives a share any value.

What does this all mean to the mutual fund investor? Just that it's fine to engage in torrid flirtation with a natural resources fund or aggressive growth fund, but limit it to a dalliance using just a tiny part of your money. Your core equity funds should also hold plenty of blue-chip stocks that pay a meaningful and rising dividend. Because when a market crash comes — and they always do — they're the shares that are most likely to fall the least and recover first.

Don't expect big dividends

Modern investors still don't ask company managers to "show them the money" in the form of a big dividend. They still appear willing to wait years for future profits and dividends — or to gamble on castles in the air, depending on how cynical you are.

Most big companies pay at least some dividends. But so much investor money is already chasing high-quality stocks that pay a decent rate that prices have been pushed sky-high. An investment in the S&P/TSX composite index (say, through the iShares S&P/RSX composite index fund) in mid-2008 would provide a limp annual dividend yield of only about 2.3 percent — in other words, if you tied $100 up in the S&P/TSX stocks, you got only $2.30 in annual dividends.

In part, that was because interest rates were low. With ten-year bonds yielding only about 3.8 percent a year, there weren't many quality investments around that produced any sort of decent income stream, so you might as well have stuck with shares.

Determining Whether Dividend and Income Funds Are Right for You

A dividend or income fund will suit you best if you meet one or more of the following tests:

✓ **You're a long-termer but you need cash now:** You need the long-term growth prospects offered by shares, but you also need to make regular withdrawals from your portfolio of investments. Many dividend funds are designed to accumulate a steady stream of cash, which they pay out regularly.

✓ **You're in a high tax bracket:** You face a high rate of tax on the income and profits earned by your investments. That might be because you already have a high income or because your investments are held in a taxable account, not a tax-deferred plan such as a registered retirement savings plan. Remember that dividends are lightly taxed, which makes them a great way to earn investment income for a taxable investor. That means the payments you get from a dividend fund won't be too badly savaged by the government.

✓ **You're not a risk taker:** You're nervous about the stock market and you feel happiest with a stock fund full of conservatively run large companies, the sort that pay lots of dividends.

But dividend funds aren't right for everyone, especially people who don't care if their investments pay out a regular income. Why bother with collecting dividends if it compromises your long-term returns?

If your aim is to build your money over many years, then you'll probably do better in a regular stock fund that's free to buy shares in all sorts of companies, including those that pay hardly anything in dividends. That way, you'll own a balanced mixture of shares that also includes some high-flying technology players and natural resource producers, and not just a portfolio of blue-chip, conservative names.

The Appealing Tax Implications of Dividends

In Chapter 23, we take a close look at how the periodic payments you get from a mutual fund are taxed. Dividend and income funds — assuming they are among the vast majority that hold mostly dividend-paying stocks — get special treatment when it comes to taxes. They can be one of the best ways of earning a stream of income that doesn't get too badly mutilated by the tax collector. To encourage Canadians to buy shares issued by Canadian corporations (to help the economy grow), dividends are taxed far more lightly than interest income, which is the sort of fixed payment you get from a bank account, bond, or fixed-term deposit such as a guaranteed investment certificate.

Crunching the numbers

As a quick-and-dirty rule, each $1 of dividend income is as good as $1.25 of interest income because the taxes on the interest-income dollar are so much higher. If you earn $125 in interest and only $100 in dividends, you'll end up with about the same amount after taxes. Dividends are tax-efficient or tax-advantaged investments, because this type of investment actually helps you keep more of your hard-earned income.

You'll know if any mutual fund you own has paid you distributions in the form of capital gains, dividends, or interest because it'll be indicated on the T3 or T5 statement of investment income you get from your fund company each year to mail in with your tax return. The calculation for reporting dividends on your tax form is a little laborious and weird, but you soon get used to it (amazing how the prospect of putting more money in one's pocket tends to fire up the old synapses). Essentially the principle is this: You "gross up" the amount of dividends received by increasing them by 25 percent and you report that amount on your tax form. But you then reduce your tax payable by a "tax credit" amounting to 16.7 percent of the dividends actually received. Don't fret: The tax form provides a step-by-step guide.

An instant dividend-paying portfolio

As we discuss in Chapter 15, index funds are one of our favourite ways to invest. And no better way to do so exists than through an exchange-traded fund (ETF). An ETF is a fund that is traded on a stock exchange — as opposed to being sold and redeemed directly by mutual fund companies. Of greater interest is the fact that its portfolio is based on a stock index, such as the Standard & Poor's/Toronto Stock Exchange composite index.

The ETF market has expanded rapidly in recent years to include funds that are based on some of the Toronto Stock Exchange's specific industry groups. One fund provides an instant portfolio of blue-chip TSX dividend-paying stocks.

The iShares Dow Jones Canada Select Dividend Index Fund holds 30 of the highest yielding dividend-paying companies in the Dow Jones Canada Total Market Index. Analysts at Dow Jones look at companies' dividend growth, yield, and average payout ratio to determine which stocks make the fund's portfolio. Its three biggest holdings in mid-2008 were Canadian Imperial Bank of Commerce, Manitoba Telecom, and National Bank of Canada.

Like most ETFs, Dow Select Dividend's MER is low, low, low — 0.5 percent, compared with 2.23 percent for the median Canadian dividend and income fund. However, performance of the fund, launched at the end of 2005, lagged behind the median fund in the category. As of mid-2008 it had a two-year compound annual return of 4.6 percent, 1.3 percentage points behind the median fund.

Understanding why dividend funds may or may not be good for your RRSP

Fund salespeople have long preached that collecting dividends within a tax-sheltered account such as a registered retirement savings plan isn't that important. That's for two reasons:

- ✔ All the income earned inside such a plan is tax-deferred anyway. And all withdrawals from the plan are heavily taxed as regular income. That means the dividend tax break is no use within an RRSP, so dividend funds — which are designed to take advantage of the tax law — arguably aren't a good fit.

- ✔ For your core equity funds in an RRSP, it may be better to buy normal equity funds rather than dividend funds because the managers of regular funds have a freer hand to play the market, rather than trying to maximize their dividend income.

But because many dividend and income funds hold big familiar companies, they can logically be treated as super-conservative equity funds that are well suited for RRSPs. Remember the 2001–2002 experience, when dividend and income funds outperformed general Canadian equity funds. The bottom line seems to be this: Check the holdings of a dividend fund, and if it's full of regular shares in big companies — as opposed to things like income trusts or other investments that are designed to throw off regular streams of cash — then it can probably be treated as a conservative equity fund.

Selecting a Winning Dividend Fund

Don't just grab the first dividend and income fund you're offered. Make sure the fund you buy comes with a reasonable management expense ratio — certainly less than the category's 2.23-percent median value. Ensure its largest holdings include the sort of shares and trust units you want to own: high-quality stocks or units of companies in sectors that are known to provide reliable dividends and other income.

Questions to ask before you buy

Here are the questions to put to your salesperson, no-load fund company, or bank employee. If you can't get a straight answer, then consider shopping elsewhere:

- ✔ What distributions has this fund paid over the past year, and how frequently?

- ✔ Is there a stated monthly distribution, and how much is it?

- ✔ Which distributions over the past year counted as dividends from taxable Canadian corporations, entitling the fund's investors to claim the dividend tax credit?

- ✔ Did any of the distributions include a return of capital — a partial refund of the investor's own money — to maintain a stated payout rate? Such returns of capital can be not only potentially misleading, but also horrendous to account for at tax time.

You can find this information easily in a fund's management report of fund performance, or MRFP, which should be available as a download from the fund company's Web site. The information will be only as current as the most recent MRFP, but because these reports come out every six months, that should be current enough to give you a good idea of what you might expect in the way of distribution types and amounts.

Two strong dividend and income funds

Here are a couple of top-quality dividend and income funds recommended by analysts at Morningstar:

- ✔ **TD Monthly Income** has done a remarkable job of giving investors the best of both worlds: high returns with relatively modest risk. Much of the fund's outstanding performance was driven by exposure to the income trust market. In recent years, the income trust market has cooled and investors shouldn't expect this fund — or any income-oriented balanced fund — to produce double-digit returns consistently. (We look at income trusts in the next section.)

  Even in the post–income trust world, you still can expect this fund to post respectable returns while paying a modest amount of income. Unlike many income-oriented funds, this fund doesn't have a fixed payout schedule. Each year TD determines how much the fund can reasonably pay out without eroding its capital base. Historically, that number has been in the 2 to 3 percent range annually. However, TD does offer different versions (H and T) of this fund that have higher fixed payout amounts of 8 percent annually if you're looking for more income.

- ✔ **CIBC Monthly Income** also has achieved outstanding returns due in large part to its considerable income trust exposure. So investors shouldn't expect this fund to reproduce that kind of performance heading forward either. The fund maintains a considerable exposure to common stocks, which should help it produce high-single-digit returns over the long run. Unlike TD Monthly Income, this fund pays a fixed six cents per share to investors each month. That works out to a respectable 4.5 to 5 percent annually.

These funds have reasonable expenses and well-regarded managers, but remember to ask plenty of questions before you invest.

The Times Are a'Changin': The Fall of Preferred Shares and Income Trusts

Just as fashion ruthlessly moves forward, making your rayon shirt an eyesore instead of a prized possession, so too does the investment world, and what was hot on Bay Street one day won't be the next. In this section we look at two investment equivalents to platform shoes and bell-bottom trousers.

Preferred shares

Time was when almost all dividend funds invested in preferred shares. But these funds are far and few between nowadays, as the preferred security is practically on the financial industry's endangered species list.

For the history books, *preferred shares* pay a fixed and usually high dividend, which is nice, but the dividend doesn't grow over time. In other words, preferred shareholders are more like lenders to a company than owners. By contrast, an ordinary or common share in a company pays a lower dividend, but the annual rate tends to increase over the years, providing an investment whose value should increase over time.

Preferred shares suit investors who want predictability but also relish the nice tax break attached to dividends. These shares pay a high fixed stated dividend, which can be reduced or omitted if the company hits turbulence — but in practice rarely is. And preferred shareholders nearly always get their dividends before common shareholders are entitled to receive a cent, hence the name.

In return for that lightly taxed and relatively generous stream of income, preferred shareholders miss out on the chance of prospering if the business booms. Preferreds nearly always stay close to their issue price, dropping a little when interest rates rise and rising when rates fall, just like bonds do. You can spot them in stock listings by their trading symbol, which always has "PR" in it. If a stock has a percentage value as part of its name, then it's a preferred share that was set up to produce that percentage yield for buyers of the stock when it was first issued.

Only a dozen or so among the 185 dividend and income funds hold a significant portion of their portfolios in preferreds. The category is now almost entirely dominated by income-oriented equity funds that derive as much as, if not more of, their returns from market performance. They load up on stocks of banks, utilities, pipelines, blue-chip industrial companies — and sometimes even growth companies that pay hardly any dividends. The manager of today's typical dividend and income fund tries to increase the value of his or her fund's units as the price of the stocks it holds rises, while also paying out at least some dividend income. Still, these funds' holdings are usually so conservative they're less volatile than regular equity funds.

Income trust funds

Until late 2006, these funds were *the* place to be in mutual funds. Everyone was hungry for the tax-efficient income these funds provided, and staid, old, slightly higher taxed dividends just didn't cut it anymore. Publicly traded companies were spinning off parts of their operations as income trusts left right and centre. Entire companies were reinventing themselves as income trusts, seemingly simply to make themselves into income-spewing, investor-friendly investment machines. But then the federal government, under pressure from proponents of the traditional stock market, put an end to the madness, levelling the taxation playing field so that owning an income trust unit was no more tax-wise than owning a dividend-paying share. (We delve into the taxation of income trusts in Chapter 23.)

However, as of mid-2008, more than 40 income trust funds were available. They're still worth a look — in fact, we suggest you evaluate them as potential investments as you would any other Canadian equity investment. After all, if an income trust's price falls precipitously, all the income in the world will be of little consequence if you've lost on your original investment. You can read more about income trusts in Chapter 5.

Chapter 17

Money Market Funds: Welcome to Sleepy Hollow

Some archaeologists and historians have an interesting theory to explain why the Romans were so successful in war, usually against massive odds (apart from Russell Crowe, that is). Bathrooms. Yes, that's right, bathrooms. The Romans liked their plumbing. Centuries before most of Western Europe had any kind of organized sanitation, the Romans were building bathhouses and sewage systems. Even in the field, they stuck to their clean-living ways. This meant their armies didn't die en masse of typhoid, cholera, and other diseases transmitted by, well, patchy hygiene. Money market funds are a bit like the humble throne in the bathroom, the white porcelain god that separates us from 15th-century Bruges with its pungent odours, annoying jesters, and unspeakable ditches down the middle of the street. They're dull, they're predictable, they're almost invisible — and they're one of the mutual fund industry's greatest inventions.

Money market funds are simply a safe parking spot for cash, designed to produce at least some sort of return. They generate a modest stream of income, especially in recent years when interest rates have been extremely low. Indeed, the median Canadian money market fund produced an anemic ten-year compound annual return of 3 percent as of spring 2008. These funds invest in government treasury bills, very short-term bonds, and other fixed-income securities that usually have less than three months to go before they mature and the issuer pays the holders their money back. Money market funds are different in structure from normal mutual funds, and the way they calculate their returns can be confusing. But just use the same rules to pick one as you do with bond funds: Buy quality and, more than ever, insist on a low management expense ratio (MER) — 1 percent annually at the very most. (The *MER* is the cost of managing a fund, and normally includes fees paid to the fund's portfolio managers, as well as marketing, sales, administration, legal, accounting, and reporting costs. These costs are charged directly to the fund, as a percentage of the fund's total assets. The fund's net asset value includes the MER.)

As with all mutual fund investing programs, do more than just insist on low costs when buying a money market fund. Lean across the table — glaring at the hapless salesperson through bulging, insane eyes — part your spit-flecked lips and demand a fund that has a very low MER. Otherwise, you won't make anything off a money market fund.

In this chapter, we show you why money market funds are a great place to hold your cash while you wait to spend or invest it. We also show you how to spot a good money market fund.

How Money Market Funds Work

Throughout this book we give you tons of grim warnings about how you can easily lose money in mutual funds because of a drop in their unit price. Well, at the risk of contradicting ourselves, that doesn't apply to the vast majority of money market funds because they are held steady at a fixed value, usually $10.

Some money market funds — especially the guaranteed type that promise to refund some or all of your money — have unit prices that do increase over time.

Keeping the unit price fixed isn't required by law, but it's the practice among fund companies. In theory, if short-term rates were to shoot up exponentially or the government's credit rating collapsed in some kind of unprecedented catastrophe, the fund company would let the value of your money market units drop. But by that time, you'll be too busy pitching bottles at the giant green spacecraft that just zapped your dog to worry much about it. In other words, woe betide the fund company that lets its money market fund units drop below their fixed value. Investors who buy this type of fund aren't known for their devil-may-care attitude to losses. So money market funds are rather like a guaranteed investment certificate: You're certain of getting your cash back, plus extra units that represent the interest you've earned along the way.

The fix isn't always in

The unit value of some money market funds does change, increasing slowly as the fund earns interest income. These are the so-called "segregated fund" or "guaranteed investment fund" versions of money market funds. Seg or guaranteed funds are funds that promise to refund most or all of the holder's original investment, as long as he or she sticks around long enough. Chapter 19 deals with segregated funds.

Mind you, with something as safe as a money market fund, such a guarantee is pretty pointless and almost certainly not worth the higher expenses charged on such funds. Some hit their investors for as much as 2 percent annually, which leaves little or nothing for unitholders after taxes and inflation are taken into account. For legal reasons to do with insurance contracts (you'd get too excited if we explained them all to you), guaranteed and segregated funds often don't give unitholders their returns in the form of extra units. They simply reinvest all interest, capital gains, and other income so that holders of the fund own units with a steadily increasing value. Yet other examples both increase their unit value and pay distributions, just like normal mutual funds. It's terribly confusing for investors, and your salesperson or bank employee could have trouble keeping up. One simple reason justifies the existence of guaranteed and segregated money market funds: They provide a temporary cash parking spot for investors in a company's other guaranteed and segregated fund families, thus avoiding switch-out fees if they were to seek an external place to temporarily store their money pending a reinvestment decision.

Your statement from the fund company should clearly show what's going on, although that's not always the case. Consider switching to another fund company or broker if you can't get a proper explanation — a clear and simple explanation of how your funds work is your inalienable right as an investor. Even if you're an alien.

You can also go to `morningstar.ca` or `globefund.com` and check the latest distributions paid by a fund. This should give you an idea of what system the fund uses.

The interest is usually calculated daily, but it's generally added to your account every month or when you sell your units. However, money market funds, like nearly all mutual funds, beat the pants off GICs because they're "liquid." That's a bit of investment industry jargon that simply means you can liquidate — turn the investment into ready cash — at a moment's notice. Unlike GICs, money market funds refund your money without penalty, usually at a day's notice.

As a guideline, the return from money market funds tends to be similar to the return from one-year GICs, particularly during shorter terms. However, in the longer term, GICs have done better; the typical five-year GIC had a 3.7 percent annualized return during the ten years ended March 2008. However, that's less than you could have gained from an investment in a balanced fund — normally a pretty cautious mix of stuff from the stock market (which is always volatile) and bonds (which usually work in great slow cycles). The median Canadian neutral balanced fund — the most conservative among the various balanced-fund categories — achieved a 4.6-percent annualized return during that ten-year period. (For more about balanced funds, refer to Chapter 13.)

The yield is just the harvest you get on your money, expressed as a percentage of what you invested. So, a madcap biotech fund might go up 50 percent in a year — at huge risk — turning $1,000 into $1,500 (always assuming you were canny enough to sell out before it crashed). For the typical money market fund, however, assuming a current yield of about 2 percent, we're talking about a return of 20 bucks for tying up $1,000 for a year.

With a money market fund, you nearly always buy a set of units at a fixed price, usually $10, and that unit price never changes. Your return comes in the form of extra units paid out to you along the way. You're not going to get wealthy soon with one of these funds. Just like bond funds, they're designed only to earn a steady and fairly predictable return, with none of the flash, risk, and potential for big gains you get with an equity fund.

Checking Up on Your Money Market Fund

Say you want to buy a money market fund but don't know what the yield over the next year is likely to be. Because most money market funds have constant prices, you need to look for a fund's current yield and effective yield. These values represent rough forecasts of what the fund, with its current portfolio, is likely to earn over the next year. Each yield figure uses a slightly different calculation, which we outline in a moment. But remember, both of these yield numbers are just estimates.

Money market funds are full of short-term stuff that matures in the next few months, so the portfolio manager can't be sure if he or she will be able to replace those T-bills and other short-term securities with new investments that will produce the same return. If rates are falling, then it will be almost impossible to do so. Don't worry about the difference between the two types of yield. Each calculation basically boils down to the same number of dollars and cents in your pocket. But just for the record, here's how to tell them apart:

✔ **Current yield:** Sometimes called the indicated yield, this shows the yield the fund earned over the past seven days, which is then "annualized" to show what the same rate of return would work out to over one whole year.

✔ **Effective yield:** The effective yield is the same annualized number, but this time it assumes that all distributions are reinvested in more units, thus achieving compounding. Because it assumes the new units are being added to your stockpile during the year, earning that extra bit of interest, the effective yield is usually a fraction of a percentage point higher than the current yield.

A fund's current yield is easy to find on all fund companies' Web sites — just look for a link to "Prices and Performance," or similar terminology. For money market funds, you'll find tables showing current yields under the Price/Yield column. Finding the effective yield isn't so easy; only a few of the fund companies' Web sites provide separate columns for current and effective yields.

When inflation and interest rates are low, no real gap exists between the two types of yield. For example, in mid-2008, the $5.1-billion CIBC Money Market Fund (Class A) quoted a current yield of 2.21 percent and an effective yield of 2.23 percent. In times of high interest rates, when compounding means the new units pile up fast, the effective yield will be quite a bit higher. But the low interest rates in 2008 meant there wasn't much difference at all.

When short-term interest rates were high — such as the early 1990s, when the returns on money market funds climbed well above 10 percent — fund companies started making a lot of noise about their "effective yields," which were much higher than the "current yield" (because the money was theoretically going to compound at high rates). But investors became so confused over which yield was which (and who can blame them?) the regulators eventually stepped in. The fund industry agreed to show both figures in its advertisements.

Why Money Markets May Not Be All They're Cracked Up to Be

Don't just assume a money market fund is the only place to park your cash — you can usually earn a full percentage point or two more annually with a low-risk short-term bond fund that has low expenses of 1 percent or less. Chapter 14 on bond funds suggests a few good candidates.

Short-term bond funds can be even better than money market funds

Canadian short-term fixed-income funds posted a median annualized return of 2.5 percent over the ten years ended June 2008 — that's nearly a full percentage point more than Canadian money market funds. The drawback, though, was slightly more volatility and the danger of losing money. That's because bond prices fall when interest rates rise, as explained in Chapter 14, although short-term bonds fall the least of all (when interest rates drop, however, they also go up the least). Money market funds, by contrast, are designed never to leave investors with a loss. For example, when interest rates rose suddenly in 1994, the average short-term bond fund suffered a loss of almost 2 percent.

Before you go plunging into a short-term bond fund, sneering and making rude gestures at the dolts lining up to buy boring old money market funds, remember that the 1990s were marked by a sharp fall in interest rates. That gave short-term bond funds an unfair advantage because bond prices were lifted by those falling rates. If rates start rising again, then short-term bond funds will have a tougher time beating money market funds. This scenario usually prompts warnings about a "bond bubble," which occurs when investors flee stocks and try to hide in bonds. If inflation goes up accompanied by a sharp rise in interest rates, a bond bubble can burst. Still, short-term bond funds are among the safest of all investments. A portfolio stuffed full of high-quality, short-term government bonds with less than five years to go before they mature (check a fund's top holdings) will ride out nearly any horror the markets can dole out.

Realistic expectations for money markets

How much can you expect to earn from a money market fund over the next year? Here's a good guideline: Check what banks are offering to pay on one-year GICs.

Over the 25 years (whew!) ended June 2008, buying one-year GICs produced an annual return of 5.4 percent while money market funds produced a similar return of 5.7 percent. To compare one-year GIC rates from all the major banks and other financial institutions, check weekend and/or Monday editions of major daily newspapers, many of which list the rates offered by virtually every deposit-taking institution on all sorts of loans and deposits, including GICs.

Pick Only the Plums: Selecting Winning Money Market Funds

Don't stay up all night picking a money market fund, because you've got a busy day ahead — a long day of sliding through sticky mud, trying to get a grip on infuriated ostriches. Money market funds tend to be pretty similar. In other words, chasing a big yield is pointless, because to get one, the manager has to take more risk. If you're buying your other mutual funds at a bank or bank-owned discount broker, simply buy the bank's money market fund. Enough competition exists in the industry to make it embarrassing for a bank to have its money market fund turn into a hound.

If you're buying through a broker or other commissioned salesperson, his or her office is probably set up to put clients into a particular money market fund, probably from the fund company the salesperson's organization does the most business with. Because money market funds are just temporary holding spots for cash — or they constitute the low-risk, low-return "cash" portion of your portfolio — one fund is pretty well as good as another.

Just make sure you can find the money market fund listed in your daily newspaper or on the Internet. That way, you know you'll be able to track your holdings and check the accuracy of your account statement.

Choosing from a mix of money market funds

Most money markets are ultrasafe, sticking to government-issued Treasury bills and bonds. Others increase the risk level very slightly, and pick up about one-fifth of a percentage point in annual yield. Either choice is fine — it depends on your personality. Here's how to tell the two options apart:

- For their very nervous clients, many fund companies offer super-conservative "T-bill" funds that buy only short-term government bonds and government Treasury bills (a type of bond with just a few months before it matures).

- For those willing to take on more risk in a cash investment, lower-quality funds — usually known simply as money market funds — exist that are allowed to increase their yield by buying things like corporate "commercial paper"; that is, short-term debt issued by big companies when they need a bit of cash to tide them over. Most of these funds really aren't dangerous at all, because the companies that issue the paper they hold are nearly always blue-chip multinationals or their Canadian subsidiaries.

However, the credit crunch that began in 2007 has cast a dark shadow over corporate cash investments, so make sure the money market fund you're considering pretty much sticks to safe and sure T-bills and other guaranteed paper.

It would take quite an economic cataclysm indeed before any major money market fund racked up losses big enough to force the bank to let the fund's unit price drop. Although some money market funds held some defaulting commercial debt assets in 2007, the fund sponsors purchased the assets from the funds in question. The bottom line is that to the typical investor, no significant difference exists between the conservative T-bill funds and the mildly more aggressive ones.

In the end, the extra bit of yield you get from a money market fund compared with a T-bill fund is very small. For example, the TD Canadian Money Market Fund, which is free to buy corporate securities, generated an annual return of 2.53 percent in the five years ended June 2008 — only slightly higher than the 2.34-percent annual return from the TD Canadian T-Bill Fund, which must stick to government debt.

World travellers: U.S. money market funds

A handful of companies also offer U.S. money market funds, either for investors who want to hold a lot of cash in U.S. dollars or for scaredy-cats who want a low-volatility investment safe from a drop in the Canadian dollar. Nearly all the funds in this group are bought and sold in U.S. dollars. The same rules apply to pick a fund. Look for low expenses if you want to end up with anything. Don't believe us? Look what happened to unfortunate investors in the Trimark Short-Term Income Fund. The fund's DSC (back-end load) units came with an MER of 1.87 percent — which left investors with an average annual return of only 1.8 percent for the five years ended March 2008, compared with 2.9 percent for the average U.S. money market fund. In other words, investors paid out more to the fund company than they got back in returns.

The median U.S. money market fund has an MER of 1.06 percent. Why pay anything more than that?

Is thin in? Watching those pesky expenses

Always remember that because the returns from money market funds are so thin, the slightest increase in expenses can leave you with nothing after taxes and inflation. So refuse to pay a sales commission when buying a money market fund. The broker or salesperson should be able to let you have it commission-free, especially if you're simply parking your money in the money market fund temporarily while you decide on a long-term home for it. Check that the money market fund offered by your bank or salesperson has produced acceptable returns. It probably has.

Remember, the median Canadian money market fund has an MER of 1.04 percent — you shouldn't be asked to pay more than that.

The lowdown on MERs

As we keep repeating over and over until readers want to shove us down a disused grease trap, the main thing to look for in a money market fund is low MERs. That can be hard in Canada because the cheapest funds, those with MERs of around 0.4 percent or less, are often "premium" funds from the banks, needing big investments of $100,000 and up, or are funds available only to certain groups such as professionals.

But if you're buying only small quantities of the fund, don't get too worked up about costs, either. If you have, say, $5,000 in a money market fund, representing 5 percent of your $100,000 portfolio, then a 1-percentage-point reduction in expenses on the money market fund means an extra $50 a year for you. Nice, sure, but not a huge deal. For convenience, you may decide just to stick with your fund company's money market product, even if it has higher expenses, and treat the extra $50 as a sort of fee. But remember that all expenses eat into your return.

Beware of empty promises

Don't bother searching endlessly for the money market fund that promises to give you a few more bucks of income. If the performance looks hot, chances are the fund company has doctored the return in some way — no doubt legally but not quite candidly. That's because in the drab world of T-bills and short-term bonds, generating any kind of extra return through fancy trading without taking on more risk is very hard. (Getting anyone to play footsie in the cafeteria with you at lunchtime is very hard, too, but let's save that for another day.) You can be pretty sure that the yield of a high-flying fund will magically revert to the middle of the pack — or worse — straight after you buy it.

Be curious, George

As always, be curious — and cautious — when some kind of "account management" fee or commission is added on to a money market fund's published expenses. If you're thinking about paying such a fee, ask to see a sample statement that at least shows clients how the fee is calculated and charged. Does the statement clearly reveal how much is taken off? Such extra charges may be legitimate and even a good deal, but they make checking on your real return a lot more complicated.

Remember that simplicity is one of the great beauties of regular mutual funds, because they publish returns and unit prices after their fees. You have a right to a clear explanation of every fee. If the fund company or salesperson doesn't respect you enough to provide you with one, then shop elsewhere.

Chapter 18

Fund Oddities: Strange Brews Sometimes Worth Tasting

*W*ith more than 8,000 retail investment funds in Canada, it shouldn't come as a surprise that some of them have pretty specific or unusual investment focuses. The variety is nothing like in the United States, where things can get so specific 65 funds invest only in debt securities issued by municipalities in Minnesota — enough to merit a special category. But the Canadian fund industry has grown enough to accommodate funds that have such specific mandates as investing in companies involved in water-supply infrastructure, or funds that build their portfolios around holdings in publicly traded stock exchanges.

In this chapter we round up a motley crew of fund oddities — funds so unusual they're difficult to compare to more traditional equity, fixed-income, or balanced funds. These also include bona fide categories such as the long-established but waning labour-sponsored group, as well as the relatively new target date or life-cycle funds. We also attempt to describe the contents of the catch-all "specialty" fund category, a dumping ground for funds so unique they can't be placed in an existing category (and aren't numerous enough to merit their own category).

Labour-Sponsored Funds: Small Business, Big Tax Break — For Now

A labour-sponsored fund is a venture capital fund that invests in strange little companies, most of which will probably fail or stagnate. Officially known as "labour-sponsored venture capital funds" (and now categorized by fund data firms as "retail venture capital" funds), they must have a formal backing from a labour union and — in theory — favour investments in companies that have unionized workforces. Private companies aren't publicly traded, which means the true market worth of the stocks the funds own is impossible to establish clearly. And labour funds' expenses are often obscene. These beauties have a few more ugly poison spikes sticking out of them, too. Their investments usually take years to mature, and you lose a huge chunk of the benefit from most of these funds unless you leave your money sitting there for almost a decade.

So why did Canadians have about $2.7 billion invested in labour-sponsored funds as of mid-2008? Two reasons: because investors in most provinces could get an attractive tax break totalling 30 percent or even more of their investment, and because the unknown ventures these funds invest in sometimes explode in value.

You need to know three main things about these funds:

✔ **You can get a sizeable tax credit:** With just about all labour funds, the federal government refunds 15 percent of your investment in the form of a tax credit — and your provincial government may also give you back the same amount. The maximum annual investment eligible for credits is usually $5,000 — so investing that amount in a labour fund that qualifies for both federal and provincial credits will immediately net you tax refunds of up to $1,500 ($750 from each government). In other words, you could end up with $5,000 worth of fund units in return for a cash outlay of only $3,500. As with contributions to RRSPs, you can usually make your purchase of a labour fund during the first 60 days of a calendar year and have the money earn tax credits for the previous year.

✔ **You must make a long commitment:** To stop people from buying labour funds, grabbing the tax credits, and then simply selling the units back to the fund, the federal government imposes an eight-year "hold period." If you cash out of the fund within that period, you have to repay the federal tax credit. That's up from a previous hold period of only five years. The government does make exceptions for illness and so on, but reckon on tying up your money for a long time.

✔ **You may find they're not so unified:** Labour funds often have few connections with the union movement — in fact, many unions want nothing to do with them, complaining that they're a sort of squalid financial mushroom thriving on vastly expensive government tax subsidies, with the money ending up in the hands of Bay Street types and non-unionized companies. Labour funds are a "dubious stock promotion scheme," according to Jim Stanford, an economist with the Canadian Auto Workers.

Alas, the big tax breaks have disappeared for investors in some provinces. In Ontario, on which the labour-fund market depends heavily, the provincial government has been whittling what used to be a 15-percent tax credit down to zero by 2011, which will leave investors with only the 15-percent federal tax credit still available for investments in these funds. And Ontario investors have been fortunate — the provincial credit originally was set to disappear completely in 2006. An industry lobby persuaded legislators to instead leave the credit in place through 2008, and then reduce it to 10 percent in 2009, 5 percent in 2010, and eliminate it entirely as of 2011. Perhaps the government will relent again, but investors apparently haven't been optimistic about this prospect — and likely are unimpressed by these funds' poor performance. Assets invested in labour-sponsored funds had decreased 23 percent to $2.7 billion as of mid-2008 since Ontario first announced it was doing away with the tax credit. And although data companies don't calculate a median return for this group of funds — saying they're not a comparable peer group because they invest in such a diverse range of companies — about half the funds showed negative compound annual returns over various periods ended mid-2008.

If you're undeterred by labour funds' shaky tax status and the considerable investment risks, be cautious and put no more than 5 percent of your money here — okay, 10 percent if your idea of a quiet evening out is partying hard at the greyhound track in a low-cut dress or snakeskin suit, clutching a fistful of grubby $20 bills.

Examining why these funds get a tax break

Labour funds operate under special rules. The concept was introduced in the 1990s, growing out of talks between the federal government and unions on how to back small businesses, which are a major source of new jobs. In return for the lavish tax breaks given to their investors, the funds must have an affiliation with a union or employee association, but in fact the connection between most labour-sponsored funds and organized labour is tenuous at best.

The main point is that labour funds buy into small Canadian businesses that would otherwise have trouble attracting investors — in return for taking on such a big risk, the unitholders get some generous tax breaks. Sometimes, they concentrate on backing businesses that have a track record of earnings and revenue, and some labour funds even seek out companies that are already listed on a stock exchange, but often the little companies in these funds tend to have a very high failure rate. In general, the small companies backed by the funds are supposed to have fewer than 500 employees and less than $50 million in assets.

Understanding the risks

Venture capital investing is notoriously risky and unpredictable, meaning that it will almost certainly take several years for the investments your fund has bought into to show any kind of profit. Venture capitalists like to talk about a "Rule of 10." By that, they mean that a portfolio of venture investments will often contain two big winners, two so-so performers, and six that end up being taken down quietly to the river in a black plastic sack. But when venture investing is hot, it can really cook.

You can't predict in advance which labour fund will hit the mother lode, however, so improve your chances by buying at least two. Most funds will let you invest as little as $1,000 or even $500, so you won't have a problem dividing up your money. Your broker may beef about the extra paperwork, and holding multiple funds is more bother for you, but this is an area where having plenty of hooks in the water by owning several funds is essential.

A big problem with labour funds is lack of choice if you live outside Ontario. A few are available for sale in several provinces, giving investors the 15-percent federal tax credit, but some provincial governments don't give purchasers of those funds a matching provincial credit.

Expenses are stiff with this group, with management expense ratios raging from just under 3 percent to an incredible 10 percent-plus. That's really expensive. At that rate, a labour fund siphons off almost half your money in just ten years, which means these funds had better earn big returns to earn their keep. And the expenses look even worse when you consider that some funds have invested only half their money — meaning that some are levying fees and expenses that amount to 10 percent of the money they've actually put into small companies. From an investor's point of view, the only justification for accepting such high expenses is the chance of earning huge returns if one of the funds' venture investments explodes in value.

Labouring toward the right fund

Here are the main points to bear in mind when picking a labour fund:

- **Think small:** Look for a smallish one with assets of less than $200 million. Any larger than that, and it'll be hard for any one super-successful investment to have much of an influence on returns. If you live in Ontario, you're spoiled for choice because more than a dozen funds offer both federal and provincial tax credits. In the rest of the country, however, you may have to settle for the local provincial fund if you want to get back the full 30-percent refund.

✔ **Remember the risk:** Remember that this is risky investing, suitable for 5 to 10 percent of your portfolio at most. Some commentators advise, sensibly, that you take the entire tax refund you get from investing in a labour fund and invest it in a solid common stock fund, a guaranteed investment certificate, or even a bond fund. That way, if the labour fund turns out to be a dud, you'll probably earn a decent return on some of the money.

✔ **Check the fund's baggage:** As always, check the fund's main holdings and read its literature carefully. Even the bland brochures should give you an idea of what the fund's main goal is — creating jobs or earning big returns for investors. After that, it's your choice as to what you think is more important. If you're buying more than one labour fund — and we recommend you do — try to get funds with different styles. Some specialize in technology stocks while others concentrate on relatively mature companies that are close to issuing shares to the public or have already listed on a stock exchange.

✔ **Recognize the reality of the return:** Don't get all worked up by promises of fabulous extra tax savings if you buy the units and put them into an RRSP — RRSP savings are available on any mutual fund, stock, or bond. Labour fund ads tout the tax credits and then, in big black letters, also talk about the extra deduction available for buying the units through an RRSP. But despite lavish ads and eye-popping figures, labour funds are nothing special in that regard. Just about every fund can be put into an RRSP.

Making an eight-year commitment

Don't bother with labour funds unless you're absolutely sure you won't need the money back for years. That's because of that eight-year hold period. Remember, if you cash out within that time frame you'll not only have to repay your federal tax credits, but also, in some cases, shell out redemption fees to the fund company.

Labour funds are suited only for your very long-term money for another reason: The value of venture capital investments traditionally forms a "J curve" (picture a hockey stick). In other words, a holding often doesn't increase in value for several years — it may even drop — but it can suddenly shoot up when a deal is struck to either sell the business to a bigger company or take the investment public by listing its shares on a stock exchange. If you cash out too soon, you risk missing out on the payoff, leaving other investors to collect the big profits.

Target Date Funds: A Gimmick that Might Make Sense

Canada's population is aging. Too many baby boomers. Our big challenge is to find a way to quit working before our eyesight and typing skills fail, and not have to live in a hovel on a diet of pet food. Perhaps by owning target date funds we'll be spared a never-ending career and/or an undignified retirement — or so proponents of such funds would have us believe.

A *target date fund* is a balanced fund of funds with an investment mandate focused on an end date — in theory, within five years of the investor's projected retirement date. Eleven fund companies offered these products as of mid-2008, with target dates at five-year intervals ranging from 2010 to 2045, depending on the company. A fund that's close to the stated retirement date will have fixed-income and cash, and one that is many years away will hold mostly equities. (Figure 18-1 illustrates how portfolios differ, depending on how near retirement is.) Some funds will begin paying out cash distributions during the last few years ahead of the maturity date. Essentially, life-cycle funds do what you and or your adviser should be doing in managing an investment portfolio over the years, assuming your goal is to have all the money available (cashable) when retirement begins.

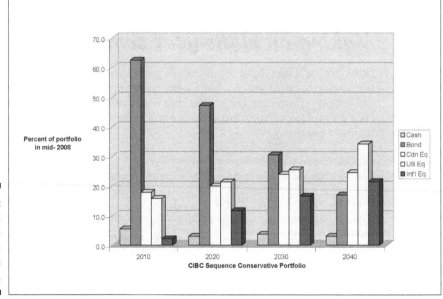

Figure 18-1: CIBC Sequence Life Cycle Funds compared.

Source: Morningstar

Considering your options

The longest-standing life-cycle mutual funds are IA Clarington's Target series, launched in early 2005. (Primerica Canada has a series of five life-cycle segregated funds that date back to 1994.) Three of the big banks (BMO, CIBC, and Scotia) have offerings in this category. (RBC has three similar funds, but they are aimed at funding post-secondary education, not retirement.) The other life-cycle players are AIM Trimark, Ethical Funds, Fidelity, London Life, Mackenzie, and Russell Investments.

The largest life-cycle mutual fund as of mid-2008 was BMO Life Stage Plus 2015, launched in June 2007. In just one year, this fund had amassed assets of more than $630 million. Not surprisingly, more assets are in funds with end dates that occur sooner (2010 to 2025) than are in the longer-term funds.

CIBC and Scotia offer two different fund portfolios for each of their life-cycle funds. CIBC's are either "conservative" or "moderate," and Scotia's versions are "conservative" and "aggressive." Table 18-1 compares the holdings in the Scotia Vision Conservative and Aggressive 2020 Portfolios.

Table 18-1	Scotia Vision Conservative and Aggressive 2020 Portfolios	
	Conservative	*Aggressive*
Cash	13.6%	10.6%
Canadian equity	31%	31.9%
U.S. and international equity	21.1%	25.9%

Not much difference there, with about 12 years remaining to retirement. But the difference between the bank's 2015 funds, with little more than seven years to go, is more pronounced. Table 18-2 spells out the difference.

Table 18-2	Scotia Vision Conservative and Aggressive 2015 Portfolios	
	Conservative	*Aggressive*
Cash	13.4%	12.4%
Canadian equity	28.7%	31.9%
U.S. and international equity	19%	24%

With the retirement date just seven years away, the 2015 aggressive portfolio has a higher cash position than its 2020 counterpart and the U.S. and international equity portion is lower. These make the portfolio less risky as the fund's liquidation date nears.

AIM Trimark launched its four Invesco Trimark Retirement Payout Portfolio funds in mid-2008. (Invesco is the name of its U.S.–based parent company.) They're different from the rest of the category because, in addition to actively managed AIM Trimark funds, their portfolios include five of Invesco's "tilted" exchange-traded funds. So a component of their return is based on the performance of U.S. and international stock indices — although as tilted funds they don't mirror the exact stock weightings of the underlining index. (Chapter 15 gives you the straight goods on tilted ETFs.)

In addition to its ClearPath group, Fidelity also has funds that take over after retirement. Its Income Replacement funds are structured to provide a regular income stream during retirement. Eleven portfolios (sold in three formats, depending on how you buy them) are available for terms of 10 to 30 years, ending in odd-numbered years. As with conventional life-cycle funds, the Income Replacement fund portfolios are built using individual Fidelity funds. Each fund's holdings are adjusted over time to ensure a monthly income stream is maintained as the maturity date draws closer.

Knowing what to look for

The life-cycle-fund concept is quite straightforward and serves as a structured and disciplined retirement investment program. Check for annual expenses, though. In some cases, MERs are fairly reasonable, considering the life-cycle portfolio adjustment service that's included. Ideally, a life-cycle fund's MER should reflect the fees of the underlying funds it holds. For example, CIBC's Sequence funds hold funds from the bank's Renaissance family. Two-thirds of the Sequence Conservative 2010 Fund is in Renaissance fixed-income funds with MERs below 2 percent. The remainder is in Canadian and U.S. equity funds with MERs ranging from 2.3 to 2.6 percent. The Sequence fund's MER seems a bargain at 2.12 percent. Even the most aggressive Sequence fund's MER is below 2.5 percent, despite being more heavily weighted in equity funds with higher MERs.

The question remains, though: Can a life-cycle fund provide the asset allocation and investment selection best suited to your specific retirement goals? For some, shopping for one-size-fits-all garments works, while others insist on a precise size. You need to decide what's right for you.

Funds with Trendy and Focused Mandates

The funds we discuss in this chapter are unusual, but they're numerous and mainstream enough to merit their own fund categories. Things get really wild and woolly in the mutual fund data surveyors' "specialty" category. You can imagine how oddball these funds are when they can't be placed in the more than three dozen categories established by the data providers. If some of these funds didn't include such intriguing names as Kyoto Planet and Criterion U.S. Buyback, they'd be lost in this classification backwater.

Some of the names reflect mandates that are in vogue, such as extreme income orientations or environmentally conscious investing. Other funds simply are so focused on a specific subsector they could not be classified among equity funds that invest in broader sectors.

The trendy nature of most of these funds means they're fleetingly popular, which suggests these funds might make poor short-term investments. However, if you feel strongly about investing in improving the world's ecological situation or renewing infrastructure, then nothing's wrong with making a "feel good" investment of, say, 5 percent or even 10 percent of your portfolio. As for funds with ultra-specific mandates, if you're able to understand the concepts behind their investment mandates, go for it — but tread very carefully and limit your investment to no more than 5 percent.

Here's a sampling of trendy and ultra-focused fund offerings:

✔ **Extreme environmental funds:** Plenty of green funds exist out there with investment strategies mainstream enough to merit classification in the various equity categories. However, some have more specialized mandates, so they are in the specialty category. Among these are the aforementioned Kyoto Planet, which invests globally in renewable energy and clean technology industries. It's not classified as a global equity fund because its mandate allows it to engage in short selling. (*Short selling* is an aggressive investing technique in which an investor "borrows" stock from a brokerage firm's inventory and sells it with the hope of repurchasing it at a lower price.)

Scotia Global Climate Change invests in companies around the world that are "expected to profit from direct or indirect actions taken by such companies to mitigate the impact of climate change on the environment." The fund's mandate is so broad within the climate-change area that the data providers classified it as a specialty fund.

Two funds even focus specifically on the water infrastructure "industry." In fact, one of them — Claymore S&P Global Water ETF — is an exchange-traded fund based on the S&P Global Water Index. The investment strategy might be a tad undiversified, but at least the annual expenses are minuscule, at 0.6 percent.

✔ **Infrastructure funds:** The developing world needs to expand and modernize its infrastructure, and this represents a huge opportunity for the industrial world's construction companies, utilities, and other firms involved in infrastructure design and implementation. Although the stated mandates of funds like Investors Global Infrastructure refer to infrastructure work done in foreign countries — often by North American firms — nothing says this or similar funds couldn't invest in companies engaged in rebuilding our own crumbling bridges, sewer systems, and other outdated public facilities.

✔ **Ultra-specific mandates:** Some funds' mandates are uber-specific — so minutely focused on one investment area or strategy they're probably best left alone in their unique little fiefdoms. But, just so you know, you can actually buy a fund that focuses on investing in shares of stock exchanges (Caldwell Exchange Fund), or one that "takes advantage of the current under-valuations in the late private or early public markets" (Marquis Bridge Fund), or even one focused exclusively in floating rate debt instruments (Trimark Floating Rate Income).

Chapter 19

Segregated Funds: Investing on Autopilot

*S*egregated funds — also sometimes known as "guaranteed investment funds" — are investment funds that promise to at least refund an investor's original investment as long as the investor stays in the fund for ten years or, well, dies. Fund salespeople who've gone forth to pitch them to cautious older customers have found that the super-safe funds are quite popular — with the investors' kids, who don't want to see their inheritance wiped out because Mom couldn't resist the allure of Brazilian junk-bond funds.

Segregated funds have attracted billions of dollars from customers who just can't bear the thought of losing their investments in the capital markets. In return, they're willing to pay much higher annual costs, as seg funds have management expense ratios that can be more than 1 percent higher than a nearly identical mutual fund. Investors are willing to swallow this extra charge for a guarantee that some observers argue is of dubious worth. The cost of this guarantee is inflated by tough rules that require insurers to set aside a sizeable amount of capital to cover the cost of these funds' guarantees. As of mid-2008, approximately 2,700 — or one-third — of the nearly 8,500 fund choices on sale in Canada were seg funds. However, seg fund assets totaled about $91 billion, compared with more than $730 billion invested in mutual funds.

In this chapter, we explain the main differences between segregated (or guaranteed funds) and regular mutual funds, set out some of the main advantages and drawbacks of seg funds, and offer a few guidelines to help you decide whether they're right for you. Throughout, we use the expression "seg funds" for both segregated funds and guaranteed investment funds (guaranteed funds is the term used by Manulife Financial, Toronto-Dominion, and some other seg-fund sponsors). Both terms mean essentially the same thing: funds that promise to refund most or all of an investor's initial outlay, if held for long enough.

Hang On to Your Hats: The Rise of the Segregated Fund

Segregated funds: What a steamy, exotic name. Surely only those wacky knockabout jesters in life insurance could have come up with such an exciting term. For years, they sold a sort of grey version of a mutual fund, often wrapped inside impenetrable life-insurance policies. The funds' assets were kept separated or "segregated" from those of the life insurance company itself, hence the name.

In principle, seg funds were much the same as mutual funds: Investors looking for growth from stocks or steady returns from bonds pooled their money in a professionally managed fund and were issued units, representing ownership of the pool, that were supposed to increase in value. Often these funds were marketed as part of frequently incomprehensible "whole life" or "universal life" insurance policies that were supposed to provide an investment return as well as protection for the customer's family.

Security with segs

Seg funds offered one advantage that their flashier Porsche-driving, model-dating, mutual fund rivals couldn't match. Regulated as insurance products, not investments, seg funds came with an attractive guarantee to refund at least 75 percent of an investor's money, as long as he or she stayed invested in the fund for a set period. This guarantee was passed on to the holder's estate in the event of the investor's death. In other words, when the funds were cashed in at the time of the holder's death, the heirs got at least 75 percent of the amount that was originally invested or the market value, whichever was higher.

The popularity of segs sag

The rising popularity of mutual funds in the late 1990s, with their easy-to-understand unit prices and relatively strong returns, left life insurers and their dreary complicated seg funds in the shade. Seg funds were usually managed extremely cautiously and they were loaded down with heavy expenses. Another big problem was the difficulty in figuring out what exactly you were buying: an investment or life insurance? The public, tired of carnivorous life insurance salespeople, listened avidly as a host of financial authors and other gurus told them to "buy term and invest the rest." The theory, which is generally a good one, goes like this: Why buy some complicated life insurance product loaded down with weird concepts like "commuted value" and "vanishing premiums" when you have no real way to be sure you're getting value for money? As for comparing the endlessly complex "whole life" policies from different companies, you might as well try to teach raccoons to play rugby.

So, the experts advised, just protect your loved ones by buying straightforward, cheap, term life insurance for a simple monthly premium and use the savings, which would otherwise have vanished into a whole-life policy, to buy regular mutual funds. That way, you're clear on exactly what you own and what you're paying. As you know we're keen on simplicity, so we agree with the strategy.

If you're a self-employed businessperson or if you have complicated tax needs, life insurance still can offer some important tax-sheltering and estate-planning benefits. So a place for "whole life" coverage still exists in some cases. Just make sure, though, that you get help in this area from a fee-paid professional such as an accountant, and don't fall for the blandishments of a commission-collecting sales rep.

A fancy fund makeover

In the late 1990s, two interesting things happened. Life insurance companies started selling seg funds that looked like mutual funds — and mutual fund companies started selling seg-fund versions of their mutual funds. Manulife Financial got the ball rolling by launching funds that essentially took well-known mutual funds from big partners such as AIM Trimark Investments, AGF Management Ltd., and Fidelity Investments Canada Ltd. and wrapped them in a nice cozy "guaranteed investment fund" blanket that pledged to return at least all the investors' original outlay if they died or if they held the funds for ten years.

The fund industry soon struck back, with CI Investments Inc. launching segregated versions of its own funds in partnership with a life insurance company. Other mutual fund players followed suit, launching seg versions of their mutual funds on which a life insurance company provided the guarantee. Soon, life insurance companies were scrambling to jazz up their stale seg offerings by forming partnerships with fund companies or hiring fancy managers of their own.

In the old days, seg funds were generally grey collections of blue-chip stocks and bonds, run by pallid people who took commuter trains every night at 5:30 sharp to their identical houses in far-off places with inspiring names like Milton, Ontario. But soon after the millennium, the insurance industry came up with much more exciting products, including seg funds that invest in emerging markets, health sciences, resource companies, the technology-crazed Nasdaq stock market, and Asian stocks. Government regulators noticed, and started to wonder whether life insurance companies had enough money to make good on the guarantees they had attached to these relatively volatile funds. They got so worried, in fact, that they forced companies to set aside extra piles of cash to cover the potential cost of providing these risky guarantees to investors.

Seg Fund Essentials

We outline the main features of seg funds here. Note that most of these funds technically count as insurance contracts, which means they involve a whole new set of jargon and concepts. We introduce some of the new terms as we go along (we know it's exciting, but please try to stay in your seat), but remember that this short description can't hope to cover every seg fund from every company.

Guaranteeing the return of your initial investment

The essential point with seg funds is their ten-year guarantee. In insurance lingo, when you buy a seg fund you've bought a "contract" that "matures" in ten years. It doesn't matter how you hold the fund: in a taxable account or a registered retirement savings plan (or some other kind of tax-sheltered account). The guarantee usually states that no matter what happens to the fund or the markets in the decade following your purchase, after ten years you're entitled to get back at least the amount of money you put into the fund or the market value of your units, whichever is greater.

Say, for instance, you bought $10,000 worth of a fund that proceeded to have an awful ten years, slashing the value of your holding to $8,000. After the period, you can go to the fund company and get your $10,000 back. If, by contrast, the fund does reasonably well, doubling the value of your hold-ing to $20,000, then you get the $20,000. Under insurance law, the guarantee must be for at least 75 percent of your investment, but many insurers and fund companies have boosted that to 100 percent for marketing reasons. However, the tough rules introduced in 2000 forced many companies to scale the guarantee back to 75 percent again, although a good selection of funds with a 100-percent guarantee is still available.

Living longer than you might

The investment-principal guarantee also applies when the annuitant (that is, the person whose life has been insured) named in the contract dies. In that case, the value of the seg fund units is paid to the policy's beneficiary (the person selected to get the death benefit). No matter when the policy was bought, the amount paid out to the beneficiary is subject to the guarantee. He or she gets either the original investment or the market value at the time of death, whichever is more.

Note that the so-called guarantee is pretty limited. It applies only after ten years or upon death. If you sell your fund units at any other time, you get only the market value, even if it's less than your purchase price. Whining to the fund company if the value of your units has collapsed after three years is pointless. They'll just make a sympathetic little face, give you an attractive key ring, and tell you to come back in seven years.

Enabling you to reset the value of successful funds

A popular feature with most of the newer seg funds was the ability to "reset" the amount covered by the guarantee, often up to twice a year. For example, say you put $10,000 into a technology-based seg fund and saw the value of your investment soar to $13,000 in six months. You could reset the value of your contract at the higher amount, so you're guaranteed to get back at least $13,000 after ten years (or your estate is guaranteed to get back at least $13,000 when you die).

The only drawback: Resetting the contract starts the clock ticking again, so you have to wait a full ten years, not nine and a half, before the contract matures. Reset features — which greatly increase the risk of seg funds for insurance companies — were a prime reason for the regulatory crackdown.

Offering asset protection

For self-employed businesspeople or professionals who potentially face lawsuits from creditors, segregated funds can be an excellent way to protect assets. Because they're an insurance contract, seg funds are normally out of the reach of creditors, as long as a spouse, parent, child, or grandchild is named as the beneficiary or the beneficiary has been named "irrevocably" (that is, their written consent must be obtained to name a new beneficiary).

Watch out, though: The beneficiary of seg funds held in an RRSP must be revocable or the investments lose their registered status. And the protection from creditors doesn't apply where a debtor has cynically shovelled assets into seg funds just to get out of paying obligations. This is a complex area, so talk to your lawyer before making decisions.

Giving to your heir apparent without the hassle

Seg funds are a great way of passing money on to heirs without hassle or fees (apart from redemption charges if you bought the funds on a deferred-load basis). Again, because they count as life insurance, the proceeds from seg funds are paid directly to your heirs when you die; they do not pass through your estate. That means the money escapes provincial probate fees, a sort of death tax in all provinces except Quebec that can run as high as 1.5 percent. And the money is usually paid out to the beneficiaries immediately, without the holdups that can plague the settlement of estates. Normal bequests are public documents, but seg fund contracts are private, so you can leave money to a charity or individual without Nosey Parker finding out about it.

Seg funds avoid probate fees, but they can be less tax-efficient than regular mutual funds when the holder dies. Normally, investment assets pass to a spouse with no taxes payable immediately on capital gains that have been earned. But a seg fund is considered to be a trust for tax purposes, so gains earned in these funds may be taxable. Be sure to talk to a knowledgeable accountant.

Because seg funds are life insurance contracts, you must buy them from an adviser who is licensed to sell life insurance, which means that not every financial planner or broker may be able to help you. However, more and more brokers and planners are taking the necessary courses to qualify to sell insurance, or they refer their clients to a colleague or local insurance agent or broker who can sell seg funds.

A Grim Reminder with Some Helpful Hints

Now, we know journalists are always producing sensationalist scare stories, but hear us out. As you get older, it becomes more likely you'll die in the near future.

At 45, a Canadian woman has an approximately 2.5-percent chance of dying in the next ten years, while a Canadian man has a 4-percent likelihood. At 55, it rises to 6 percent for women and 10 percent for men. By 65, it shoots up to 15 percent and 26 percent, respectively. And at 75, Canadian women have a 38-percent chance of dying in the next decade — but for men, well, the chance they'll be throwing a seven in the great craps game of life before ten lacrosse seasons have come and gone is 55 percent. (Those figures, by the way, are based on Statistics Canada numbers reported by mathematicians Moshe Milevsky and Thomas Salisbury in a 2006 study, Asset Allocation and the Transition to Income: The Importance of Product Allocation in the Retirement Risk Zone.)

The fact that older investors are more likely to die means it gets riskier for the fund companies to guarantee a refund of the amount they put into a seg fund. So, many companies reduce or restrict the guarantee for older investors. For example, some don't allow resets of the death benefit guarantee when the annuitant has turned 75. And when the annuitant has turned 90, the death benefit guarantee may be reduced.

Mutual funds must obtain their unitholders' consent to increase fees, but seg funds are pretty well free to charge what they like. Seg funds are complicated beasts, and their "information folders," the prospectus-like documents that set out their features, are tough to read. You have to buy them through a licensed insurance salesperson, so take your time and find an experienced agent or broker whom you trust. You'll need an expert on your side to figure out the often-horrendous complexities.

Figuring Out How Much this Certainty Costs

How much extra do you pay for the guarantee? For volatile funds, the difference can be several percentage points of your investment each year — slicing into returns like a giant weighted machete cutting rancid butter — but if you shop aggressively and buy sane, high-quality funds, you may be able to get the coverage at a reasonable cost. Check out Table 19-1, which shows the median (or midpoint) annual management expense ratio (MER) for regular mutual funds and then segregated funds in five key categories.

One of the things that makes insurance companies most nervous is, clearly, foreign stock investing, with its added risk in the form of currency swings — on global equity seg funds, insurers cost almost 0.6 of a percentage point more. For investments closer to home, they get less cagey.

Reality check for seg funds

Check out how one segregated fund has fared against the normal mutual funds it's supposed to track. Manulife Financial launched its MLI Fidelity Canadian Asset Allocation GIF Fund 1 in 1997. The fund was pitched as a conservative way to achieve much the same performance as the Fidelity Canadian Asset Allocation Fund, a fund that switches among stocks, bonds, and cash in an effort to achieve high total returns.

At the cost of a higher MER, currently 3.41 percent compared with 2.28 percent for the Fidelity fund, investors in the GIF got the usual guaranteed return of at least their original investment after ten years or upon death. The Fidelity fund, by contrast, could in theory lose money over ten years, leaving unitholders in the red. The

Manulife GIF funds were a huge marketing success: By the end of 1999, Manulife Fidelity Canadian Asset Allocation GIF's assets had ballooned to $750 million, making it Canada's seventh-biggest seg fund at that time.

The GIF hasn't done a bad job of tracking the Fidelity fund. As of March 2008, an investor who put $10,000 into the fund on inception (January 1997) was sitting on $22,338, or a cumulative 123 percent return on his or her investment. The same $10,000 investment in the Fidelity fund grew to $24,689, or 145 percent. In other words, the Manulife fund has done a reasonable job of tracking the Fidelity fund, with the difference in returns attributable to its extra annual costs of more than a percentage point.

On Canadian balanced funds, normally a fairly stable stew of bonds and stocks, insurers apparently ask less than half of a percentage point in extra MER. They charge roughly the same premium for providing the (limited, remember) pledge on Canadian stocks. Of course, looking at category medians or averages doesn't highlight some examples of seg funds with pretty spectacular MERs. How does 5.8 percent annually on the seg version of a Toronto-Dominion Bank health-industry fund sound? That's half your money in a decade. The mutual version of the same fund charges an MER less than one-half as much. This, of course, demonstrates the cost of insuring an investment in a risky investment area like biotechnology. As for bond funds, charging an annual premium of more than one-half of a percentage point to guarantee against losses might seem exorbitant, given the relatively low volatility of bond portfolios. Nonetheless, buying some kind of guarantee might well be a good idea if inflation returns in a big way, potentially sending bond prices tumbling for years.

The gap between mutual and seg money market funds is smaller — 0.35 of a percentage point. Yet this seems severe when you consider the safety of this type of investment. Money market seg funds exist only for the purpose of keeping an investor's money within a particular fund family, thus avoiding switch-out fees for an investor who wants to park his or her money and later reinvest within that family of seg funds.

Table 19-1	The High Price of Peace of Mind	
	Median MERs (in percent)	
Fund Type	*Regular Funds*	*Segregated Funds*
Global Equity	2.60	3.18
Canadian Equity	2.34	2.80
Canadian Neutral Balanced	2.30	2.77
Canadian Fixed Income	1.48	2.13
Canadian Money Market	0.96	1.31

Source: Morningstar Canada

Taking a Closer Look at the "Deal" with Segs

Many commentators have argued forcefully that those costly guarantees are ripoffs when it comes to bond funds and of dubious benefit for balanced funds, which are supposed to be sedate portfolios that avoid losses. After all, in the 25 full calendar years from 1983 through 2007, the median Canadian fixed-income mutual fund lost money only twice, a drop of 6.1 percent in 1994 and another of 2.2 percent in 1999. The median Canadian neutral balanced mutual fund had only four losing years, falling 1.9 percent in 1990, 3.1 percent in 1994, 1 percent in 2001, and 5.4 percent in 2002.

Given the long-term tendency of stocks to rise, it's rare, too, to find any kind of equity fund that loses money over ten years. That makes it unlikely you'll ever need to collect on the ten-year maturity guarantee (which promises to at least refund your investment if you've held the fund for a decade). Among equity funds of significant size — we'll define these as those with assets of $100 million or more — only 23 of 236 failed to make money during the ten years ended February 2008.

Admittedly, a lot of flea-bitten funds get buried within median and average statistics, as a result of the fund industry's habit of quietly folding underperformers into their better-performing sister funds. This "survivorship bias," which results in merged and otherwise discontinued funds — many of them truly awful — vanishing from the record, is notorious for casting a rosy glow over the industry's performance past. However, data firm Morningstar calculates indices that wipe out survivorship bias and, equally important, produce a weighted average return for all mutual fund categories. (We take a closer look at the Morningstar Canada Fund Indices in Chapter 21.)

If you decide high-MER seg funds are a scam because mutual funds rarely lose money over a decade, you may be missing the point. Over shorter periods mutual funds are perfectly capable of losing money, and lots of it. Some 80 of 472 equity funds lost money over the three years ended February 2008. For older investors who are worried about dying just as their funds are going into the tank, taking thousands of dollars off the value of their estate, a segregated fund guarantee is mighty comforting. At least on death the full value of the original investment goes to the heirs (not that we'd give the slack-jawed gum-chewing brats anything, but that's just crusty old lovable Andrew's take on things).

To Seg or Not to Seg: Are They for You?

The bottom line with seg funds is almost certainly that they're best suited for older or unwell investors who have a reasonable probability of passing away in the next few years. Seg funds' protection from creditors also makes them very attractive to self-employed businesspeople and entrepreneurs.

Here are two examples, adapted from material produced by AIM Trimark, of older investors who seem well suited for seg funds.

The first is a 67-year-old woman with four nieces and three nephews to whom she wants to leave money without legal hassles and probate fees. She puts $50,000 into a seg fund. If she dies after five years and the value of her deposit has risen to $85,000, her beneficiaries get $85,000, minus any withdrawals or redemption fees if she bought the funds on a back-end-load basis. But say the market has slumped and the value of her contract is only $43,000. Then her beneficiaries get the guaranteed amount of $50,000, again minus redemption fees.

The other example is a 61-year-old, self-employed engineer who's two years from retirement. He's repelled by the low interest rates available on guaranteed investment certificates but he doesn't want to put his money at risk just before he retires. So he invests $100,000 in seg funds. If it grows to $230,000 in ten years, when the contract matures, he gets $230,000. But if the value of his fund drops to $80,000 at maturity, he gets his original $100,000, minus any withdrawals.

Then consider the estate-planning advantages of seg funds, especially the relative simplicity of passing on money to a beneficiary by simply putting it in a seg fund. Don't get too excited about saving on probate fees, though, because the higher management fees on seg funds will quickly wipe out that advantage.

Choosing a seg fund really comes down to the famous "pillow factor." Just how well can you sleep at night knowing your money is in danger? If you're really afraid of losses, then seg funds may well be your thing, despite their higher management expense ratio. The emotional security is sometimes worth the higher MERs.

Chapter 20

Fund Packages:
One-Stop Shopping

*W*e're always being hassled and badgered to think for ourselves in our workplaces — so isn't it nice to just regress to a vegetative state once in a while? Well, mutual fund companies and stockbrokers are keen students of human weakness and they've noticed that many investors like to be presented with simple one-decision products that they can just buy and forget about.

Hence the emergence of fund packages, also known as *wraps* and *funds of funds.* Brokers, bank employees, and financial planners enjoy selling them. These funds are nice and simple to pitch. And because they have built-in diversification, the salespeople won't have to explain why the Rust-Encrusted Highly Indebted Declining Heavy Industry Recovery Value Fund is at the bottom of the performance table once again.

In this chapter, we describe the main types of preselected fund packages and list some of their advantages and disadvantages.

The Flavours Fund Packages Come In

A *fund package* is a group of individual mutual funds selected by a fund company or money manager for the purpose of providing the investor with a diversified fund portfolio in a single product. It's structured as an individual fund (or "wrap") that has a portfolio made up only of individual mutual funds, usually drawn from the sponsoring firm's fund lineup. Depending on its investment objectives, a package typically will hold one or more equity funds, a bond fund, and a money market fund (as the cash component).

Fund companies, banks, stockbrokers, insurance companies, fund managers, and financial planning firms have come up with a bewildering range of fund combinations that claim to take care of your every need, eliminating the need to pick and choose your own funds. Sometimes these are called "managed accounts."

Checking out the risk categories

Typically, before you're sold a fund package, you'll be asked to fill out a questionnaire that establishes how much risk you can stand and what sort of annual return you're demanding. From there, the salesperson, bank employee, or fund company representative simply takes your money and sticks it into a suitable package, usually straight off the shelf but sometimes supposedly designed for your needs.

You'll probably be offered something that falls into one of these three risk categories:

- **Conservative:** The safest packages of all, they're all about conserving capital while offering a reasonable flow of income from bonds or Treasury bills, and perhaps the chance of some capital gains from stocks. (Remember that "income" in this context refers to the steady interest payments generated by bonds, money that you simply plow back into the same kind of investment.)

  These conservative packages are usually full of funds that invest in *bonds* — which are debts owed by governments and big companies — and money market securities — which are short-term borrowings by the government and large corporations.

- **Moderate:** The next step up on the volatility scale, these packages are pretty similar to the typical balanced fund. They're for investors who don't mind the occasional loss in return for the higher returns that stocks and long-term bonds offer. Generally, their mixture of stocks and bonds will be close to one-half each, with a cash anchor of about 5 percent.

- **Growth:** These packages own mostly stocks and typically have only a small portion of their assets, usually 25 percent or less, in bond and money market funds, with the rest in equities. You'll be steered into these mixtures only if you've indicated on the questionnaire that you won't be needing to cash in any of the investment for several years. If your "horizon" is long term, the theory goes, you shouldn't be worried by a nasty dip in the value of your holdings in the short term.

  The most entertaining growth packages, naturally, are those with "aggressive" in their name. Much as we love to think of these being bought by shaven-headed former paratroopers with drinking problems, it simply denotes a mixture that puts as little as 10 percent of your assets into bonds and holds lots of volatile stuff such as emerging markets and technology companies.

Check out Chapter 4, where we help you determine what type of investor you are. If you're a saver, you're best suited for a conservative package. Balanced investors, consider a moderate package. Growth packages, unsurprisingly, are best suited to growth investors.

Sticking with Canada or going global

Whether you stay true to the maple leaf or go global depends partly on what you think will happen to currencies, and of course on your time horizon. If the Canadian dollar tanks, then it would be better to have your money outside the country. If it goes up, then it's better to keep a lot of your investments Canadian. But it's impossible to know in advance what will happen to foreign exchange rates.

For short-term and medium-term savings, an all-Canadian package of investments is probably fine because you plan to spend the money relatively soon and you'll be spending it in Canadian dollars. But with long-term equity packages, make sure you get at least some global stock action. It spreads your risk by giving you a more mixed bag of investments, and great companies to invest in exist all around the world. And you also need to protect yourself against a drop in the Canadian dollar.

What to Find Out Before You Buy

Be sure to pose these stumpers to anyone who tries to peddle a fund portfolio to you. This section reviews the two essential questions to ask.

How much will this cost me?

With some of these preselected mixtures, you have to pay the regular fees and expenses of the funds included in the service plus an extra fee for the package itself that can run as high as 1 percent annually.

Adding another 1 percent in yearly costs is a heavy weight to put on your portfolio, especially if some of the equity funds in the package already have management expense ratios (MERs) of more than 2.5 percent. Many brokers and financial planners sell their own private wrap or asset allocation products that use funds that charge low or no management fees. But in this case, the client pays a separate fee — often listed directly on her or his statement — to cover the asset allocation service.

In theory, costs you incur trying to earn investment income are tax-deductible, so you may be able to claim fund management fees against taxes. Some vendors like to make a big song and dance about this advantage. But that applies only to fees that are charged separately to the investor and not simply deducted from the fund. Ordinary mutual fund charges and fees are quietly taken out of the fund's assets by the manager and can't be claimed as a cost. However, though they're not directly deductible, ordinary fees do reduce your taxable capital gains and income by cutting into the return you get from your funds, so the fees are ultimately deductible, too.

Although it's great to see package fees broken down openly on your statement instead of having them buried in the management expense ratio, make sure you realize what you're paying — because it can be confusing. Funds that charge you expenses separately instead of taking them out of your annual return present another problem. Because they ignore expenses and costs when they report those returns, they'll often seem to be doing better than funds that handle fees and costs in the normal way, by extracting them before they report performance.

How do I know how well I'm doing?

Many of these services don't publish their returns publicly, and even if they do the names are often so similar it can be hard to remember what you own. Some fund companies even establish a sort of imaginary unit price, simply for the purpose of calculating performance. That's mostly because mutual fund data firms like Globe Interactive and Morningstar use special software for working out a fund's returns. Essentially, their systems determine performance by calculating the changes in the price of a unit, taking into account any distributions for unitholders along the way. For example, if you check out the portfolios available from CIBC, you'll notice they have unit prices. In fact, when you buy into these services, you sometimes buy each fund in the package separately with its own unit price, in the normal way. The units shown for the package may simply be there for ease of calculating returns.

The account statement you receive semi-annually, quarterly, or monthly for any service should make your returns absolutely clear, so ask to see a sample before you sign up. Don't be fobbed off by vague excuses. If the salesperson or bank employee can't demonstrate that your returns will be clearly reported, avoid the product.

The Upside of Fund Packages

The idea of simply handing over your cash to let professionals decide the asset mix can be wonderfully attractive. And fund packages offer a number of other important advantages:

- ✔ **Dealing with only one fund company:** You don't have to juggle account statements and tax slips from several sellers. Most investors, with their busy lives, loathe getting piles of mail from fund companies.

- ✔ **Automatic rebalancing:** You don't have to rejig your funds if strong returns or big losses throw the asset mix of your portfolio out of whack. Many packages are periodically rebalanced by the company so that clients don't end up with too much of their money riding on just one type of investment.

For example, say you've put $100,000 into a sedate portfolio made up equally of bond funds and stock funds. If the stock market slides by 20 percent but interest rates stay unchanged, your stock funds will probably be worth $40,000 while your bond funds will still be worth $50,000. To maintain your 50/50 mix, the portfolio service will redeem about $5,000 worth of bond funds and put the money into stocks instead, to restore the equal balance.

✔ **Charging reasonable fees:** Because they use regular mutual funds that are subject to public scrutiny and fairly tight securities laws, the widely available fund packages charge fees that are usually reasonable, at least when you compare them to the charges that trust companies or lawyers can levy for looking after assets.

The Downside of Fund Packages

Letting someone else pick your funds for you does have its drawbacks. Here are a few:

✔ **An unexciting way to invest:** It's boring and Big Brotherish. All you get is the same gruel-like return earned by everyone else who buys the same package, with no real clue as to which fund did well and which one barked your money away. It's more interesting to be an informed consumer who can tell that, for example, bonds were up while international equities were down, just by looking at your account statement.

✔ **Extra costs:** If extra costs are levied, they eat into your return, especially when tacked on top of the underlying mutual funds' fees and expenses.

✔ **Tax implications of rebalancing:** The regular portfolio rebalancing by the fund company can trigger taxable capital gains distributions for investors holding the package of funds outside a tax-deferred account such as an RRSP. Fund companies maintain that these distributions will generally be small because they're simply readjusting the asset mix rather than turning the fund inside out, but taxable payouts add unpredictability and can cut into your real, after-tax return.

✔ **Unreported returns:** Be very wary before you buy into any fund or managed investment whose returns and unit price aren't published regularly in the newspapers. Remember, sunlight disinfects: If the performance isn't publicly reported alongside that of big regular mutual funds, making comparisons simple, then you can never really be sure you're not stuck with a dog.

✔ **Constricted by your funds:** If you're in pooled or house-brand funds that are sold only through a particular brokerage or financial planning firm, then moving your money elsewhere can be troublesome because your new broker or planner might be unwilling to add this fund to his or her product lineup. (A *pooled fund* is similar to a mutual fund, except it is sold on an institutional basis by offering memorandum rather than by prospectus, and requires a high minimum investment, often $300,000 or more.)

✔ **Great potential confusion:** Working out how you're doing or even what package you own can be tricky, given the confusing multiplicity of products with similar names. Web sites and brochures can be vague on how the systems actually work, and salespeople are hard-pressed to keep up with the flood of new offerings. And a whole bunch of transactions may be reported to you on your statement, just as though you had ordered them, when the portfolio is automatically rebalanced or a fund is dropped from the mixture. If you're not completely sure you understand what you're buying, better to steer clear.

Just about every fund seller claims that its asset allocation strategies are best, and comparing them is just about impossible. That's because the returns produced by any system tell only half the story. The other half is how much risk did the portfolio take on and how violent were the swings. To provide a crude example, a portfolio that made 12 percent a year for five years might look superior to one that generated a return of just 6 percent annually. But if it turns out that the first portfolio was exclusively invested in super-risky, early-stage, biotechnology shares while the second held mostly government bonds, then the second portfolio probably did a better job — earning a good profit relative to the low level of risk it incurred.

Before buying a fund package from a bank or other seller, try to get the goods on how well it's been doing from a third-party online source like Morningstar.ca or Globefund.com. Before you hand over any money, make sure you can actually find the package at one of these sources. That way, you'll be able to track your returns easily from month to month without relying solely on your account statement from the company.

Don't worry too much about trying to figure out the difference between one company's Nervous Nellie Never-Lose-a-Penny-of-My-Money Portfolio and another fund seller's Shaky Sue Can't Stand the Slightest Suspicion of Suffering a Slump Asset Allocation Service. The big thing, as usual, is to look for low costs, so you know you're getting reasonable value, and clear reporting so you at least know how you're doing.

Steering Clear of the Hype

Packages have become an extremely popular product for financial advisers to sell. They transfer the investment selection decisions to portfolio-management experts within their firm or at a fund company of another third-party firm. The adviser's main role is to help you determine the right asset allocation — the breakdown among equities, fixed income, and cash.

Advisers who pitch fund packages will extol the benefits of professional portfolio management and the discipline this brings. They will talk about portfolio "rebalancing," which the package's managers will take care of at regular intervals — often quarterly — to ensure the asset allocation is correct. Advisers will all but guarantee you are much better off in a package as opposed to a collection of individually selected funds. But take all such claims with a big swig of salty vinegar. Investment wizards are infallible only until they blow it, and the explosion can be spectacular. The market and economy have a delightful way of throwing weird slimy curveballs that completely fool the number-crunchers.

The truth is, when banks and other fund sellers pitch these packages, what they're really trying to do is eliminate the need for you to pick any other fund seller's wares. They'd much rather you stuck to their product line than mix and match funds from different sellers. So they offer their super-simple, off-the-shelf packages that relieve you of the need to choose your mutual funds and that tempt you to go with their stuff.

Some companies even sell packages that also include other companies' funds. Even Investors Group, the country's biggest fund complex and a bastion of the in-house product approach, has packages that include *third-party funds* — funds from other managers. However, you'll notice that third-party funds usually come from companies such as Fidelity Investments Canada or AGF Management that pay a sales commission to the people who put the package together. These packages may include good funds, but they also carry the same disadvantages as other pre-mixed fund selections. That is, their costs can be high and it's hard to know which fund is doing well for you and which is sinking like a lead submarine.

Preselected packages of funds are convenient, but you're not guaranteed that the fund company, bank, or broker has got the mix right. And the packages can make it hard to know how well you're doing or even what exactly you own. Better to buy a varied selection of high-quality, low-cost funds, monitor the mix yourself, and adjust it when one asset class either soars or falls out of bed.

Down, boy

If the salesperson has sold his or her clients a pre-mixed package containing a selection of funds holding cash, bonds, and stocks, chances are that at least something in the casserole will be doing all right — so a dog's slimy wet nose won't stand out so much.

Fund packages offer another advantage for fund sellers: It's easy to tell if an individual fund you own is an underperformer, but it's pretty well impossible to tell if your pre-mixed fund package isn't doing its job. That's because packages are virtually impossible to compare with each other. These things use so many different rules and structures that they're like lobsters and cantaloupes.

Meanwhile, quite a lot of nonsense gets said about the magical results of combining funds in these packages. Andrew once wrote the following about a fund in a *Globe and Mail* article: "You could travel to the worst-run Canadian Tire store in the country, root around at the back of the filthy warehouse and dig out the wettest and most disgusting bag of salt. Then you could dress up the salt in a suit and tie, and give it an expense account, a pair of wire-rim glasses, and a nice office in Winnipeg. And it would do a better job of picking U.S. stocks than these guys." Someone from the company called Andrew to gripe that he was being unfair, because the fund fitted in some mystical way with the rest of the seller's funds. But bad returns are bad returns, no matter how you cut 'em.

Taking a Look at a Decent Fund Package

Canadian Imperial Bank of Commerce offers packages, under the Managed Portfolio nameplate, that are among the better buys. They impose no extra fees beyond the charges and costs of the underlying CIBC funds.

Table 20-1 gives a breakdown of how their balanced package invests — half in growth and half in income investments.

Table 20-1	Anatomy of a Fund Package: CIBC Managed Balanced Portfolio
Fund	**Percentage of Package**
Income funds	
CIBC Canadian Short-Term Bond Index Fund	15%
CIBC Canadian Bond Fund	20%
CIBC Global Monthly Income Fund	15%
Growth funds	
CIBC Canadian Index Fund	7%
CIBC Canadian Equity Value Fund	9%
CIBC U.S. Equity Index Fund	7%
CIBC U.S. Small Companies Fund	4%
CIBC Disciplined U.S. Equity Fund	7%
CIBC European Equity Fund	6%
CIBC Far East Prosperity Fund	2%
CIBC Disciplined International Equity Fund	8%

Part IV

The Nuts and Bolts of Keeping Your Portfolio Going

The 5th Wave

By Rich Tennant

"My portfolio is gonna take a hit for this."

In this part . . .

We supply some maintenance tips to help make sure your fund portfolio ticks over nicely. We introduce you to the odd cackling symphony of voices on the Internet, all of them trying to talk to you about funds. But don't worry: We also suggest ways of cutting through the cant to find valuable information. We describe the wonderful RRSP, with its ability to keep the tax hounds at bay. And, for your funds that are exposed to taxes, we show you the basic methods of working out how much you have to pay.

Chapter 21

The Internet: The Place to Go for Fund Information

*D*on't get us wrong. The best place to start your fund familiarization journey is right here, reading this book in your favourite armchair or at the dining table, highlighting away. You won't find a substitute for the comfort of hard copy when you're first getting acquainted with a new and complex subject.

But after you're done reading this book and it has taken on the appearance of an old shoe, the pages well worn from careful reading and notations, you need to roll up your sleeves, fire up that infernal machine, peer into the screen, move the mouse, tap on the keyboard — and get specific. The Internet has become, bar none, *the* place to find out about mutual funds. So while this book is a great place to get started, for the most up-to-date fund information, the Web is the place to be.

Independent Sources: Where to Get the Honest Goods

Third-party mutual fund Web sites are where to start your search. They're perhaps the most useful places to mine fund information because they don't sell investments; their business is just providing you with information. The major sites let you set up a portfolio of funds — and, in some cases, other investment securities such as stocks and bonds. Fund and securities prices are updated daily, enabling you to track your investments — or any collection of investments you wish. In some cases, the Web sites can produce detailed charts and tables of one or more portfolios.

Taking a look at the top two

Globefund.com and Morningstar.ca are the country's leading mutual fund information Web sites. Although some of you may want to check out other sites (we recommend a few later in this section), if you'd rather not bother, you'll do fine with these two.

We're trying to be objective here, but we need to come clean. Andrew is a host and commentator with the Business News Network (BNN), the financial news television outlet owned by CTV Globemedia, which also owns Globefund.com. Matthew used to work for Morningstar, and was in charge of the firm's Web site content. Not to worry, though — most investors, advisers, and fund company people will agree that these Web sites (and the databases that fuel them, as well as affiliated but separate desktop software products) set the bar for mutual fund information in this country.

Globefund.com

You can easily find a fund at Globefund.com, which offers information on every mutual and segregated fund sold in Canada. You can look up an individual fund by typing its name in the Search field, or search for funds by category or by sponsoring company. The site offers a detailed report for each fund, showing rates of return over the various periods ranging from one month to 20 years, portfolio asset allocation summaries by overall asset class (stocks, bonds, cash), geographic area and (for stocks) industry group, and the portfolio's top-ten individual holdings. You can create charts of a fund's performance over a variety of time frames, and compare it against a benchmark index.

The site rates funds that have a two-year or longer record according to its Globe Five Star system. Funds at the top of six categories get the highest rating. The categories are:

- ✔ Growth (primarily mid-size and large-cap Canadian equity funds)
- ✔ Growth and income (primarily balanced, dividend, and asset allocation funds)
- ✔ International growth (foreign equity funds)

✔ Aggressive growth (primarily small-cap, geographic, and specialty funds)

✔ Income (fixed income and mortgage funds)

✔ Capital preservation (Canadian and foreign money market funds)

In addition to following mutual funds, the site tracks more than 1,000 Canadian and American exchange-traded funds at its useful ETF Centre.

Because they're traded like stocks, you can buy ETFs in the United States even though you don't live there, unlike mutual funds. (For more on ETFs, refer to Chapter 15.)

For stock and bond information, click over to Globeinvestor.com. If your portfolio includes both funds and individual securities, you can keep an eye on them in one spot using the Globe Portfolio system.

Globefund benefits hugely from the extensive resource of *The Globe and Mail* newspaper and its data affiliate Globe Interactive. In addition to having access to a sea of performance and other data, you can access recent articles on mutual funds from the newspaper, notably regular contributions from *The Globe*'s respected personal finance columnist Rob Carrick. You also get glimpses of editorial content from the GlobeInvestorGold.com "premium" (as in you have to pay for it) Web site, including articles by respected fund expert Gordon Pape.

Although Globefund.com provides most of what the typical fund investor needs, you can access a lot more information by subscribing to `Globe InvestorGold.com`, including full access to articles on investing published in the newspaper. Look for the Globe Plus icons on Globefund.com to find out more.

Morningstar.ca

The Canadian unit of the longtime U.S. mutual fund tracking giant offers an array of data on the more than 8,000 mutual, segregated, and other investment funds sold in this country. This site is up to date and extremely comprehensive in its presentation.

Enter a fund's name in the Search field and you'll be treated to an impressively detailed fund report. The Portfolio page provides a pie chart with the fund's overall asset allocation (stocks, bonds, cash, and so on), followed by lists showing allocation among industry sectors and the top-25 individual securities holdings. You can get much of this information from other data providers, but go to Morningstar.ca to produce a (free) table comparing the asset allocation of all funds in a specific asset category.

Morningstar rates funds that have a track record of three years or longer, assigning one to five stars. Funds are rated in relation to their peers — other qualifying funds in their asset category, of which 42 exist. These categories are the official ones supervised by the Canadian Investment Funds Standards Committee, an independent group made up of database firm executives and other impartial industry observers. The rating is based on a risk-adjusted return, which combines rate of return and a risk measure based on the fund's unit-value volatility.

In addition, you can peruse the Fund Analyst Picks — funds Morningstar's analysts have deemed to be worth a serious look. This process goes far beyond the firm's well-known Morningstar Ratings, because they are chosen based on not just their numbers but also a qualitative review by the analyst team. There were 65 Fund Analyst Picks as of mid-2008.

Another helpful tool is the Morningstar fund indices. At first glance, these look like category averages, but in fact they're much more useful than that. Morningstar calculates weighted average rates of return for each of the 42 categories. A *weighted average* is far more useful than the simple average you see quoted most everywhere else because it assigns more importance to the larger funds within a category, and less to the smaller ones. The degree of a fund's contribution to the index return is determined by the size of its total assets. Better still, each Morningstar Fund Index is corrected for *survivorship bias,* which means the values include the impact of returns of funds that no longer are active funds (such as those that were closed down and/or combined with other funds). These indices also weed out funds that report returns before fees. Simply put, the Morningstar fund indices provide the most accurate snapshot of how funds in a certain category have fared over the years.

Morningstar.ca's reports set it apart from the rest of the Internet pack. Morningstar is the only independent Web site operator in Canada to provide analysts' reports on individual funds. These reports are prepared according to a rigorous research framework, which ensures each fund is fairly measured against its peers. After the research has been completed, the analysts don't hold any punches, telling a particular fund's story in sometimes brutal clarity. You won't find reports on all the funds you're interested in, but the choice is pretty impressive — the firm's team of analysts covers several hundred funds. The reports are timely, too; reports remain posted for a year or so, and are removed if they're not updated by that time.

Morningstar.ca has other unique article content, including profiles of hundreds of portfolio managers and the must-read weekly Fund Watch column that covers virtually every news development of note in the investment funds industry.

The site is free, although an even more detailed version is available to investment advisers at MorningstarAdvisor.ca. A premium version of Morningstar.ca is in the works, so keep an eye out for it. It will charge a fee, but if you have a thirst for endless data, you may find it's worth the money.

What ever happened to paper?

Until a few years ago, a great way to get started in mutual fund investing was to go to your local mega-bookstore, head for the business section, browse for an hour or so, and pick a couple of volumes with the right content and tone to buy. A month or so (and a few colour highlighter pens) later, you'd be knowledgeable enough about fund investing to call a broker or financial planner — or, if you were really on top of the topic, a discount broker or other direct seller.

Although we still recommend including a bookseller in your fund-research pilgrimage — after all, you're reading this book — bookstore shelves have almost nothing left for the Canadian fund investor. Sure, the business section is as vast as ever, but most of those books are about the stock market, portfolio management, financial planning, or other money-related topics. You'll come across plenty of mutual fund books, too, but almost all of these are of real use only to American investors. They'll contain interesting stuff on portfolio diversification and the benefits of long-term investing, but these books constantly refer to U.S. fund products you can't buy unless you're a U.S. resident.

The news media remain a useful source of mutual fund information, with the *Globe and Mail*, the *Financial Post,* and other large newspapers frequently publishing stories on the risks (and sometimes the benefits) of fund investing. But the papers no longer include monthly fund performance reports in their print editions, referring readers to their Internet sites. Magazines like *MoneySense* and *Canadian Business* have excellent reading on the subject too, but they have a lot of other ground to cover in their monthly and special issues.

Worth looking out for, though, is *MoneySense*'s *Honour Roll: Canada's Best Mutual Funds,* an annual report that produces a list of 100 funds its contributors deem to be worthwhile. Much of the report is also available online, as we report in the section "Independent Sources: Where to Get the Honest Goods."

Checking out other sites worth a visit

Between Globefund and Morningstar, you're set for independent mutual fund information. But, we know some people are information junkies — if you're one of those people, we recommend bookmarking these sites.

Canadian Business Online

The mutual funds section of this wide-ranging Web site (www.canadian business.com) — the online portal for Rogers Communications Inc.'s various financial publications, including *Canadian Business* and *MoneySense* magazines — contains a lot of interesting reading and analysis. It's fairly buried, so you'll have to access it via the "Your Money" tab at the top of the home page. (Alternatively, simply type "Moneysense.ca" into your browser and save a step or two.) When you find the mutual funds section, you can access an extensive fund selector tool that brings up numeric information along with articles related to fund investing.

Most notable on the site is *MoneySense*'s annual Honour Roll of the best mutual funds. This is an exhaustive analytical project, undertaken for *MoneySense* by independent analyst Suzane Abboud of FundScope Ltd. The Honour Roll includes funds that have performed consistently well over the long term, without experiencing big swings during up and down markets, in six asset areas: Canadian equity, U.S. equity, Canadian balanced, global equity, small-cap equity, and Canadian bonds.

Fundlibrary.com

Fund Library, one of the first mutual fund Web sites in Canada, offers a wide range of services. It has a set of powerful fund comparison tools, using data supplied by Fundata, which also supplies Globefund and Morningstar with their information. The site offers more fund-list display options for free than what's available on Morningstar or Globefund. These include an unusual tool that lets you see which funds are invested in any of 95 countries. For instance, did you know that, as of mid-2008, 417 funds had a least some money invested in Egypt? Unfortunately, we were unable to find any means of sorting funds by other forms of asset allocation. Looking up individual fund companies or portfolio management teams is easy, but these aren't necessarily the same firm as the fund sponsor.

Fund Library has plenty of original editorial content, including regular columns by its editor, Levi Folk. You can also find manager interviews, "Value Picks" reports on individual funds, and even some sponsored personal finance content here. The site also features a lively discussion forum.

Lipper Leaders

Lipper Inc., one of Morningstar's biggest competitors in the United States, set up shop in Canada recently at www.lipperleaders.com. Like Fundata, its business is selling data, and it doesn't offer a Web site laden with fund-lookup tools. The site does, however, rank funds according to its Lipper Leaders fund rating system, which, similar to the Morningstar and Globe systems, assigns "Leader" ratings to funds measured against peer groups. Lipper Leader ratings are calculated for five different *metrics* or analysis areas: total return, consistent return, preservation, expense, and tax efficiency.

Unlike their competitors' ratings, Lipper Leaders are assigned using an even 20-percent peer-group division. For example, the top 20 percent of funds (ranked by specific criteria) in a category receive a rating of 1.

Other independent sites worth a look

Still hungry for more? A number of other Canadian Web sites offer interesting mutual fund content, including the following:

✔ **CanadianFundWatch.com:** This sometimes quirky Web site is run by investor advocate Ken Kivenko and consists almost entirely of his commentaries, which tend to lash out at the fund industry's favourite whipping topics such as high management expense ratios (MERs) and closet indexing (where supposedly active funds actually shadow their benchmark index). The site also features explanatory pieces on such analytical measures as the Sharpe Ratio, a widely used assessment of a fund's return relative to a risk-free cash investment (a government Treasury bill).

✔ **Bylo Selhi:** Before you scratch your head over the name behind this Web site (www.bylo.org), just say it slowly: "Buy low, sell high." Bylo Selhi is the pen name of a financial adviser. Under this pseudonym, he's a well-known contributor to discussion forums and an advocate of do-it-yourself investing. The site contains commentaries, how-to articles, and lists of funds that are deemed by Mr. — or is it *Ms.*? — Selhi to provide good value thanks to low MERs. Other sections provide links to numerous articles, published in Canada and elsewhere, related to Selhi's investment themes.

The Regulatory Jungle: When You Need Official Stuff

Sometimes going to the government or an official industry organization for information is unavoidable. At least in this case you don't have to take a number and line up.

The Investment Funds Institute of Canada

The Web site of the Investment Funds Institute of Canada (IFIC), the trade group that represents mutual fund companies (www.ific.ca), is a great place for data junkies who want to know how much money is invested in a particular fund category, or which fund companies are the biggest (or the smallest, or the fastest-growing). The site has a useful Investor Resource Centre, which contains articles on mutual fund taxation, RRSPs, and other topics. You can also check out a detailed member directory, where you can find contact information and Web site addresses.

Not every fund company is an IFIC member. Excluded are insurance companies (which operate segregated funds and are members of the Canadian Life and Health Insurance Association), as well as a few mutual fund companies, big and small, which for one reason or another have chosen not to be members. (By "big," we mean really big — like CI Funds.)

Investor Education Fund

Some good (Ontario) government money went into building the Investor Edu–cation Fund's Web site (www.investored.ca), which has a lengthy section on mutual funds. (Actually, some of the funding came from fines and other payments from wrongdoings in the securities industry!) The Ontario Securities Commission established the Investor Education Fund to broaden investor education.

Of particular interest is the Mutual Fund Fee Impact Calculator, accessed from the site's home page. This tool works out how big a bite sales loads and MERs will take out of an individual fund investment. Usually these costs are expressed only as percentages; this calculator shows the actual dollars gob-bled up by the various fees charged on a typical fund investment over time.

Mutual Fund Dealers Association of Canada

This Web site (www.mfda.ca) of the Mutual Fund Dealers Association of Canada might be of use — but unlikely of interest. The MFDA is a subset of the Investment Dealers Association that regulates brokerage and finan-cial planning firms licensed to sell mutual funds, as opposed to investment securities in general. You'll want to go here only if you need information on an MFDA-member firm or about the MFDA Investor Protection Corporation, which is a sort of insurance policy that protects you, the investor, should your broker or planner go broke (don't laugh — it happens).

The System for Electronic Document Analysis and Retrieval (SEDAR)

SEDAR has nothing to do with trees or any related earthy analogies about branching out and growing your investments. In fact, it's the address of a Web site (www.sedar.com) that is about as dull and lifeless as they come. However, its content is extremely important, if not exciting. SEDAR is run by the Canadian Securities Administrators (which represents provincial securi-ties commissions) and contains every public document, report, and filing a fund manager (or any publicly traded company) produces.

SEDAR is a little cumbersome to use at first, but after you get the hang of it you can find most anything that's ever been filed with a securities commission in Canada. That includes prospectuses, financial statements, annual information forms, and those valuable new documents, management reports of fund per-formance. You can search by date range, company name, or type of document. When you unearth what you need, you can download it as a PDF file.

Fund Company Sites: Useful Information, But Mind the Context

If you love glossy brochures and pamphlets and keep them around for easy reference "just in case," or laboriously file them away in careful order, then you'll love fund company Web sites. On the other hand, if you're the type who tosses marketing glossies in the wastebasket as soon as they arrive, you'll also appreciate the Internet for its inherent lack of paper burden.

Most fund companies have invested mightily in their Web sites. Yes, they still produce masses of paper promotion as well, but the Internet increasingly is becoming their main marketing tool. They're also fast becoming an alternative to paper statements, with investors and advisers alike now able to access account information online.

An efficient way to find a company's Web site is to simply type its name into an Internet search engine. You also can use the Investment Funds Institute of Canada's directory of mutual fund company sites at `www.ific.ca`.

On a typical big-company Web site, you'll find:

- ✔ **Forms:** Many company Web sites offer downloadable forms for new account applications, account transfers, pre-authorized chequing (PAC) schemes, and systematic withdrawal plans (SWP). Too bad you might still need the help of a fund company official or your adviser to figure out how to complete them!

- ✔ **Marketing-oriented material:** In addition to the expected promotional material, many companies offer detailed profiles on individual funds and portfolio managers. Of even greater use are records (both recent and longer term) of daily fund prices, distributions, and performance.

- ✔ **Information above and beyond the call:** Some companies, for example AGF, go to the unusual extent of revealing information that's normally left buried in various legal documents. Kudos to AGF for providing a table on the history of the firm's fund mergers, closings, and acquisitions, making it easy for investors to understand the genesis of the company's funds.

- ✔ **Personal finance information:** Many firms' Web sites offer articles on financial planning topics such as basic investing principles, RRSPs, education savings plans, and taxation. You'll also come across calculators (to compute RRSP contributions, say, or the power of compound interest) and other financial-planning tools.

Sometimes the personal finance information that fund companies provide is objective, but occasionally the content is skewed toward their products and marketing approach.

✔ **Regulatory documents:** As we explain in Chapter 3, the twice-a-year management reports of fund performance (MRFPs) are very useful pieces of information. You'll find them more easily on a company site than on SEDAR, the government site we look at in the previous section. You'll still have to dig around a little to find the MRFPs, though. Don't expect a big red button labeled "MRFP" at the top of the home page. Too bad everyone can't present these via straightforward links, such as BMO's "Prospectuses, Reports & Other Information" link or the Bank of Nova Scotia's "Downloadable Documents" link. In most cases, you'll have to sleuth through smokescreens like Mackenzie's "Marketing Material Library" or Dynamic's "Financial Planning Centre" to locate MRFP downloads.

Brokers and Planners: Only the Basics

You'll find only very basic information on mutual fund investing at most full-service investment dealers' Web sites. One exception is RBC Dominion Securities, which offers a useful overview on its site (rbcds.com). But discount brokerages, which want you to operate on your own and simply buy and sell products through them (see Chapter 6), offer a wealth of fund information. The following discount brokerages offer Morningstar research tools on their Web sites (in some cases only to their registered clients):

✔ BMO InvestorLine (bmoinvestorline.com)

✔ RBC Direct Investing (rbcdirectinvesting.com)

✔ TD Waterhouse (tdwaterhouse.ca)

CIBC Investor's Edge (investorsedge.cibc.com) has a fund research package powered by GlobeInvestorGold.

Investing without the Net?

Using the Internet doesn't guarantee you'll make money from your portfolio — the same old rules of buying quality funds with low expenses and conservative holdings still apply. So don't worry if you're not using the Net to invest. You can build an excellent portfolio of funds without ever firing up a browser. In fact, as some hapless investors have found, the Web has given birth to a whole new generation of scam artists. And it's certainly created a tidal wave of confusing marketing clutter. But the Internet also gives you far more control over your portfolio by allowing you to check your portfolio whenever you want and, if you do business with a discount broker, to buy and sell funds at any time.

Chapter 22

RRSPs: Fertilizer for Your Mutual Funds

Coffee and cigarettes, Saturday night and fighting, tight leather and fun — some things just go together. And mutual funds are a powerful combination with Canada's beloved registered retirement savings plan (RRSP), a tax-deferred account in which your investments pile up without molestation from the government. In this chapter, we explain why it's a great idea to fill up your RRSP as a first step when buying funds, and we also look at the sort of funds you should put into your plan. The chapter also offers a brief rundown of the rules of RRSPs. They can be horrendously complex, but in essence they're simple — just stick your money in, buy top-quality funds, and watch your nest egg grow and grow.

Pour It In and Watch It Grow: Understanding RRSPs

An RRSP is like a warehouse for investments and assets in which they can accumulate tax-free until you take the money out and spend it. At that stage, you have to treat the withdrawals as income, and pay taxes on them. But the idea is that you won't care about having to share some of the loot with Ottawa at that stage because the money will have grown tax-free to such a huge pile and also because you'll be in a nice low tax bracket (because your income will be lower in retirement).

So an RRSP isn't an investment in itself — you don't "buy" an RRSP — but rather a tax-privileged account in which you hold investments and assets. Don't even think about it too much. Just go ahead and open an RRSP account. It's one of the great tax breaks Canadians get, for two reasons:

- **The money you put in comes off your income for tax purposes:** The government's attitude is that money you put into an RRSP is cash you've diverted from your income for the moment — or deferred, in the jargon — so you don't have to pay tax on it. That's why taxpayers who've contributed to their RRSPs the previous year get back tax refunds, or returns of taxes they already paid.

- **Your investments accumulate tax-free within the plan:** This is the real reason why RRSPs are so powerful. The dollars in there are supercharged because the interest, dividends, and capital gains they attract are free of tax. Added to the pile, those earnings go on to earn their own cute little baby earnings, which in turn produce their own offspring, and so it goes. And tax-free compounding of investment returns is a wonder of the modern world.

Claiming a tax refund for the cash you put into a plan is wonderfully simple and perhaps the most enjoyable thing about an RRSP (although watching your balance climb steadily is also fun). And the refund can be a fair amount of money. If your top tax bracket is 40 percent (that is, the government takes away 40 percent of the uppermost portion of your income), then a $5,000 RRSP contribution can earn you a refund of $2,000.

Even the saddest and least organized financial planner in Canada can open an RRSP for you and handle your contributions. Ottawa makes it simple. Your tax return clearly asks if you've contributed to an RRSP and then invites you to deduct the amount from your income. And, helpfully, the government mails you a slip along with your tax refund or tax bill each spring showing exactly how much you can contribute for the current year.

Figuring out how much you can put in your RRSP

Actually, it's a good thing the tax authorities tell you how much room — or maximum possible contribution — you have. That's because for people who are in a pension scheme at work, the RRSP contribution limits are complicated to calculate. If you're in a pension plan, you're already getting tax relief on the money you contribute to that scheme, and your employer may also be helping out, so policymakers water down the amount you can plow into your RRSP.

If you're not in a pension plan, the maximum contribution is up to 18 percent of the income you earned the previous year. However, regardless of that figure, an annual dollar limit applies, which is $20,000 for the 2008 taxation year, $21,000 for 2009, and $22,000 for 2010. Thereafter, it's supposed to be indexed to inflation — that is, the maximum contribution will increase each year in line with the general rise in prices. (The "great thereafter" is never actually reached because, fortunately for tax-break-starved Canadians, the government tends to come back and increase the RRSP limits every few years or so.)

If you're in a pension scheme, then your maximum contribution is reduced by something called the pension adjustment, which is the value the tax authorities assign to the value of the pension benefit you build up each year — and it's then used to reduce your maximum RRSP contribution. Your pension adjustment is reported to you each year on the T4 tax slip you get from your employer. The T4 shows the income you earned and the tax paid during the latest year.

If your income is roughly $111,000 or more, you're entitled to contribute the full $20,000 for 2008 — as long as you're not in a pension plan. But if you are, and the tax people decide that the value of the pension benefit you build up during the year is, say, $5,000, then your maximum contribution is reduced by that amount, to $15,000. Still, that's not too shabby. If you can't afford to contribute that much, you needn't waste the unused amount. The government lets you "bank" the amount you can't afford to contribute to use in a future year. So if you could muster only $10,000 for 2008, you add the unused amount — $5,000 if you were in the pension situation described above, otherwise $10,000 — to your contribution limit in 2009 or a future year. In effect, you can create a balance of unused contribution room that can be used as an additional RRSP contribution above and beyond your limit in any future year.

You have even more RRSP contribution leeway. The tax department will let you put in an extra $2,000 each year without being required to withdraw that amount and pay a penalty (the taxpayer's version of a fine).

The deadline for making an RRSP contribution that is tax-deductible for a particular year is 60 days following the end of the year in question — normally March 1. So most people make a 2008 RRSP contribution during 2009. Being procrastinators, millions of people leave their RRSP contribution until those two months, and that's why you see a hysterical flood of RRSP advertising and hype in January and February.

It all sounds a bit daunting, but don't worry. You can find out how much you're allowed to contribute to your RRSP for a particular year simply by checking the Notice of Tax Assessment the government sends you a month or so after you file your income tax return. For example, your 2007 assessment includes a section that tells you how much you will be allowed to contribute for 2008 — that is, by the March 1, 2009, deadline. So take note of this information before you file away that nasty little document.

Understanding the power of tax deferral

Getting a tax refund for contributing to your RRSP is nice, but the even more powerful attraction of RRSPs is the way that income earned within the plan is also tax-deferred. It piles up year after year without the Canada Revenue Agency sticking its claws in along the way.

Investment income such as interest and dividends, as well as capital gains — a fancy name for trading profits — can pile up tax-free inside an RRSP, which makes an RRSP the ideal place to put your mutual funds. That's because, as we explain in Chapter 23, funds throw off their income and capital gains to unitholders each year in the form of distributions. *Distributions* are payments your fund makes to you. You can take them as a cheque or as more units. Most people take the payouts in the form of new units, but it doesn't matter; the distributions are taxable just the same — unless they're earned in a tax-deferred plan such as an RRSP.

You can be sure that a bond or other income-oriented fund will generate a steady stream of distributions (that's what they're designed to do), and equity funds have a habit of suddenly producing big capital gains for their investors — which can be painful if you don't hold the fund in a tax-deferred account.

Given long enough, money that compounds tax-free grows at a frightening pace. But it's a good sort of scary, if you know what we mean. For example, as shown in Figure 22-1:

- ✔ Let's say you invested $6,000 each year in an ordinary account that earned 5 percent annually, but you also had to pay 40 percent of the return each year in tax. The money would grow to about $231,000 in 25 years.

- ✔ If you invested that $6,000 in an RRSP at the same rate of return, where it built up tax-free, then you'd have nearly $307,000 after 25 years.

So, when you take the money out of that whopping quarter-million-dollar RRSP, you'll want to avoid having to pay tax on every penny of it. The idea, of course, is that by that stage you will have quit working, so you're in a low tax bracket. But always remember that while the magic of tax-free compounding within an RRSP does produce wonderful growth, the dollars inside the plan have annoying little strings attached.

Where to Buy Your RRSP

Buying an RRSP is simple because banks, brokers, and fund companies just love them. The money tends to be long-term retirement savings that won't be withdrawn for years, so it sits there producing a stream of fees for the lucky firm that gets to hold it. And it's a massive industry: Statistics Canada reports

Canadians have more than a half-trillion dollars sitting in RRSPs. Six in ten families had an RRSP account, with a median value of about $25,000. The median contribution in 2006 was $2,730. Contributions in 2006 topped $34 billion, up 6 percent from 2005. However, that represented only 7 percent of the total RRSP contribution room available to Canadians — which means a staggering $450 billion or so of unused contributions is out there because wage slaves can't or won't find the dough.

You have three basic choices when setting up an RRSP. Here's the triple play:

✔ **Basic banking:** You can stumble into a bank, trust company, or credit union and ask for a basic RRSP account that holds that particular institution's mutual funds and other offerings, usually guaranteed investment certificates (refer to Chapter 5).

Limited choice of investments is the problem with doing this, but the simplicity and convenience make it ideal for investors who are just starting out. So if you're looking for convenience, fire ahead and open up a simple plan at a bank. As you learn more and your assets grow, it's pretty simple to move the holdings later into another RRSP at a full-service broker or discount broker plan for a fee of about $100 (the delighted institution that's getting your money will often pay the fee for you).

Banks offer a wide selection of index funds that track the entire market at low cost to the unitholders; an RRSP full of index funds with a smaller portion of ordinary actively managed funds is a wise choice for nearly any investor. Bank funds are *no-load* — they sell directly to investors and do not charge a sales commission. No-load funds also are sold by a handful of independent companies. They, too, will be happy to set up an RRSP on their books for you.

✔ **From your planner:** If you go to a commission-paid financial planner, he or she may put your investment into a fund company's RRSP. That's an RRSP set up on the books of the fund company, which almost always holds just that company's funds. It's an easy option for the salesperson because the fund manager handles all of the administration and registration of the plan with the government. Once again, though, limited choice is a problem from your point of view. But a fund company RRSP is handy for investors who don't want to fiddle around too much with their portfolios, because the fund company does all the bookkeeping.

Not all planners will limit you to a fund company–sponsored RRSP. Some have arrangements with an outside trust company or other service provider that let them offer independent RRSPs and normal taxable accounts that can hold funds from a variety of fund companies.

✔ **Self-directed:** The final, best, and increasingly popular way to do it is to start up a self-directed RRSP at a discount brokerage company. This is the very finest type of RRSP because you're free to hold virtually anything, instead of limiting your portfolio to the wares of just one company. Check out the next section for more.

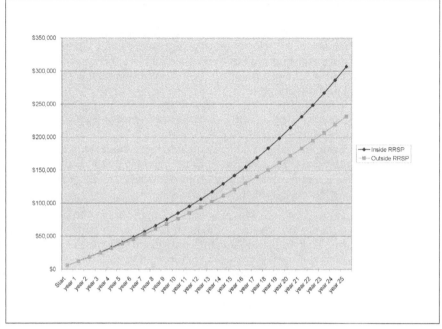

Figure 22-1: $6,000 invested at 5 percent for 25 years, untaxed and taxed values.

The Beautiful Garden That Is the Self-Directed RRSP

Just about everyone should have a self-directed RRSP because, well, these things are marvellous. The traditional RRSP offered by a bank or fund manager is basically a vehicle for holding just their stuff. But with a self-directed plan, you're free to roam the world. A self-directed RRSP is a plan in which you're free to hold just about anything. It's about the only way to own stocks or bonds within an RRSP and to load up on funds from a multiplicity of companies.

Setting up a self-directed RRSP is easy — remember that brokers welcome this type of business, because it tends to represent long-term money that'll be on their books for decades. And the term self-directed often doesn't apply, because many investors have a full-service broker who helps them pick what should go into their plan. However, self-directed RRSPs are ideally suited for discount brokerages because discounters tend to have a large selection of funds, available for low or no sales commissions. See Chapter 6 for more on discounters.

Expect to pay a maximum of $100 for most plans annually. Lots of fund sellers and discount brokers charge less or waive the charge altogether if your account is big enough, so be sure and ask them to do so if you're investing $10,000 or more.

Don't worry that opening a self-directed plan means you have to become a stock market wizard. Stick to the rules for fund selection in this book (which we cover in Chapter 10) and you'll almost certainly do okay. You don't have to start playing stocks directly: Lots of investors hold nothing but conservative mutual funds in their self-directed plans.

And don't be shy about transferring assets from other plans into your self-directed plan. The old brokerage firm or bank that's seeing your money depart its coffers will sometimes drag its feet on the paperwork (getting nasty shoe marks all over it). But after a few weeks, if a delay drags on that long, you can simply threaten politely to call the Investment Dealers Association of Canada, the Toronto-based lobby group that regulates the industry. That usually speeds things up a bit.

If you're moving assets from an existing plan over to the self-directed RRSP, the new brokerage firm may tell you that its systems won't accommodate some or all of your old funds. In that case, you may have to sell the funds in the old account and just move the cash proceeds over. That's a hassle, but it shouldn't cost you anything in taxes because the transaction is taking place within an RRSP, shielding any capital gains. (Refer to "Pour It In and Watch It Grow: Understanding RRSPs" for more about RRSPs and taxes.)

Planting the Most Fragrant Flower: Choosing Funds for Your RRSP

The overriding rule for investments inside your RRSP should be *Insist on Quality* — leave the wacky speculative stuff for the money that's not earmarked to support you in your dotage. That means buying conservative equity and bond funds, and going easy on emerging markets funds, volatile single-industry funds, and small-company funds.

The dollars inside your plan should be treated as sacrosanct — all incense and white cloth — because they're irreplaceable. Because you are restricted in how much you can contribute to an RRSP over the years, when a magical compounding RRSP dollar has been lost on a slump in the Brazilian market, it can't be restored. Chapter 4 offers two suggested RRSP portfolios, and just about any bank or mutual fund now has a proprietary system for suggesting the asset mix in your plan. (Beware of fund packages, however, which we discuss in Chapter 20.)

With this type of long-term investing, the costs and fees charged by the funds and fund mixtures assume ever-greater importance. So own at least some index funds in your plan. Your RRSP is too important to have it spoiled by some Lexus-driving turkey who can't keep up with the market.

Including international investments

Until recently, investing money in an RRSP was severely handicapped by an evil restriction known as the foreign content limit. This meant your RRSP could contain a maximum of 30 percent foreign investments. Cloaked in patriotic reason, in fact this served as a prop for the Canadian stock market and put severe restrictions on how Canadians could use one of the few tax breaks available. But the government washed the foreign content rules away in one fell swoop in its 2006 budget, opening the door completely to investing in foreign stocks and other worldwide markets.

Of course, the non-geographic restrictions remain in place: An eligible stock must be listed on an exchange approved by the Canada Revenue Agency, and bonds must be issued by a government or related agency, or if it is a corporate issue it must be rated as "investment quality." (See Chapter 14 for more on bonds.) And so on.

The deep-sixing of the foreign content limit also freed fund investors from having to fathom a complex fund version that emerged in the late 1990s to serve as an end run around the rules. Fund companies came up with flocks of "clone" products that were foreign but used financial witchcraft to count as Canadian, through the use of futures contracts on existing foreign funds. It was an unspeakably complicated arrangement that few investors understood. Mercifully, the clones quickly disappeared after the rule change, with units of these funds being rolled over to the underlying funds.

Mixing the right assets

As with other forms of investing, your asset mix is almost certain to get more cautious as you get older and closer to taking money out of your plan rather than putting it in. For nearly everyone, that means more bonds and cash and fewer stocks.

Many experts say you should put your bond funds into your RRSP if you're a long-term investor, and the numbers seem to indicate that they're right. That's because bond funds earn and throw off a constant stream of interest, which attracts murderous rates of tax.

Funds usually pay distributions in the form in which they receive the money from their investments. So interest earned by a fund is paid as a distribution that's taxable as interest in the investor's hands. Capital gains — the polite term for trading profits — are paid out as capital gain distributions, and dividends earned by a fund are paid out as dividend distributions to the investor.

Equity funds are mainly about buying and selling stocks so they generate capital gains distributions — and only one-half of a capital gain is taxed in the hands of the investor. Equity funds also produce dividends from Canadian companies — payouts of the company's profits to shareholders — which are also lightly taxed. So, funds that produce distributions in the form of dividends or capital gains are reasonably tax-efficient, or lightly taxed, making them more suitable than bond funds for an open or taxable account. (Tax efficiency is a value computed by fund data firms that captures the percentage of the pre-tax return that is retained by a hypothetical investor after accounting for taxes on distributions. See Chapter 23 for more on this.)

In other words, equity funds are often better than bond funds when it comes to investing outside your RRSP. Have a look at Table 22-1, which compares pre- and after-tax returns, as well as tax efficiency (assuming you continue to own the fund), for three Bank of Montreal funds. Say you'd invested in BMO Equity Index Fund, a big index fund with low portfolio turnover because it simply tracks stocks in the S&P/TSX composite index, in mid-1998. If you held the fund for ten years in an RRSP, by mid-2008 your compound annual return would have been 8.1 percent. But if you'd been paying tax along the way, you'd have ended up with a 7.9-percent "tax-adjusted" return. That's not bad, as this fund had a low portfolio turnover rate during those 10 years and this was very tax efficient. By contrast, the return for BMO Bond Fund held outside an RRSP was only about half as good as the return inside an RRSP.

Table 22-1	Pre- and after-tax compound annual returns for three BMO funds, 1998–2008		
Fund	*Pre-Tax Return*	*After-Tax Return*	*Tax Efficiency*
BMO Equity Index	8.1%	7.9%	97.3%
BMO Equity	9.4%	8.4%	89.3%
BMO Bond	4.3%	2.2%	51.0%

Source: Morningstar

Now every rule has its exceptions, and quadruply so when it comes to taxes and investing. An equity fund that pays big distributions year after year, while producing solid returns as well, may be an excellent candidate for your RRSP because you'll be shielding those payouts from tax. You can get an idea whether the fund manager is in the habit of paying out lots of capital gains by looking at one of the new fund prospectuses or by checking with your salesperson.

But don't get all bogged down in theories: Remember to put top-quality stuff into your RRSP and you'll likely do fine, whether it's bonds or stocks. The market has an old saying that you should never let tax strategies blind you to the merits or faults of an investment. Nobody's ever wished she'd had more to drink the night before — and nobody's ever regretted holding a well-managed equity fund in an RRSP over many years, no matter how small the distributions.

Chapter 23

Taxes: Timing Is Everything

A lot of investment writing and theorizing seem to take place in an airy-fairy world in which everybody is beautifully dressed and articulate, no one ever eats with her mouth open, all decisions are perfectly rational, and nobody ever has to pay taxes. In fact, the stock and bond markets are rather squalid places driven by terror and avarice, in which nondescript people swap sleazy favours. And taxes end up grinding us all down remorselessly. Unless mutual fund unitholders are investing through a tax-deferred plan, the government often goes after them mercilessly. In this chapter, we outline how to count the cost of taxes, and we look at a couple of methods of reducing the pain.

The Wacky World of Fund Distributions

Now this stuff will get a little complicated, but bear with us because it's worth knowing and we should be able to cut through it pretty quickly. Mutual funds, as you know, hold all kinds of company shares, bonds, and cash — and sometimes derivatives, those strange financial deals based on options and futures, which are promises to buy or sell something at a certain price.

All the time, cash is piling up in the fund from three main sources:

✓ Every year, the stocks pay dividends to the fund — which are payouts to the shareholders of a portion of the company's profit.

✔ Meanwhile, the bonds and cash, which are loans to government and big companies, keep earning interest income.

✔ The fund also earns capital gains — which are essentially trading profits generated by buying low and selling high — when it sells stocks, bonds, and derivatives.

In general, no fund hangs on to these streams of income and capital gains because, if it did, the fund itself would have to pay tax on them, reducing its total return. So just about all mutual funds pay out the interest and dividend income and capital gains to their unitholders in the form of so-called distributions, letting them deal with the tax.

The investors have to pay tax on the income and gains at their own personal rate. It's more sensible to have the unitholders, rather than the fund, pay the tax because many of the unitholders may not even be taxable personally. Those investors can collect the distributions and not owe a penny to Ottawa. And investors who hold the fund in a registered retirement savings plan (RRSP) — a tax-deferred holding tank in which investments can grow tax-free — don't have to pay tax on the distributions immediately, so it would be a waste of money for the fund to pay taxes on their behalf. Other unitholders may have low incomes, meaning that their tax rates are low or zero.

Paying out distributions to fundholders

Here is where things begin to get Druidical — when a fund pays out a distribution, it reduces the cash value of each of its own units. Let's say the fund has total assets of $100 million and 10 million units outstanding, or in the hands of investors. Then each unit has a net asset value per unit — or price — of $10 ($100 million divided by 10 million). Now say the manager pays out $20 million in capital gains to the unitholders. That's $2 for every unit ($20 million divided by 10 million units outstanding). If all of them took it in cash, then the value of the fund's assets would drop to $80 million. It still has 10 million units — outstanding, though, so the value or price of each falls to $8 ($80 million divided by 8 million), after taking away the value of the $2 distribution.

Table 23-1 shows what happens to your cash if you're a unitholder in the fund and you have 100 units.

In other words, you start out owning 100 units, which are worth $10 each, for a total holding of $1,000. The fund declares a distribution of $2 a unit, which you elect to take in cash. You then still hold 100 units, but the value of each has dropped by $2 to $8, which leaves you with $800 worth of units. But you also have the $200 in cash ($2 for each of your units), which means you still have a total holding of $1,000.

Table 23-1	What If You Take the Distribution in Cash?			
Units Held	Unit Price	Value of Units Held	Cash in Hand	Total Holding
Before Distribution				
100	$10	$1,000	Zero	$1,000
After Distribution				
125	$8	$800	$200	$1,000

But most people just put the money back into the fund. One of the great advantages of mutual funds is the fact that you can automatically reinvest your income and capital gains in more units, which go to bolster your account and earn even higher streams of income and gains in the future. It's a no-brainer, as we like to say in frontal-lobe surgery. That's what long-term investors do — take their distributions in the form of more units.

So let's say you follow that course. You don't get cash but more units. Their value has dropped by $2 each, but that's fine because the investor now owns more of them. This scenario is shown in Table 23-2.

Table 23-1	What If You Take the Distribution in Cash?			
Units Held	Unit Price	Value of Units Held	Cash in Hand	Total Holding
Before Distribution				
100	$10	$1,000	Zero	$1,000
After Distribution				
125	$8	$1,000	$200	$1,000

You get an extra 25 units valued at $8 each, which increases your unit total to 125. The units are now worth just $8 each, though, so you still have a total holding of $1,000. As you can see, a distribution isn't really a windfall or a payout to you. It reduces the value of each unit you hold, so it's more like a reshuffling of your investment in the fund.

Note that if you hold funds in a discount brokerage account, you may have an alarming experience when you get your statement for December 31. Your fund units may have fallen sharply, reflecting the value of a distribution, but there might be no sign of any extra units in your account to make up for it. So it sometimes looks as though the value of your investment has slumped. That's actually just an administrative glitch: The lines of communication aren't always very good between discount brokers and the fund companies at the end of the year, when the fund industry is scrambling to calculate the distributions. Your broker's system may not record the distributions until mid-January or so, after you've gotten your December statement. However, the error should be fixed by the time you get your statement for January 31.

A fund can easily lose money during a calendar year (because its unit price dropped) but also pay out distributions to unitholders because the fund manager earned interest or dividend income or made some capital gains by selling a stock or bond. Taxable unitholders find themselves in the galling position of having to pay taxes on their investment in a fund, even though it lost them money. Gee, thanks. For example, Brandes Canadian Equity, a small-cap fund, was 2007's worst performing Canadian equity fund. Nevertheless, it still made a distribution of 72 cents a unit in December. And Trimark Canadian Endeavour — with a 14.7 percent loss in 2007 the third worst overall among domestic equity funds — paid out near a dollar per unit.

Watching out for tax exposure

Many equity and balanced funds pay out their capital gains distributions in December, and bond funds and other income funds usually pay out interest income quarterly or even monthly. Funds that seek bond interest, dividends, and other regular income nearly always pay it straight out to unitholders. So, bond, dividend, and other income funds by their nature pay a lot of distributions every year, exposing taxable investors to lots of tax on the income. So hold them inside a tax-sheltered plan when you can, unless you need the regular payments.

By contrast, equity funds can go years without paying any distributions at all because the manager hasn't generated enough trading profits. That can be for a number of good reasons, though. The fund may have simply bought a bunch of good companies and hung on to them without selling the shares, nicely increasing its value per unit. In 2007, one-quarter of domestic equity funds did not make a distribution.

The taxation of funds is cruelly complicated because a host of factors can influence it. But with stock funds, the basic rule is this: The more trading done by the fund, the bigger the distributions and the higher your tax bill (again, if investing outside an RRSP). However, sometimes the need for distributions is eliminated because of the way investors move into or out of the fund. Or a fund manager can sometimes sell shares and then buy them back immediately, again reducing the tax liability of the fund.

Fund companies often make a song and dance about the fact that a fund hasn't paid much in distributions in recent years — reducing the tax bill for unitholders — because its manager tends to hold stocks for long periods. Instead of selling shares and earning trading profits that must be paid out in big distributions, some managers try to simply hold good stocks for long periods, increasing the fund's unit value. But always be wary: A takeover bid or drastic change in a company's fortunes might force the manager to sell the stock, forcing the fund to pay out a big distribution.

Fund companies say the lack of annual payouts helps you to defer paying taxes until you sell the fund's units. That may be true, but remember that taxation shouldn't be the first thing you consider when making an investment — the fund should be suitable in other ways, too. However, if you're deciding which fund to hold in a taxable account — that is, an account that isn't an RRSP or some other tax-deferred plan — then a fund that doesn't do much trading is often the best choice. If the fund uses a definite buy-and-hold style, the fund company's litera-ture will usually say so. And as we explain later, equity index funds — funds that simply track the whole stock market — are a great buy-and-hold investment.

So if you're trying to decide which funds you should put into your RRSP, the income fund is often the best choice because the distributions can just pile up in there tax-free until you take the money out.

Because a big capital gains distribution produces an apparent abrupt fall in a fund's unit price at the end of the year, mutual fund investors sometimes get a fright. Every year, fund companies get worried phone calls from investors asking why their fund's units seem to have plunged. However, they needn't worry: Yes, the unit price has fallen, but the investor has received more units.

Determining what distributions your fund has declared

Finding out what distributions your fund has declared is easy. On Globefund. com, follow these steps:

1. Type the fund's name in the search field and click the Go button.

2. Select the class of fund you want and click on its name.

3. Scroll down to near the bottom of the page to the Distribution Report, a table that shows distribution amounts for each of the past six quarters.

Finding your fund's distribution history is similarly easy at Morningstar.ca:

1. Type the fund's name in the Quicktake Reports search field to pull up the report for that fund.

2. Select the class of the fund your want, and click View Report.

3. Click on the Tax Analysis tab at the top of the report page and, on the page that appears, scroll down to the Distribution History section, which is a table showing total annual distributions for each of the past five years plus the current year to date.

Both sites provide breakdowns of the various types of distributions — dividends, income, and capital gains — and Morningstar also gives return-of-capital distributions. You can also go to the fund company's Web site. Mackenzie Financial, for example, provides a handy "Distributions" button atop its home page.

Paying Taxes on Fund Distributions

Here's the rub. No matter whether the investor takes the distributions in the form of cash or reinvests them in more units, they're taxable just the same — as long as the fund is held in an open (that is, taxable) account and not a tax-deferred plan such as an RRSP. Always remember that none of this stuff applies if you hold your fund in an RRSP, but the distributions are ultimately taxable when you start taking money out of the plan. At that stage, any money you withdraw is taxed as income, just as though you earned it at your normal job.

Enjoying tax breaks on Canadian content

The fact that RRSP withdrawals are taxed like normal income can be a disadvantage because the money gets no special treatment, even if it was originally earned as capital gains or dividends from a Canadian company. That's a pity, because normally dividends from Canadian corporations and capital gains are eligible for the following special tax breaks:

✔ Canadian dividends received by investors get the "federal dividend tax credit," essentially a reduction of the tax you pay to encourage investment in Canadian companies and to reflect the fact that corporations have already been taxed. That means taxation of dividends is relatively low. As of mid-2008, an Ontario investor with $75,000 in taxable income faced a tax rate of only 13.8 percent on each extra dollar of dividends earned compared with 39.4 percent on interest income, according to accounting firm Ernst & Young. In Alberta the rates were 5.6 percent and 32.0 percent, respectively.

✔ You must include only half of a capital gain in your taxable income. That makes it even more attractive to hold equity funds outside your RRSP, because their capital gains distributions aren't heavily taxed in the hands of investors. As of 2002, an Ontario taxpayer with $70,000 of taxable income had to pay tax of only 19.7 percent on each extra dollar of capital gains. Albertans paid capital gains tax at 16.0 percent.

Getting tax slips

Don't worry: Your fund company will send you tax slips each year showing how much in interest income, dividends, and capital gains distributions you should report in the appropriate place on your tax form.

If you hold the fund in an RRSP or other tax-deferred plan, you don't get tax slips because you don't pay tax on the distributions.

You may get two types of tax slips:

✔ A T3 if the fund you hold is a mutual fund trust, which most funds are. If you hold several funds with one company, you'll probably get just one consolidated T3, but it should have a breakdown on the back showing which fund paid you which sort of distribution.

✔ A T5 if your fund is itself a corporation, issuing shares instead of units. That's a less flexible type of structure, and most funds these days are trusts.

Paying Taxes When You Sell or Exchange

If you sell or redeem some of your fund units at a higher price than you paid, and the fund is held in a taxable account, then you're liable for capital gains tax on the profit you made. The same applies even if you just do an exchange or switch — moving money from one fund to another. As far as the tax authorities are concerned, an exchange is the same as selling Fund A and then buying Fund B. What you do with the proceeds of the sale is irrelevant — if selling the first fund generates a capital gain, then you have to pay taxes on it.

Checking out tax-skirting fund structures

A few companies, such as CI Fund Management Inc., Mackenzie, and AGF Management Ltd., have set up funds that are organized in "classes" or versions that are designed to let you switch from fund to fund without generating capital gains for tax purposes. Technically, they're actually units of the same fund, although one is the Canadian equity class, the next is the bond class, and so on, each with its own cute baby unit price. You can use this fund structure and jump from fund to fund, avoiding taxes on any capital gains along the way. After all, a capital gain is produced when a fund has gone up — and that's why you bought it in the first place.

Many fund marketers have jumped on the tax-free switching bandwagon. But they've gone much further than that, bringing out ever more complicated products. Here are just a couple:

- ✔ Fidelity Investments Canada, Mackenzie, and Franklin Templeton Investments started selling classes of existing funds that make a steady payout to investors who want to gradually withdraw their money from their funds — but a lot of the distribution is in the form of *return of capital* or a refund of the investor's own money. That means no tax is payable right then — but it's added to the investor's profit for capital gains purposes when the units are sold. In Chapter 13, we talk about the new balanced funds designed to distribute income to unitholders that also use this technique.

- ✔ Mackenzie (and no doubt others) sells bond funds that distribute interest that normally would attract a heavy tax rate — nearly 40 percent in the Ontario example above. But, by swapping a lot of e-mails with other chaps who went to Upper Canada College, they've figured out a way to turn the interest payments into capital gains for unitholders — and those are often taxed at just 16 percent.

These new tax-managing structures may turn out to be great deals for investors, but they add a level of complexity. Make sure you understand before you buy — or at least get an adviser who you're sure knows which number goes where.

Working through capital gain calculations

So how much tax do you face when you sell units of a mutual fund in a "taxable" account that's not an RRSP or similar tax-deferred plan? Look at the example of the investor who holds 100 units of a fund — say she paid $8 a unit. If she sells half of those units for $10 each, then her account will look something like this:

Purchase   100 units at $8 for total investment of $800

And six months later:

Sell   50 units at $10 for total proceeds of $500

Hold   50 units at $10 for total holding of $500

The units sold for $500 cost the investor $400 originally, so she has to report a capital gain of $100, only half of which must be included in taxable income for the year. The investor also still holds another 50 units.

When the investor was working out the capital gain on the sales, it was necessary to establish the cost base or original cost of the units. That was simple to do because it represented just half of the initial investment. But when you've made more than one purchase of the fund, things become more complex and you have to work out an adjusted cost base (ACB). Here's an example:

Purchase	100 units at $8 for an investment of $800
Purchase	Another 100 units at $10 for investment of $1,000

The investor now holds 200 units, which cost a total of $1,800, so her ACB is $1,800, or $9 per unit ($1,800 divided by 200).

Sell	100 units at $13 for proceeds of $1,300

The 100 units that were sold at $13 have an ACB of $9 each. That means they were sold for a profit of $4 each, so the investor has generated a capital gain of $400. And she also still holds 100 units, whose ACB base remains at $9 per unit.

If you get distributions and reinvest them in more units, then that represents yet another purchase of the fund — so you add the value of the distribution to your cost base. And always make sure that you do increase the ACB by the value of reinvested distributions, because if you don't you could face double taxation.

One more complication: Say the investor incurs a "back-end" commission when she sells the fund — that's a sales charge levied on the proceeds of the sale or redemption of the fund.

Sell	50 units at $13 for proceeds of $650, incurring a 5-percent redemption charge

The investor's proceeds from the sale have been reduced by 5 percent, to $617.50. That means, for tax purposes, she's received only $12.35 per unit.

Unfortunately, fund companies say they don't have the systems or information necessary to provide you with an accurate ACB for your units for tax purposes. That means the unit cost shown on your account statement may not be an accurate guide, so keep full records of any reinvested distributions or purchases or sales. Things can get horrendously complex if you have a regular purchase plan, which involves buying units at different prices at different times, or if you've done a lot of switching around. But the basic principle remains: The cost of your units is any money you spent to buy them, plus the value of reinvested distributions. And selling some of your units doesn't affect the ACB per unit of the ones that remain.

Several fund companies offer excellent general information on mutual fund taxation. For example, you can download the Mackenzie Mutual Fund Tax Guide from Mackenzie Financial's Web site (go to the Planning Tools section of www.mackenziefinancial.com). AIC Ltd.'s Web site (www.aic.com) has useful information on taxation in its Tax Smart section.

Avoiding fund purchases near year-end

If you're tempted to celebrate the holidays by throwing a few thousand into an equity mutual fund in a taxable account, it might be a good idea to hold off until you're struggling through your blinding hangover in early January. That's because many funds pay out big capital gains distributions at the end of the year. Even if you buy the fund just before the distribution, you're on the hook for capital gains tax on that distribution. Here's an exaggerated example:

> **Purchase** 100 units at $8 for total investment of $800 on December 10.

> **Receive distribution:** If the fund pays out $2 a unit a few days later, its unit price will drop to about $6. If you reinvest the distribution, you'll end up with 133 units. But you'll also have incurred $200 in taxable capital gains.

In a sense, you're simply paying the tax early because the reinvested distribution is added on to your ACB, which reduces your eventual capital gain when you sell. But most people would rather defer paying tax, thank you very much, so it would have been better to wait until after the distribution was made and then buy the fund. That way, your $800 would have gotten you the same 133 units, but you wouldn't have faced that annoying capital gains bill.

Index Funds and ETFs: A Tax-Efficient Investment

One type of fund that's virtually guaranteed to produce very little in the way of distributions is the equity index fund (bond index funds throw off piles of income, just like regular bond funds). Index funds — and their lower-cost cousins, exchange-traded funds (ETFs) — don't try to buy and sell stocks in pursuit of capital gains; they just hold every stock in the index. (See Chapter 15 for more on index funds and ETFs.) So their stream of capital gains distributions is usually small or non-existent. Yes, they may flow through some of the dividend income they receive and they may have to declare capital distributions if a major company in the index is taken over or dropped from the benchmark, forcing the index fund to sell it and book a gain. But just like buying good stocks and holding them for years, putting index funds in your non-RRSP portfolio is a highly tax-efficient strategy.

Taxes are a blind spot for the fund industry. Most investors probably find it virtually impossible to calculate the ACB of the units accurately. And the performance published for funds invariably shows only the returns earned by a non-taxable investor. Both problems may be insoluble because everybody's tax situation is different; however, once again, buying an index fund solves a lot of your problems. The other solution is to find the adviser from heaven: one who goes to the trouble of calculating ACBs for you.

A Few More Ideas for Tax Savings

For the average Canadian, the RRSP is the Rolls-Royce of tax planning. Not only does money grow tax-free within the plan, but you also get to write off each year's contributions against your taxable income. The write-off is known as a deduction. (We look at RRSPs in greater detail in Chapter 22.)

You can shield your investments, including mutual funds, from taxes through a few other simple methods. Two of the most popular are used to build capital for a child — often to go to college or university — so they're useful for parents and grandparents. The last option we discuss is brand new, so you can be the first on your block to try it!

Informal trusts or in-trust accounts

Informal trusts or *in-trust accounts* are investment accounts set up for the benefit of a child or beneficiary. The person who supplies the money is called the donor. Income earned by the account, such as dividends, is still taxable in the donor's hands. But capital gains can be taxable in the child's hands, and the child presumably has such a low income that he or she pays hardly any tax.

The fact that capital gains are taxable in the child's hands makes in-trust accounts ideal homes for equity mutual funds, because they usually produce capital gains distributions rather than interest income or lots of dividends.

(See "The Wacky World of Fund Distributions" in this chapter for more information.) Contributing money to the account doesn't give you a tax deduction. When the child reaches 18 or 19 (depending on the province), he or she is free to do anything with the money.

Brokers and mutual fund companies have offered informal trusts for years. When setting them up, be careful to make sure the "trustee" — the person overseeing the account on behalf of the beneficiary — is not the same as the donor. Otherwise, the tax people may refuse to have the capital gains taxable in the child's hands. And don't forget that money put into the in-trust account belongs to the child forever: You can't get it back. That means the kid might just choose to squander it at 18 or 19. By law, you can't do anything about it.

Registered education savings plans

Registered education savings plans (RESPs) are more formal government-registered schemes (with, you guessed it, ridiculously complicated rules) in which investment income and capital gains add up tax-free. As with informal trusts, no deduction applies for contributions. While no annual limit on contributions exists, you can contribute only up to $50,000 per child in a lifetime. Contributions may be made for up to 31 years from the date the plan was first set up, and the deadline for terminating a plan is 35 years from the set-up date.

The federal government offers a major plus for RESP investors in the form of its Canada Education Savings Grant (CESG), which Ottawa adds to the RESP. The grant is 20 percent of the first $2,500 contributed per child annually, so it's a maximum of $500 per year. The maximum grant for each kid is $7,200. Some provinces provide additional grants.

Note that the rules for RESPs have been changed a number of times, so keep an eye on federal and provincial budgets and other government announcements for any future amendments.

Three basic types of RESP exist:

- ✓ A so-called scholarship trust where your money is pooled with that of other parents by a money manager. The fees, complicated rules, and super-conservative investments (mostly bonds) of these trusts mean that we would avoid them.

- ✓ RESP accounts offered by mutual fund companies, aimed at getting you to buy their funds. They're fine, but the investment selection is limited.

- ✓ Self-directed RESPs offered at brokers and discount brokers, which can buy stocks, bonds, and cash. Because of flexibility we would go with the self-directed option, but investors who want simplicity often stick to a fund company RESP.

With an RESP, if the child doesn't go to university or college you can get back your contributions but you must refund any CESG grants. You then pay tax on any accumulated investment income, but you can move $50,000 of it into your RRSP if you still have the contribution room. Contribution room is the limited amount you can put into an RRSP each year, and any quota you don't use can be made up in a subsequent year. For much more on RRSPs, see Chapter 22.

A new acronym for the masses: The TFSA

In 2008, the federal government wheeled out a new tax-saving vehicle, the tax-free savings account (TFSA). Its title pretty much explains how it works: Starting in 2009, you can invest up to $5,000 a year into a TFSA account and it's allowed to grow tax-free for as long as you like. This amount will be adjusted each year based on the inflation rate, rounded up or down to the nearest $500. The same investments that are eligible for an RRSP are eligible for a TFSA (refer to Chapter 22 for more).

Before you get all excited about the RRSP's sexy sibling coming to town, take a deep breath and understand an important difference: You won't get a tax deduction for your contribution. Its appeal grows, however, after you realize that not only will your money be allowed to grow sheltered from tax, you won't have to pay tax when you withdraw it from the account. Of course, without a tax deduction going in you're investing after-tax money in it, so it would be double taxation if you did have to pay tax on the way out.

How much the TFSA benefits we tax-weary Canadians remains to be seen — $5,000 a year doesn't seem like much, particularly when stacked up to the annual RRSP limit, which is nearing the $20,000 mark.

Part V
The Part of Tens

The 5th Wave   By Rich Tennant

"I knew they were writing their own vows, but I expected quotes from Robert Frost poems, not mutual fund company prospectuses."

In this part . . .

Feeling intimidated by a salesperson — or even an office bore, the lad with the protruding teeth who claims to be the all-knowing oracle of investing? Whip out this part, and you'll find enough ammunition to blow 'em away permanently. Here are three collections of factoids, each with ten entries. We provide a handy checklist you can turn to when you're hiring a salesperson, and a list to consult if you're wondering whether to dump one. We also list ten investing blunders that just about everyone makes — including fund guidebook authors.

Chapter 24

Ten Questions to Ask a Potential Financial Adviser

*ots of us are uncomfortable with being assertive with salespeople.
Hey, we're polite Canadians, after all. But you need to get some things
straight before you hand over a penny to an investment adviser. Ask these
ten questions and jot down notes to look over later. If the answers you
receive are hazy, think seriously about looking for somebody else.

How Do You Get Paid?

This is the first thing to find out from an adviser, because it usually dictates
where you'll hold your account and what kind of investment he or she will
suggest. If the adviser is paid by the hour (not common in Canada), then his
or her advice should be reasonably impartial and you will have at least an
idea of how much you'll be paying. But if the adviser makes a living by earning sales commissions then getting you to buy a product is his or her bottom
line. A commission-paid planner or broker will try to get you to move your
money over to his or her firm or to a mutual fund company account on which
the firm earns commissions — that's known as asset capture.

Some commission-paid advisers won't want to discuss the subject of how
they get paid. They're not being dishonest; skilled brokers often avoid
depressing topics (such as commissions) and confusing statistics (such as
rates of return) until they believe they have won your trust. They will first
sell you on the concept of the fund — investing in big, stable, undervalued
companies, for example — and then get down to the mechanics of how to
buy it. But don't fall for the line. If you don't get a straight answer on commissions, then go elsewhere.

What Do You Think of My Financial Situation?

Ask for a quick version of the sort of financial strategy the adviser recommends for you. Listen carefully to the way he or she expresses ideas. Even after a brief interview, an experienced adviser should have a reasonable notion of your financial health and priorities and should be able to make a couple of sensible suggestions. The adviser can't give you a definitive financial prescription without knowing your goals, assets, income potential, and liabilities. But the sort of questions that he or she asks, and the interest shown in your problems, will tell you whether the planner or broker is comfortable with you as a client.

Will You Sell Me Index Funds and Low-Cost, No-Load Funds?

Funds with low expenses are the very best way to accumulate wealth. Unfortunately, too many stockbrokers and planners won't sell them because the bargain-priced funds don't pay enough in commissions. That's not necessarily because the salespeople are greedy: They have to make a living. But a good planner or broker should be prepared to fix you up with a mixture of low-expense, no-load funds and regular load or commission-charging funds. Some planning firms and brokers don't even carry low-cost funds, claiming that their administrative systems can't handle them. In that case, try a firm with a full range of products.

What Will You Do for Me?

"Financial planning" means something different to everyone. Get a clear idea of what your planner or adviser will do for you and how many times a year you can expect to meet. Ideally, there'll be an organized calendar, so that tasks such as making a registered retirement savings plan contribution and reviewing your portfolio are dealt with in a predictable way. If you go away from the initial meeting with the impression that all this person wants to do is sell you a few mutual funds, then that's probably all you'll get.

Can You Help with Income-Splitting and Tax Deferral?

Canadians pay a lot of tax, but many opportunities to lessen the burden exist through simple tax deferral and income-splitting devices, such as spousal RRSPs. An adviser who's not a tax enthusiast isn't worth hiring. Tax deferral is postponing payment of taxes, usually by diverting income into a tax-sheltered account such as an RRSP. Income-splitting usually involves shifting income to a spouse or child who's in a low tax bracket. Make sure the adviser is able to set up a RESP and is happy talking about tax-avoidance methods in detail.

Avoidance is the legal practice of minimizing the tax you pay, but evasion is illegal tax-dodging.

Can I Talk to Some of Your Clients?

The best reference is from someone you know, but asking to talk to satisfied customers never hurts. Confidentiality rules will probably prevent an adviser from giving out names, but he or she should be able to get someone to call you. If the adviser can't think of a single customer who'd be willing to do that, then how much loyalty does he or she inspire?

What Do You Think of the Market?

The ideal answer to this question is: "I don't know." You're hiring someone to help manage your savings here, not to accompany you to Las Vegas. Mutual funds enable brokers and advisers to do what they're good at — selling investments to people — while relieving them of the need to pretend they know how to pick stocks. After all, why should they? It's far more honest for an adviser to admit he or she can't beat the market and then sell you a "managed money" product run by someone who is trained to do the job.

Nothing's wrong with a potential adviser having an opinion on share prices, and talking about the market isn't a crime. But if you get a stream of investing theories and stock tips, then you're talking to a frustrated portfolio manager and not someone who's going to help build your financial future.

What Training Do You Have?

Insist on some kind of specialized training. All mutual fund salespeople have to pass a basic funds course to obtain the licence, but that's fairly bare-bones. Also check that the planner has obtained a specific financial planning qualification. An under-qualified planner or adviser could miss out on some tax-deferral or wealth-building techniques he or she hasn't heard of. But if a planner isn't a member of Advocis or the Institute of Advanced Financial Planners, then ask why.

How Long Have You Been Doing This?

Let someone else give a beginner his or her first big break. Financial planning and stockbrokerages take in hordes of people every year, chew 'em up, and spit lots out. Don't hire someone who shouldn't have been in the industry in the first place. Go with a veteran with experience. An adviser who's dealt with scores of clients is far more likely to know some neat tricks and ways of cutting red tape.

Can I See a Sample Client Statement?

If you're buying through a financial planner or mutual fund dealer, then expect to get a twice-yearly account statement from the mutual fund companies you're dealing with. But the salesperson's firm should also give you a consolidated account statement showing all your holdings. Check that it's professionally produced and easy to read. Many aren't.

If you invest with a traditional stockbroker, then you may just get a statement from the brokerage firm, and not the fund company. Ask to see an example of a statement.

Chapter 25

Ten Signs You Need to Fire Your Financial Adviser

· ·

*M*aybe they just say this to fool us into thinking they're human, but senior executives often claim that firing someone is the hardest thing they have to do. And for an investor, dumping an adviser is also tough. A salesperson's ego and livelihood are tied up in getting and keeping clients, so losing your account can feel like a punch in the stomach.

The circumstances are rarely cut-and-dried. Most investment advisers are a mixture of good and bad, just like the rest of us. But some clear signs indicate that it's time to move on, and this chapter offers ten classics. These signs apply mostly to commission-paid salespeople — because they have the greatest potential for conflict of interest — but drop a fee-only adviser if he or she develops any of these bad habits.

Produces Rotten Returns

We're amazed at how many clients hang on with a broker or planner through years of poor investment performance, often languishing in mutual funds that consistently lag the market and rival funds. Yes, measuring performance is tricky, especially if you've been sold a confusing package of funds that can't be compared with other investments. Your funds should show up fairly consistently in the middle of the pack or higher. One year of poor performance is acceptable because good managers often hold stocks that are out of fashion. But develop itchy feet if it happens again. Fund managers can be left behind by the times, after all. Hot funds may fall to the bottom of the league — but bad funds stay that way. If you have an awful year in which most or all of your funds are near the back of the pack, then ask for a clear explanation from your adviser. If none is forthcoming, consider moving your account.

Nobody expects a broker or planner to be a genius at picking funds. But all too often, poor returns are caused by simple mistakes such as putting too much money into funds with the same style, betting too heavily on one asset class (stocks or bonds), or chasing risky specialty funds that are too volatile for an investor's core savings.

Pesters You to Buy New Products after the Firm Is Taken Over

Be wary if your adviser's firm changes hands and your salesperson suddenly starts pushing a new line of funds, possibly an "in-house" brand or other limited-distribution product. These funds may be excellent — and you can be sure there'll be a fancy sales pitch — but the firm's new owners may be pressuring your adviser to switch as many clients as possible to the new lineup. You may pay extra costs. In general, stick with widely available mutual funds that can be transferred later to a new brokerage or financial planner if you decide to change. Alternatively, the new funds may be available everywhere, but the firm's new management may have struck a special distribution deal. Remember, if you switch you'll probably be on the hook for commissions.

Switches Firms Frequently

An adviser who doesn't stay put is usually someone with whom employers aren't happy — and that's a sure indication of trouble. The problem may be fairly innocent — poor recordkeeping, for instance — or it could be as serious as putting clients into unsuitable investments. Whatever it is, by the adviser's second or third move you should probably part company.

Financial planners and stockbrokers are independent businesspeople with their own book of clients. They join a brokerage firm or mutual fund dealership because it provides an office, administrative support, and credibility. So your adviser will almost certainly try to take you and your account along if a move happens. But don't follow blindly. Talk to the firm's office manager to see if another broker or planner suits you and your investing style.

Be warned, though, that things can get tangled when you pit your adviser against her firm. The firm will also want to hang on to your business, so the salesperson's old boss may falsely imply that there was something not quite right with the departing employee. In other words, investors often find themselves in a tug-of-greed, with both parties battling over "who owns the assets" — yes, that's the industry phrase, even though we're really talking about your money here. We're afraid you'll just have to use your judgment. If the adviser has provided excellent service, then move your money to his or her new firm. Good advisers are hard to find.

Keeps Asking for Power of Attorney or Discretionary Authority

Be very wary if an adviser seems excessively keen to get power of attorney or discretionary authority over your money — legal terms that denote giving him or her the ability to make decisions without consulting you. Even if you find the whole investing process overwhelming, giving the job of choosing and selling securities to a trusted friend, relative, or even your lawyer is usually preferable.

Cases of fraud, exploitation, and deception by brokers almost always involve abuse of discretionary authority over clients' accounts. In fact, it's questionable whether you should ever give such sweeping powers to a salesperson.

Doesn't Listen to You

People in the investment game tend to come out with a spiel, while brushing aside or ignoring questions. To some extent, they have been trained to do this. Clients often ask questions just for the sake of saying something, the reasoning goes, and if the query is genuinely important they'll raise it again later.

But advisers who just don't want to hear from you are all too common. Andrew has sat in rooms and heard brokers set out a plan for a prospective investor after asking only one or two questions. If you feel that your adviser isn't listening to you, then he or she probably isn't. Time to find someone who will.

Doesn't Return Your Phone Calls

Andrew can't begin to count the number of phone calls he's fielded from confused investors who can't even get through to their brokers to obtain answers to simple questions. Brokers and planners are salespeople, remember, which means that they're fuelled by new conquests. According to some astute observers, people who go into sales are in fact approval junkies: Every time they get a prospect to say yes, it represents validation of them and not the product.

Junkies are annoying, though. Brokers and planners often neglect their former clients, perhaps because the accounts are too small to generate much in the way of commissions and perhaps because the thrill of the chase is gone. You deserve better. If you can't get hold of your adviser easily, then look for someone else.

Suggests "Unregistered" Investments or Other Strange Stuff

If your adviser recommends some unregistered investments, head for the hills. If a fund doesn't come with a regular simplified prospectus — the legal document setting out the dangers and potential of the fund — and isn't supported by annual and semi-annual management reports of fund performance, then you're probably going into the deal unprotected. If the investment is offered by an insurance company, however, it should be from a company you've heard of and it should come with a prospectus-like document called an information folder.

A few "high net worth" funds for the rich generally require a minimum investment of up to $150,000. These are sold more like stocks, with the risks and terms set out in a document called an offering memorandum. They may be good investments, but always check with an accountant or a lawyer. A professional's fee of a few hundred dollars can save you lots of grief.

One of the most common frauds involves offering unlisted stocks, usually with the promise that they'll soon be trading on a proper exchange and that the price will shoot up when that happens. Or an unscrupulous broker will offer "notes" that purport to carry lavish rates of interest. The scam nearly always contains the implication that you're being let in on the deal in a slightly seedy way — "I shouldn't be telling you this, but. . . ." In fact, an old saying exists among fraud artists: "You can't cheat an honest man." So if your salesperson even hints that buying into a deal involves bending the rules, then move your money immediately.

Keeps Wanting You to Buy and Sell Investments

Excessive trading — known as churning in the investment industry — is a classic sign of a greedy salesperson who views you as a lucrative source of commissions rather than as a long-term customer. If your adviser moves your money to a new fund company and if you buy the funds on a back-end-load basis — incurring a sales commission that applies only if you sell within a set number of years — then the salesperson gets up to 5 percent of your investment. That's $1,000 if you move $20,000. So always ask why when the adviser suggests you sell. You can be less suspicious about moves between funds sold by the same company because they don't usually generate a commission for the adviser, although some fund salespeople charge a "switch fee" of 2 percent. Such transfer fees aren't justifiable, so refuse to pay them.

Funds are supposed to be long-term holdings — at least five years for an equity fund. That's because the stock market often dips for extended periods and because a good money manager's investment style can easily stop working for a year or longer. Perhaps your adviser can present a compelling reason to sell — a loss of a fund manager or a drastic change in a fund's holdings, for example. In that case, it may be wise to go along with the suggestion. The adviser's knowledge is what you're paying for, after all. But remember that when you move money to a new fund company or buy a new stock, it's payday for your adviser.

Keeps Making Recordkeeping Mistakes

The investment business is so sales-driven that paperwork and reporting of transactions are often far down the priority list. Every investor (including us) encounters mistakes and incorrectly executed orders. Check your account statement and transaction slips religiously.

The profit margins in the financial planning business aren't huge, so many small firms can't afford elaborate back offices or administration systems. But why should that be your problem? If you find that your adviser or firm is constantly getting things wrong, then don't accept the frustration. Move your money to someone who's more professional. And act quickly if you notice that money is missing from your account. Don't be fobbed off with claims that the money is in transit or tied up in red tape. If you can't get written confirmation of the whereabouts of every penny, then talk to the adviser's manager.

Won't Abandon Pet Theories

Some investment advisers are gold fanatics, some are bond nuts ("I don't like to see anything in an RRSP but fixed-income securities"), and some think they're all-knowing about the stock market. If your salesperson keeps repeating the same mantra no matter what's happening to your portfolio, then consider a change.

The history of the market is littered with those who hung on for dear life, insisting that their particular stocks or ideas "will come back." Advisers and brokers become incredibly attached to these beliefs, even at the cost of losing clients. If you think your adviser has a one-track mind, then get off at the next station.

Chapter 26

Ten Mistakes Investors Make

*W*e're sure we've been guilty of every blunder on this list, so please don't accuse us of lecturing you. Investing is hard because you have to conquer not only inflation, endless sneaky expenses, and taxes, but also your own innate fear and greed. Here are ten warning signs your personal demons are sabotaging your quest for wealth.

Diversifying Too Much

Buying 20 different funds and assuming you can't lose because you've covered all the bases is pointless. Sure, you're certain to own something that's going up — but a chaotic portfolio like that is also bound to contain lots of funds that hold very similar investments. And the more funds you own, the closer your returns will be to the index or market in general — so why not just buy index funds and be done with it? Keep things simple by limiting yourself to a few index funds (one Canadian, one U.S., and one international) plus a few conservative equity funds. That way, you won't be paying multiple management fees to everyone and his beagle in return for mediocre returns that track the market, minus expenses.

Diversifying Too Little

Betting the whole lot on one pony can be tempting. But look at what the professionals do and you'll notice they always own lots of different stuff. If your portfolio isn't a broad mixture of top-quality bonds and conservative stocks, then you're probably going to come off at the first fence. Remember the old rule: Own your age in bonds and cash. So, according to the traditional saw, a 40-year-old should have just 60 percent of her money in stocks. That seems overly conservative to many people in our go-go age, where retirees can look forward to 25 years or more after quitting work. But if you don't own at least some bonds, then you're walking a tightrope — with a noose around your neck.

Procrastinating

Invest $200 a month for 20 years at an 8-percent annual rate of return and you'll end up with more than $113,000. But wait five years before starting, and you're looking at less than $69,000. So get going now. Ten years hence, you don't want to be looking back at today . . . and regretting you didn't just pick up the phone.

Being Apathetic

Allowing your portfolio to slide into mediocrity is so easy — you might ignore your awful funds, perhaps, or let the cash component build up too high. Personal finances aren't exactly a blast, so we're all tempted to leave things to the forces of continental drift. But just a few dull hours of work once or twice a year can make all the difference between a well-adjusted, balanced portfolio and a neglected mess.

Hanging on to Bad Investments

Refusing to sell a bad fund or stock is the true mark of the hopeless amateur — Andrew should know, because he's done it many times. Unfortunately, no green light comes on when it's time to get out. But one thing's for sure — the price you paid is completely irrelevant. Waiting "until it's back where I bought it" is one of the most damaging things you can do to your wealth. Sell it, absorb the lesson, and move on.

Taking Cash out of Your RRSP

When contribution room to an RRSP has been used up, it can't be replaced. Just like brain cells. So think long and hard about cashing in any of those supercharged dollars nestling within your plan. You not only pay taxes, and high ones at that, on the withdrawal, but also give up years of tax-free growth. Withdrawing money for a down payment on a house under the Home Buyers' Plan is a little less harmful, because Ottawa lets you put the cash back in. But you're still probably giving up years of tax-sheltered income within the RRSP because the money isn't there to earn it.

Ignoring Expenses

Those extra one or two percentage points in mutual fund fees and costs seem so unimportant — but they ultimately represent a huge chunk of your retirement savings. Remember that over 20 years, an extra one percentage point in annual expenses eats up one-fifth of the total accumulated capital. Do yourself a favour and go with some low-cost managers — look for a maximum expense ratio of about 1.5 percent on equity funds.

Failing to Plan for Taxes

Remember that the mutual fund returns that appear in the papers were earned in a magical tax-free land of hugs, kisses, and happy pixies. In the real world — hellish places like your neighbourhood, for example — people have to pay taxes. So beware of holding bonds, bond funds, and other income-paying investments in a taxable account. To minimize the taxes you pay, opt for professional advice, unless your finances are extremely straightforward. Tax accountants know perfectly legal tricks that you don't.

Obsessing about Insignificant Fees

If you're happy with an adviser or fund company, then don't get all irate about a $75 RRSP administration fee. Just pay it if your returns are good and your other expenses are low. People in the fund business will tell you that clients happily pay out hundreds or even thousands in management fees without even noticing — but they fly into a rage if presented with a $25 bill for transferring an account. Remember that the fund company or broker who's truly the cheapest may also be the one who nags you for a "nuisance fee" — but at least it's out in the open. By contrast, a fund that's dinging you for huge expenses each year might seem to be absorbing all of those annoying charges itself. But don't worry, you're paying.

Waiting until the Market Looks Better

Ignore this one if you're a psychic. But for the rest of us, attempting to divine the direction of the market is like trying to catch the wind. The movement of share prices is as intangible and random as the weather, or it may as well be.

The fund industry will tell you that "the time to invest is when you have the money." In other words, trying to jump on and off stocks is pointless. And, for once, the fund sellers' homilies are right on the mark. The evidence is overwhelming that market timing is a futile exercise, so grit your teeth and invest. As they used to say in an annoying Irish lottery ad: "If you're not in, you can't win."

Index

• E •

• F •

• J •

• K •

• L •

• **N** •

• **O** •

• W •

CPSIA information can be obtained
at www.ICGtesting.com
Printed in the USA
BVHW080957250119
538629BV00009B/73/P

9 780470 157640